Connections

Connections

Writing, Reading, and Critical Thinking

Second Edition

Tammy Montgomery Boeck
Folsom Lake College

Megan C. Rainey
Cosumnes River College

PEARSON
Longman

New York • San Francisco • Boston
London • Toronto • Sydney • Tokyo • Singapore • Madrid
Mexico City • Munich • Paris • Cape Town • Hong Kong • Montreal

Vice President and Editor-in-Chief: Joseph Terry
Senior Acquisitions Editor: Susan Kunchandy
Development Editor: Janice Wiggins-Clark
Senior Marketing Manager: Melanie Craig
Senior Supplements Editor: Donna Campion
Production Manager: Denise Phillip
Project Coordination, Text Design, and Electronic Page Makeup: WestWords, Inc.
Cover Designer/Manager: Wendy Ann Fredericks
Cover Photo: ©Michael Tcherevkoff Ltd./GettyImages, Inc.
Photo Researcher: WestWords, Inc.
Manufacturing Buyer: Al Dorsey
Printer and Binder: Courier Corporation
Cover Printer: Phoenix Color Corporation

Library of Congress Cataloging-in-Publication Data

Boeck, Tammy.
    Connections: writing, reading, and critical thinking / Tammy L. Boeck, Megan C. Rainey.
        p. cm.
    Includes bibliographical references and index.
    ISBN 0-321-10374-2
    1. English language—Rhetoric. 2. Critical thinking—Problems, exercises, etc. 3. Report
writing—Problems, exercises, etc. 4. College readers. I. Rainey, Megan II. Title.

PE1408.B573 2003
808'.0427—dc21   2003045815

Please visit our website at http://www.ablongman.com

ISBN 0-321-10374-2

3 4 5 6 7 8 9 10—CRW—06 05 04

This book is dedicated to:

Our students at
Cosumnes River College
Folsom Lake College
West Valley College
California State University, Sacramento

Daniel

Bethany

John

The three graces—Brienna Faith, Keely Catherine, and Ann Marie

Brief Contents

Detailed Contents

Readings by Theme

Preface for Instructors

Welcome to the second edition of *Connections!* Whether new to the text or a veteran of the first edition, you'll find *Connections* offers instructors flexibility and a number of exciting features—all designed to provoke student thought and empower student writing.

The second edition of *Connections* continues to promote writing, reading, and critical thinking as interrelated skills. Because proficiency in these skills is expected of college students, *Connections* introduces students to effective processes for developing their skills and achieving collegiate-level proficiency in reading and writing. Although more traditional writing texts often separate writing, reading, and critical thinking tasks and ask students to practice them in isolation, we've found that real progress in student writing occurs when these processes are *connected*.

Instructors who use this text will find the support they require to engage student interest and guide students through chapters that integrate critical reading and thinking skills, writing skills, and sentence work. The second text in a three-book developmental writing series, *Connections* would traditionally be called a "paragraph-to-essay text." However, after students study the reading process and learn how to summarize what they've read in Chapters 1–3, they move on to studying the writing process in Chapter 4. Then, from Chapter 5 forward, they practice their reading and writing processes as they complete progressively more challenging reading and essay assignments. Paragraphs are taught in the context of essay preparation. Sentence work is taught within the context of the paragraph. Thus, no time is wasted trying to get students to apply to their writing what they learned in drill and exercise work. With *Connections*, students engage in authentic essay assignments while learning about paragraphs, focus, development, organization, analysis, and sentence clarity.

The result: developmental writers too often marginalized in the college classroom join the ranks of their fellow students, wrestling meaning out of challenging texts, providing support for their opinions, and constructing well-developed essays that respond to the issues raised.

In response to our colleagues' suggestions, we've revised, updated, and expanded several features in the second edition.

- Sentence practice has been expanded through the text. A new or expanded set of exercises appears at the end of every chapter (1–8). In addition to sentence basics, coordinators and subordinators, and sentence combining exercises, sentence practice now covers phrases, clausal patterns, and parallelism in student writing.
- The chapters are sleeker now. Assignments are fewer, yet more substantial. Some of the readings have been replaced or moved to the Supplemental Readings section (as optional readings).
- Some chapters have been reorganized or redeveloped. Chapter 2 maintains a sharper focus on the shape of academic writing and how to summarize academic texts. Chapters 6 and 7 have been refurbished. Dated topics (such as the V-chip) have been deleted whereas hot topics (such as privacy and the role of surveillance technology) have been added to generate student interest and provoke discussion.
- More student writing samples have been included for study.
- A "Get Involved!" feature has been added to the text that directs students to additional resources and encourages them to move beyond the confines of the textbook to discover information on their own. Students are encouraged to watch films, complete online activities, interview people, and conduct research.
- The Supplemental Readings section has been overhauled. Many of the journalistic pieces from the first edition have been replaced with more challenging, academic readings. These readings have been selected to serve as alternate or additional readings to accompany the writing assignments throughout the text.
- A new section titled "Understanding, Correcting, and Avoiding Sentence Errors" has been added in the back of the text. This section shows students how to recognize, correct, and avoid the most common sentence errors.

Although the progression of the writing, reading, and critical thinking instruction remains consistent with the first edition, the second edition offers new and updated features to enrich the quality of instruction. Because students are often enrolled in courses requiring essays and reports, they are eager to see how the pieces of writing instruction come together and apply to their courses. In other words, they seek an authentic college-level approach to improving writing skills. *Connections* provides such an approach.

GOALS OF THIS TEXT

Connections aims to help developmental writers achieve their collegiate and workplace goals by sharpening their reading, writing, and critical thinking skills.

Sharpen Study Skills   For students to succeed in college, they must take notes, organize their work, seek tutorial help, use computers, understand the features of their textbooks, use dictionaries, and summarize other texts. The second edition of *Connections* begins with a review of these basic study skills.

Engage Students as Participants in College   The thematic approach to each chapter in *Connections*—along with journal assignments, discussion questions, activities, readings, critical thinking questions, and writing assignments—fosters an empowering learning environment. Through the repeated reading and writing processes used in *Connections*, students learn to approach a subject critically and from an academic perspective. They also learn the value of others' points of view. As a result, students find themselves participants in a collective learning process.

Sharpen Reading and Critical Thinking Skills   Although *Connections* is a writing text with a writing emphasis, critical reading and thinking are major components. Better readers and thinkers are also better writers. Students who use *Connections* will learn how to approach their readings (through an effective *process* in which they preview, anticipate, read and reread, think about, and summarize their readings) in order to wrestle meaning out of difficult texts. They will also analyze audience, purpose, development, focus, organization, and effective sentence structure in their readings, and then apply newly discovered strategies to their own writing.

Sharpen Writing Skills   *Connections* emphasizes the writing process as key to generating meaningful text. Researchers such as Mina Shaughnessy (see "Beyond the Sentence" in *Errors and Expectations*) have shown that as inexperienced writers learn an effective process for completing writing assignments, they are able to create essays with improved focus, development, organization, and clarity. Individual elements (e.g., topic sentences) and skills (e.g., focus) must be taught and studied, but all the practicing and studying should be done within authentic writing tasks.

Chapter 4 outlines this writing process and Chapters 5–8 repeat it. As a result, students leave the text with a clear sense of the process writers follow to achieve clarity. Even the sentence work is woven into the writing process. The grammar exercises connect in topic to the themes of the chapters, and the exercises prepare students for the unique sentence challenges each writing assignment brings.

CONTENT OVERVIEW

A resource for student writers, the second edition of *Connections* provides tools and support in six sections of instruction. While promoting a progression of skill development, the text is designed to be flexible. Instructors can select from chapters or segments of chapters that address their students' particular needs. A collection of syllabi can be found in the *Instructor's Manual*.

Section I Establishes The Writing-Reading-Critical Thinking Connection
Chapter 1 introduces the writing-reading-critical thinking connection and offers an overview of study skills, such as taking notes, keeping a notebook, and using the dictionary. It also explains the different types of assignments in the text—journals, activities, readings, questions for critical thought, and writing assignments.

Because students will encounter a variety of texts in college, Chapter 2 introduces the unique characteristics of academic and journalistic writing and teaches students how to summarize both types of text. Chapter 3 explores the PARTS of the reading process: Preview, Anticipate, Read and Reread, Think Critically About, and Summarize. Developing an effective writing process is the focus of Chapter 4, which takes students through the recursive process that leads from discovery to drafting, revising, and editing.

Sentence work (appearing at the end of each chapter) encourages students to develop sentence skills within the context of their own writing and reinforces each chapter's focus and theme. In Chapters 1–4, students will review sentence basics: verbs, subjects, clauses and phrases.

Section II Develops the Writing-Reading-Critical Thinking Connection
Emphasizing a discrete writing skill per chapter—focus, development, organization, and analysis—Chapters 5 through 8 teach students how

to construct coherent, unified paragraphs and essays. In each chapter, students engage in discussions, activities, and readings that lead directly to writing assignments. They investigate heroes in Chapter 5, then examine *focus* in their writing as they select particular heroes and *focus* on their heroic qualities in their essays. They weigh the pros and cons of television in Chapter 6 and focus on *development* in their writing. In Chapter 7, students explore technology and the effects of new forms of surveillance technology while developing their *organizational* skills. Finally, in Chapter 8, they *analyze* and write about music and poetry.

Sentence work continues to appear at the end of each chapter and to connect to thematic content. In these chapters, however, the sentence work moves beyond the basics, focusing sometimes on the unique rhetorical challenges that come with each writing assignment and at other times focusing more generally on complex sentence patterns. In Chapter 5, for example, students review pronouns and parallelism, for the assignment on heroes calls for students to rely on pronouns and create descriptions. Since Chapter 6 offers students their most challenging argumentative essay, the sentence work helps students learn to use subordinators, concessions, and transitions effectively. Chapters 7–8 offer the most challenging reading and writing assignments in *Connections* and, similarly, the sentence work challenges students to create complex sentences by embedding phrases and joining clauses.

Section III Provides Supplemental Readings to Complement Writing Assignments   Representing diversity in culture and thought, this collection of substantive articles, essays, and poems reinforces the themes presented in Chapters 1 through 8. Readings on the value of language, education, relationships, role models, education, television, and technology serve as alternates or additions to those in the chapters, offering students additional perspectives on issues and offering instructors greater flexibility in preparing assignments.

Section IV Offers Additional Skill-Building Instruction   Designed to enhance reading and writing instruction, this section contains chapters on study skills, basic skills, outside sources, and timed writing. The chapters can be assigned to individuals needing extra help or to the entire class. In Discovering Your Learning Styles, students find out how they learn best and how to utilize study skills that complement their own styles. Mini-chapters—Using the Dictionary, Building Your

Vocabulary, Spelling Matters, and Reading Aloud—offer instruction and reinforcement activities that lead to increased vocabulary as well as stronger reading and writing skills. In Using Outside Sources, students learn how to integrate quotations and cite sources in their essays as they write. Then, in a final subsection, Writing in Class/Writing the Argument, students examine the challenges of in-class writing and learn how to read a prompt, budget time, plan, draft, revise, and edit in a set amount of time.

Section V Addresses the Most Common Sentence Errors and Teaches Students How to Correct and Then Avoid Them   Students will follow a process for understanding and correcting common sentence errors. Through completing the exercises in this section, students will learn to recognize, correct, and avoid verb form, verb tense, and subject-verb agreement errors. In addition, they will learn to recognize, correct, and avoid fragments, run-ons, and comma splices.

Section VI Contains Easy Reference Charts for Review   At a glance, students have access to a list of right-word choices, capitalization rules, and punctuation rules.

FEATURES

The following features of *Connections* support students' development as writers and contribute to their writing success in college and the workplace:

Academic Focus   Students engage in the kinds of critical reading and writing activities—summarizing, discussing, and analyzing—they'll encounter in other college classes.

Flexibility   Six distinct sections and eight distinct chapters allow instructors to select writing instruction according to skill level and subject matter.

Chapter Preview Pages   Main topics for each chapter appear highlighted on each opening page of Chapters 1 through 8, providing an instant overview of the chapter and preparing students to engage the chapter.

Coverage of Study Skills   Chapter 1 offers instruction in taking notes, keeping a notebook, working with a tutor, and using computers. Section IV includes instruction in using the dictionary, building vocabulary, spelling, reading aloud, and using outside sources.

Learning Styles   In Discovering Your Learning Styles, students find out how they learn best and how to utilize study skills that complement their individual styles. The activities throughout *Connections* engage visual, auditory, tactile, and kinesthetic learners.

Integrated Sentence Skills Support   Sentence work connects to each chapter's theme and readings and challenges students to inductively learn the parts of speech and basic rules of written language. In the sections entitled Your Own Writing, students create new sentences and apply instruction to current writing assignments.

Reading Skills Support   Students are taught effective reading strategies through the PARTS—**P**review, **A**nticipate, **R**ead and Reread, **T**hink Critically About, and **S**ummarize—of the reading process. Prereading activities appear at the beginning of most readings, with questions for critical thought following the readings. Glossed vocabulary words occur at the end of readings in Chapters 1 and 2 as students develop their dictionary skills.

Writing Assignments Linked to Readings   Students read, analyze, and summarize articles from magazines and newspapers, textbook excerpts, song lyrics, poems, and essays as they consider and develop their own perspectives on the issues presented.

Level-Appropriate, High-Interest Multicultural Readings   Readings from academic and other sources reflect contemporary issues and diverse opinions on issues such as dating and marriage, the characteristics of a hero, the effects of television, the impact of new surveillance technologies on citizens' privacy, and more. Representing a variety of styles and sources, these pieces vary in length and difficulty.

Supplemental Readings   An additional set of readings near the end of the text provides supplements or alternatives to those in Chapters 1–8.

Student Writing Samples   Examples of successful student writing appear throughout the text.

Writing Skills Support   Students engage in a step-by-step writing process. Journals, prereading questions, readings, questions for critical thought, and workshop activities assist students in moving from the discovery phase through the brainstorming, drafting, revising, and editing phases of this process. Students are encouraged throughout the text to take advantage of tutorial assistance and their school's computer or writing lab.

Opportunities for Collaboration   Activities, journals, discussion questions, and draft workshops provide ample opportunities for group discussion and collaboration and help students recognize the value of establishing a writing community.

In-Class Writing Support   Writing in Class/Writing the Argument teaches students how to read a prompt, budget time, outline, draft, revise, and edit under pressure. A segment devoted to writing the argumentative essay is cmphasized.

Easy Reference Rules   Easy-to-read charts help students check punctuation rules, capitalization rules, and right-word choices.

Using Outside Sources   This unique chapter gives students basic instruction in integrating sources, using quotations, and citing source information in their writing.

Glossary   Definitions for terms appearing in bold are listed for easy reference.

THE OTHER TEXTS IN THIS SERIES

Connections is the second text in a three-book developmental writing series.

Book One, *Expressions* (copyright 2003), is for students three levels below freshman composition. Books at this level are traditionally created as sentence-to-paragraph books. *Expressions,* however, is built on the same premise as *Connections:* developmental writers learn best when reading, writing, and critical thinking tasks are woven together. *Expressions* initiates the developmental writer into the world of college by offering a survey of different types of written expression (diaries, letters, academic paragraphs, autobiographies, fairy tales, and academic essays). As students study the readings, they build their awareness of purpose, audience, and style. The writing assignments, then, offer students opportunities to write academic paragraphs in response to the readings or to practice the genres themselves. Because *Expressions* is meant to prepare students for the kind of work found in *Connections*, *Expressions* devotes significant time to study skills, vocabulary building, and sentence work. Unique features include Skill Spotlights (on such subjects as brainstorming and making your writing interesting with detail), Sentence Style activities that draw sentences from the readings, and Computer Notes.

Book Three in this series, *Interpretations* (scheduled for publication in 2004), is for the advanced developmental writer. This essay-level writing text challenges students to read, write, and think critically as it prepares them for entry into freshman composition. Students will spend significant time studying, summarizing, and interpreting current controversial issues in their reading and writing assignments. In addition, they will gain experience in writing in the humanities as they interpret literature, art, and film. Finally, reading, writing, and critical thinking work relates to corresponding sentence-level work. Not only will students practice traditional punctuation and usage in their writing, but they will also develop the ability to integrate a variety of sentence structures to make their writing more interesting and effective.

TEACHING AND LEARNING PACKAGE

The Instructor's Manual

The *Instructor's Manual* offers an updated discussion of the underlying pedagogy and an overview of features in *Connections*. The manual also offers diagnostic materials, sample syllabi, in-class writing assignments, sentence work answers, and chapter-by-chapter support materials: chapter previews, preparation suggestions, overhead transparencies for class discussion activities, brainstorming and support activities, and a detailed, day-to-day lesson plan for one or two major assignments per chapter. For ordering, the ISBN is 0-321-10372-6.

In addition to the *Instructor's Manual,* many other skills-based supplements are available for both instructors and students. All of these supplements are available either free or at greatly reduced prices.

For Additional Reading and Reference

The Dictionary Deal   Two dictionaries can be shrink-wrapped with this text at a nominal fee. *The New American Webster Handy College Dictionary* is a paperback reference text with more than 100,000 entries. *Merriam Webster's Collegiate Dictionary,* tenth edition, is a hardback reference with a citation file of more than 14.5 million examples of English words drawn from actual use. For more information on how to shrink-wrap a dictionary with your text, please contact your Longman sales representative.

Penguin Academics: *Twenty-Five Great Essays, Fifty Great Essays,* **and** *One Hundred Great Essays,* **edited by Robert DiYanni**   These alphabetically organized essay collections are published as part of the "Penguin Academics" series of low-cost, high-quality offerings intended for use in introductory college courses. All essays were selected for their teachability, both as models for writing and for their usefulness as springboards for student writing. For more information on how to shrink-wrap one of these anthologies with your text, please contact your Longman sales consultant.

100 Things to Write About   This 100-page book contains 100 individual assignments for writing on a variety of topics and in a wide range of formats, from expressive to analytical. Ask your Longman sales representative for a sample copy. 0-673-98239-4

Newsweek **Alliance**   Instructors may choose to shrink-wrap a 12-week subscription to *Newsweek* with any Longman text. The price of the subscription is 59 cents per issue (a total of $7.08 for the subscription). Available with the subscription is a free "Interactive Guide to *Newsweek*"—a workbook for students who are using the text. In addition, *Newsweek* provides a wide variety of instructor supplements free to teachers, including maps, Skills Builders, and weekly quizzes. For more information on the *Newsweek* program, please contact your Longman sales representative.

Electronic and Online Offerings

The Longman Writer's Warehouse   The innovative and exciting on-line supplement is the perfect accompaniment to any developmental writing course. Developed by developmental English instructors specially for developing writers, The Writer's Warehouse covers every part of the writing process. Also included are journaling capabilities, multimedia activities, diagnostic tests, an interactive handbook, and a complete instructor's manual. The Writer's Warehouse requires no space on your school's server; rather, students complete and store their work on the Longman server, and are able to access it, revise it, and continue working at any time. For more details about how to shrink-wrap a free subscription to The Writer's Warehouse with this text, please consult your Longman sales representative. For a free guided tour of the site, visit *http://longmanwriterswarehouse.com*

The *Writer's ToolKit Plus*   This CD-ROM offers a wealth of tutorial, exercise, and reference material for writers. It is compatible with either a PC or Macintosh platform, and is flexible enough to be used either occasionally for practice or regularly in class lab sessions. For information on how to bundle this CD-ROM free with your text, please contact your Longman sales representative.

The *Longman Electronic Newsletter*   Twice a month during the spring and fall, instructors who have subscribed receive a free copy of the *Longman Developmental English Newsletter* in their e-mailbox. Written by experienced classroom instructors, the newsletter offers teaching tips, classroom activities, book reviews, and more. To subscribe, send an e-mail to *BasicSkills@ablongman.com.*

Research Navigator Guide for English   Designed to teach students how to conduct high-quality online research and to document it properly, Research Navigator Guide provides discipline-specific academic resources, in addition to helpful tips on the writing process, online research, and finding and citing valid sources. Free when packaged with any Longman text, Research Navigator Guide includes an access code to Research Navigator™—providing access to thousands of academic journals and periodicals, the NY Times Search by Subject Archive, Link Library, Library Guides, and more. 0-321-20277-5

For Instructors

Electronic Test Bank for Writing   This electronic test bank features more than 5,000 questions in all areas of writing, from grammar to paragraphing, through essay writing, research, and documentation. With this easy-to-use CD-ROM, instructors simply choose questions from the electronic test bank, then print out the completed test for distribution. CD-ROM: 0-321-08117-X Print version: 0-321-08486-1

Competency Profile Test Bank, **Second Edition**   This series of 60 objective tests covers ten general areas of English competency: fragments; comma splices and run-ons; pronouns; commas; and capitalization. Each test is available in remedial, standard, and advanced versions. Available as reproducible sheets or in computerized versions. Free to instructors. Paper version: 0-321-02224-6

Diagnostic and Editing Tests and Exercises, **Sixth Edition**   This collection of diagnostic tests helps instructors assess students' competence in Standard Written English for purpose of placement or to gauge progress. Available as reproducible sheets or in computerized versions, and free to instructors. Paper: 0-321-19647-3. CD-ROM: 0-321-19645-7

ESL Worksheets, **Third Edition**   These reproducible worksheets provide ESL students with extra practice in areas they find the most troublesome. A diagnostic test and post-test are provided, along with answer keys and suggested topics for writing. Free to adopters. 0-321-07765-2

Longman Editing Exercises   54 pages of paragraph editing exercises give students extra practice using grammar skills in the context of longer passages. Free when packaged with any Longman title. 0-205-31792-8 Answer key: 0-205-31797-9

80 Practices   A collection of reproducible, ten-item exercises that provide additional practices for specific grammatical usage problems, such as comma splices, capitalization, and pronouns. Includes an answer key, and free to adopters. 0-673-53422-7

CLAST Test Package, **Fourth Edition**   These two 40-item objective tests evaluate students' readiness for the CLAST exams. Strategies for teaching CLAST preparedness are included. Free with any Longman English title. Reproducible sheets: 0-321-01950-4

TASP Test Package, **Third Edition**   These 12 practice pre-tests and post-tests assess the same reading and writing skills covered in the TASP examination. Free with any Longman English title. Reproducible sheets: 0-321-01959-8

Teaching Online: Internet Research, Conversation, and Composition, **Second Edition**   Ideal for instructors who have never surfed the Net, this easy-to-follow guide offers basic definitions, numerous examples, and step-by-step information about finding and using Internet sources. Free to adopters. 0-321-01957-1

Using Portfolios   This supplement offers teachers a brief introduction to teaching with portfolios in composition courses. This essential guide addresses the pedagogical and evaluative use of portfolios, and offers practical suggestions for implementing a portfolio evaluation system in a writing class. 0-321-08412-8

The Longman Instructor Planner   This all-in-one resource for instructors includes monthly and weekly planning sheets, to-do lists, student contact forms, attendance rosters, a gradebook, an address/phone book, and a mini almanac. Ask your Longman sales representative for a free copy. 0-321-09247-3

For Students

Researching Online, **Fifth Edition**   A perfect companion for a new age, this indispensable new supplement helps students navigate the Internet. Adapted from *Teaching Online,* the instructor's Internet guide, *Researching Online* speaks directly to students, giving them detailed, step-by-step instructions for performing electronic searches. Available free when shrink-wrapped with this text. 0-321-09277-5

Learning Together: An Introduction to Collaborative Theory   This brief guide to the fundamentals of collaborative learning teaches students how to work effectively in groups, how to revise with peer response, and how to co-author a paper or report. Shrink-wrapped free with this text. 0-673-46848-8

A Guide for Peer Response, **Second Edition**   This guide offers students forms for peer critiques, including general guidelines and specific forms for different stages in the writing process. Also appropriate for freshman-level course. Free to adopters. 0-321-01948-2

Ten Practices of Highly Successful Students   This popular supplement helps students learn crucial study skills, offering concise tips for a successful career in college. Topics include time management, test-taking, reading critically, stress, and motivation. 0-205-30769-8

The Longman Student Planner   This daily planner for students includes daily, weekly, and monthly calendars, as well as class schedules and mini-almanac of useful information. It is the perfect accompaniment to a Longman reading or study skills textbook, and is available free to students when shrink-wrapped with this text. 0-321-04573-4

The Longman Writer's Journal   This journal for writers, free with any Longman English text, offers students a place to think, write, and react. For an examination copy, contact your Longman sales consultant. 0-321-08639-2

The Longman Researcher's Journal   This journal for writers and researchers, free with this text, helps students plan, schedule, write, and revise their research project. An all-in-one resource for first-time researchers, the journal guides students gently through the research process. 0-321-09530-8

The Longman Writer's Portfolio   This unique supplement provides students with a space to plan, think about, and present their work. The portfolio includes an assessing/organizing area (including a grammar diagnostic test, a spelling quiz, and project planning worksheets), a before-and-during-writing area (including peer review sheets, editing checklists, writing self-evaluations, and a personal editing profile), and an after-writing area (including a progress chart, a final table of contents, and a final assessment). Ask your Longman sales representative for ISBN 0-321-10765-9.

State-Specific Supplements

[For Florida Adoptions] *Thinking Through the Test,* **by D.J. Henry** This special workbook, prepared specially for students in Florida, offers ample skill and practice exercises to help students prep for the Florida State Exit Exam. To shrink-wrap this workbook free with your textbook, please contact your Longman sales representative. Available in two versions: with answers and without answers. Also available: Two laminated grids (one for reading, one for writing) that can serve as handy references for students preparing for the Florida State Exit Exam.

[For New York Adoptions] *Preparing for the CUNY-ACT Reading and Writing Test,* **edited by Patricia Licklider**   This booklet, prepared by reading and writing faculty from across the CUNY system, is designed to help students prepare for the CUNY-ACT exit test. It includes test-taking tips, reading passages, typical exam questions, and sample writing prompts to help students become familiar with each portion of the test.

[For Texas Adoptions] *The Longman TASP Study Guide,* **by Jeanette Harris**   Created specifically for students in Texas, this study guide includes straightforward explanations and numerous practice exercises to help students prepare for the reading and writing sections of the Texas Academic Skills Program Test. To shrink-wrap this workbook free with your textbook, please contact your Longman sales representative. 0-321-20271-6

The Longman Series of Monographs for Developmental Educators

Ask your Longman sales consultant for a free copy of these monographs written by experts in their fields.

#1: *The Longman Guide to Classroom Management*   Written by Joannis Flatley of St. Philip's College, the first in Longman's new series of monographs for developmental English instructors focuses on issues of classroom etiquette, providing guidance on dealing with unruly, unengaged, disruptive, or uncooperative students. Ask your Longman sales representative for a free copy. 0-321-09246-5

#2: *The Longman Guide to Community Service-Learning in the English Classroom and Beyond*   Written by Elizabeth Rodriguez Kessler of California State University, Northridge, this is the second monograph in Longman's series for developmental educators. It provides a definition and history of service-learning, as well as an overview of how service-learning can be integrated effectively into the college classroom. 0-321-12749-8

ACKNOWLEDGMENTS

Many thanks to those who've supported both the first and second editions of *Connections*. We appreciate the continued support of Longman Publishers and the Developmental English editorial team, who have guided us through both editions. We wish to thank Janice Wiggins-Clark, our developmental editor on the second edition, who has offered genuine support and sound advice. Likewise, we want to thank Meegan Thompson for administrative support, Melanie Craig for marketing, and Caroline Gloodt for text permissions. Credit goes to our production manager Denise Phillip for overseeing publication of the second edition, Donna Campion, senior supplements manager, and Cyndy Taylor, supplements editor, for their work on the *Instructor's Manual*. In addition, we appreciate the support of Patrick Burt, production editor, and the staff at WestWords, Inc., who have helped to produce a quality text.

We're grateful for the perspectives offered by our colleague-reviewers:

Alice Adams, Glendale Community College

Alan Ainsworth, Houston Community College

Dennis Chowenhill, Chabot College

Robert Fuhrel, Community College of Southern Nevada

Sugie Goen, San Francisco State University

Susanmarie Harrington, Indiana University-Purdue University at Indianapolis

Linda Houston, The Ohio State University Agricultural Technical Institute

Peggy Karsten, Ridgewater College

Laura Knight, Mercer County Community College

Mary Ann Lee, Longview Community College

Randall Popken, Tarleton State University

Harvey Rubenstein, Hudson County Community College

Valerie Russell, Valencia Community College

Athene Sallee, Forsyth Technical Community College

Mary Sauer, Indiana University-Purdue University at Indianapolis

Nancy Taylor, California State University, Northridge

Ben Thomserson, Crafton Hills College

We've implemented many of their suggestions in the revision of the text.

And we're grateful to our colleagues who reviewed the final version of the first edition. Please know that you've helped to establish the standard for the second edition:

Christine Barkley, Palomar College

Gwyn Enright, San Diego City College

Marilyn Kennedy, Orange Coast College

John Lundquist, Golden West College

Amy F. Penne, Parkland College

We also appreciate the guidance of team members who made the first edition possible. Our thanks to David Cohen, our developmental editor for the first edition, whose advice contributed to the text's success; to Jennifer Krasula for responding to our every need; to Melanie Craig for marketing; and to Caroline Gloodt for securing permissions. Likewise, Denise Phillip, production manager, and researchers Joanne Polster/PhotoSearch, Inc., and Karen Pugliano deserve credit for their roles in the construction of the first edition. We're grateful, too, for the help of Tatiana Zaza, Donna Campion, Belinda Yong, and Christine White in the development of the *Instructor's Manual* that accompanied the first edition. And we appreciate Nan Lewis-Schulz, senior production editor at Thompson Steele, Inc., for managing the production stage for the first edition.

Others who contributed to the first edition include Mollie Burroughs, who generously compiled the index; Lisa Abraham and Sean Colcleasure, who helped pilot materials; Lisa Marchand, who contributed a writing prompt; and Milenko Vlaisavljevic, who contributed his talents in photography and design.

We also wish to acknowledge the contributions of our colleagues, friends, and family members whose continued support has sustained us through the development of two editions of the text.

Special thanks to Dr. Stephanie Tucker of California State University, Sacramento, whose inspirational teaching and insight into the needs of developmental writers fueled our desire to create this text.

Finally, we'd like to thank our students at Cosumnes River College, Folsom Lake College, West Valley College, and California State University, Sacramento, for being open to new materials and a new approach. We especially wish to acknowledge those students who've contributed essays, paragraphs, or sentences to the text: Jennifer Arch, Allison Baxter, Melody Bruley, Diony Fernandez, Paul Gregorio, Maria Gonzales, Keisha Harris, Ruth Hathaway, Doris Maysonet, Stacy Michel, Aura Northy, Parris Ray, Rector Sajor, and Miguel Viera. Your willingness to share your work with others makes this a better, more collaborative text.

Tammy Montgomery Boeck
Megan C. Rainey

A Note to Students

Dear Student,

Welcome to a challenging and dynamic textbook that will help you further develop your academic writing skills. If you are used to doing drill work and fill-in-the blank exercises in your English courses, you will be surprised by what you find here. We wrote this book to engage you in interesting, challenging topics that encourage discussion and lead to discovery. Our goal is to guide you through the realistic and productive reading and writing processes that help you write thoughtful essays.

The title of the text is *Connections* because we have connected all the links of the communication chain—so that each piece of work you do makes sense and leads to honest, meaningful communication. You'll learn strategies for approaching and responding to writing topics and for stating, explaining, and proving your claims in your essays. In other words, you'll learn what experienced writers know—that to write well, you must engage in an effective writing process, a process that also involves critical reading and thinking.

The Premise of This Book

Connections is built on the premise that developing good writing skills requires you to connect three key elements:

Writing—The First Link

It is obvious that developing strong writing skills requires you to write. But what if you don't have much confidence in your ability to write? What if you aren't sure what to write about? What if you're in the class to learn how to write essays, reports, summaries, or other work required in college and on the job? Just where should you begin?

For many years, students were asked to fill in blanks and do many, many sentence drills. However, research shows that such approaches only slightly improve a person's writing skill and may, in fact, discourage the writer who may not see the value of the drills or be able to apply the concepts in the exercises to his or her own writing. That's why fill-in-the-blank work is used only as an occasional method of warming up in *Connections*.

Instead, you will focus on journal assignments, summaries, and essay assignments. These writing activities are designed to stimulate thought and help you develop opinions about the issues raised in the text. Rather than just writing *about* an issue you may be unfamiliar with, you'll actively *engage* that issue in your writing. Even the sentence work connects to the issues and requires you to write out whole sentences or paragraphs. This combination of writing activities provides a productive approach to developing writing skills. Yet, these types of assignments aren't enough by themselves.

Reading—The Second Link

Writing assignments must be linked to reading assignments. Working on both reading and writing skills at the same time will speed up your progress in developing stronger language skills. The reading work you do in this book will help you build your vocabulary, become more familiar with the forms of academic and journalistic writing, understand writing styles and techniques, and learn information you can use in your essays. You'll also work on your summarizing skills.

Critical Thinking—The Third Link

The final link, critical thinking, connects to both reading and writing. Critical thinking work helps you analyze the issues and make sense of the readings so that you can develop ideas worth communicating in your essays. Critical thinking also helps you make important choices about what to include in or exclude from your writing.

Connecting the Links

Of course, simply having each link present between the front and back covers of this book is not enough. The links must actually be joined. In Chapters 1 through 4, you'll learn more about each link and how they should connect when you are working on your reading and writing skills. In these chapters, you'll also learn about the reading and writing processes—the necessary steps for approaching and completing your reading and writing work successfully. Then the links are dynamically connected in Chapters 5 through 8—the essay chapters—as each chapter focuses on one theme: heroes, television, technology, and poetry and music. All the discussion activities, questions for critical thought, journal responses, readings, writing assignments, and sentence exercises stay focused on the theme in the chapter. Each piece of work you do as you complete an assignment will connect to the next, and you'll be able to watch your own writing process develop as you construct your essays.

Goals

As you work on effectively connecting these links, you'll be working toward these specific goals:

Writing Goals

- Develop an effective writing process.
- Write focused essays with clear thesis statements and topic sentences.
- Write thoughtful, developed essays.
- Write well-organized essays.
- Write clear, well-shaped sentences.

Reading Goals

- Develop an effective reading process.
- Broaden your knowledge of how essays and other readings are shaped.
- Improve your vocabulary and your approach to vocabulary.
- Increase your knowledge of writing styles and techniques.

Critical Thinking Goals

- Sharpen your questioning and thinking skills so that you better understand readings and analyze complex topics.
- Improve your ability to make good choices when writing your own essays.

Connecting the links and working toward these goals will be challenging, but this text offers you the tools and the guided steps to lead you to success.

Good luck!

Tammy Montgomery Boeck
Megan C. Rainey

Establishing the Connections

This section of Connections *will help you understand the writing-reading-critical thinking connection and will help you sharpen your study skills. You'll also study the shapes of essays and journalistic writing and then learn to summarize texts. The final two chapters explain the reading and writing processes and offer you many opportunities to practice these processes.*

The Writing-Reading-Critical Thinking Connection

Main Topics

- Making the writing-reading-critical thinking connection

- Considering audience and purpose in effective communication

- Reviewing your history as a writer, reader, and critical thinker

- Establishing reading, writing, and critical thinking goals for the semester

- Taking notes, keeping a notebook, and working with a tutor

- Understanding the text, the assignments, and the sentence work

- Identifying, describing, and defining verbs

Beetle Bailey

Sacramento Bee, Jan. 11, 1999, C:6

You may believe that the ability to write well is something that you're either born with or not. However, the fact is that successful writers develop their writing skills in much the same way as sculptors develop their artistic skills. Just as the sculptor begins with a lump of clay and then kneads, massages, and molds it into a vase or other object, so the writer begins with a cluster of ideas to explore, develop, and shape into an essay.

Of course, with practice the sculptor becomes skilled at shaping the clay. In the same way, the writer becomes skilled at writing through practicing the craft. Like anyone learning a craft, the writer needs the right tools and techniques to fashion the work. This chapter will provide you with the tools. Future chapters will help you develop the techniques. While you read this chapter and those that follow, think in terms of sculptor and clay, writer and words, as you shape thoughts and ideas into expression.

INTRODUCING THE CONNECTIONS

This textbook may have surprised you. You may have expected it to begin with a series of grammar exercises or a description of how to start typing your first paragraph. Although most writing textbooks start with writing sentences or paragraphs, this text is different. *Connections* was designed with the conviction that writing skills are developed through the linking of reading, writing, and critical thinking. Perhaps you've heard the saying "A chain is only as strong as its weakest link." It's a reminder that each link must be strong enough to hold its share of the weight.

What does this comparison suggest in terms of your writing skills? To become an effective writer, you must strengthen not only your writing, but also your reading and critical thinking skills. In this section, you'll examine and practice the **writing-reading-critical thinking connection.**

As you read this chapter and those that follow, you'll need to keep a dictionary, loose-leaf notebook, pen, and highlighter ready. The margins throughout the text have been left blank so that you'll have room to write down any thoughts, questions, or notes as you read.

The Writing Link

Writing serves many functions. In your personal life, it may help you reflect on your experiences, explore ideas, and discover new ones. It's also a form of communication. From office memos to e-mail, from term papers to love letters, we often find ourselves writing. (Even the *Beetle Bailey* comic on page 2 has Private Bailey attempting to communicate with his sergeant through writing.) You've probably already discovered the need for strong writing skills. In fact, you may have discovered that writing well is one key to your future success.

Journal Assignment

The journal assignments in this text are opportunities for you to express yourself thoughtfully and freely. Concentrate on exploring ideas and don't worry about spelling, punctuation, grammar, or style.

A Writer Today

Think of some ways in which writing is a part of your life. How many things, personal or professional, have you had to write in the past few days or weeks? What might you have to write in the future? Respond to these questions in your notebook.

Your History as a Writer   Although strong writing skills are required of both students and employees, many people lack confidence in their writing. If you don't enjoy writing, a look at your own history as a writer may show when, why, and how your apprehensions about writing developed. Or, if you're one of the lucky people who finds writing fun and easy, your history may reveal how you developed a more positive view toward writing.

Journal Assignment

Your History as a Writer

In your notebook, trace your development as a writer. How far back can you remember writing? Try to remember what it was like to write in grade school for a teacher, parent, or friend. Explain what you were writing about and whom it was for. How did you feel about your writing at that time? What kind of feedback (if any) did you receive?

Now answer the same set of questions for your writing in your middle school years and your high school years. Finally, describe your writing experiences since high school. Overall, would you say your experiences have been positive or negative? Explain.

The Reading Link

Now let's take a look at the second link in our chain of connections: *reading.* Like writing, reading is a part of our daily lives. Even the most basic street sign is impossible to understand when you don't know how to read it (unless it's accompanied by a picture). If you've ever traveled to a country where you didn't speak the language, then you've probably discovered how much we rely on our reading skills.

We read all the time, often without thinking about it. At the grocery store, for instance, we may stop to read a label to make sure a product doesn't contain too much fat. Or we may browse through a newspaper or magazine while waiting for a doctor or dentist appointment. In fact, if you've had the opportunity to surf the Web, then you may be reading e-mail or other documents from all over the world.

Journal Assignment

A Reader Today

Think of some ways in which reading is a part of your daily life. How many things, personal or professional, have you read in the past few days or weeks? How important are strong reading skills for success in today's world?

Your History as a Reader   As you did earlier with "Your History as a Writer," take time now to consider your history as a reader. If you have always enjoyed reading, your history should show what you like to read and how you gained your love for reading. If you haven't enjoyed reading in the past, your history may show when, why, and how your concerns about reading developed.

Journal Assignment

Your History as a Reader

Think about your own history as a reader. Did anyone (a parent, teacher, friend, or sibling) read to you as a child? How old were you when you first began to read on your own? Did you enjoy reading as a young person? Why, or why not? If you didn't read much, what activities probably took the place of reading in your life? Can you recall any book that you especially appreciated? (If you don't remember the title, tell what happened in the book.)

Get Involved!

Read "The Most Precious Gift" on pages 390–394. On a sheet of paper, first describe Robert Howard Allen's history of reading as he grew up. Then explain how his reading as a child affected his life as an adult. Discuss your explanation with classmates.

Making the Writing-Reading Connection

To be a good writer, you must be a good reader. Reading helps you understand concepts and ideas while providing information to use in your

Notes

writing. Reading also helps you learn the techniques of good writing. This joining of skills is what we call the writing-reading connection.

- **We often respond to reading through writing.**

    At work: You might be asked to read a report and write a summary of it for your supervisor.

    At school: Many exams require you to read a short article and then write an essay in response.

    At home: After reading an e-mail you've received, you might respond by writing and sending your own e-mail.

- **We read to gather ideas we might want to write about.**

A slash (/) between words such as maternity/paternity usually means "or."

    At work: Perhaps as a personnel manager, you need to write a memo explaining new laws concerning maternity/paternity leave. You would first need to read government information about these new laws.

    At school: If your history instructor wants a research paper on an American hero, you would need to read books, essays, and articles to gather the necessary information.

    At home: Perhaps you want your medical insurance provider to pay for your X-rays. You would need to read your insurance plan materials before writing a letter to the company.

- **When we write, we expect to be read.**

    At work: If you write a proposal suggesting that the company pay the tuition costs for employees who take college courses, you expect someone to read your ideas.

    At school: After you've diligently worked on your English essay about music lyrics, you expect your instructor to read it.

    At home: When you leave a note reminding your roommate that rent was due two days ago, you expect her to read it (and also pay the rent).

Activity

Activities in the text are designed to help you practice new concepts. In this activity, you'll practice making the writing-reading connection.

Even Abby Makes the Connection

This activity offers you an entertaining chance to practice the writing-reading connection. Whenever people write to the advice column *Dear Abby,* they hope "Abby" will *read* about their dilemmas and *write* in response. Begin by reading the *Dear Abby* selection below, then follow the instructions after the reading.

Dear Abby:

I dated "James" for 18 months before he proposed. Our wedding is set for the fall of next year. James is loving, considerate, and honest. However, we're completely opposite in our tastes and interests. I am romantic, artistic, and impulsive. He is practical, predictable, and stable.

I was happy with this relationship until a couple of months ago, when I went out to lunch several times with a single man I'll call "John." (We work together.) What began as a casual friendship seems to be developing into more. The attraction is mutual. We share the same values, the same likes and dislikes, and we often think alike. When I look at him, I see myself, so we're very compatible.

John, however, has a less-than-perfect past. He's been in some bad relationships and is twice divorced. He has a troubled family history and two teenagers in therapy with numerous unresolved problems.

Abby, we both realize we won't remain "just friends" if we continue going out to lunch, etc. John hasn't mentioned marriage, but he has told me that he wants me in his life.

I think I love them both. James is safe, John is exciting. John knows about my fiancé, but James doesn't have a clue. Should I go through with the wedding because I'm certain that James would be a good husband, or should I take my chances that John and I will find happiness together?

—Bewitched, Bewildered, and Bothered

As seen in *Dear Abby* by Abigail Van Buren a.k.a. Jeanne Phillips and founded by her mother Pauline Phillips. © Universal Press Syndicate. Reprinted with permission. All rights reserved.

1. Think about Bewitched's predicament and how she might solve it. Then respond in your notebook with a letter of advice. Begin your letter with the greeting "Dear Bewitched."

2. Compare your advice with a classmate's before continuing to the next step.

Notes

Get Involved!

With a classmate, go to the library or computer lab on campus and log on to the *Dear Abby* website, which is located at www.uexpress.com/ dearabby/viewda.cfm. (Or find Abby's column in your local newspaper.) Read Abby's advice for the day and discuss it with your partner. Share your responses to Abby's advice with classmates.

3. Now read Dear Abby's advice, which follows. Was your advice similar? Do you agree or disagree with her advice? What do you think Abby considers as she forms responses to letters like the one from Bewitched?

4. What was your classmate's response? How did you and your classmate arrive at your responses? Discuss the similarities and differences in advice.

Dear Bewitched:

If you are attracted to John, it's obvious that you are not in love with James. You would be doing James an enormous favor if you broke the engagement and freed him to find a woman who would love and appreciate him. And the sooner the better.

—Abby

As seen in *Dear Abby* by Abigail Van Buren a.k.a. Jeanne Phillips and founded by her mother Pauline Phillips. © Universal Press Syndicate. Reprinted with permission. All rights reserved.

The Critical Thinking Link

Although strong writing and reading skills are important to your success, your ability to **think critically** about issues or ideas is equally important. When you use your critical thinking skills, you look beyond the surface of an issue or action and examine the purpose or motivation behind it.

In terms of the *Dear Abby* activity, you used your critical thinking skills if you not only considered Bewitched's behavior but also carefully examined and evaluated her motivations and desires. As you can see from Abby's response, Abby looked beyond the obvious symptom—Bewitched was attracted to another man—to what Abby believed is the main issue: Bewitched wasn't really in love with her fiancé. And although you may have judged Bewitched's motivations and actions differently, if you examined them carefully and took the time to consider the viewpoints of others *before* writing your response, you were thinking critically.

Critical Thinkers

- consider different views and possibilities when looking at an issue or problem,

- consider the possible reasons or motivations behind issues or actions,
- question the ideas presented before agreeing, disagreeing, or seeking an alternative, and
- question ideas and seek new ideas.

Critical thinkers use their ability to reason—questioning, evaluating, and judging every issue or idea they read, discuss, and write about.

Don't Believe Everything You Read or Hear It would be a scary and confusing world *if we believed everything we read or heard.* Sometimes even reliable sources have to be questioned.

- After reading only a few advertisements, we might believe that the only road to happiness, power, and beauty is to buy new cars, jewelry, and clothing.
- If we read one essay in favor of the death penalty and believed it, and then read another essay against the death penalty and believed it, we would be very confused.
- If we believed everything we heard, we might panic, as some 1.7 million people did on Halloween in 1938 during a radio presentation of H. G. Wells's *War of the Worlds.* (They believed Martians were invading Earth because they trusted the powerful medium of radio.)

Think Before You Write Consider how difficult or even embarrassing it would be to write without carefully thinking through ideas first.

- A writer who dives into an essay on the death penalty without careful thinking (critical thinking) might waste significant time by writing things he doesn't believe or that don't make sense.
- A writer who reads about the death penalty, thinks about it, discusses it, and then takes a side on the issue is prepared to write what he believes.

Consider Audience and Purpose With a few exceptions, most of your writing is directed at a specific audience for a specific purpose.

- Your **audience** includes anyone you intend to communicate to.
- Your **purpose** is your reason for writing and should be the driving force behind your writing.

Whether you are composing a letter to a loved one or writing a report for your employer, you use your critical thinking skills and consider

Notes

your audience and purpose. Doing so ensures that you convey your ideas to your audience in a way that allows you to be heard.

> ### Activity
>
> ### Analyzing Audience and Purpose
>
> Review the *Beetle Bailey* comic strip from page 2 of this chapter. In it, Beetle Bailey, the main character, has presented to his sergeant a written list of reasons why he should be given the day off. With a partner, answer the following questions:
>
> 1. What is Beetle's purpose for writing?
>
> 2. Who is his audience?
>
> 3. Is he successful in getting his message across? Why, or why not?
>
> 4. How might Beetle be more effective in his future communication with the sergeant?
>
> 5. What advice about audience and purpose would you offer Beetle for the next time he tries to communicate in writing?

There's a simple message behind the *Beetle Bailey* strip that can help you with your writing: Think critically about audience and purpose to communicate effectively.

> ### Journal Assignment
> ### Your History as a Critical Thinker
>
> Reflect on times when you've used your critical thinking skills. Were any of them connected to reading and/or writing? Did any instructors or employers encourage critical thinking? How did they encourage you? What has been your response to activities requiring critical thinking? Write about your experiences as a critical thinker.

Making the Writing-Reading-Critical Thinking Connection

Now it's time to use the writing-reading-critical thinking chain we've constructed. This chain can give you the power to learn new ideas and to say new things. Although the links can be separated and used individually, when connected they make your communication more interesting and powerful. The most important tasks in college and at work will require you to use this chain.

Activity

Making the Connection

In this activity, you will read, think critically, and write. With your classmates, review the following quotation:

Writing is the act of saying "I," of imposing oneself upon other people, of saying listen to me, see it my way, change your mind.
> —*Joan Didion (1934–), American novelist and essayist*

1. Think about what Didion is saying about writing. Considering what she does for a living, why would she believe this?

2. Look up the word *imposing* in your dictionary to see what it means, then discuss your thoughts with classmates. Put Didion's idea in your own words.

3. Discuss with your classmates how you might use writing, "the act of saying 'I,'" in your future at college and work. Be sure to take notes.

Journal Assignment

Your Goals as a Writer, Reader, and Critical Thinker

Take time to *reread* interesting sections of this first chapter, your journals, your class notes, and Didion's preceding quotation. *Think* about the skills you want to gain in this class and how you might use them. Consider what some of your classmates have said. Consider what past instructors have said. Consider, honestly, your strengths and weaknesses. *Write* down your goals as a writer, reader, and critical thinker.

TOOLS FOR MAKING THE CONNECTIONS

Now that you've established your writing, reading, and critical thinking goals, you're ready to learn some strategies for achieving your goals. In this section, you'll learn how to

- take lecture notes and use the "Notes" column in the text,
- put together a notebook of your writing assignments,
- make the most of a good tutor,
- use the computer to become a more efficient writer, and
- use the glossary and index.

By applying these strategies, you'll strengthen not only your writing, reading, and critical thinking skills, but also your study skills.

Taking Notes

You'll get much more out of your reading and lectures if you learn to take notes well since taking notes is one way to be an active participant in the reading, writing, and critical thinking processes. By taking notes, you aren't simply absorbing information. You're involved in the process of actively listening and identifying the most important points, then transcribing those points into writing that makes sense to you so that you can review the information later.

Sometimes taking notes is as simple as leaving a check next to an interesting idea in your reading. In other cases, taking notes involves writing out the speaker's main points while listening to a lecture. In this section, you'll learn how to take notes when reading and while listening.

Writing in the Margins: Becoming a More Active Reader   One simple way to become a more active reader is to make notes in book margins as you read. Does this suggestion surprise you? If so, you were probably taught *not* to write in your textbooks in elementary or secondary school. Since textbooks were usually passed down from one class to the next, or sold at the end of the school year, you may have been told to keep the margins clean. However, effective readers usually write in the margins of their textbooks. You should feel free to use the margins of your own books for restating main ideas, responding to what you've read, or making connections to other books or articles you've read.

In the following excerpt from his essay, "How to Mark a Book," Mortimer Adler, the founder of the Great Books Program, explains why marking up books is important.

> Why is marking a book indispensable to reading? First, it keeps you awake. (And I don't mean merely conscious; I mean wide awake.) In the second place, reading, if it is active, is thinking, and thinking tends to express itself in words, spoken or written. The marked book is usually the thought-through

book. Finally, writing helps you remember the thoughts you had, or the thoughts the author expressed.

—Saturday Review, 1940

Adler suggests, as do other reading experts, that the act of writing in response to reading helps you think through and retain ideas. And if you've made notes next to important ideas in the text, you can easily refer back to these ideas when you review. For study purposes, marking your book makes sense. If you get into the habit of noting important points or ideas in your text, then you'll be a step ahead when it's time to study for an exam.

Using the "Notes" Column in This Text   Because we understand the importance of being an active reader, this text provides an ongoing "Notes" column in the margins. This column gives you a place to record your immediate reactions to a reading, jot down questions that come to mind as you read, identify main points, or brainstorm ideas for your writing. In short, the "Notes" column is meant to encourage you to become a more active reader.

To give you an idea of how you might use the "Notes" column, we've included the first three paragraphs of an essay that appears in the textbook *America and Its People*. Note the reader's comments in the margin of the text.

The Modern Family
by James Kirby Martin et al.

This selection appeared in the American history book, *America and Its People*.

1   Does a father have the right to give his children his last name even if his wife objects? Can an expectant mother obtain an abortion without her husband's permission? Should a teenager, unhappy with her parents' restrictions on her smoking, dating, and choice of friends, be allowed to have herself placed in a foster home? Should a childless couple be permitted to hire a "surrogate mother" to be artificially inseminated and carry a child to delivery? These are among the questions that the nation's courts have had to wrestle with as the nature of American family life has, in the course of a generation, been revolutionized.

2   During the 1950s, the Cleavers on the television show *Leave It to Beaver* epitomized the American family. In 1960, over 70 percent of all

Notes

These are interesting questions. I wonder if all of them will be answered in the body of the essay. The essay appears to be about the American family.

"Epitomize": to be a typical example. Were the Cleavers really a typical American family? Maybe the writers mean simply that most families then had a father, mother, and children.

Notes

American households were like the Cleavers: made up of a breadwinner father, a homemaker mother, and their kids. Today, "traditional" families with a working husband, [a homemaker], and one or more children make up less than 15 percent of the nation's households. And as America's families have changed, the image of the family portrayed on television has changed accordingly. . . .

True, the family has changed: divorce rate, single-parent households, couples living together are all higher now than in the '50s or '60s.

3   Profound changes have reshaped American family life in recent years. In a decade, divorce rates doubled. The number of divorces today is twice as high as in 1966 and three times higher than in 1950. The rapid upsurge in the divorce rates contributed to a dramatic increase in the number of single-parent households. . . . The number of households consisting of a single woman and her children has tripled since 1960. A sharp increase in female-headed homes has been accompanied by a startling increase in the number of couples cohabitating outside of marriage. The number of unmarried couples living together has quadrupled since 1970.

It's clear from the reader's margin notes that she engaged in her reading. She speculated about what the reading would cover, she looked up an unfamiliar term and put the definition where she will see it when she reviews, and she asked questions and made comments that show she had thought about the reading.

Although this reader made extensive comments in the "Notes" column, this isn't always necessary. Let's look at another brief selection marked in a different way.

—topic sentence

—support: facts and statistics

—creative wrap-up

Television is the most popular of the popular media. Indeed, if Nielsen research and other studies are correct, there are few things that Americans do more than they watch television. On average, each household has a TV on almost fifty hours a week. Forty percent of households eat dinner with the set on. Individually, Americans watch an average of thirty hours a week. We begin peering at TV through the bars of cribs and continue looking at it through the cataracts of old age.

—Joshua Meyrowitz, from "Television: The Shared Arena"

In this case, the reader used the "Notes" column for labeling the parts of the paragraph as opposed to making comments on the reading. The point is to use the "Notes" column as needed. *You* are the one who decides how to use the margins.

Additional Ideas for Engaging with Your Reading

Not every book comes equipped with a "Notes" column. However, most books have enough of a margin or some blank pages at the ends of chapters that you can use for notetaking. Here are some of Adler's pointers for marking not just your textbooks, but any book you may read.

Notes

1. <u>*Underlining:*</u> of major points, of important or forceful statements.

2. *Vertical lines at the margin:* to emphasize a statement already underlined.

   ‖

3. *Star, asterisk, or other doo-dad at the margin:* to be used sparingly, to emphasize the . . . most important statements . . . .

   *

4. *Numbers in the margin:* to indicate the sequence of points the author makes in developing a single argument.

   1, 2, 3

5. *Numbers of other pages in the margin:* to indicate where else in the book the author made points relevant to the point marked; to tie up the ideas in a book, which, though they may be separated by many pages, belong together.

   see page 67

6. *Circling key words or phrases.*

   critical thinking

7. *Writing in the margin, or at the top or bottom of the page, for the sake of:* recording questions (and perhaps answers) which a passage raised in your mind; reducing a complicated discussion to a simple statement; or recording the sequence of major points right through the books.

As you actively engage in your reading, you should freely adapt Adler's suggestions to fit your needs as a reader.

Becoming a More Active Listener   From the moment you walk into a classroom, you're expected to listen to and remember what the instructor says. But remembering everything the instructor says is quite a task. You've probably been told how important it is to take notes. But taking notes effectively is easier said than done. To take useful notes, you must first learn how to listen.

In his article "Learning to Listen," William H. Armstrong (who has taught history for over 50 years) briefly explains the history of the lecture and the difficulties people have in listening.

> Before books and printing, the primary element in acquiring knowledge was listening. A "lecture" originally meant a "reading" from some precious manuscript. The reader read slowly and stopped to explain difficult passages to his listeners. The process has changed; reading is no doubt the primary element in acquiring knowledge, but listening remains the second most important element.

Notes

Why is listening . . . the most difficult of the learning processes? The practices of seeing (reading), writing, and thinking are exercised within the person. But listening takes on the complexity of the listener having to coordinate their mental powers with an outside force—the person or thing to which the listener is listening. This demands the discipline of subjecting the mind of the listener to that of the speaker.

The second problem in learning to listen arises from lack of associated control. When you learn to read, your eyes control the speed with which you read. When you write there is actual physical control in your hand. In thinking, the analysis of thought travels at exactly the speed capacity of your mind. But when you begin to train yourself to be a good listener, you are faced with a difficulty not unlike that of trying to drive a car without brakes. You can think four times as fast as the average teacher can speak.

Only by demanding of yourself the most unswerving concentration and discipline can you hold your mind on the track of the speaker. This can be accomplished if the listener uses the free time to think around the topic—"listening between the lines" as it is sometimes called. It consists of anticipating the teacher's next point, summarizing what has been said, questioning in silence the accuracy or importance of what is being taught, putting the teacher's thoughts into one's own words, and trying to discern the test or examination questions that will be formed from this material.

If you find your mind wandering after only a few minutes of class, you need to work on developing your concentration. Armstrong suggests that you begin by concentrating for the first ten minutes of every class period. As you focus on the instructor or task at hand, block out other sounds that might keep you from listening. Then, as your ability to listen develops, extend your period of concentration. Eventually, you'll be able to stay focused for the entire class period. Taking notes will help you stay focused.

Taking Lecture Notes   This is the scenario in many classrooms: The instructor begins speaking when the class period starts, and students write down the most important points. Later, they will review their notes when it's time to take the midterm or final. Sounds easy enough, doesn't it? But taking effective notes (as you may have discovered) can be quite challenging.

Here are some tips (from Armstrong and other instructors) for taking lecture notes:

- *Be a good listener.* If you aren't listening, you can't possibly take good notes.

Notes

- *Be prepared.* You need the tools with you, ready, in order to take lecture notes. This means blank paper and pencil or pen in hand when class starts.

- *Listen for clues* in the lecture that suggest an important point is being made. Remember, you can't write down everything the instructor says. Trying to do so will only frustrate you. Listen for the repeated phrases "the important point" or "we must remember." When you hear such clues, be ready to write.

- *Watch the overhead or chalkboard.* If the instructor displays or lists points, write those down. The instructor wouldn't write them down if they weren't important.

- *Don't break your concentration* to worry about spelling or grammar.

- *Ask the instructor for help* at the end of the class if you miss an important point or need something clarified.

- *Review and fill in your notes* after a lecture so that you don't forget what you've heard.

- *File your notes* in an organized manner (in your notebook) so that they're in place when you need to study them.

Journal Assignment

Taking Effective Lecture Notes

Taking effective lecture notes can help you get better grades. Reflect on how you've taken notes in the past. Then consider what you've learned about listening and taking notes in this chapter. Which strategies do you intend to use in your next class? How will you use these strategies to improve your reading, writing, and critical thinking skills?

Keeping a Notebook

Being well organized is another key to success. The well-organized person carefully files away important papers and assignments so that they're easily found when needed. By learning to organize a notebook, you'll not only develop your organization and study skills, you'll simplify your life. The idea is to make your own life easier by keeping journal entries, reading questions, class activities, writing assignments, and other work handy.

Notes

To begin, you'll need a three-ring binder (1½- to 2-inch width), a package of dividers, and loose-leaf paper.

Two Basic Methods of Organization   There are many ways to organize a notebook, but we'll focus on two specific ways—organizing by process and organizing by assignment. No matter which method you use, your course syllabus should appear first in your notebook.

When one assignment builds on another, it helps to *organize your work by process*. The idea is to organize assignments as you complete them so that you can see your writing develop through a chapter. Begin by filling out a divider for each chapter. Then, under each chapter divider, keep every assignment you complete—from activities to reading questions to journals to drafts—filed in order of completion. Also include any pages of your own: questions about the assignment, brainstorming activities, outlines, or any articles you discover and want to add to your body of research. Include your early rough drafts, developing drafts, and later drafts in order of completion. Also include a copy of your final drafts as well as the graded drafts returned by your instructor. As you complete each chapter, you'll be able to flip through the assignments and easily see how your essays developed.

Another approach is to *organize your work by assignment*. In this case, you store journal entries under one divider, reading questions under another, sentence work under another, and so on. If you choose this approach, consider using the following headings:

a. Journal Assignments

b. Reading Questions

c. Class Activities

d. Lecture Notes

e. Writing Assignments

f. Sentence Work

g. Vocabulary

(other sections as needed)

If you use this approach, the "Writing Assignments" section should still store—from beginning to end—all the drafts of your essays. As you store these drafts, you'll begin to understand and develop your own process for writing. Also in this writing assignments section, jot down any thoughts or reactions you have to the assignments or any questions you have about the assignments so that you can ask your instructor. Feel free to include any pages of your own brainstorming—clustering, listing, freewriting—on the topic. Also include early outlines, rough drafts, developing drafts, and later drafts. Finally, store a copy of your final draft as well as the graded draft returned by your instructor. As the semester progresses, this section of your notebook will become the largest. At a glance, you'll be able to see how your essays developed.

Making the Most of a Good Tutor

As a supplement to your assigned work, we recommend that you see a tutor. Your reading and writing skills will improve much more quickly if you can discuss your work frequently outside of class. And although study groups made up of students from your class are an excellent idea, too, it is important to discuss your work with a more experienced writer. This is where tutors come in.

Whether you are feeling secure or insecure about your reading and writing skills, you can benefit from tutorial assistance. (Even professional writers hire editors to help them rethink and revise portions of their writing.) However, it's extremely important that you have a clear idea about what you can expect from a tutoring session. A tutor who does too much for you can actually slow down your growth as a reader, writer, and thinker. You'll want to find a tutor who offers guidance and tools for success while encouraging you to do the work yourself. Here are things to look for in a good tutor.

A Good Tutor Should

- be on time and ready to help you.
- listen carefully to you and your concerns about writing.
- ask you questions about your assignment, your deadlines, and your concerns.
- probably comment first on the global aspects of your writing: your focus, development, and organization.
- respond honestly to your writing.
- discuss some possible ways to improve weak spots, but let you do the actual improvements.

- explain a grammatical error to you and different ways to correct it, but have you identify and fix it in your own writing.
- tell you how many spelling errors he or she sees, but let you find the errors and fix them yourself.

A Good Tutor Should Not

- waste your time by being consistently late or by talking about things unrelated to the writing task.
- rewrite sections of your paper or give you the "right words" to say. (Yours are the right words and ideas.)
- proofread your paper by marking and correcting your grammar, punctuation, and spelling mistakes.

Finding a Good Tutor   To find a good tutor, go to the writing center, the computer lab, your English instructor, or your college counselor to ask for a referral. Most colleges have some kind of tutorial service available at little to no cost. It's up to you, however, to use your college's system to your advantage. If you begin working with a tutor and discover that he or she isn't listening to or understanding your needs, then don't waste your time. Arrange to work with another tutor.

Making the Most of a Tutoring Session   The more enthusiasm and interest you put into your tutoring sessions, the more you'll get out of them. Think about it from the tutor's perspective for a moment. A tutor often works one-on-one with students for several hours in a single day. If you were a tutor, wouldn't you feel energized by those students who arrived at their sessions prepared to work? Here are some tips on how you can be a good tutee:

- *See the tutor on a regular basis.* Have a set appointment time, if possible, for once or twice a week. Be on time.
- *Set goals with the tutor.* Discuss and write down your strengths and weaknesses as a reader and writer. Prioritize your writing goals. Review this list with your instructor after your instructor has had time to evaluate some of your writing. Revise your goal list as your instructor suggests. (Review this list at midterm with your instructor.)
- *Bring in and discuss readings.* Discuss vocabulary words, main ideas, and interesting points.

- *Bring in and discuss the actual writing assignment.* Make sure you understand the requirements of the writing assignment.
- *Brainstorm ideas for your writing assignments.*
- *Show drafts to your tutor.* Ask what is the strongest part of the draft and what is the weakest. (Consider your list of goals for improvement.)
- *Write a short to-do list each week* before you leave the tutoring session. Make an agreement about what you will bring with you next time.

Because your time with a tutor is limited, be on time—with materials organized—and ready to work. Plan to ask questions and share concerns about your writing.

Using Computers

In college and on the job, you will be expected to type most of what you write. You'll become a more efficient writer if you begin the practice of writing your essays on a computer. You don't need to know any fancy computer tricks to benefit from using a computer. You only need to know a few basic commands, which you can learn in the computer lab on your campus. You will also need to know how to type or be willing to learn. (Most college computer labs have computers equipped with typing tutorials.)

Here is a number of tasks that you can complete easily on the computer.

- Freely pour out ideas to discover what you're thinking.
- Move paragraphs and sentences with ease.
- Add and delete information without having to retype your entire essay.
- Check word definitions with the computer's dictionary.
- Check spelling with the computer's spell-check program.

Overall, the computer is faster and more efficient than the typewriter. If you're unsure about where the computer lab is on your campus, ask your instructor or counselor. Both should be able to direct you to this important resource.

Using the Glossary and Index

This book provides two additional resources for writers that you should know about. The first one is the *glossary*. Whenever an important term

Get Involved!

Investigate one of the resources available to students on your campus. For example, look into day care, counseling, tutoring, or financial aid services. Or visit the library or a computer lab. Report back to your classmates, telling them important features of the service: hours, location, eligibility requirements, and so on.

Notes   is mentioned for the first time, it will appear in boldface. The definitions of these boldfaced terms are listed alphabetically in the glossary (page 541). In this chapter, you have encountered several boldface terms. Take a moment to look up the meaning of two of these terms in the glossary: **audience** and **purpose**.

You can also find out information and the location of other terms, authors used in the text, or general subjects by looking in the *subject index* (page 553) or *author-title index* (page 561). Terms in the index, as in the glossary, are listed in alphabetical order. Look up *audience* and *purpose* in the subject index to see where these terms appear in the text.

UNDERSTANDING THE TEXT

Now that you've reviewed the tools and some basic strategies for college success, we'd like to explain how this text works.

An Overview of the Text

This text is divided into six basic areas of instruction. The first section will help you understand how writing, reading, and critical thinking connect. The second will give you practice in making these connections. The third contains supplemental readings that will allow you to further explore these connections. The fourth, fifth, and sixth will offer additional resources to help you refine these connections.

Section I: Establishing the Connections
  Chapter 1: The Writing-Reading-Critical Thinking Connection
  Chapter 2: The Structure of Writing and How to Summarize Texts
  Chapter 3: Examining the Reading Process
  Chapter 4: Examining the Writing Process
Section II: Employing the Connections
  Chapter 5: Writing About Heroes
  Chapter 6: Writing About Television
  Chapter 7: Writing About Technology
  Chapter 8: Writing About Music and Poetry
Section III: Supplemental Readings
Section IV: Skill Builders
  Discovering Your Learning Style
  Using the Dictionary

Notes

Understanding the Assignments

You'll encounter several types of assignments in this text: journals, activities, readings, and essays. Each type of assignment has been created to teach you something about the relationship between reading, writing, and critical thinking, and each offers you practice in applying what you've learned.

Journal Assignments   Usually consisting of a series of questions, **journals** are designed to get you thinking critically about a topic or issue. These are "freewriting zones." In other words, journal assignments provide you the opportunity to explore your ideas on paper. They're much like a diary in that you're allowed to write honestly without fear of judgment. Your instructor may write back in response to your journal but will not judge your ideas or point out grammatical errors.

To give you an idea of what a student journal entry looks like, two student journals on goals are reprinted on the following page. You'll notice that each student's personal writing goals are different although both students are concerned with improving their writing.

Notes

> The skills I wish to gain from this class are simple. First of all, I would like to express myself better as a writer, so that I get good grades on essays and term papers. I know that I'm a good student, but English has always been a bit scary for me. I have a hard time writing ideas under pressure, but let me get in my car and ideas for writing seem to jump out of my head. As a reader, my goals are to continue reading for knowledge and pleasure. As a critical thinker, my goals are to consider a diverse amount of information and then make rational and intelligent decisions. For the larger part of my life, most of my decisions were made around my emotions or what I was feeling instead of thinking. Today I like to think things through.
>
> —*Allison Baxter*

> I know in fact that writing, reading, and critical thinking are the skills that I need to gain and improve in this class. I use these skills on my daily activities such as in school reading books and writing homework assignments and at work communicating with other employees to read and write procedures, reports, and instructions. In addition, reading and writing are very useful in some other ways such as when applying for a new job, writing a resume, traveling with directions, reading menus or labels, and so on. As far as the critical thinking, it may help me to organize things, solve problems and find solutions, and determine better ideas and make improvements. . . . My goal is to increase my knowledge in writing, reading, and most especially thinking to lead me to a higher career.
>
> —*Rector Sajor*

Activities   Within the text, **activities** help you put into practice new writing concepts or ideas. In the *Dear Abby* activity earlier in this chapter, for instance, you were asked to practice the writing-reading connection. Future chapters include such activities as writing summaries, organizing ideas with cue cards, and sharing rough drafts on heroes. As you'll discover, this text offers a variety of individual and group activities all designed to help you practice new concepts.

Here's one student's response to the *Dear Abby* activity from pages 6–8. She read Bewitched's letter and responded as she believed Abby would have responded.

Notes

> Dear Bewitched,
>
> I believe you have quite a hard decision to make. But of all that you've told me, I have to wonder why you would even consider leaving a relationship with a man who is as loving, considerate, and honest as James. John is just offering fun with no commitment.
>
> When the smoke clears, after all the fun you have had with John, you'll have to deal with two troubled teens, a history of divorces, and a man who believes in cheating.
>
> But if James doesn't turn you on anymore, it's obvious that you're not quite ready for commitment or marriage. James deserves someone who is honest, loving, and considerate, too.
>
> —*Maria Gonzalez*

Reading Assignments and Readings Beginning in Chapter 3, readings are preceded by **Reading Assignments**. These assignments will help you practice some of the steps of the reading process that you will learn about in Chapter 3: previewing, anticipating, reading, and rereading.

Then, following each Reading Assignment, you'll find a selected **reading** to complement the writing assignment and chapter theme. For instance, Chapter 5 focuses on heroes, so in that chapter you'll discover a selection of readings on heroes including a personal essay entitled "A Hero in My Family," another essay entitled "Move Over, Barney" that suggests we replace our children's cartoon heroes with real ones, and a newspaper article on Rosa Parks, the woman considered to be the mother of the Civil Rights movement. Although these readings are tied directly to the writing assignments, there's no doubt that as you complete them, you'll be developing your reading skills also.

Note: In Chapter 2, challenging vocabulary is listed before the readings. In later chapters, after some vocabulary instruction, you will become responsible for keeping your own vocabulary list for the readings.

Questions for Critical Thought Following the readings in the text, **Questions for Critical Thought** help you understand and analyze what you've read. They help you think critically about the writer's message as well as the strategies used to convey the message to the reader. They also serve as springboards to class discussion. When responding to these questions, you may discover ideas to use in your writing assignments. Such questions bolster reading comprehension and strengthen critical thinking and discussion skills.

Writing Assignments   You will practice several forms of writing in Chapters 1 through 3—journals, activities, and summaries. Then in Chapter 4 you'll encounter a more formal form of **writing assignment,** the **essay.** In brief, the essay is an organized, multiparagraph piece of writing in which the writer focuses on and develops a particular issue or theme—for a specific audience, for a specific purpose.

Each writing assignment will take you through a series of stages that will help you develop and improve your writing. And you'll write essays on a wide range of contemporary issues and topics: advertisements, heroes, television, technology, music, and poetry.

Understanding the Sentence Work

Throughout this text, sentence practice material (also called **sentence work**) will help you learn to develop and refine your sentences. You may find the work here different from the grammar exercises you've done before. For one thing, you'll be creating many of your own sentences as you practice what you've learned. Also, the practice segments are closely connected to the readings and issues discussed in the chapters. These grammar segments, which appear at the end of each chapter, are designed to help you continue developing your writing, reading, and critical thinking skills.

The Hows and Whys   When you learn how to drive a car, you don't have to know the names of all the parts of the car or how the car was assembled. You do, however, need to know a few key terms: emergency brake, hazard lights, high beams. You also need to know how to use these items. As you become a more experienced driver, you easily pick up more knowledge. For example, you learn how to check the fluids and change the oil. Many people who love cars and driving continue to learn even more about the technical aspects of cars: What is a flange gasket? How do you replace a flange gasket?

How does all of this apply to you as a writer? First, remember that you are a writer because you already know some important basics about writing. For example, you know thousands of words, and you've written these words in various forms—letters, essays, reports—over the years.

The exercises in this text will help you learn or get a better handle on *key writing terms* that will help you shape clear and effective sentences. You don't need to recite definitions of *all* the parts of speech, but knowing these terms will help you develop more control over your writing. That way, when you turn in essays to your instructor (or reports to your boss), you won't feel like you just turned over your prized car to a mechanic who knows everything when you know too little.

Completing the Sentence Exercises   You'll find that the exercises in this text call for you to read and research material, create and discuss ideas, and practice your reading-writing-critical thinking skills. These are the most effective methods for learning about sentences. You'll be exploring, and the more energy you put into your explorations, the better the results you will see.

As you complete the exercises, you'll discover that writing good sentences will become second nature for you, and you'll gain the ability to discuss your writing with others. Throughout this book, you'll continue to pick up more terminology and more ways of shaping sentences. In the end, you'll leave your class knowing that you have better control over your sentences and, consequently, the thoughts you choose to communicate.

SUMMARY OF CHAPTER 1

In Chapter 1 you've learned about the writing-reading-critical thinking connection. In particular, you've reviewed

- the importance of each connection as you've explored your history as a writer, reader, and critical thinker;
- the tools necessary for "making the connections" successfully this semester: taking and keeping notes, keeping a notebook, and making the most of a good tutor; and
- how the text works.

Notes

INTRODUCTION TO VERBS

The Complete Sentence
Identifying and Supplying Verbs
Describing and Defining Verbs

The sentence work in this book begins with verbs because verbs are one of the key ingredients to sentences. You might even call the verb the heart of the sentence because understanding and identifying verbs will help you understand and identify all the other elements in a sentence. In this chapter, you'll first consider the sentence as a whole. Then you'll zero in on the verb and how it functions in a sentence.

The Complete Sentence

To understand the sentence, you'll need to be familiar with a few key terms.

- A **complete sentence** will have a subject and a verb and will express a complete idea.
- A **subject** is a person, place, thing, or idea that is performing an action or that is being described.
- A **verb** expresses the action in the sentence or links the subject to descriptive information.
- The **predicate** is the verb and everything that comes after the verb.

In these complete sentences, verbs are underlined twice, and subjects are underlined once.

The <u>woman</u> <u>wrote</u> to Dear Abby.

<u>Dear Abby</u> <u>gave</u> advice.

The <u>newspaper</u> <u>is</u> on the table.

In the next set of sentences, predicates are underlined twice, and subjects are underlined once.

<u>Collin</u> <u>laughed at my response.</u>

The <u>woman</u> <u>canceled the wedding.</u>

The <u>man</u> <u>was sad.</u>

Identifying and Supplying Verbs

Identifying and understanding verbs will help you talk about and gain better control over your sentences. The exercises that follow will give you practice identifying and supplying verbs.

Practice #1   Supplying Verbs, Part One

Rewrite sentences 1–9 by adding verbs that make sense. (Try not to add the same verb to more than one sentence.) Underline the verbs twice. The first one is done for you.

1. Mary and Joe __*fell*__ in love in Paris.
2. One day, Joe _____ at the top of his lungs, "Marry me, Mary!"
3. But Mary _____ having many boyfriends.
4. She _____ the idea of settling down right away.
5. Joe _____ this was strange.
6. He _____ that all women wanted to get married as soon as possible.
7. Mary _____ Joe to wait for a few years and let her date for a while longer.
8. Joe _____ tired of waiting after about six months.
9. Mary and Joe _____ up.

Practice #2   Supplying Verbs, Part Two

- Copy all the sentences in the following exercise (even the sentences that aren't missing any words).
- Add the missing verbs.
- Because there is more than one way to complete some of these sentences, experiment to find verbs that fit the best.
- Your finished product should be three paragraphs long. (Be sure to *indent* your paragraphs. This means that the beginning of each paragraph should be "pushed in" five spaces so that your reader will know that a new paragraph is starting. You can use your *tab* key on your computer keyboard to indent.)
- Some verbs consist of more than one part. If part of a verb has been provided for you, it has already been underlined. And when complete verbs have been supplied, they have been underlined as well.
- Underline every verb twice in the paragraphs you write.

    Most people <u>think</u> monogamy <u>means</u> staying with one partner (a husband, a wife, a boyfriend, or a girlfriend). The opposite <u>would be</u> polygamy, which

Notes

__means__ having more than one partner at a time (dating or being married to several people at one time). __Are__ these definitions *scientifically* accurate? And __are__ humans __meant__ to be monogamous? According to Deborah Blum, a science writer, scientists __have made__ a lot of interesting discoveries in this area.

Blum _____ that monogamy __doesn't__ necessarily _____ anything to do with sex. Monogamy _____ more about commitment. That __is__, according to scientists, monogamous animal couples __may sleep__ around, but they always __come__ home to each other. They _____ for the babies together, they __defend__ their homes and babies together, and so on. Interestingly, scientists _____ that only 3 percent of the world's mammals _____ monogamous. Blum __reports__, "Birds, lizards, and some loyal fish species __are__ the most likely to stay together." And she __adds__, "Before the rise of moralistic religions, such as Christianity, more than 70 percent of the world's societies __could be classified__ as polygamous."

You __can__ often _____ which species __are__ monogamous just by looking at them. Monogamous couples _____ alike, so much so that without looking at their sex organs, you probably __can't__ _____ them apart! Polygamous animals, on the other hand, __will__ _____ quite different. One example of a polygamous animal __is__ the peacock. Male peacocks, for instance, _____ beautiful feathers whereas the females _____ quite plain feathers. And polygamous animals _____ very different roles. Females _____ care of the young. Males _____ their families from danger. Scientists __point__ out that humans __don't look__ monogamous. Men usually _____ larger bodies. Women tend to have softer curves and smaller frames. But consider this . . . our

bodies seem to be more alike now than they were 300,000 years ago when

"male skeletons were nearly twice the size of female ones." We seem to be

becoming more alike!

Describing and Defining Verbs

Now that you've had some practice at identifying and supplying verbs,
you'll work on describing and defining verbs.

Practice #3   Quick Verb Quiz

Be sure to look at your paragraphs in the section "Identifying and
Supplying Verbs" when you are looking for the answers to this quiz.

1. Can a verb be made up of more than one word?
2. Can a sentence have more than one verb?

Practice #4   Creating a Draft of a Verb Definition

On a separate piece of paper, try your hand at forming the rest of the
following definition:

Verbs are words that _____.

- Don't look up the answer in a dictionary or grammar book! Look
  at what you've done in the sentence work in this chapter and develop a definition *in your own words*.
- Share your definition with at least one classmate and see if you
  can improve your own definition.
- This is your first attempt to define *verb* on your own. Consider
  this a "working definition." That is, you'll be changing and improving this definition in later exercises.

Your Own Writing: Introduction to Verbs

Copy part or all of a journal response you have completed in this chapter. Then underline your verbs twice. Exchange your sentences with a
classmate. Have you underlined *all* the verbs? Have you underlined the
correct words? Discuss any confusing sentences with your classmates
and your instructor.

Notes

IDENTIFYING SPECIFIC KINDS OF VERBS

Action Verbs
Linking Verbs
Helping Verbs
Revising Your Definition of Verbs

So far, you have practiced identifying verbs, and you have gotten a sense of what a verb is and how it works within the sentence. Now you're ready to look at several specific types of verbs: action, linking, and helping.

Action Verbs

One type of verb is called the *action verb*. An **action verb** expresses activity or movement.

Practice #5   Male and Female Roles
Copy and complete sentences 1–4, and you'll begin to see how action verbs work. Be sure to underline the verbs twice.

Some believe that men and women should have clear, defined roles in the household.

1. Women <u>make</u> the food.
2. Men _____ the lawns.
3. Daughters _____ the dirty clothes.
4. Sons _____ the oil in the car.

Linking Verbs

The words you supplied in Practice #1 and Practice #5 are *action verbs:* they represent movement, work, or someone doing something. Another kind of verb is called a *linking verb*. A linking verb, as you'll see, doesn't show action. A **linking verb** connects (or links) the subject to information in the sentence.

A chart of the linking verbs follows.

Practice #6   Traditional Values
Rewrite and complete sentences 1–8 using a different linking verb for each sentence. (The first one is done for you.) Be sure all the linking verbs you choose would make sense if the eight sentences were

written as one paragraph. (You may want to refer to the chart below when searching for the best linking verb.)

   Traditional values <u>are</u> important to some people.

1. He <u>is</u> happy in the kitchen.
2. He thinks that the kitchen _____ wonderful when bread is baking.
3. She _____ eager to work in the yard.
4. She _____ anxious if she must stay in the house all day.
5. The young woman _____ exhilarated working as a stockbroker.
6. The young father _____ happy caring for the children all day.
7. He _____ content to be a house husband.
8. She _____ fulfilled to be the breadwinner.

All forms of "to be"
   is
   am
   are
   was
   were

Words associated with our five senses
   look
   sound
   smell
   feel
   taste

A few others
   appear
   seem
   become
   grow
   turn
   prove
   remain

These verbs must be followed by descriptive information or a noun that renames a subject when they are acting as linking verbs.

Identifying Specific Kinds of Verbs

Notes

As you can see from Practice #6, linking verbs often help you express feelings or describe things. They don't show action. They link the subject to a description or feeling.

Linking verbs work well when you are describing a feeling or appearance. However, sometimes when you are revising your writing, you'll want to look for places where you can use an action verb instead of a linking verb. This is especially important when you are writing about an action or event and want to add energy to your description and information.

Practice #7   Ocean Scene

In the following exercises, revise the sentences by replacing the linking verb that is underlined twice with an action verb. Besides changing the verb, you may also change and add other words too. Be creative and have fun making the sentences more lively and vivid.

Example: I was on the roof.
• I sat cross-legged on the roof.

When changing the verb, try to use single-word verbs. For example use *sat* instead of *was sitting.*

1. The splintery brown shingles <u>were</u> scratchy on my legs.
2. The house <u>was</u> on a cliff by the coast.
3. The seagulls <u>were</u> loud.
4. The sandpipers <u>were</u> at the water's edge.
5. A small white sailboat <u>was</u> out near the edge of the world.
6. A group of children <u>were</u> on the beach.
7. A dog <u>was</u> in the water.
8. A kite <u>was</u> in the sky.
9. A couple <u>was</u> near the pier.
10. The fog <u>was</u> in the distance.

Practice #8   Using Action Verbs

Write five sentences of your own that use *only* action verbs. Be sure to underline these verbs twice and check your work with a classmate.

Hint: Try to describe activities. It's okay to write about five unrelated activities.

Identifying Specific Kinds of Verbs

Practice #9   Using Linking Verbs

Now write five sentences of your own that use *only* linking verbs. Be sure to underline these verbs twice and check your work with a classmate.

Hint: You may want to write about feelings or descriptions. The sentences don't need to connect to one another.

Practice #10   Creating an Action Paragraph

Now, here's your chance to flex your verb muscles: write a paragraph that uses only action verbs. (All sentences should relate to one another and flow.) This will probably be easier if you write about some sort of activity—such as picnicking at the park or playing basketball. Any activity will do. To be successful at this, follow these directions carefully:

a. List at least three *specific* topics you might write about. Then circle the one that seems most promising.

b. Draft a paragraph using mainly action verbs. Write at least five sentences that fit together. Then underline all verbs. (Don't try to use only action verbs at this point. For now, focus on getting your ideas written down.)

c. Go back and check all your verbs. Circle any linking verbs you may have used.

d. Change the sentences with linking verbs so that you can use action verbs instead.

e. Rewrite your paragraph. The final version of your paragraph should be neatly written with no spelling errors.

f. Underline all verbs twice.

Helping Verbs

A **helping verb** is a verb that works with another verb to create a complete verb. Here is a list of some helping verbs:

do	*does*
did	*can*
could	*may*
might	*will*
would	*shall*
should	*must*

Notes

is	*am*
are	*was*
were	

Some of these verbs can work alone as regular verbs, or they can work with others as helping verbs. (*Note: Is, am, are, was,* and *were* can be linking verbs or helping verbs, depending on how they are used in a sentence.*) In the following sentences, each complete verb (made of a helping verb and another verb) is underlined twice:

She <u>is working</u> on her English homework.

He <u>did discuss</u> his ideas with his classmates.

He <u>might finish</u> his essay tonight.

The instructor <u>has canceled</u> class.

The students <u>had been hoping</u> for a break.
[Sometimes a complete verb consists of two helping verbs *plus* another verb.]

They <u>do</u> not <u>mind</u> missing one class.
["Not" and "never" sometimes come between the parts of the verb.]

<u>Will</u> we <u>meet</u> next week?
[In a question, the parts of the verb are often separated, with the subject in between.]

Practice #11   Carla Reads

In the paragraph that follows, identify the verbs by underlining them twice. After you have checked your work with a classmate and feel that you have identified all the verbs, highlight the complete verbs that are made up of a helping verb *plus* another verb. The first two sentences are done for you.

Carla <u>enjoys</u> reading. Right now, she <u>is shopping</u> for two new novels. She will read them both in about two weeks. She learned to love books as a child. Her grandmother took care of her after school. Carla's grandmother would finish her household chores at about 4:30 P.M. each day. Then they would cuddle on the couch, and they would read for at least an hour. They read every kind of book: fairy tales, mysteries, nonfiction. Carla's grandmother's eyesight isn't very good anymore. Now Carla reads to Grandma every Saturday afternoon.

Practice #12   Using Helping Verbs

Create ten original sentences in which you use a helping verb with another verb. Underline your complete verbs twice.

Revising Your Definition of Verbs

You have learned to identify action, linking, and helping verbs, and you've learned why writers sometimes choose to use action verbs and sometimes choose to use linking verbs. It is time now to revise your earlier definition of verbs and make it better by adding new information.

Practice #13   Revise Your Verb Definition

Take a look at your earlier definition of verbs. Rewrite that definition by making it clearer and adding new information. Share your new information with your classmates or work as a whole class to develop a class definition.

Your Own Writing: Identifying Specific Kinds of Verbs

Copy two paragraphs from one of the journal responses you wrote for this chapter and underline the verbs twice.

- Mark action verbs with an "A."

- Mark linking verbs with an "L."

- Highlight verbs that are made of a helping verb plus another verb.

- If you see places where changing a linking verb to an action verb would make your writing clearer and more lively, make the necessary revisions.

Identifying Specific Kinds of Verbs

The Structure of Writing and How to Summarize Texts

Main Topics

- Examining the structure of writing

- Building summary skills

- Reading, writing, and thinking about relationships

- Manipulating verb tense

- Identifying verb imposters and prepositional phrases

Your reading and writing assignments will become easier as you begin to understand the structure of writing and how to summarize. Let's begin by considering how the structure of an item reveals its function.

First, visualize a skyscraper and a sports stadium. Although both hold many people, these buildings have been designed for different reasons and to serve different functions. The skyscraper may have a small base since it must fit within a city block, but lack of ground space is made up for in the number of stories. Inside are offices and cubicles, allowing many people to work on individual jobs. The sports stadium, however, may take up several acres of land. With its stadium seating, it's designed to give the most people the best possible view of a game.

Just as the structures of these buildings suggest their functions, so the structure of a piece of writing tells you about its function. In this chapter, you'll examine several types of writing—essays, textbook excerpts, and news articles—and discover how their structures reveal their functions.

Once you've analyzed several forms of writing, you'll be ready to write a summary. When you summarize, you retell the main points and important supporting points of essays, textbook excerpts, or articles. As you learn to summarize, you'll produce condensed versions of documents that express the author's meaning. In your classes, if you get into the habit of summarizing chapters as you complete them, you'll have a summary from each chapter to study when it's time for a test. In the workplace, if you have developed strong summary skills, you'll be able to summarize documents and present them in condensed form to your boss or colleagues. In this chapter, you'll develop the techniques for writing effective summaries.

UNDERSTANDING THE STRUCTURE OF ACADEMIC WRITING

Academic writing, such as an essay or textbook chapter, usually appears as a group of paragraphs working together to prove a point, explain an issue, describe a process, or relate an incident. Normally this group of paragraphs follows a specific organizational structure and may be broken into three basic parts: the introduction, the body, and the conclusion.

The **introduction** (the opening paragraph or two of the essay) explains what the essay will be about and suggests the order and direction of the paragraphs that will follow. The **body** of the essay (usually made up of several paragraphs) supports whatever claim has been

Notes

established in the introduction. The **conclusion** (the final paragraph) summarizes the most important points made in the body or restates the writer's claim from the beginning of the essay, while at the same time drawing the essay to a close. Many textbook chapters and most of the essays you'll read and write in college follow this basic format.

It may help you to think of an essay or textbook chapter as a passenger train. In the same way that an engine pulls the various cars of the train toward a specific destination, an essay's introduction powers the body paragraphs and conclusion toward a specific point the writer is trying to make. And though a train's cars are different (there could be a sleeper car, a dining car, and a baggage car), they are all being pulled in the same direction along the same track.

Each body paragraph of an essay, too, though proving different points and containing different kinds of evidence, is guided by the introduction. Finally, as the caboose signals the end of the train, the conclusion signals the end of the essay.

EXAMINING AN ESSAY

Get Involved!

Rent and watch a modern romantic comedy such as *Tortilla Soup* (2001) starring Hector Elizondo and Constance Marie and directed by Maria Ripoll. In your next class meeting, discuss the role of romantic love in the relationships portrayed in the film.

Consider the structure of an academic essay and how it works as you read the following selection. This essay first appeared in a book entitled *Human Intimacy* by Frank D. Cox. In the essay, Cox explains America's fascination with romantic love. As you read, pay close attention to the essay's parts—introduction, body, and conclusion—which are labeled.

In this chapter, words you may not be familiar with are listed before the readings by paragraph (par.) with their definitions.

Terms and definitions:

Par. 1 *romantic love:* an idealized version of love involving perfect mates

Par. 5 *pithy:* forceful and brief

The *introduction* of an essay appears first. Here the writer introduces the subject and explains what the essay will be about.

Romantic Love

by Frank D. Cox

1   For many Americans the idea of *romantic love* most influences their thoughts about attraction and intimacy. This concept of love encompasses such ideas as "love at first sight," "the one and only love," "lifelong commitment," "I can't live without him/her," "the perfect mate," and so forth.

2 In essence the concept of romantic love supplies a set of idealized images by which we can judge the object of our love as well as the quality of the relationship. Unfortunately, such romanticized images usually bear little relationship to the real world. Often we project our beliefs onto another person, exaggerating the characteristics that match the qualities we are looking for and masking those that do not. That is, we transform the other person into an unreal hero or heroine to fit our personal concept of a romantic marital partner. Thus we often fall in love with our own romantic ideas rather than with a real human being.

3 For example, the traditional romantic ideals dictate a strong, confident, protective role for a man and a charming, loving, dependent role for a woman. A woman accepting this stereotype will tend to overlook and deny dependent needs of her mate. She will tend to repress independent qualities in herself. Love for her means each correctly fulfilling the proper role. The same holds true for a man who has traditional romantic ideals.

4 Those who "fall in love with love" in this way will suffer disappointment when their partner's "real person" begins to emerge. Rather than meet this emerging person with joy and enthusiasm, partners who hold romanticized ideals may reject reality in favor of their stereotypical images. They may begin to search again for a love object, rejecting the real-life partner as unworthy or changed. Dating and broad premarital experience with the opposite sex can help correct much of this romantic idealism.

5 When people fall in love with their romanticized expectations rather than with their partner, they may either reject the partner or attempt to change the partner into the romantic ideal. John Robert Clark has a *pithy* description of the first action:

> In learning how to love a plain human being today, as during the romantic movement, what we usually want unconsciously is a fancy human being with no flaws. When the mental picture we have of someone we love is colored by wishes of childhood, we may love the picture rather than the real person behind it. Naturally, we are disappointed in the person we love if he does not conform to our picture. Since this kind of disappointment has no doubt happened to us before, one might suppose we would tear up the picture and start all over. On the contrary, we keep the picture and tear up the person. Small wonder that divorce courts are full of couples who never gave themselves a chance to know the real person behind the pictures in their lives.[1]

6 The second action, attempting to change one's spouse, also leads to trouble. Making changes is difficult, and the person being asked to do so may resent the demand or may not wish to change.

---

[1] John Robert Clark, *The Importance of Being Imperfect* (New York: McKay, 1961), 18.

Notes

Note: This author introduces the subject of his essay in the first *two* paragraphs.

The *body* paragraphs of the essay appear next. In each body paragraph, the author makes a specific point that helps to support the main idea of the essay.

Notes

The *conclusion* appears at the end of the essay. In it, the writer may summarize the main points of the essay or explain what he or she has learned. Its main job is to draw the essay to a close.

7   Generally, romantic love's rose-colored glasses tend to distort the real world, especially the mate, thereby creating a barrier to happiness. This is not to deny that romantic love can add to an intimate relationship. Romance will bring excitement, emotional highs, and color to one's relationship. From there one can move toward a more mature love relationship. As emotional, intellectual, social, and physical intimacy develops romance takes its place as one of several aspects of the relationship, not the only one.

A CLOSER LOOK AT THE PARTS

Now that you've read "Romantic Love" and have identified the three basic parts of the essay, you're ready to examine these parts more closely.

The Introduction Powers the Essay

As we mentioned, most academic writing (such as essays and textbook chapters) starts with an introduction, a paragraph or two that establishes the subject of the essay and the essay's route or direction—much like an engine powers the cars of a train along a track. Here you can tell your reader what to expect in your essay. Typically the introduction begins with general information and becomes more specific toward the end.

Look back to the introduction of Cox's "Romantic Love." Note how Cox first mentions romantic love in general, then describes it in more detail, and finally states his opinion on how ideas about love affect relationships.

The Thesis Guides the Essay

At the very end of an introduction, you'll often find a specific statement or two that convey the author's main idea for the entire essay or chapter. This is called the **thesis statement,** and its job is to keep an essay on track as it heads toward its destination.

Activity

Identifying the Thesis

Underline the thesis statement in "Romantic Love." In your own words, write in your notebook what the author intends to talk about in his essay. Share your ideas with a classmate.

The Body Paragraphs Carry the Evidence   *Notes*

The middle paragraphs of an essay that follow the introduction are called **body paragraphs.** Body paragraphs, like the cars of a train, contain cargo or passengers in the form of evidence and support.

Body paragraphs have a particular structure, too. They usually start with a general statement—called a **topic sentence**—that introduces the main idea of the paragraph. (Sometimes it takes more than one sentence to tell what the paragraph will be about, so a paragraph topic may be introduced in one or more sentences.) The rest of the paragraph supplies more specific pieces of information or examples that support the topic sentence.

Activity

Identifying Topic Sentences

Review the body paragraphs in "Romantic Love" and then complete the following tasks.

1. After reviewing, go back and highlight the topic sentences—the general statements that begin the body paragraphs. In your notebook, write down the body paragraph numbers (3–6), and next to each number write down *in your own words* what the author says each paragraph will be about. Compare your ideas to a classmate's to see if you agree. Discuss any differences.

2. Further down on your sheet of paper, make a separate list called "specific support." Then list any examples or details you find in the body paragraphs. How many specific pieces of support did you find? Which paragraph contains the most support? Compare your findings with a classmate's.

The Conclusion Signals Completion

Finally, at the end of the essay or chapter, there is often a concluding paragraph or section that sums up what has been said earlier and that helps the reader "make sense" of the entire piece. Here, as the writer, you can tell the reader what you've learned from writing the essay and what you want the reader to learn from your essay. In other words, the conclusion's job is to signal the end of the essay.

Notes

Activities

Examining the Conclusion

Look back at the conclusion of "Romantic Love." In your notebook, list the main points in the conclusion. Did Cox repeat all of the main points at the end of the essay? What does Cox want you to learn from his essay?

Diagramming the Essay

With a partner or two, create a picture or diagram of an essay. Consider the structure of an essay. Besides drawing a train, how else might you illustrate an essay? You may want to use different colors and shapes to show where the general statements are and where specific information appears.

For class discussion: Share your diagrams.

Journal Assignment

Making the Pieces Fit

Now that you've read about the structure of academic writing and studied Frank Cox's essay, you're ready to take another look at the *Peanuts* cartoon on page 38. In a few sentences, explain what is happening in the cartoon and how successful you think Linus and Snoopy will be and why. Now, imagine that Linus and Snoopy are actually working on an academic essay. What are the pieces of an essay that they would be working with? Explain why they wouldn't be able to create a clear essay using their energetic method of making things fit.

THE WRITER'S PURPOSE AND AUDIENCE

So far, you've considered the structure of an essay and how it works. But an essay's message is important as well. For instance, Frank Cox uses the essay form to explain to his audience (his readers) how Americans influenced by the notion of romantic love may "fall in love with [their] own romantic ideas rather than with a real human being." His purpose (reason) for writing the essay? To help people establish realistic expectations when choosing partners. Like Cox, every writer has a purpose for writing, as well as a message to convey to a chosen audience. The essay form that we've examined in this chapter is one of the possible ways for writers to send their messages.

Questions for Critical Thought   *Notes*

Questions for Critical Thought help you examine the writer's message as well as the strategies used to convey that message to the reader. (Note that some questions contain more than one part.)

"Romantic Love"

Respond in your notebook to the questions that follow. Be prepared to discuss your responses with classmates.

1. How does Frank Cox define *romantic love?*

2. a. Do you believe in "love at first sight" or a "one and only love"?

    b. Do you have an idealized view of your perfect mate? Or, if you don't *now*, did you *ever* have an idealized view of a perfect mate? What is/was this view?

3. Do you agree that romantic love influences most people when they are selecting a mate? Why, or why not?

4. What does Cox say is a more realistic view of a mate or marriage?

5. Who might be included in Cox's audience? How might his audience respond to his message?

EXAMINING A TEXTBOOK CHAPTER

Academic writing in the form of textbook chapters or sections often follows the same basic format as an essay. This is especially true in textbooks for courses such as history, sociology, anthropology, and psychology. These texts must include a range of important information in a form that is easy for students to follow.

In each segment of a textbook chapter, there should be an introductory paragraph or two, supporting body paragraphs, and a conclusion (or concluding remarks). The following textbook **excerpt** (selected passage) comes from the chapter, "Families," which appears in *Sociology: A Brief Introduction* by Alex Thio.

Terms and definitions:

Par. 1 *diligently:* applying effort consistently

Par. 2 *chivalrous:* courteous and gentlemanly

Par. 3 *spontaneity:* the quality of being ready at a moment's notice; *seclusive:* isolated

Get Involved!

Rent and watch the film *The Family Man* (2000) starring Nicolas Cage and Téa Leoni and directed by Brett Ratner. In your next class meeting, share your reactions to the film and discuss what it has to say about the American family and family values.

N o t e s

Par. 4 *courting:* dating that leads to marriage; *"playing the field"*: casually dating a number of people

Par. 5 *nuclear family:* a family consisting of a father, a mother, and their children

Par. 6 *irrationally:* illogically; *intrinsic:* essential, inner; *extrinsic:* outer; *pragmatic:* practical; *overt:* open and observable

Par. 7 *fervent:* passionately sincere

Preparing for Marriage
by Alex Thio

In the *introduction,* the writer of the textbook section introduces the main ideas of the section.

1   Most people do not consciously prepare themselves for marriage or *diligently* seek a person to marry. Instead, they engage in activities that gradually build up a momentum that launches them into marriage. They date, they fall in love, and in each of these steps they usually follow patterns set by society.

The first *subsection* (which focuses on one of the main ideas) is identified by boldface. Clearly, the writer will focus on dating practices. This subsection is part of the body of the textbook selection.

2   **The Dating Ritual**   Developed largely after World War I came to an end in 1918, the U.S. custom of dating has spread to many industrial countries. It has also changed in the United States in the last two decades. Before the 1970s, dating was more formal. Males had to ask for a date at least several days in advance. It was usually the male who decided where to go, paid for the date, opened doors, and was supposed to be *chivalrous.* The couple often went to an event, such as a movie, dance, concert, or ball game.

3   Today, dating has become more casual. In fact, the word "date" now sounds a bit old-fashioned to many young people. Usually you do not have to call somebody and ask for a date. "Getting together" or "hanging around" is more likely. *Spontaneity* is the name of the game. A young man may meet a young woman at a snack bar and strike up a brief conversation with her. If he bumps into her a day or two later, he may ask if she wants to go along to the beach, to the library, or to have a hamburger. Males and females are also more likely today than in the past to hang around—get involved in a group activity—rather than pair off for some *seclusive* intimacy. Neither has the responsibility to ask the other out, which spares them much of the anxiety of formal dating. Getting together has also become less dominated by males. Females are more likely than before to ask a male out, to suggest activities, pay the expenses, or initiate sexual intimacies. Premarital sex has also increased, but it tends to reflect true feelings and desires rather than the need for the male to prove himself or for the female to show gratitude (Strong and DeVault, 1992).

The names and years appearing in parentheses (Strong and DeVault, 1992) are references to research used by Thio in the textbook.

4   The functions of dating, however, have remained pretty constant. It is still a form of entertainment. More important, dating provides opportunities for learning to get along with members of the opposite sex—to develop companionship, friendship, and intimacy. Finally, it offers opportunities for *courting,* for falling in love with one's future spouse. *"Playing the field"* does not lead to a higher probability of marital success, though. Those who have married their first and only sweetheart are just as likely to have an enduring and satisfying marriage as those who have married only after dating many people (Whyte, 1992).

Notes

Note the word "finally." This signals the writer's final point and concluding remark about dating.

5   **Romantic Love**   Asked why they want to get married, Americans usually say, "Because I am in love." In U.S. society, love between husband and wife is the foundation of the *nuclear family.* In fact, young people are most reluctant to marry someone if they do not love the person even though the person has all the right qualities they desire. . . .

The second subsection (which focuses on a main idea from the introduction) is identified by boldface as well. This subsection is a part of the body of the textbook selection.

6   But does romantic love really cause people to choose their mates *irrationally?* Many studies have suggested that the irrationality of love has been greatly exaggerated. An analysis of these studies has led William Kephart and Davor Jedlicka (1988) to reach this conclusion: "Movies and television to the contrary, U.S. youth do not habitually fall in love with unworthy or undesirable characters. In fact, [they] normally make rather sound choices." In one study, when people in love were asked, "Does your head rule your heart, or does your heart rule your head?" 60 percent answered, "The head rules." Apparently, romantic love is not the same as infatuation, which involves physical attraction to a person and a tendency to idealize that person. Romantic love is less emotionalized, but it is expected to provide *intrinsic* satisfactions, such as happiness, closeness, personal growth, and sexual satisfaction. These differ from the *extrinsic* rewards offered by a *pragmatic* loveless marriage—rewards such as good earnings, a nice house, well-prepared meals, and *overt* respect.

7   In the United States over the last 30 years, the belief in romantic love as the basis for marriage has grown more *fervent* than before. In several studies in the 1960s, 1970s, and 1980s, college men and women were asked, "If a person had all the other qualities you desired, would you marry this person if you were not in love with him/her?" [In the 1980s], as opposed to earlier decades, a greater proportion of young people [said] no (Simpson, Campbell, and Berscheid, 1986).

The writer wraps up this subsection with a concluding remark.

A CLOSER LOOK AT THE PARTS

Like the essay, the textbook chapter contains the basic elements of academic writing—introduction, body, and conclusion. However, there is a difference between the essay "Romantic Love" and the textbook

Notes
selection "Preparing for Marriage." Textbook chapters often contain section headings and subheadings in bold to keep information clearly organized. It's easy to see how such headings work.

Under the general heading of "Preparing for Marriage," the author gives a quick overview of the section. The two subsections, "The Dating Ritual" and "Romantic Love," which offer different aspects of the main topic, are presented in an organized manner—one topic at a time. Textbook headings and subheadings show the general topic of the section, give easy references to specific information, and help readers anticipate what sections will be about.

Activity

Examining Headings and Subheadings

1. The heading of this textbook section is "Preparing for Marriage." Highlight the two subheadings. Notice that the two subheadings (or subsections) are introduced in the opening paragraph of the section. Explain how the writer sets up the two subsections in the introduction.

2. Examine the chapter of another textbook. (Look at a history, psychology, sociology, or other textbook that presents large sections of information.) Read the chapter, then write down the chapter's headings and subheadings. Explain how the writer has organized the information under headings and subheadings.

The Introduction and Thesis

Textbook sections and chapters—like the essay—contain an introduction that lets the reader know what information will be covered. In fact, it's important for the textbook writer to state the thesis or main idea of each chapter clearly so that students can follow the chapter discussion easily.

Activity

Identifying the Thesis

After rereading the introduction, in your own words, write down the thesis of "Preparing for Marriage." What does the introduction tell us the excerpt will be about?

The Body Paragraphs

The body paragraphs of a textbook chapter often begin with topic sentences like those in the essay. They are followed by support in the form of examples, details, quotations, and other evidence.

Activity

Identifying Topic Sentences

Review the body paragraphs in "Preparing for Marriage" and then complete the tasks below.

1. Highlight the topic sentence(s) in each body paragraph. (Keep in mind that sometimes it takes more than one sentence to introduce the paragraph topic.) Then, in your own words, write down what each paragraph is about.

2. Also in your notebook, make a "specific support" list. Go back through the selection and write down examples, details, quotations, and other forms of support. Which of the paragraphs contains the most support? Share your findings with a classmate.

The Conclusion

Most textbook chapters end with a summary. You may have noticed, for example, that Chapter 1 of *Connections* ends with a summary of the entire chapter. However, within each section or subsection of a chapter, you should be able to identify a concluding remark or two that draws that section or subsection to a close.

Activities

Examining the Conclusion

Review the concluding remarks in each subsection of "Preparing for Marriage." Does Thio repeat all of the main points of the body paragraphs from "The Dating Ritual"? What does Thio want you to learn about dating? Does Thio repeat the main points of "Romantic Love"? What does he want you to learn about romantic love?

Comparing the Structure of Academic Writing

1. Compare the structures of Thio's "Preparing for Marriage" and Cox's "Romantic Love." How are their shapes similar? How are they different?

Notes

2. Compare the structure of "Preparing for Marriage" to a chapter or section in another college textbook. How are their shapes similar? How are they different? Does the section you've chosen contain headings and subheadings similar to those in "Preparing for Marriage"?

THE WRITER'S PURPOSE AND AUDIENCE

Although the essay "Romantic Love" was written to convince people to establish more realistic expectations when choosing partners, the textbook selection "Preparing for Marriage" was written to inform. If you look back through the selection, you will see that Thio has compiled source information (studies and research) and has presented concepts differently than Cox. As you respond to the questions that follow, consider why Thio's writing would serve a different audience and purpose than Cox's might.

Questions for Critical Thought

"Preparing for Marriage"

1. According to Thio, do most people consciously prepare for marriage? What leads people to eventually marry?

2. How has dating in the United States changed in the last twenty years? What was it like before the 1970s? In what ways is it different today? What hasn't changed about dating? What's dating really for?

3. According to Thio, what is "the foundation of the nuclear family"?

4. What part, if any, does romantic love play in American marriages, according to Thio's findings?

5. Does Thio's presentation of romantic love agree with Cox's view in "Romantic Love"? Do both Thio and Cox think that people need to be more realistic in choosing partners? If so, why? If not, why not?

6. What is Thio's purpose in writing "Preparing for Marriage"? Who would be his audience?

Journal Assignment

Making the Writing-Reading-Critical Thinking Connection

Compare dating, romantic love, and marriage in the past and present. Is dating today the same as it was in your parents' or grandparents' youth? Did romantic love play a part in their choices of mates? Do you consider romantic love to be important to your own relationships? In your notebook, write about what you believe to be the ideal approach to love and/or marriage based upon what you've read and experienced.

LEARNING TO SUMMARIZE ESSAYS AND TEXTBOOK CHAPTERS

Now that you've learned how academic writing works, you're ready to learn how to summarize this form of writing. As you learn to summarize, you'll begin to produce condensed versions of documents for study purposes, for workplace reports, and for your own writing.

What Is a Summary?

A **summary** is basically a *concise retelling of the main points of a longer piece of writing*. Your job in writing a summary is to relay the author's most important points without including your own opinion on the subject. (Although your opinion isn't included when you are writing a summary, your opinion is a welcome and important part of reading questions, journal responses, essays, and other assignments.)

Points to Remember About Summaries

- Summaries should be much shorter than what you are summarizing.

- Summaries should include all main points and important supporting details—not just what you liked best. Nonessential details and examples should be left out.

- Summaries should include, when possible, the author's name and the title of what you're summarizing (and the date and place of publication, if available).

- Summaries should be written in your own words (paraphrased), not copied—to avoid *plagiarizing* the author's work. (You may include an occasional quotation for impact.)

- Summaries should not include your reactions to the text.

Plagiarism is the act of using someone else's words as your own without giving proper credit to the author. If you use a word-for-word phrase or sentence from the original, you must place it in quotation marks and credit the author.

A Sample Summary

To give you an idea of what a summary looks like and how it works, reread "Romantic Love" on pages 40–42. Then study this list of important points.

Notes

- Many Americans are influenced more by the notion of *romantic love* than any other concept of love.
- Romantic love is an idealized version of love, a fairy tale–like view of love with expectations to match.
- The problem is that people who see love only from this perspective may "fall in love with [their] own romantic ideas rather than with a real human being."
- These people will find it nearly impossible to be happy with a mate since no one can fulfill their romantic notions.
- A mate may be expected to fulfill a stereotypical role in order to live up to his or her lover's ideal image of a mate.
- A female lover may expect her male lover to be the strong silent type, whereas a male lover may expect his female lover to be the passive yet charming type.
- Lovers who expect their mates to live up to stereotypes are bound to be disappointed when the mate begins displaying characteristics that go against the stereotypes.
- If not careful, these lovers may reject partner after partner since no one will ever fit the idealized version.
- Or these lovers may expect their mates to conform to the idealized image, an impossible and painful task.
- Romantic love isn't all bad. It can add delight to a relationship, especially in the beginning. But it should exist in a balance with other attributes such as intellect.

—Opening statement includes author, title, and main idea.

—Quotation emphasizes main idea.

—Important supporting point follows.

—Most important points appear through summary in logical order.

Summary   In his essay "Romantic Love," author Frank Cox explains that Americans are more influenced by the notion of romantic love—a fairy-tale version of love—than by any other concept of love. According to Cox, those who view love solely from this perspective may "fall in love with [their] own romantic ideas rather than with a real human being." These people will idealize their relationships and may even expect partners to fulfill stereotypical images like the strong, silent type for men or the passive-yet-charming type for women. When partners inevitably begin to display characteristics that go against the stereotypes, these people can't help but be disappointed. They may even try to force mates to conform to their ideal images. If not careful, these disappointed lovers will reject partner after partner since no one ever fits the ideal. Still, Cox sees romantic love as a positive part of a new relationship. But he cautions that as the relationship matures, a couple should move toward balancing romantic love with emotional, intellectual, social, and physical intimacy.

Notes

—Author's conclusions are relayed.

WRITING THE ACADEMIC SUMMARY

As you examined how the typical essay or textbook chapter is constructed, you discovered that general information appeared in certain places and specific information in others. You learned, for instance, that in most cases the introduction offers an overview of the essay or chapter, so it contains mainly general information.

You've learned, too, that each body paragraph usually (though not always) begins with a topic sentence, a general statement that tells what the paragraph will be about. This topic sentence is followed by details and examples, specific information that helps prove the main point of the paragraph. And you've examined the process one writer went through to summarize Cox's "Romantic Love."

What, then, are the stages of effective summary writing?

Step One: Distinguishing between general and specific information

Step Two: Identifying the main points

Step Three: Drafting the summary

Step Four: Revising the summary

You'll read about and practice each of these steps in the following section.

Note: Summaries may be more than one paragraph long depending on the length of the original document. However, most of the summary assignments in this text call for a single paragraph.

Distinguishing Between General and Specific Information

Learning to tell the difference between the general and specific statements is the first step in learning to summarize academic writing. Most of the academic writing you'll encounter contains both general and specific information. General statements usually give the reader an overview of the essay or a particular paragraph. Specific statements offer examples, statistics, quotations, or other forms of evidence to support the more general statements. Why is it important for you to be able to distinguish between general and specific information? As you develop this skill, you'll begin to see how main ideas appear in various forms of writing. This will help you understand your readings, prepare for exams, and summarize. Read this paragraph

Notes   from the essay titled, "The Modern Family." (*Note:* General information has been identified by a "G" in the "Notes" column, and specific information has been identified by an "S.")

G   During the 1950s, the Cleavers on the television show *Leave It to Beaver* epitomized the American family. In 1960, over 70 percent of all American households were like the Cleavers: made up of a breadwinner father, a home-
S   maker mother, and their kids. Today, "traditional" families with a working husband, [a homemaker], and one or more children make up less than 15 percent of the nation's households. And as America's families have changed, the image
G   of the family portrayed on television has changed accordingly. . . .
—James Kirby Martin et al., from America and Its People

The topic sentence of this paragraph offers a general statement about what the authors believe a typical American family used to be like. This statement is followed by specific information in the form of statistics—"In 1960, over 70 percent of all American households were like the Cleavers"—and a definition of the traditional American family: "a breadwinner father, a homemaker mother, and their kids." The statistical information and definition are followed by a final general statement suggesting that images on television reflect changes in the American family.

Activity

Distinguishing Between General and Specific Information in "The Modern Family"

1. Read the paragraph below. (This is another paragraph from the essay, "The Modern Family.")

   Profound changes have reshaped American family life in recent years. In a decade, divorce rates doubled. The number of divorces today is twice as high as in 1966 and three times higher than in 1950. The rapid upsurge in the divorce rates contributed to a dramatic increase in the number of single-parent households. . . . The number of households consisting of a single woman and her children has tripled since 1960. A sharp increase in female-headed homes has been accompanied by a startling increase in the number of couples cohabitating outside of marriage. The number of unmarried couples living together has quadrupled since 1970.

2. Write "G" beside general statements and "S" beside specific statements.

3. Write down any words or phrases (such as "for example") that indicate that specific support will follow.

Identifying the Main Points

What if you were asked by your instructor to summarize or retell what you had learned from the excerpt "Preparing for Marriage" (pages 46–47)? What would you say? You certainly wouldn't want to repeat the whole thing. And you wouldn't just randomly choose a few sentences to read. You would pick out the most important statements and *put them in your own words*. Although this may seem hard to do, with practice it'll become easier. Identifying the main points is the second step in the summary writing process.

Activity

Identifying Main Points in "Preparing for Marriage"

1. Mark the general and specific statements in "Preparing for Marriage." Which statements appear to be the most important, or main, ideas? Highlight only these statements and review them carefully. Leave out details.

2. Now set the excerpt aside and from memory make a list of these main ideas. (You don't need to quote them exactly. In fact, you should put these main points in your own words.)

3. Go back to the excerpt and double-check to see that you've included all of the main points. Add necessary information to your list.

Drafting the Summary

Once you have made a list of the main points, you are ready for step three, writing your summary. Remember that your summary should

- open with a statement that introduces what is being summarized (including author and title),
- provide an overview of the piece,
- include all of the main points (even those you may not agree with), and
- end with the author's conclusions on the subject.

Activity

Drafting a Summary of "Preparing for Marriage"

Drawing from your list of main ideas, write a summary of "Preparing for Marriage." First, include the author, title, and main idea of the piece. Follow with the most important points. End with the author's conclusions on the subject.

Notes

Revising the Summary

After completing a draft of your summary, it's time to move to step four of the process. To do this, you must look back at the document you're summarizing to make sure you have accurately explained the main ideas as the author intended. If you discover that you have not explained an idea correctly, then you need to **revise** (rewrite) parts of your summary to more accurately reflect the main ideas presented in the original piece.

> ### *Activity*
>
> #### *Revising Your Summary of "Preparing for Marriage"*
>
> Return to "Preparing for Marriage." Compare the main ideas that you high-lighted to those you have relayed in your summary. Have you explained the most important points accurately? If not, revise your summary to reflect the main ideas in the original.

UNDERSTANDING THE STRUCTURE OF JOURNALISTIC WRITING

Besides academic writing, there are other forms of professional writing, such as **journalism** (news writing and reporting), that you probably encounter on a daily basis. If you read the newspaper or a weekly or monthly magazine, then you've already come across many different types of writing. In this section, you will examine two types of newspaper articles, the feature story and the column. As you read both, consider what the unique structure of each offers the reader.

EXAMINING A FEATURE STORY

A **feature story** is a newspaper article that presents and discusses a timely issue. It does not follow the same format as the essay or text-book chapter. News writers know that they must "hook" their readers with an interesting opening statement. Once they snag their audience, they must provide manageable "bites" of information because busy readers are probably reading their papers over morning coffee. In fact, that's one of the reasons the paragraphs are short, sometimes only a sentence or two in length.

Another reason for the short paragraphs has to do with the way a newspaper is laid out into **columns** (several long, vertical rows of

writing on a news page). Newspaper columns are long and thin, so
paragraphs must be kept short. Otherwise, a paragraph might go on
for an entire column, which could result in readers losing their place
in the reading. Finally, journalistic style doesn't call for the same
level of explanation and development that academic style requires,
so shorter paragraphs are acceptable.

The feature story, "Modern Marriage" by William R. Macklin, appeared in the *Sacramento Bee* newspaper. In it, Macklin compares traditional matrimony (marriage) to other forms of commitment.

Terms and definitions:

Par. 1 *companionate love:* love shared by partners; *marital fidelity:*
faithfulness in marriage

Par. 2 *jibe:* agree; *archaic:* ancient

Par. 5 *mandate:* command; *diligent:* hardworking

Par. 8 *think tank:* group formed to solve a problem

Par. 14 *clans:* family groups united by common interests

Par. 15 *Industrial Revolution:* a surge in the economy in late eighteenth century England resulting from the use of machinery; *gender roles:* expected behavior for males or females

Par. 16 *socializing:* behavioral training for social situations

Par. 24 *protracted:* long and drawn out

Par. 28 *matrimonial contracts:* signed marriage agreements

Par. 29 *monogamy:* commitment to one partner

Par. 30 *unsavory:* offensive

Par. 31 *paradigm:* pattern, model, or example

Modern Marriage
by William R. Macklin

This feature story appeared in the *Sacramento Bee* newspaper, January 30, 1999.

1   In theory, at least, few things in modern life are as uncomplicated as
traditional matrimony. A devoted couple take a vow to love, honor and
comfort, and then after champagne toasts and a toss of the bride's
bouquet, they head off for a lifetime of *companionate love* and *marital
fidelity.*

2   But theory and reality don't always *jibe,* and so it's no surprise that
old-fashioned matrimony has its critics, observers who say that the

institution of marriage is so *archaic* and unworkable that it's time to throw out the whole thing.

3   Nancy Saunders, a psychologist who has a family practice in the Philadelphia area, is one of them. . . .

4   "Society can no longer support what we think of as marriage," says Saunders. "When marriages come crashing to an end, as 50 percent of them do, there is a sense that the couple failed. That's not really true."

5   Saunders, who is divorced, says it's unrealistic to expect couples to balance contemporary work demands and heightened desires for personal happiness against a lifelong marital *mandate* to be faithful lovers, *diligent* parents and tireless helpmates.

6   That might have worked 100 years ago, when lifespans were shorter, or 50 years ago, when the majority of married women were economically dependent on their husbands, or even 30 years ago, when getting home on time for dinner was a daily priority, Saunders suggests. Now, she says, the traditional requirement that couples remain together "in sickness and in health . . . as long as you both shall live," often masks long years of bitter unhappiness.

7   Saunders believes that long-term, committed relationships still are the best hope for the care and support of children. But she favors doing away with traditional matrimony. Instead, she suggests individualized marriage contracts that would allow couples to custom-design their relationships with the full support and recognition of the state.

8   For Linda Chavez, head of a Washington *think tank* that studies family issues, however, the problem is not that traditional marriage doesn't work. It's that people don't work hard enough at traditional marriage.

9   The president of the conservative Center for Equal Opportunity in Washington, Chavez resents the suggestion that marriage is a failing institution.

10   "Perhaps what we really need is for people to rethink their sense of responsibility and consider more than their personal happiness," says Chavez, who has been married for 31 years. "I think that marriage as an institution has worked quite well, especially for raising children."

11   That's not surprising, given that marriage began as a way of protecting and supporting the young.

12   George Becker, a sociologist at Vanderbilt University in Nashville and a specialist in the sociology of the family, says that early Western civilizations viewed marriage as a way to provide stability and safety for children during their long maturation period.

13   Not because people loved babies, but because children were a crucial source of labor.

14　"Early *clans* farmed the land and needed a lot of workers," Becker says. "And so you essentially needed a relationship that would ensure having children and make sure that they survived to provide the labor."

15　The concept of romantic love as the basis for marriage was virtually unknown to most working people before the 18th century, and the nuclear family emerged only in the 19th century, after the *Industrial Revolution,* Becker says. As a result, marriage has been slow to accommodate shifting personal expectations or to anticipate changes in *gender roles.*

16　"We are not adequately *socializing* men to pick up the slack around the house," Becker says. "It's a social lag. So many women are realizing, 'Hey, who needs this guy? I am doing everything by myself, earning a living, and then coming home and cleaning up the house.' It's no longer enough for a man to go out and get the bacon. He now has to cook it and help clean up after."

17　And what became of marriage as a public trust?

18　Becker says increased mobility and the growth of a national "cult of individuality" have left most marriages isolated from the cultural and societal pressures that have historically enforced the standards expressed in the traditional marriage vow.

19　That didn't happen to John and Vee Stanbach.

20　They were born one week apart in Wildwood Crest, N.J., met on the boardwalk when they were 17, and got married after a five-year courtship.

21　They believe, fiercely, in traditional marriage, indeed view it as a public trust, and say they would never do anything to lose the respect of their community.

22　The Stanbachs are 78 and have been married 55 years.

23　"A lot of our friends have been married 50 years and better," Vee says.

24　The Stanbachs say their marriage has survived because they avoid *protracted* arguments, rarely spend time apart, and never forget, as Vee says, that "marriage is forever."

25　And, they feel that the failure of a marriage, any marriage, is a cause for sadness.

26　"It breaks my heart that they couldn't persevere and work things out," says Vee.

27　What worked for the Stanbachs probably would work for most couples if everyone lived their entire lives in one place and rarely encountered contemporary social and personal pressures, says Saunders.

28　In the long run, though, the only way to help modern couples be happier is to "get rid of this huge muck we call marriage," Saunders says, and to allow couples to enter into *matrimonial contracts* that lay out the exact terms of their relationship.

29　Saunders says that such contracts—which might or might not include *monogamy,* lifelong commitment, or even living in the same

Notes

home—should be entirely legal and that divorce action should take into account the terms of such contracts.

30   Saunders says that parenting contracts would be a strong start toward establishing a new type of marital bond based on the idea that couples have a right to dictate the terms of their marriages, even when those terms seem *unsavory* or troubling to those outside the relationship.

31   "We need a *paradigm* shift," she says. "We would do ourselves and society a tremendous favor if we would ask, 'What are the realistic tasks a committed relationship should accomplish? . . . What should a marriage have to do to last through all the changes?'"

A CLOSER LOOK AT THE PARTS

Although it doesn't have the same structure as the essay or textbook chapter, the newspaper article does contain some of the same components. All contain an introduction, body, and conclusion.

Activity

Labeling the Parts

Go back through "Modern Marriage," and in the "Notes" column label the introduction, body, and conclusion. (Remember, an introduction may be longer than one paragraph.)

The Introduction Is Called the Lead

Whereas the essay contains a more formal introduction, a newspaper article begins with what is called the **lead.** The lead, the opening statement of an article, is often an intriguing or dynamic sentence or two designed to interest the reader. At other times, it is a statement of fact or the main point of the article. Without a clever or intriguing lead, newspaper writers risk losing their audience. In "Modern Marriage," Macklin presents a lead with a twist.

Activities

Examining the Lead

1. Review the opening two paragraphs of "Modern Marriage." How does Macklin attempt to draw in the reader? After reading paragraph 1, what did you think the article would be about? When you read the second paragraph, how did your view change?

2. Read a front-page newspaper story from today's paper. Write down the lead. How has the writer tried to draw you into the article? What does the lead suggest the article will be about? Is the lead similar to or different from the lead in Macklin's article?

Identifying the Thesis

Now that you've examined the introduction/lead, in your own words, write down the thesis of "Modern Marriage." What does the introduction suggest the article will be about?

The Body Paragraphs Are Shorter

The body paragraphs of a newspaper article are shorter than those appearing in an essay. Some paragraphs, in fact, may be only a sentence long. As in the essay, there are paragraph breaks to identify when new ideas are presented. But there are paragraph breaks for other reasons as well:

- To set off a quotation or a set of facts
- To transition the reader from one idea to another
- To emphasize a certain point
- To simply keep the paragraphs short

In "Modern Marriage," Macklin begins a new paragraph each time he presents someone else's point of view. He also begins new paragraphs to emphasize quotations and to help readers make the transition from one idea to another. Keep in mind, too, that paragraphs in journalistic writing don't always contain topic sentences.

The Conclusion

In the conclusion of a journalistic piece, writers try to bring their ideas full circle. Usually, the journalistic piece will end with a final thought or quotation rather than with a summary of the main points.

Activities

Examining the Conclusion

Review the conclusion of "Modern Marriage." Explain how Macklin concludes his feature story. Does Macklin's conclusion emphasize a particular point of view on marriage? Or does Macklin's article summarize the various views?

> ### Comparing the Structure of Academic and Journalistic Writing
>
> 1. Compare the structures of Macklin's "Modern Marriage" and Cox's "Romantic Love." How are their shapes similar? How are they different?
>
> 2. Now compare the structures of "Modern Marriage" and another newspaper article. How are their shapes similar? How are they different? What have you learned about newspaper articles that you didn't know before?

THE WRITER'S PURPOSE AND AUDIENCE

The journalist has the same goal as any other writer—to convey a particular message to the reader. In "Modern Marriage," Macklin presents various sides of an issue to get readers to think about and perhaps reconsider their views on the issue of marriage. By quoting a variety of experts, it's clear that Macklin intends to present a range of views. Still, there may be a clue to his own perspective in the way in which he presents the "experts." Consider Macklin's perspective as you answer the questions that follow.

Questions for Critical Thought

"Modern Marriage"

1. According to Macklin, what do critics say about marriage?

2. What does psychologist Nancy Saunders believe about traditional marriage? What does she suggest as an alternative?

3. Does Linda Chavez, president of the Center for Equal Opportunity, agree with Saunders? What does Chavez believe?

4. In the article, sociologist George Becker explains early Western views of marriage. How did early Western marriages differ from modern marriages?

5. Did romantic love play a part in the mate selection process in early Western civilization? Why, or why not?

6. What is John and Vee Stanbach's position on marriage? Do you agree or disagree?

7. Psychologist Saunders believes in marriage contracts. What might be negotiated in such a contract? How might the contract work?

8. Consider each of the experts and their perspectives. Who does Macklin quote most often? Which expert does he begin with? Which does he end with? Which does he emphasize most? What message do you think Macklin is conveying?

Notes

> ### *Journal Assignment*
>
> ### *Making the Writing-Reading-Critical Thinking Connection*
>
> Consider the differing views on marriage in "Modern Marriage." Is marriage outdated, as Saunders believes? Or is it worth keeping, as the Stanbachs believe? Are there other ways to handle a long-term, committed relationship? Would any other options work just as well as, if not better than, marriage? In your notebook, write out your view on marriage.

EXAMINING A NEWSPAPER COLUMN

A **column** is an article in which a **columnist** (writer) expresses his or her own views on current issues, events, or concerns. Many newspapers have columnists who write opinion pieces on a daily or weekly basis for their papers. Some columnists—like the late Mike Royko—express strong opinions on controversial issues like capital punishment or gun control. Others—like syndicated columnist Dave Barry—write humorous pieces on the human condition.

The newspaper column is shaped like other news articles, beginning with a lead that draws the reader into the story. It is followed by short paragraphs that usually contain a combination of discussion, dialogue, and evidence. Such articles are written to inform, to explain, to persuade, or sometimes simply to entertain. The column that follows appeared in the *Daily Northwestern*, a publication of Northwestern University. Writer Maggie Bandur offers a blend of discussion and dialogue laced with humor as she challenges women to defy female stereotyping.

Terms and definitions:

Par. 1 *Victoria's Secret catalog*: a mail order catalog specializing in women's undergarments and lingerie; *objectification of women*: the treatment of women as objects; *scantily clad*: barely clothed

Par. 2 *antiquated*: outdated; *stereotypes of women*: oversimplified patterns of belief about women

Get Involved!

Review the definition of a feature story on page 56 and compare it to the definition on this page of a column. Find an example of a feature story and a column in your local newspaper. Bring them to class and explain how they fit the two definitions.

Notes   Par. 3 *ogling:* staring; *not synonymous with:* not the same as;
fared: done
Par. 4 *defy:* go against
Par. 5 *credence:* validity

Women Play the Roles Men Want to See
by Maggie Bandur

This column appeared in the *Daily Northwestern*, Northwestern University, January 23, 1996.

1   A favorite assignment of media courses is to have students analyze advertisements. Without fail, some boy will bring in a picture from the *Victoria's Secret catalog* as an example of the *objectification of women.* Does it objectify women? Considering how many sex-starved, male dorm residents steal the mailroom's copies to check out the *scantily clad* women wearing submissive, come-hither looks, I would have to say "yes." The male-dominated society's lack of respect for women is alive and well!

2   What is not always pointed out, but should be, is that the catalog is marketed to women. And this type of marketing apparently works. The women are just as excited as the men on the day it arrives. Many *antiquated* attitudes and *stereotypes of women* persist because men still have a lot of power. But what makes it hard to destroy the stereotypes is that some women still go along with them.

3   Sometimes, I'm one of those women. As much as I hate the fact that men think women are stupid, I have on occasion played dumb to get male assistance. As much as I am offended by male *ogling,* there have been times when I have worn tight clothing and endured the agony of heels so that men would pay attention to me. (Keep in mind, of course, that attention is *not synonymous with* being touched.) As saddened as I am at how many women will let men treat them horribly, I haven't *fared* much better. As much as I try not to give in to all the stereotypes and societal expectations, I sometimes do, but I don't think I am alone.

4   In high school, when my friends and I would go out to dinner, none of the girls would want the guys to see us actually eating. Ordering anything more than a salad and a Diet Coke would supposedly insure that all the boys would think you were a cow. Every once in a while, the other girls and I would agree that this was ridiculous, that we were hungry, and that we would order whatever we darn well pleased. We'd get to the table and I, like a fool, would order first. "Hamburger and chocolate milk shake, please." And then those traitors would all order salads and Diet Cokes. If four or five girls can't work together on a trip to a restaurant, can all womankind join together to *defy* male expectations? If everyone dressed com-

fortably, let themselves reach the weight their bodies wanted, and stubbornly refused to give men the time of day until they treated women with the respect they deserved, men would come around a whole helluva lot faster. But there is always someone who is going to order that Diet Coke.

5   Sometimes it's easier to play along, and some people will; but in the long run it's better for all women if you don't. Every woman who embraces a stereotype—even if it is as a tool to get ahead in the world that men have made harder for women—is giving that stereotype more *credence.*

6   It may take a while before I have the strength to resist every dictate of male society, but I am trying. I have almost accepted the fact that I will always be forty to fifty pounds heavier than supermodels my height, and I can almost get through a large meal with a man without apologizing for eating. Small victories, I will admit, but at least it's a start.

A CLOSER LOOK AT THE PARTS

The writer's column is shaped like the feature story or other news article. It contains a lead, short paragraphs, and a conclusion.

Activity

Labeling the Parts

Read "Women Play the Roles Men Want to See" a second time. In the "Notes" column, label the lead, body paragraphs, and conclusion. (Remember, an introduction may be longer than one paragraph.)

The Lead

"Women Play the Roles Men Want to See" contains a lead that "snags" readers and compels them to read. In fact, if readers read only the lead, they might believe the article was going to focus on one issue when it is in fact concerned with another.

Activities

Examining the Lead

1. Review the lead in "Women Play the Roles Men Want to See." How does Bandur "hook" the reader in the opening paragraph? If you had read just the opening paragraph but not the body, what would you have believed the author was writing about?

Notes

2. Compare the leads in "Women Play the Roles Men Want to See" and "Modern Marriage." How are the two approaches similar? How are they different?

Identifying the Thesis

After examining the lead, write down in your own words the thesis of "Women Play the Roles Men Want to See." What does the full introduction (the first two paragraphs) suggest this column will be about?

The Body Paragraphs

Because Bandur uses a conversational approach (as though she's talking directly to the reader), she relies on discussion and personal examples in the body paragraphs to make her points. Review the body paragraphs to see which ones contain topic sentences.

The Conclusion

As you discovered in "Modern Marriage," the writer's goal in the journalistic piece (as in the essay or textbook chapter) is to bring ideas full circle. Such a piece ends with a final thought or quotation. A column such as Bandur's ends less often with a summary.

Activities

Examining the Conclusion

Return to the conclusion of "Women Play the Roles Men Want to See." Consider Bandur's approach to her conclusion. Does she emphasize a particular point in the conclusion? Or does she summarize the points she's made in the article?

Comparing the Shapes of Journalistic Writing

Compare the shape of "Women Play the Roles Men Want to See" to that of "Modern Marriage." How are their shapes similar? How are they different?

THE WRITER'S PURPOSE AND AUDIENCE

Writers must think about their message and how best to communicate their ideas to specific audiences. Consider, for example, what you might say and how you might express yourself if you were writing a cover letter for your resume. If you are writing a letter to a close friend, however, you will discuss different topics and use different vocabulary. Similarly, Bandur carefully considered the message she wanted to communicate to her readers, and she presented that message with words and examples her intended audience would find interesting.

Notes

Questions for Critical Thought

"Women Play the Roles Men Want to See"

1. According to Bandur, what do men expect women to look like?

2. Does Bandur believe that men are the only ones who try to make women match this stereotype? Explain why Bandur believes it's so hard to get rid of stereotypical views of women.

3. Bandur admits to having played into some of these stereotypes herself. Do you believe that women in society today defy or follow the expectations encouraged by images such as the stereotypical supermodel? Explain.

4. What is the main message of Bandur's column? Mark parts of the text that point to this message.

5. Describe the readers in Bandur's audience. Consider these questions as you describe the readers: Where was this column published? Who would relate best to her examples? What specific words from Bandur's column give us clues about her audience? Your answers to these questions should help you make some thoughtful guesses about the ages and interests of her readers.

Journal Assignment

Making the Writing-Reading-Critical Thinking Connection

Explain what Bandur means when she says that it's "easier to play along" but "better for all women if you don't." Would you say this is useful advice for women? Respond honestly to the article.

WRITING THE JOURNALISTIC SUMMARY

Earlier in this chapter, you discovered the ways in which journalistic writing differs from academic writing. You learned, for example, that most newspaper or magazine articles begin with a lead that is followed by short body paragraphs that may or may not have topic sentences. Such articles often conclude with a final remark or a quotation that circles back to the lead.

You may be surprised to find out that you will use the same four steps that you followed for summarizing academic writing when you summarize journalistic writing. The steps appear here for review:

Step One: Distinguishing between general and specific information

Step Two: Identifying main points

Step Three: Drafting the summary

Step Four: Revising the summary

Distinguishing Between General and Specific Information

Because the body paragraphs of articles do not always contain topic sentences, summarizing articles is made easier when you begin by identifying general and specific information, which is step one of the summary process. Return to the activity "Labeling the Parts" following the article "Modern Marriage" (pages 57–60). Review what you identified as the introduction, body, and conclusion. Use this information as you complete the summary activity below.

Activity

> *Distinguishing Between General and Specific Statements in "Modern Marriage"*
>
> 1. Read the essay a second time, and as you read, mark general statements with "G." Then identify the statements that contain specific information and mark each with an "S."
>
> 2. Write down any clues that suggest that specific information follows.

Identifying the Main Points

In distinguishing between general and specific information, you are preparing to write your summary. Remember, the main ideas in a magazine or newspaper article usually appear in general statements just as they did in academic writing. Identifying these main ideas is the second stage of the summary process.

Activity

Identifying Main Points in "Modern Marriage"

1. Look back at how you've marked general and specific statements in "Modern Marriage." Which statements appear to be the most important, or main, ideas? Highlight only these statements and review them carefully. Leave out the details.

2. Set the article aside, and from memory write a list of the main points. (Don't worry about getting them down exactly. These should be in your own words.)

3. Return to the article and check to see if you've included all of the main points on your list. Add any you left out.

Drafting the Summary

Putting the main points into paragraph form is step three. Keep in mind that a summary should begin with a statement that gives an overview of the article and includes the article's author and title. In order for a summary to be effective, it must include all of the main points and end with the author's conclusions.

Activity

Drafting a Summary of "Modern Marriage"

Draft a summary using the list of main ideas you wrote down in the activity "Identifying Main Points." First, introduce the author, title, and overall main idea of the article. Follow with the most important points. End your summary with the author's conclusions on the subject.

Revising the Summary

After writing a draft of your summary, it's important to return to the article and check to make sure that you have explained the author's main ideas accurately. This is step four of the process.

Activity

Revising Your Summary of "Modern Marriage"

Review the article "Modern Marriage" again (pages 57–60). Compare the main ideas you highlighted earlier to those that appear in your summary

Notes   now. Have you included the most important points? If not, revise your summary to agree with the original.

PRACTICING SUMMARY SKILLS

Knowing how to summarize will help you at work, at home, and in your classes. On the job, you may be asked to summarize documents and reports. At home, you might have to summarize the problems you have had with a product in a letter to the Better Business Bureau. In your classes, you will probably be asked to write summaries of textbook chapters or essays. Writing summaries of textbook chapters you have been assigned will also help you strengthen study skills and prepare for tests.

Activity

Put Your New Summary Skills to Work

1. Choose a section from one of your textbooks from another class, and then write a short summary. Be prepared to show your instructor the actual section in your textbook as well as how you marked general and specific information and identified main ideas. (This is a good way to get a jump on your reading for other classes.)

2. Write a summary of Maggie Bandur's "Women Play the Roles Men Want to See" from pages 64–65. Be prepared to show your instructor how you marked general and specific information and identified main points.

3. Choose a magazine or newspaper article, and then write a short summary. In addition to your summary, be prepared to show your instructor the actual article and how you marked general and specific information and identified main ideas.

4. Read the textbook excerpt, "Sexual Revolution, Cohabitation, and the Rise of Singles," located in Supplemental Readings on pages 395–397. Then summarize the excerpt. Be prepared to show your instructor how you marked general and specific information and identified main ideas.

5. Read the magazine article, "Sex Has Many Accents," located in Supplemental Readings on pages 398–400. Summarize the article. Be prepared to show your instructor how you marked general and specific information and identified main ideas.

TIME TO REFLECT

> ### *Journal Assignment*
> ### *Your Progress as a Writer, Reader, and Critical Thinker*
> Spend a few minutes *reviewing* sections of the chapter that you found in-teresting or helpful. Look back at any notes you took, comments in the "Notes" column, journals, activities, and readings. *Think* about your sum-mary skills and how they are improving already. *Write* down those things you've learned from this chapter that you hadn't known before. In what ways will you *apply* this new knowledge?

SUMMARY OF CHAPTER 2

In Chapter 2, as you considered the themes of dating, marriage, and gender roles and stereotypes, you also

- examined the structure of essays, textbook chapters, and newspa-per articles;
- practiced distinguishing between general and specific ideas; and
- practiced summarizing essays, textbook chapters, and newspaper articles.

Notes

VERB TENSE

Verbs Tell Time
Revising Your Definition of Verbs

Thus far in your sentence work, you've practiced identifying verbs, and you've considered the differences between action, linking, and helping verbs. In this section, you'll learn about a unique characteristic verbs possess that makes identifying them easier.

Verbs Tell Time

Verbs possess a unique characteristic: they tell time. **Verb tense** tells when the action (or linking) takes place. The simple verb tenses are the past, present, and future tenses. You should know, too, that verbs are the only words that change form when the tense changes.

Here are some examples of how verbs change when the tense changes.

Today I walk.	Today I sing.
Yesterday I walked.	Yesterday I sang.
Tomorrow I will walk.	Tomorrow I will sing.

Practice #1 Grandmother, The Feminist

Read this paragraph, and then answer the questions that follow.

My grandmother was a feminist of her own design. She kept the living room clean, organized, and beautifully decorated. The appearance of the living room was important to her because she often served afternoon tea to local politicians. The rest of the house, however, was never clean. She baked wonderful cookies and pies to serve to guests. On the other hand, she never cooked dinner for her family. Many years ago, she said to me that she was interested in local and foreign politics. She said, "I had to be a good hostess in order to be involved in interesting political discussions. But I was never a good housekeeper. Your grandfather understood me. He didn't like coming home to no dinner. However, our marriage survived because he let me be me."

1. When did most of the action in this paragraph take place? (Today? In the past? In the future?)
2. How do you know? Write down specific words from the paragraph that help you understand when the story occurs.

3. Did you find all of the words that help you understand when the story occurs? Check with a classmate.

4. Are the verbs in the present tense, past tense, or future tense? Underline verbs twice.

Practice #2   Manipulating Verb Tense

1. Rewrite the paragraph in Practice #1 as though the events are happening right now. Remove words as necessary.

2. Underline the verbs twice.

3. What tense are the verbs in now?

Practice #3   The Woman of My Dreams

• Read the following paragraph.

• Rewrite it in the future tense. To make verbs tell *future* time, add *will* before the **base form** of the verb. The base form of a verb is the verb with no special endings like *-ed* or *-ly*. At the beginning of the paragraph, change *today* to *tomorrow*.

• Underline your future tense verbs twice. Be sure to underline the entire verb (*will* + _____).

Example: She <u>understands</u> physics. (present tense)

    She <u>*will* understand</u> physics. (future tense)

Today I met the woman of my dreams. She wants to split all the responsibilities right down the middle. She pays for half of everything. She asks me out sometimes. On other occasions, I plan the dates. She spends time alone with her friends. She encourages me to go out with my friends. She is a confident, secure woman. I appreciate those qualities.

Revising Your Definition of Verbs

Remember

• All verbs can change tense.

• Only verbs can change tense.

To figure out if a word is a verb, use the **test of time.** This means that you place the word *today, yesterday,* or *tomorrow* at the beginning of a sentence and see which word (or words) change. Any word that changes is a verb. (Don't be fooled by words that *look* like verbs. Use the test of time.)

Verb Imposters and Prepositional Phrases

Notes

Here is an example of how you could use the test of time to figure out the verb of this sentence:

Many couples attend the marriage workshop.

- *Yesterday,* many couples attended the marriage workshop.
- *Today,* many couples attend the marriage workshop.
- *Tomorrow,* many couples will attend the marriage workshop.

The only word that changes in these sentences is *attend,* so *attend* must be the verb.

Practice #4   Revise Your Verb Definition

Revise your definition of a verb to include your knowledge of verb tense. Use as many sentences as necessary to express your definition of a verb.

Your Own Writing: Verb Tense

Copy a paragraph from your own writing (a journal or summary) and underline the verbs twice.

- Use the test of time if you are unsure about which words are verbs.

VERB IMPOSTERS AND PREPOSITIONAL PHRASES

Imposter #1: Present Participles (-ing Words)
Imposter #2: Infinitives (To + Verb Combinations)
Prepositional Phrases
Revising Your Definition of Verbs

Using the test of time can really help when searching for the verb, and knowing which words are verbs can help you avoid a variety of sentence errors. Besides using the test of time to identify verbs, you should also be aware of two kinds of **imposters**—words that look like verbs but really aren't. When searching for the verb in a sentence, you can make your task easier by eliminating the imposters.

Imposter #1: Present Participles (-ing Words)

A word ending in *-ing* like *snowing* or *talking* is called a **present participle**. Present participles cannot change tenses, so they cannot be verbs all by themselves. However, present participles can work as verbs *if* they get some help. In the following sentences, you'll find a present participle that is not a verb and then one that is a verb.

a. <u>Communicating</u> is important to a healthy marriage.

b. Marge and Kevin <u>are communicating</u> better.

In sentence (a), *communicating* cannot change tense and still make sense in the sentence. Therefore, it isn't a verb. It does not make sense to say, "[Yesterday] communicated is important to a healthy marriage."

In sentence (b), *are communicating* can change tense to *were communicating* or *will communicate* when we use the test of time. The following sentences do make sense.

Marge and Kevin were communicating better.

Marge and Kevin will communicate better.

Thus, *are communicating* acts as a verb in sentence (b). *Note:* When you have a helper verb and another word, only the helper verb will change *tense* although the other word may change *form*. (For example, compare *were communicating* to *will communicate*.)

Practice #5   The House Husband

Put brackets around the present participle imposters in the paragraph below. Then underline the verbs twice.

Many men are choosing the role of "house husband" today. Dusting, vacuuming, and cooking are just some of the daily chores the house husband is responsible for. On weekdays, he rises at 6:00 A.M. to cook breakfast and drive the children to school. Then he spends his afternoons running errands and driving the children to after-school activities. He devotes his evenings to helping the children with their homework and then to tucking them into bed. Around midnight, after stapling all the PTA newsletters, he finds himself ready to fall into bed. Although he considers it exhausting, he finds his chosen profession rewarding at the same time.

Notes

Imposter #2: Infinitives (to + verb combinations)

An **infinitive** is a phrase that consists of *to* + a verb. Infinitives cannot change tenses, so they cannot be verbs. In these examples, complete verbs are underlined twice and brackets are around the infinitives.

Some women <u>choose</u> [to enter] traditional career fields.

Others <u>break</u> gender barriers [to become] firefighters or police officers.

I <u>want</u> [to study] psychology.

Jason <u>has offered</u> [to share] his lecture notes.

Practice #6   A Business Leader Speaks

- Read the following paragraph.
- Put brackets around the infinitives and present participle imposters.
- Rewrite each sentence and change the tense to future tense. Begin the paragraph with *tomorrow.*
- Notice that the infinitives and present participle imposters don't change. They cannot change tense. Therefore, they cannot be verbs.
- Underline the verbs twice.

  A group of business leaders spoke at a special lunch for business majors attending University of California, Berkeley. I was one of those people giving a speech. I didn't focus my speech on which business classes to take. And I didn't focus on which magazines or newspapers to read. Instead, I emphasized the importance of learning to write well. My intention was to get business majors to realize the importance of good communication and thinking skills.

Prepositional Phrases

You now know that you must ignore imposters when looking for verbs. A **prepositional phrase**, which is a group of words consisting of a preposition and its object, is another group of words that you can eliminate when searching for verbs.

How can you spot prepositional phrases? There are so many prepositions that you shouldn't try to memorize them, but you can learn to recognize them. They usually suggest location, time, or belonging. In the following examples, the preposition is in italics and the object follows.

Location	Time	Belonging
in the dark woods	*at* four o'clock	*by* William Shakespeare
at the old farm	*before* noon	*of* my family
on the table	*after* dark	

Notes

The *object* of the preposition follows the preposition and may consist of one or more words.

Sometimes words in a prepositional phrase may look like verbs. However, words in a prepositional phrase cannot be the verb(s) for the sentence.

Consider this sentence from Frank D. Cox's essay:

> For many Americans the idea of romantic love most influences their thoughts about attraction and intimacy.

Finding the verb in this sentence can be a little tricky. But if you place brackets around any prepositional phrases, you'll find the verb is easier to identify. You can put brackets around *For many Americans, of romantic love,* and *about attraction and intimacy* because these are prepositional phrases. Only *the idea* and *most influences their thoughts* remain. The only word here that will change tense when you use the test of time is *influences*. So *influences* must be the verb.

> [For many Americans] the idea [of romantic love] most <u>influences</u> their thoughts [about attraction and intimacy.]

Practice #7   Verbs and Nonverbs in Cox's Paragraph

In the paragraph from Cox's essay that follows, put brackets around present participle imposters, infinitive imposters, and prepositional phrases. Underline the verbs twice. Use the *test of time* to test verbs when necessary. The first sentence is done for you.

> [For example,] the traditional romantic ideals <u>dictate</u> a strong, confident, protective role [for a man] and a [charming,] [loving,] dependent role [for a woman.] A woman accepting this stereotype will tend to overlook and deny dependent needs of her mate. She will tend to repress independent qualities in herself. Love for her means each correctly fulfilling the proper role. The same holds true for a man who has traditional romantic ideals.

When there are two or more infinitives in a sentence, sometimes only the first *to* is written. For example in this paragraph, you'll see *to overlook and deny.* The *to* before *deny* has been left out but *deny* is still part of an infinitive.

Verb Imposters and Prepositional Phrases

Notes

Practice #8   Verbs and Nonverbs in Bandur's Paragraph

In the paragraph from Bandur's column that follows, put brackets around present participle imposters, infinitive imposters, and prepositional phrases. Underline the verbs twice. Be careful to include helping verbs and exclude imposters. (Use the test of time to identify verbs when you are in doubt.)

> A favorite assignment of media courses is to have students analyze advertisements. Without fail, some boy will bring in a picture from the *Victoria's Secret catalog* as an example of the *objectification of women*. Does it objectify women? Considering how many sex-starved, male dorm residents steal the mailroom's copies to check out the *scantily clad* women wearing submissive, come-hither looks, I would have to say "yes." The male-dominated society's lack of respect for women is alive and well!

Revising Your Definition of Verbs

In this last section on verbs, you have studied two kinds of imposters and you have studied prepositional phrases. You are now ready to further refine your definition of verbs.

Practice #9   Revise Your Verb Definition

Revise your definition of a verb to include your knowledge of imposters and prepositional phrases. Use as many sentences as necessary to express your definition of a verb.

Your Own Writing: Verb Imposters and Prepositional Phrases

- Copy two paragraphs from your own writing (a journal or summary).
- Underline the verbs twice.
- Put brackets around present participle imposters. (Remember, if the present participle has a helping verb, it is working as a verb.)
- Put brackets around infinitives.
- Put brackets around prepositional phrases.

Examining the Reading Process

Main Topics

- Examining the PARTS of the reading process

- Practicing the reading process

- Responding to texts

- Using the dictionary and building your vocabulary

- Reading about people's roles in society

- Identifying subjects in your sentences

Calvin and Hobbes   by Bill Watterson

The Essential Calvin & Hobbes Treasury, Andrews & McMeel (Universal)

Notes

Reading is the process of gathering meaning from the letters, words, and sentences printed on a page (or a computer screen). In this chapter, you'll learn strategies that will help you better understand and remember what you read. In addition, as you read and absorb information about style, vocabulary, and writing technique, you'll begin to apply what you've learned to your own writing. Quite simply, the more you practice your reading skills, the better your reading and writing will become.

THE PARTS OF AN EFFECTIVE READING PROCESS

Experienced readers aren't necessarily speed readers. In fact, they take their time when reading and often reread to reach understanding. They use what's known as the **reading process,** a series of steps that helps them comprehend (understand) and retain (remember) what they have read. This process may be divided into five basic **PARTS,** or stages. As you begin to practice using the PARTS of the reading process, you will become a more confident reader.

Preview

Experienced readers **preview** their reading by looking at author, title, length, and topic sentences. They also review any subheadings, charts, pictures, or diagrams that accompany the reading. This previewing helps prepare them for the information to come.

Anticipate

Experienced readers know they will need to read the text more than once, so during the preview stage, they **anticipate** (expect or guess) what the reading will be about. Then as they read through the first time, they think about what will logically come next. Readers who have these expectations when they read stay interested and focused.

Read and Reread

As you read through this text, be sure to use the "Notes" column to record your questions, any new terms, and comments.

During their first **read,** successful readers move through the text quickly. They jot down questions and note words they don't recognize although they won't answer these questions or look up definitions yet. Then they **reread** slowly, answer their own questions, and look up the meanings of any words they don't know or haven't figured out. At this stage, readers also take the time to highlight important points and make written comments in the margins of the reading or on note paper.

Think Critically

Experienced readers also **think critically** about their reading. They discuss important points or answer critical thinking questions as they begin to "make sense" of the reading. These activities help readers understand the author's message and purpose, remember important ideas, and examine writing techniques that they can use in their own writing.

Summarize

Finally, experienced readers take the time to **summarize** (restate in their own words) so that they can easily review the main points of their reading.

This process may seem like hard work if you've never done it before. However, as you become a more experienced reader, you'll begin to use the PARTS of the reading process without even thinking about them.

Get Involved!

Interview a reading instructor on your college campus (or review your notes or textbook if you are currently in a reading class). Create a list of five important tips for effective reading to share with your classmates.

Journal Assignment

Responding to Calvin and Susie

Review Bill Watterson's *Calvin and Hobbes* comic strip on page 79. Which of the two characters, Calvin or Susie, appears to be the more experienced reader? How does each character feel about books? Are both views valid? What have you learned about reading and about readers from this strip?

ENGAGING IN THE READING PROCESS

To help you see how the reading process works, you'll look at one reader's preview, anticipation, and first reading of "The Struggle to Be an All-American Girl," written by Elizabeth Wong. After reviewing the first two parts of the reading process, you'll read the article yourself. Then you'll complete the stages of the reading process by rereading, thinking critically about, and summarizing the writer's main points.

One Reader's Preview and Anticipation

[*The reader's thoughts are italicized and in brackets.*] The reader's written responses appear in plain text.

Preview   [This column appeared in the newspaper, so I expect short paragraphs and few topic sentences. I'll look quickly at the

Notes

title, the author, and the first two paragraphs to get an idea of what the column is about.] The title suggests that the writer is struggling because she wants to be an "all-American girl." As I look over the column, I can see that the writer's mom made both of her children attend Chinese school. Also, the writer's first name is Elizabeth, but her last name is Wong. So her parents may be from China, but she was probably born in America. Maybe that's why she's struggling.

Anticipate   Overall, Wong seems to be frustrated. She wasn't happy going to Chinese school. She just wanted to be American.

[*As I read, I'll underline words that I plan to look up. I'll also place questions in the "Notes" column that I plan to answer when I read through the second time.*]

One Reader's First Read

Following the preview and anticipation stages of the process, the reader reads through the column quickly, jotting questions in the margin and highlighting or underlining unknown words.

Activity

The First Read

Read "The Struggle to Be an All-American Girl." As you read, look at one reader's questions in the "Notes" column and notice which vocabulary words the reader has underlined.

The Struggle to Be an All-American Girl
by Elizabeth Wong

This column appeared in the *Los Angeles Times* in 1980.

1   It's still there, the Chinese school on Yale Street where my brother and I used to go. Despite the new coat of paint and the high wire fence, the school I knew 10 years ago remains remarkably, <u>stoically</u> the same.

2   Every day at 5 P.M., instead of playing with our fourth- and fifth-grade friends or sneaking out to the empty lot to hunt ghosts and animal bones, my brother and I had to go to Chinese school. No amount of kicking, screaming, or pleading could <u>dissuade</u> my mother, who was solidly determined to have us learn the language of our heritage.

Notes

3   Forcibly, she walked us the seven long, hilly blocks from our home to school, depositing our defiant tearful faces before the stern principal. My only memory of him is that he swayed on his heels like a palm tree, and he always clasped his impatient twitching hands behind his back. I recognized him as a repressed maniacal child killer, and knew that if we ever saw his hands we'd be in big trouble.

I'm wondering why Wong's mother insisted they learn Chinese against their will.

4   We all sat in little chairs in an empty auditorium. The room smelled like Chinese medicine, and imported faraway mustiness. Like ancient mothballs or dirty closets. I hated that smell. I favored crisp new scents. Like the soft French perfume that my American teacher wore in public school.

5   Although the emphasis at the school was mainly language—speaking, reading, writing—the lessons always began with an exercise in politeness. With the entrance of the teacher, the best student would tap a bell and everyone would get up, <u>kowtow</u>, and chant, "sing san ho," the phonetic for "How are you, teacher?"

6   Being ten years old, I had better things to learn than <u>ideographs</u> copied painstakingly in lines that ran right to left from the top of a *moc but,* a real ink pen that had to be held in an awkward way if blotches were to be avoided. After all, I could do the multiplication tables, name the satellites of Mars, and write reports on *Little Women* and *Black Beauty.* Nancy Drew, my favorite book heroine, never spoke Chinese.

7   The language was a source of embarrassment. More times than not, I had tried to <u>disassociate</u> myself from the nagging loud voice that followed me wherever I wandered in the nearby American supermarket outside Chinatown. The voice belonged to my grandmother, a fragile woman in her seventies who could outshout the best of the street vendors. Her humor was <u>raunchy</u>, her Chinese rhythmless, patternless. It was quick, it was loud, it was unbeautiful. It was not like the quiet, lilting romance of French or the gentle refinement of the American South. Chinese sounded <u>pedestrian</u>. Public.

Why does Wong think Chinese is pedestrian? What does she mean by pedestrian?

8   In Chinatown, the comings and goings of hundreds of Chinese on their daily tasks sounded <u>chaotic</u> and <u>frenzied</u>. I did not want to be thought of as mad, as talking gibberish. When I spoke English, people nodded at me, smiled sweetly, said encouraging words. Even the people in my culture would cluck and say that I'd do well in life. "My, doesn't she move her lips fast," they would say, meaning that I'd be able to keep up with the world outside Chinatown.

Notes

Why was Wong's brother so bothered by his mother's mistakes in English?

Why was she allowed to stop going to Chinese school? Why is she sad at the end? Didn't she get what she wanted?

9   My brother was even more <u>fanatical</u> than I about speaking English. He was especially hard on my mother, criticizing her, often cruelly, for her pidgin speech—smatterings of Chinese scattered like chop suey in her conversation. "It's not 'What it is,' Mom," he'd say in exasperation. "It's 'What is it, what is it, what is it!'" Sometimes Mom might leave out an occasional "the" or "a," or perhaps a verb of being. He would stop her in mid-sentence: "Say it again, Mom. Say it right." When he tripped over his own tongue, he'd blame it on her: "See, Mom, it's all your fault. You set a bad example."

10   After two years of writing with a *moc but* and reciting words with multiples of meanings, I finally was granted a cultural divorce. I was permitted to stop Chinese school.

11   I thought of myself as <u>multicultural</u>. I preferred tacos to egg rolls; I enjoyed Cinco de Mayo more than Chinese New Year.

12   At last, I was one of you; I wasn't one of them.

13   Sadly, I still am.

REREAD, THINK CRITICALLY, AND SUMMARIZE

Reread   Following a quick first read, the reader reads the column a second time, slowing down to more closely consider the writer's meaning. Then the reader looks up meanings of unfamiliar terms and answers her own questions from the first reading.

Activity

Reread

Reread Wong's essay, looking up the meanings of any words you don't know or can't figure out. Write definitions in your notebook, in the "Notes" column, or on notecards. Also, write responses to the first reader's questions in the "Notes" column.

Think Critically   As you read through the article a second time, you should have begun to carefully consider the writer's message and purpose. This stage of the process also involves answering critical thinking questions and/or discussing important points with classmates after you have completed your second read.

Questions for Critical Thought

"The Struggle to Be an All-American Girl"

1. Why would Wong's mother have wanted her children to attend Chinese school?

2. Why might Wong have rebelled against going to Chinese school? In your opinion, should she have been forced to attend? Why, or why not?

3. What are some of the reasons why Wong seemed to be embarrassed by her grandmother's Chinese? Are these the same reasons why Wong's brother became upset when their mother made mistakes in English?

4. The title of the article suggests that Wong was "struggling to be an all-American girl." What does she mean by this? Did she reach her goal? What evidence does she offer as proof?

5. What does Wong mean in paragraph 10 when she says, "I finally was granted a cultural divorce"? Does the word "divorce" accurately describe what happened?

6. Why does Wong use the word "sadly" in paragraph 13? In your opinion, does she have reason to be sad?

7. Because Wong's article appeared in a newspaper, we can assume that it was directed at a general audience. In your opinion, what message does she wish to share with her audience?

Summarize   Finally, it's a good idea to summarize what you've read. As you discovered in Chapter 2, summarizing not only helps you remember what you've read, but it also can be a resource for your own writing.

Activity

Summarize

Summarize Wong's article. Remember that when you are summarizing a newspaper article, you need to look for main ideas rather than topic sentences. Write a list of these main ideas. Then write a brief summary of the article. Be sure to include author, title, and place of publication.

RESPONDING TO READING

A **response** is a thoughtful reaction to what you've read. In a response, the writer refers back to the article, essay, or textbook chapter, and then comments on the most important or most intriguing ideas. It differs from the more organized summary, which requires the writer to include only the author's main points. Also, a response differs from the essays you'll be writing. In an essay, the writer states a thesis in the introduction and then supports that thesis in the paragraphs that follow. In a response, the writer has the freedom to move from one idea to another and back again, perhaps to explore several aspects of an issue or just to think on paper. You've been writing responses as you've worked your way through the first two chapters of this text. When you're asked to write your opinion in the form of reading questions, journals, or other assignments, you're writing a response.

Journal Assignment

Respond to "The Struggle to Be an All-American Girl"

Write a 10- to 15-minute response to Wong's article. You might write about the importance of your own cultural heritage, an experience of your own that is similar to or different from Wong's, or another issue connected to the article.

BUILDING YOUR VOCABULARY

One of the most important benefits of reading is improving your vocabulary. Your vocabulary will naturally grow as you look up new terms and figure out words as you read. But if you haven't had much practice using the dictionary, looking up words can be pretty frustrating, especially when there are several possible definitions listed for a single word. Also, new words are easy to forget if you don't have a plan for reviewing them. In the following discussion, you'll learn some techniques for developing your vocabulary.

Using the Dictionary to Find Word Meanings

If you were unsure of what *pedestrian* means in paragraph 7 of Wong's article, then you probably looked it up in your dictionary.

The voice belonged to my grandmother, a fragile woman in her seventies who could outshout the best of the street vendors. Her humor was raunchy, her Chinese rhythmless, patternless. It was quick, it was loud, it was unbeautiful. It was not like the quiet, lilting romance of French or the gentle refinement of the American South. Chinese sounded *pedestrian*. Public.

Notes

This entry is from *The American Heritage Dictionary:*

pe·des·tri·an (pə-dĕs'trē-ən) *n.* A person traveling on foot; walker.— *adj.* **1.** Of, relating to, or made for pedestrians. **2.** Going or performed on foot: *a pedestrian journey.* **3.** Undistinguished; ordinary: *pedestrian prose.* [Lat. *pedester,* going on foot < *pedes,* a pedestrian < *pes,* foot.]— **pe·des´·tri·an·ism** *n.*

When you look at a dictionary entry, you can't just pick any part of the entry and apply that information to the word and sentence you are interested in. *Pedestrian,* for example, can be a noun (person, place, or thing) or an adjective (a word used to describe a noun). The *n* (meaning noun) and *adj* (meaning adjective) in the entry tell us that. In order to choose the correct meaning, you have to figure out how the word you want to define is being used. In the quotation, *pedestrian* is being used as an adjective because it describes the noun *Chinese.*

Once you know how the word is being used, then you can look at the possible definitions. Three are listed following *adj.* Numbers one and two relate to someone walking, but we can see that the sentence doesn't refer to walking. However, number three offers a different meaning: "Undistinguished; ordinary." These two words help describe how Grandmother's Chinese sounded to Wong. It sounded ordinary and unimportant. Remember, when looking up a word like *pedestrian,* you should think about how it works in the sentence.

You should also consider the words and sentences surrounding *pedestrian.* For example, look at the word *public,* which follows *pedestrian* in paragraph 7 (page 83). When something is *public,* it's exposed to all. It's not special. Wong's use of *public* following *pedestrian* emphasizes the idea that her grandmother's Chinese sounded ordinary and unimportant to Wong. Then consider how Wong describes other languages and dialects in the same paragraph: "the quiet, lilting romance of French" and "the gentle refinement of the American South." Words such as *refinement* and *romance* contrast with *pedestrian* and *public,* revealing that Wong thought other languages were beautiful in comparison to her grandmother's. By considering the surrounding words and sentences, we're better able to understand what *pedestrian* means and how Wong felt.

Notes

Activity

Finding Meanings in the Dictionary

The paragraph that follows is from a personal essay, "Navigating My Eerie Landscape Alone," in which writer Jim Bobryk talks about living with blindness. (You'll read the entire essay later in this chapter.) Practice your dictionary skills by finding definitions for the words in italics.

> I was driving home for lunch on what seemed to be an increasingly foggy day, although the perky radio deejay said it was clear and sunny. After I finished my lunch, I realized that I couldn't see across the room to my front door. I had battled *glaucoma* for 20 years. Suddenly, without warning, my eyes had *hemorrhaged*.

Write down the definitions for these terms. Explain how knowing these terms helps you better understand what happened to Jim Bobryk.

Finding Definitions in the Writing

Often, unfamiliar words in a reading are immediately followed by their definitions. This is particularly true in a textbook when the writer must introduce several new concepts within a single chapter. Note how the definition follows the term *feminism* in this example:

A complete version of this textbook excerpt by Thompson and Hickey appears in Supplemental Readings, pages 401–403.

> The struggle for women's rights has been a long and hard-fought battle in the United States. The first major wave of **feminism,** *an ideology aimed at eliminating patriarchy in support of equality between the sexes,* was linked to the pre–Civil War abolitionist movement.
>
> —William E. Thompson and Joseph V. Hickey, from
> "Feminism: The Struggle for Gender Equality"

Recognizing Context Clues

In addition to using your dictionary or finding definitions in the text, you should try to figure out the meaning of an unfamiliar word by looking at the **context,** the writing in which the word appears. This means that you think about the entire sentence in which the unfamiliar word appears, and you also consider the sentences before and after it. Nearby words and other sentences often give you clues about what the unknown word means.

For example, the word *patriarchal* in the following textbook excerpt on the Puritans might be unfamiliar to you. Consider what this word means by looking at the sentence that precedes it.

> Families cared for the destitute and elderly; they took in orphans; and they housed servants and apprentices—all under one roof and subject to the authority of the father.
>
> The Puritans carried *patriarchal* values across the Atlantic and planted them in America. . . .
>
> —*James Kirby Martin et al., from "Seventeenth Century Roles for Puritan Men, Women, and Children"*

In this case, the last phrase of the first paragraph, "all under one roof and *subject to the authority of the father,*" sets up the idea of *patriarchal* values. Now that you see this connection, it is clear that the term *patriarchal* connects to the idea that males were in charge of the Puritan family.

Reexamine the paragraph example from the previous section, "Finding Definitions in the Writing" (reprinted again below). Note that though the word *feminism* has been defined in the example, there are at least two other words, *ideology* and *patriarchy,* that you may find unfamiliar.

> The struggle for women's rights has been a long and hard-fought battle in the United States. The first major wave of **feminism,** *an ideology aimed at eliminating patriarchy in support of equality between the sexes,* was linked to the pre–Civil War abolitionist movement.

However, you may have recognized that the word *patriarchy* is a form of the word *patriarchal,* which you've already discovered has something to do with males being in charge. So now you can see that feminism means "eliminating male superiority" (patriarchy) in favor of supporting "equality between the sexes." When figuring out words in context, then, you should look for variations of words you already know. In this case, the only other term you would need to look up would be *ideology.* But before you do, ask yourself what other words might be forms of this term.

Activity

Finding Meaning in Context

Read the paragraph that follows. Look at the context of the word *matrilineal.* What discussion follows the introduction of this term? Based on the sentences surrounding it, what do you think it means?

Notes

A complete version of Menon's article appears in Supplemental Readings, pages 405–407.

Meghalaya, a district tucked away in the remote northeastern corner of India, is home to the Khasi, one of the largest surviving *matrilineal* societies in the world. In this hill tribe of nearly 650,000, descent is traced through the mother's line and women have an honored place in the society. Here, baby girls are quite welcome, and, some argue, even more highly prized than boys. Since the woman's family holds the cards when arranging a marriage, the question of dowry—paying a man's family for accepting the "burden" of a wife—would never even arise. No social stigma is attached to women, whether they choose to divorce, remarry, or stay single.

—*Kavita Menon, from "In India, Men Challenge a Matrilineal Society"*

Figuring out a word in context will save you time and energy while developing your critical thinking skills. However, the most important reason to develop this skill is so that you'll gain a better understanding of the meaning of the word and how it works in a particular sentence, paragraph, or essay.

Keeping a Vocabulary Notebook

Assign a section of your notebook to vocabulary. Writing down new words, definitions, and other related information will help you build your vocabulary. But writing down such information is not enough. To help you make these terms a part of your life, you need to review your vocabulary section regularly. You must also practice using these new words in your own writing.

Use the vocabulary section of your notebook to write down and define unfamiliar words you come across in all of your classes—not just your English class. Your list should contain

- the sentence that the word appeared in,
- the meaning in context (if possible),
- how the word works in the sentence, and
- the dictionary definition.

Here is an example of how to list a word.

The new term —— *dissuade*

The sentence in which the term appeared —— "No amount of kicking, screaming, or pleading could <u>dissuade</u> my mother, who was solidly determined to have us learn the language of our heritage."

Definition based on context —— I know that "persuade" means to convince someone to do something. "Dissuade" must mean to make someone not do something.

Verb   ——Type of word

Pronunciation: (dĭs•wād')   ——Pronunciation

Definition: To deter from course or action.   ——Definition

Other forms of the word: dissuader (noun)   ——Other forms

Paraphrased: Nothing Wong did could keep her mother from in-   ⎤ Word meaning in
sisting that Wong and her brother learn Chinese.   ⎦ context—in your own
                                                                    words

Activity   *Notes*

> ### Vocabulary Notebook
>
> Return to Elizabeth Wong's article, "The Struggle to Be an All-American
> Girl." Write any words that were new to you in the vocabulary section of
> your notebook. Be sure to include the definition as well as other related in-
> formation. In addition, log any other new terms from this section, "Building
> Your Vocabulary." Consider logging the following terms: *pedestrian, glau-
> coma, hemorrhaged, patriarchal* or *patriarchy,* and *matrilineal.*

Remember, writing this information will help you learn new words
and review and study them. Also, you must *practice using your new
words* if they are to become a part of your expanding vocabulary. Try using these new words as you answer questions or respond in journal assignments. In the chapters to come, plan to include them in your essays.

PRACTICING THE READING PROCESS

So far in this chapter, you've studied the PARTS of the reading process
and have explored some strategies for using the dictionary and building your vocabulary. You're ready now to begin practicing what you've
learned. In the reading assignments that follow, you'll encounter many
of the writing structures you explored in Chapter 2. In addition, you'll
have the opportunity to practice and develop your reading-writing-
critical thinking connection as you explore people's roles in society.

READING THE PERSONAL NARRATIVE

In "The Struggle to Be an All-American Girl" earlier in the chapter,
you encountered a type of writing called the personal narrative. In a
personal narrative, an individual recounts an event or series of events
from his or her own life, usually to make a point or to help the reader

Notes

better understand an issue. In Wong's case, she retold her story about wanting to be "an all-American girl" so that she could tell what she had learned from her experience—that it's important to remember your own cultural heritage. In the essay that follows, writer Jim Bobryk shares his personal experience.

Reading Assignment: *"Navigating My Eerie Landscape Alone"*

Preview   This is a personal narrative that appeared in a popular magazine. You can assume that it will follow journalistic format, with shorter paragraphs and few topic sentences. Review the title, the quotation underneath the title, and the first two paragraphs.

Anticipate   What do you think this personal narrative will be about? Use the "Notes" column to record your answer.

Read   Now read the entire article quickly and continue to anticipate as you read. Highlight unfamiliar terms and jot down any questions in the margins. (Remember, because you're reading quickly, it's all right not to understand everything the first time through.)

Navigating My Eerie Landscape Alone
by Jim Bobryk

"Unless I ask for help, strangers are so afraid of doing the wrong thing that they do nothing at all."

This *Newsweek* article, by writer and executive Jim Bobryk, appeared on March 18, 1999.

1   Now, as I stroll down the street, my right forefinger extends five feet in front of me, feeling the ground where my feet will walk.

2   Before, my right hand would have been on a steering wheel as I went down the street. I drove to work, found shortcuts in strange cities, picked up my two daughters after school. Those were the days when I ran my finger down a phone-book page and never dialed Information. When I read novels and couldn't sleep until I had finished the last page. Those were the nights when I could point out a shooting star before it finished scraping across the dark sky. And when I could go to the movies and it didn't matter if it was a foreign film or not.

3   But all this changed about seven years ago. I was driving home for lunch on what seemed to be an increasingly foggy day, although the perky radio deejay said it was clear and sunny. After I finished my lunch, I realized that I couldn't see across the room to my front door. I

had battled glaucoma for 20 years. Suddenly, without warning, my eyes had hemorrhaged.

4   I will never regain any of my lost sight. I see things through a porthole covered in wax paper. I now have no vision in my left eye and only slight vision in my right. A minefield of blind spots make people and cars suddenly appear and vanish. I have no depth perception. Objects are not closer and farther; they're larger and smaller. Steps, curbs and floors all flow on the same flat plane. My world has shapes but no features. Friends are mannequins in the fog until I recognize their voices. Printed words look like ants writhing on the pages. Doorways are unlit mine shafts. This is not a place for the fainthearted.

5   My cane is my navigator in this eerie landscape. It is a hollow fiberglass stick with white reflector paint and a broad red band at the tip. It folds up tightly into four 15-inch sections, which can then be slipped into a black holster that attaches to my belt with Velcro.

6   Adults—unless they're preoccupied or in a hurry—will step aside without comment when they see me coming. Small children will either be scooped up apologetically or steered away by their parents. Only teenagers sometimes try to play chicken, threatening to collide with me and then veering out of the way at the last moment.

7   While I'm wielding my stick, strangers are often afraid to communicate with me. I don't take this personally—anymore. Certainly they can't be afraid that I'll lash at them with my rod. (Take *that,* you hapless sighted person! Whack!) No, they're probably more afraid *for* me. Don't startle the sword swallower. Don't tickle the baton twirler.

8   The trick for the sighted person is to balance courtesy with concern. Should he go out of his way or should he get out of the way? Will his friendliness be misconstrued by the disabled as pity? Will an offer of help sound patronizing? These anxieties are exaggerated by not knowing the etiquette in dealing with the disabled. A sighted person will do nothing rather than take the risk of offending the blind. Still, I refuse to take a dim view of all this.

9   When I peer over my cane and ask for help, no one ever cowers in fear. In fact, I think people are waiting for me to give them the green light to help. It makes us feel good to help.

10   When I ask for a small favor, I often get more assistance than I ever expect. Clerks will find my required forms and fill them out for me. A group of people will parade me across a dangerous intersection. A salesclerk will read the price tag for me and then hunt for the item on sale. I'm no Don Juan, but strange (and possibly exotic) women will take my hand and walk me through dark rooms, mysterious train stations and foreign airports. Cabbies wait and make sure I make it safely into lobbies.

Notes

11   It's not like it's inconvenient for friends to help me get around. Hey, have disabled parking placard—will travel. Christmas shopping? Take me to the mall and I'll get us front-row parking. Late for the game? *No problema.* We'll be parking by the stadium entrance. And if some inconsiderate interloper does park in the blue zone without a permit, he'll either be running after a fleeing tow truck or paying a big fine.

12   Worried about those age lines showing? Not with me looking. Put down that industrial-strength Oil of Olay. To me, your skin looks as clean and smooth as it was back in the days when you thought suntanning was a good idea.

13   So you see, I'm a good guy to know. I just carry a cane, that's all.

14   None of this is to make light of going blind. Being blind is dark and depressing. When you see me walking with my cane you may think I'm lost as I ricochet down the street. But you'll find more things in life if you don't travel in a straight line.

Reread   Once you've completed a first reading, read Bobryk's narrative a second time. Slow down to answer your own questions and look up the meanings of any words you don't know or can't figure out. Add these to the vocabulary section of your notebook.

Here is a list of words to get you started. Be sure to include any other unfamiliar terms and definitions. (You may skip any of the terms that you're familiar with already.)

Par. 3: glaucoma; hemorrhaged

Par. 4: porthole; minefield; mannequins

Par. 5: eerie

Par. 7: wielding

Par. 8: misconstrued; etiquette

Par. 11: interloper

Par. 14: ricochet

Think Critically, Summarize, and Respond   The questions and activities that follow will help you develop your reading skills as you complete the reading process.

Questions for Critical Thought

"Navigating My Eerie Landscape Alone"

1. What caused Jim Bobryk to lose his sight?

2. Bobryk explains that his cane is now his "navigator." What does he mean by this?

3. In what ways has Bobryk's life changed as a result of his losing his eyesight?

4. Bobryk explains that "strangers are often afraid to communicate" with him, but when he asks for assistance, he finds that people are more than willing to help. How does he account for these different forms of treatment?

5. Identify two places in the article where Bobryk uses humor to make his point. Why would a writer use humor to make a serious point?

6. Bobryk states, "I'm a good guy to know. I just carry a cane, that's all." What does he want his audience to understand from this statement?

7. Bobryk's article appeared in *Newsweek* magazine. Who would most likely be included in his audience? What overall point or message do you believe Bobryk conveys in this article?

Activity

Summarize "Navigating My Eerie Landscape Alone"

After making a list of the main points and most important supporting points, write a summary of Bobryk's article. Be sure to include author, title of article, and where it was published. Also include a general statement telling what the article is about, followed by its main points. When you've finished a draft of your summary, return to the article to check for accuracy and revise as necessary.

Journal Assignment

Respond to "Navigating My Eerie Landscape Alone"

Take ten to 15 minutes to respond to Bobryk's article. You might comment on Bobryk's use of humor in the piece. (Look back at paragraphs 7, 9, 10, and 11.) You could write about a similar experience of your own or of someone you know. You might also write about what you have learned from Bobryk's article.

Get Involved!

Rent and watch the film *At First Sight* (1999) starring Val Kilmer and Mira Sorvino and directed by Henry Winkler. In the film, a blind man has an operation that gives him sight. Prepare to discuss in your next class how the main character's life changes as a result of the operation. Also be ready to discuss how this character's experience compares to the real-life experience of Jim Bobryk.

READING TEXTBOOK CHAPTERS

In Chapter 2 you studied the structure of textbook chapters. You know that this type of writing follows basic essay format and contains an introduction and clear thesis that lead the reader through the chapter. A textbook chapter's body paragraphs usually consist of topic sentences followed by supporting detail and explanation. Most end with at least a concluding remark. This section includes an excerpt (portion) of a chapter from a history textbook that explores people's roles in our society. (For an excerpt from a sociology textbook that is also on people's roles in society, see "Feminism: The Struggle for Gender Equality" in Supplemental Readings, pages 401–404.)

Reading Assignment:
"Seventeenth-Century Roles for Puritan Men, Women, and Children"

Get Involved!

Before reading this textbook excerpt, go to the library or the Internet and gather information about the Puritans. Share the information with your classmates.

Preview   This segment comes from a history textbook, so you know that it will follow the expected format of a clear introduction, body paragraphs, and concluding remarks. Review the title, author, and introductory information. Then read the opening paragraphs as well as the topic sentences throughout the piece.

Anticipate   After reviewing the introduction and topic sentences, what do you believe this textbook selection will be about? Use the "Notes" column to record your answer.

Read   Quickly read through the excerpt. Anticipate what information will appear next as you read. Be sure to highlight unfamiliar terms and write any questions you may have in the margins.

Seventeenth-Century Roles for Puritan Men, Women, and Children
by James Kirby Martin et al.

This selection appeared in the history textbook, *America and Its People.*

Note: This selection was written by more than one author. The first author's name is followed by "et al.," a Latin phrase that means "and others."

1   The early Puritans looked at their mission as a family undertaking, and they referred to families as "little commonwealths." Not only were families to "be fruitful and multiply," but they also served as agencies of education and religious instruction as well as centers of vocational training and social welfare. Families cared for the destitute and elderly; they took in orphans; and they housed servants and apprentices—all under one roof and subject to the authority of the father.

2   The Puritans carried *patriarchal* values across the Atlantic and planted them in America. New England law, reflecting its English base,

Copyright © 2004 by Pearson Education, Inc.

subscribed to the doctrine of *coverture,* or subordinating the legal identity of women in their husbands, who were the undisputed heads of households. Unless there were prenuptial agreements, all property brought by women to marriages belonged to their mates. Husbands, who by custom and law directed their families in prayer and scripture reading, were responsible for assuring decency and good order in family life. They also represented their families in all community political, economic, and religious activities.

3   Wives also had major family responsibilities. "For though the husband be the head of the wife," the Reverend Samuel Willard explained, "yet she is the head of the family." It was the particular calling of mothers to nurture their children in godly living, as well as to perform many other tasks—tending gardens, brewing beer, raising chickens, cooking, spinning, and sewing—when not helping in the planting and harvesting of crops.

4   Most Puritan marriages functioned in at least outward harmony. If serious problems arose, local churches and courts intervened to end the turmoil. Puritan law, again reflecting English precedent, made divorce quite difficult. The process required the petitioning of assemblies for bills of separation, and the only legal grounds were bigamy, desertion, and adultery. A handful of women, most likely battered or abandoned wives, effected their own divorces by setting up separate residences. On occasion the courts brought unruly husbands under control, for example, a Maine husband who brutally clubbed his wife for refusing to feed the family pig. There were instances when wives defied patriarchalism, including one case involving a Massachusetts woman who faced community censure for beating her husband and even "egging her children to help her, bidding them knock him in the head."

5   Family friction arose from other sources as well, some of which stemmed from the absolute control that fathers exercised over property and inheritances. If sons wanted to marry and establish separate households, they had to conform to the will of their fathers, who controlled the land. Family patriarchs normally delayed the passing of property until sons had reached their mid-twenties and selected mates acceptable to parents. Delayed inheritances help to explain why so many New Englanders did not marry until several years after puberty. Since parents also bestowed dowries on daughters as their contributions to new family units, romantic love had less to do with mate selection than parental desires to unite particular family names and estates.

6   Puritans expected brides and grooms to learn to love one another as they went about their duty of conceiving and raising the next gen-

Notes

eration of children. In most cases spouses did develop lasting affection for one another, as captured by the gifted Puritan poetess Anne Bradstreet in 1666 when she wrote to her "dear and loving Husband":

If ever two were one, then surely we.
If ever man were lov'd by wife, then thee;
If ever wife was happy in a man,
Compare with me the women if you can.

7   Young adults who openly defied patriarchal authority were rare. Those who did could expect to hear what one angry Bay Colony father told his unwanted son-in-law: "As you married her without my consent, you shall keep her without my help." Also unusual were instances of illegitimate children, despite the lengthy gap between puberty and marriage. As measured by illegitimate births, premarital sex could not have been that common in early New England, not a surprising finding among people living in closely controlled communities and seeking to honor the Almighty by reforming human society.

Reread   Complete a second, slower reading of the textbook excerpt. Respond to questions you wrote in the margins during your first reading. Look up terms and record their definitions in your notebook.

Consider adding the following terms to your vocabulary list. Remember to try to figure out the word in its context. Then use the dictionary to verify its meaning.

Par. 1: "little commonwealths" (look up the term "commonwealth"); apprentices

Par. 2: patriarchal; coverture; prenuptial agreement

Par. 5: dowries

Think Critically, Summarize, and Respond   Continue the reading process as you think critically, summarize, and respond to what you've read.

Questions for Critical Thought

"Seventeenth-Century Roles. . . ."

1. The reader is told that Puritan society was a patriarchal society. Explain how this society operated.

2. Look up the word "commonwealth." Write out the meaning. Explain what you believe the authors mean when they say Puritan families operated as "little commonwealths."

3. What does the command "be fruitful and multiply" mean? Where   *Notes*
   might this command have come from? Why did the Puritans believe
   and obey it?

4. According to the selection, what were the husband's responsibilities
   or duties in the early Puritan household? What were the wife's?

5. Look back at the term *coverture* and its definition in paragraph 2.
   How were Puritan women affected by the doctrine of *coverture?*

6. Describe what early Puritan marriages were like. Did they seem to
   work? What happened if trouble developed in a Puritan marriage?

7. Did romantic love play a large part in the selection of a mate in
   those days? Why, or why not?

8. What might have happened to a son or daughter who rebelled against
   his or her father's wishes in marriage?

9. Was premarital sex a common occurrence in early Puritan New
   England? Why, or why not?

10. In what ways has the family changed since early Puritan times?

11. Who would be the audience for this piece? What is the authors'
    purpose in presenting this reading to this particular audience?

Activity

Summarize "Seventeenth-Century Roles. . . ."

Write a summary of this excerpt. Because it follows essay form, you can
check for a thesis in the introduction and main ideas in the topic sentences.
Begin by listing the most important points. Open your summary with the excerpt's overall main idea. Follow with the most important points. Look back
at the excerpt to make sure you've included all of the main ideas. Don't forget to identify the author, title, and textbook.

Journal Assignment

Respond to "Seventeenth-Century Roles. . . ."

Spend ten to 15 minutes responding to this excerpt. Consider the
positive and negative aspects of love and marriage in the past and
present. Think about how modern views compare to Puritan views. You

Notes

might write about what you believe to be the ideal approach to love and/or marriage. You might write about a time when love and marriage worked best, or respond to something else in the text that interests you.

READING MAGAZINE AND NEWSPAPER ARTICLES

To read an opposing viewpoint, see Kavita Menon's article, "In India, Men Challenge a Matrilineal Society," Supplemental Readings, pages 405–407.

Back in Chapter 2, you examined the shape and function of a feature story and newspaper column. In this chapter, you'll practice the reading process on a feature story about unequal pay for equal work. Keep in mind that newspaper articles contain shorter paragraphs and fewer topic sentences than the textbook excerpt you've just read.

Reading Assignment: *"Not a Two-Bit Problem"*

Preview This feature story appeared in a newspaper, so you should expect an opening statement (the lead), short paragraphs, and few topic sentences. Begin by reviewing the title, author, publication information, and opening paragraphs.

Anticipate What do you believe this article will be about? Use the "Notes" column to record your thoughts.

Read Quickly read the article. As you read, highlight unfamiliar words and write your questions in the "Notes" column.

Not a Two-Bit Problem

Women earn about 75 cents for every dollar men receive.
Here are several reasons why.

by Dave Murphy

This feature story was written for the *San Francisco Examiner* newspaper, April 11, 1999.

Get Involved!

Find the latest information on the wage gap online at the National Committee on Pay Equity's Website: www.feminist.com/ fairpay/peinfo.htm. Do women still earn 75 cents for every dollar men earn? Share your findings with your class.

1   The typical full-time female worker earns about 75 cents for every dollar that the typical man earns. Is that a misleading statistic—or an indicator that women still are a long way from workplace equality, 36 years after the federal Equal Pay Act was passed?

2   Yes, on both counts.

3   The federal government statistic is misleading because it simply compares the median earnings of all full-time workers of both sexes, not taking into account experience, education, ability or even the

Copyright © 2004 by Pearson Education, Inc.

type of job involved. Women were at 74 cents per men's dollar in 1997, the last year that figures are available. In the first quarter of 1998, the figure rose to 76 cents, mainly because of increases in the minimum wage.

4   "We would not say that all of that is pure discrimination," says Susan Bianchi-Sand, executive director of the National Committee on Pay Equity in Washington, D.C.

5   According to figures from the committee's Web site (feminist.com/fair-pay.htm), women were at only 60 percent of men's earnings until 1980, but increased to 72 percent by 1990.

6   "The reason the gap has actually closed is that men's wages have stagnated," Bianchi-Sand says. "You don't close the gap by holding men's wages down. No one is interested in that."

7   The Economic Policy Institute in Washington says that through 1997, the inflation-adjusted median wages for women had grown just 0.8 percent during the 1990s. Men's wages had fallen 6.7 percent.

8   Although the wage gap is a flawed statistic, experts say women still are being underpaid for several reasons—including discrimination. In the late 1980s, the President's Council of Economic Advisors found that 12 cents of the wage gap could not be explained, says Kelly Jenkins-Pultz, policy advisor to the director of the Department of Labor's Women's Bureau.

9   The AFL-CIO's Web site for working women (aflcio.org/women) points to wage gaps in a variety of jobs. It says, for example, that female attorneys earn nearly $300 a week less than male attorneys, and female professors are paid $170 a week less than male professors.

10   Bianchi-Sand says much of the gap is because many jobs traditionally held by women don't pay as well as jobs traditionally held by men.

11   "It's a lot about attitude, which in some cases translates into overt discrimination," she says. "Attitudes are harder to change than laws, it appears."

12   Sometimes discrimination laws are of little help because they apply only to jobs that have workers of both sexes, Bianchi-Sand says. She explains that social workers (typically female) have many of the same duties as probation officers (typically male), but are paid substantially less. That is not discrimination under the law because they are different jobs.

13   Among jobs available to people without a college degree, many of the highest paying involve danger or physical labor. Those jobs are traditionally held by men—in some cases because few women want them.

14   Jenkins-Pultz agrees that many women are in low-wage jobs like cashiers and secretaries, or in low-wage industries like service and child care. Still, she is encouraged because more women are ending up in

Notes

managerial and administrative jobs, or in high-paying professional jobs like doctors and lawyers.

15   "They're not nontraditional jobs for women anymore," she says.

16   Jenkins-Pultz also is encouraged because more bachelor's degrees now are being awarded to women than men, and more women are developing the kind of work experience that can get them better jobs. She says women traditionally have had less education and less work experience than men, two legitimate reasons for part of the wage gap.

17   Three other factors can contribute to the gap: perception, pricing, and parenthood. Here's how:

18   **Perception:** Sometimes even those who agree that women are discriminated against don't recognize that they're part of the problem.

19   A 1997 Romac International survey of human resources executives found that 52 percent believed that women were being paid less than men for comparable work, but only 21 percent thought it was happening in their own companies.

20   **Pricing:** Sometimes female workers don't negotiate as hard or as well for a high salary as their male counterparts do. Or they may find other aspects of the job that are worth more to them than money.

21   Leon A. Farley, a San Francisco executive search consultant for 27 years, says men and women earning more than $500,000 a year tend to emphasize compensation equally. For those whose compensation is $150,000 to $500,000, however, he sees men pushing harder for the extra pay than women do.

22   Some of it is because of family, Farley says. More of the women in that category have spouses who also work, so they may be more concerned with a good opportunity or other benefits than with bringing in extra money.

23   Age can be a factor as well. Although he acknowledges there are plenty of exceptions, Farley says younger women—who grew up playing sports and being encouraged to compete more than their mothers had been—are more likely to push for equal wages. . . .

24   **Parenthood:** When families have children, mothers are far more likely than fathers to leave the work force for several years to raise the kids. When people leave the work force for several years, their skills get rusty and their careers suffer.

25   But the problem goes deeper than that, Bianchi-Sand says.

26   It's a vicious circle. Because of the fear that female employees will have children and leave, she says, some employers won't give women the same training or opportunities that men receive. So the women don't do as well and don't earn as much money.

27   So when married couples have to decide which parent should stay home to raise the children, it makes perfect sense for the spouse with the lower income to stay home—and for the spouse who stays employed to emphasize money more than before.

Reread   Take the time to read Murphy's article again. Read slowly and think about the issues Murphy has raised. As you read carefully, be sure to answer your questions in the "Notes" column and take the time to define any unknown words.

Here are words to consider adding to the vocabulary section of your notebook. Be sure to consider context clues, then verify the meanings by looking up unfamiliar words in your dictionary.

Title: two-bit

Par. 6: stagnated

Par. 11: overt

Par. 16: legitimate

Par. 21: compensation

Think Critically, Summarize, and Respond   Continue to move through the reading process as you complete the activities and questions for critical thought.

Questions for Critical Thought

"Not a Two-Bit Problem"

1. Why does Murphy pose a question in the opening paragraph? Is this an effective strategy for beginning an article? Why, or why not?

2. Government statistics show that a female worker earns approximately 75 cents for every dollar that a male worker makes. Why, according to Murphy, is this figure misleading?

3. What are some of the reasons given to explain why women are still underpaid?

4. How does perception contribute to the gap in wages? How does pricing? How does parenthood?

5. What, if anything, should be done about this difference in wages?

6. Who is the audience for this article? In your opinion, what is the writer's reason for having written this article?

Notes

Activity

Summarize "Not a Two-Bit Problem"

Now that you've discussed the article, summarize the main points. Begin by listing them. Then write your summary from this list. Be sure to include a general opening statement about the article and include author, title, and publication information. Return to the article to check your facts. Make any necessary revisions.

Journal Assignment

Respond to "Not a Two-Bit Problem"

Take ten to 15 minutes to respond to Murphy's article. Consider the current difference in wages. Think about the explanations given for this difference and who suffers as a result. You may write about something from the article that you find interesting. You may also write about your personal experience or the experiences of others you know.

TIME TO REFLECT

Journal Assignment

Your Progress as a Writer, Reader, and Critical Thinker

Think about the chapter and the skills you have developed, then respond in your journal by discussing

- new reading skills you have begun to develop,
- how using the reading process will help you become a better reader and writer,
- the kinds of writing activities you found most helpful, and
- new reading and writing goals.

SUMMARY OF CHAPTER 3

In Chapter 3, you have examined the strategies used by effective readers and the PARTS of an effective reading process:

Preview

Anticipate

Read and reread

Think critically

Summarize

You have also

- contemplated and responded to a variety of challenging readings about people's roles in society,
- learned to use your dictionary and search for context clues to discover meanings of unknown words and phrases,
- learned the importance of retaining new words to build your vocabulary, and
- started logging definitions in a section of your notebook for easy review.

As you continue to practice the stages of the reading process and become a more experienced reader, you'll not only see your reading skills improve, but your writing and critical thinking skills as well.

Notes   # INTRODUCTION TO SUBJECTS

Identifying Subjects
Subjects Are Nouns or Pronouns
–ing Words Can Be Subjects
Subjects and Prepositional Phrases
Multiple Subjects

Now that you have learned the importance of verbs and how to identify them in your sentences, it's time to turn to the next major ingredient of a sentence: the *subject*. The subject of a sentence is the person or thing the sentence is about. The subject performs the action expressed by the verb, or it is linked to other information by the verb. In these examples, the verbs are underlined twice and the subjects are underlined once:

I wrote an essay.

My classmates gave me suggestions.

At the end of class, the instructor collected our drafts.

Identifying Subjects

To identify the subject of a sentence, ask, "Who?" or "What?" about each verb. In the following example, the verb is underlined twice.

I like funny books.

Question: Who *likes?*

Answer: *I*

The answer to your question is the subject of that sentence.

I like funny books.

One verb can have more than one subject, and one subject can have more than one verb.

Elizabeth Wong and Amy Tan write about Chinese culture.

Question: Who *writes?*

Answer: *Elizabeth Wong and Amy Tan*

Elizabeth Wong and Amy Tan write about Chinese culture.

The essay entertains and informs readers.

Question: What *entertains and informs?*

Answer: *essay*

The essay entertains and informs readers.

Sometimes it is easier to find the subject if you ask "Who?" or "What?" after the entire *predicate*. The predicate of a sentence is the verb and all the words attached to the verb.

Notes

To help me study vocabulary, I <u>created some vocabulary flashcards</u>.

Question: Who *created some vocabulary flashcards?*

Answer: *I*

To help me study vocabulary, <u>I</u> <u>created some vocabulary flashcards</u>.

Practice #1   Jim Bobryk's Essay

- In the following sentences, identify the verbs and underline them twice.
- Remember not to let "imposters" fool you. Infinitives like *to win* won't be verbs. Present participles (words ending in *–ing*) can be verbs only if they have helpers with them. Be sure to underline the whole verb.
- Then, ask the "Who?" or "What?" question, identify the subjects, and underline them once.

Example: Jim Bobryk lost his sight.

Jim Bobryk <u>lost</u> his sight.

Question: Who <u>*lost his sight?*</u>

Answer: *Jim Bobryk*

- <u>Jim Bobryk</u> <u>lost</u> his sight.

1. I added the word *glaucoma* to my vocabulary list.
2. Unfortunately, people are sometimes afraid to help blind people.
3. Bobryk's essay reminded me to look beyond a person's disability.
4. People don't want to be reduced to just one characteristic.
5. For instance, I don't want to be labeled by just my skin color.
6. I am many things: a man, a father, a sports enthusiast, a restaurant manager, and an Italian American.
7. No one wants to be discriminated against.
8. The *Newsweek* article educated people about the feelings of at least one disabled person.
9. I would like to learn to use humor in my writing.
10. An entertaining essay will keep a reader's interest.
11. Bobryk's description of losing his sight was vivid and frightening.

Notes

Subjects Are Nouns or Pronouns

The subject in a sentence is either a noun or a pronoun. As you may know, a **noun** names a person, place, thing, or idea: tree, book, happiness, Mom, Fred, fighting. A **pronoun** is a word that can take the place of a noun: it, he, she, me, I, you, we, us, they. (See pages 216–225 for more on pronouns.) In the following sentences, the nouns and pronouns are highlighted. If they are used as subjects, they are also underlined once. Verbs are underlined twice.

> I reread the article.
>
> Jessie found the main points after reading it again.
>
> The instructor reminded us to edit carefully.

Practice #2   The Study Group

In the following sentences,

- find the verbs and underline them twice,
- highlight all nouns and pronouns, and
- ask the "Who?" or "What?" question and underline the subjects once.

1. The instructor assigned four readings on water pollution.
2. Four students decided to form a study group.
3. The students followed the reading process.
4. First, they previewed and anticipated.
5. Then, they read the articles quickly, marking unknown words.
6. Next, they reread the articles, looking up definitions and making notes in the margins.
7. Finally, the students met to discuss the readings.
8. Frank summarized each reading.
9. He did a good job of finding most of the main points.
10. The other students took notes and added some missing points.
11. Susan asked a few questions about one of the readings.
12. She had found some of the technical vocabulary to be confusing.
13. Stuart had created some practice questions for them to work on.
14. On the day of the exam, they felt well prepared.

–ing *Words Can Be Subjects*

You have learned that *-ing* words cannot be verbs unless they have helper verbs. So what are *-ing* words when they don't have helper verbs? Well, they can act as nouns and in some of those cases they can be subjects. Another name for an *–ing* word that is working as a noun is **gerund.**

In the following sentences, the *–ing* word (gerund) is working as an *–ing* noun but not as a subject. The nouns are highlighted. The subjects are underlined once, and the verbs are underlined twice.

I enjoy skiing.

Lisa and Sam love driving to the coast.

The doctor suggested counting sheep.

In the following sentences, the *–ing* words (gerunds) are nouns, and they are working as subjects. The subjects are underlined once, and the verbs are underlined twice.

Writing this paper was a challenge.

Editing takes patience.

Drinking too much coffee isn't good for me.

Practice #3   Writing

1. Highlight all of the nouns in sentences a–d.

   a. The class discusses the topic.
   b. The student writes in his journal.
   c. The instructor assigns a reading.
   d. The student reads the essay and answers the discussion questions.

2. Some of the nouns you highlighted in sentences a–d are also the subjects of those sentences. Underline the verbs in those sentences twice, and then ask your "Who?" or "What?" questions to find the subjects. Underline the subjects once.

3. Underline the verbs in the following sentences twice, and then ask your "Who?" or "What?" questions to find the subjects. Underline the subjects once. You may want to discuss these sentences with your class.

   a. Writing takes a lot of time.
   b. Expressing your thoughts is not always easy.

c. However, communicating with the written word gives you power.

d. Reading is another key to power.

4. Look at one of your readings from this class or from another class and find two more sentences that have *-ing* words as the subjects. Write these sentences down. Underline the verb twice and the subject once.

Subjects and Prepositional Phrases

Remember, a prepositional phrase consists of a preposition, its object, and any words in between. In these examples, the preposition is underlined and the object is highlighted.

<u>in</u> the brick building

<u>on</u> the neighbor's roof

<u>by</u> the author

<u>for</u> one week

When you are looking for the subject of a sentence, you will want to ignore the prepositional phrases because your subject cannot be in a prepositional phrase. In the following sentences, the subjects are underlined once. The verbs are underlined twice, and the prepositional phrases have been crossed out.

<u>Grading standards</u> ~~at their school~~ <u>are</u> tough.

<u>Computers</u> ~~in the classroom~~ <u>are</u> an asset ~~to writing students~~.

A <u>tutor</u> ~~from one~~ ~~of the learning centers~~ <u>helps</u> dedicated students.

~~In his article~~, <u>Francis</u> <u>explained</u> the significance ~~of the statistics~~.

Practice #4   **Puritans and Kids**

In the following sentences,

- underline the verb twice;
- cross out the prepositional phrases;
- ask your "Who?" or "What?" question; and
- when you find the subject, underline it once.

The first sentence is done for you.

~~In "Seventeenth-Century Roles for Puritan Men, Women, and Children,"~~ the authors describe Puritan family life. Perhaps we could learn something from the Puritans. Men shouldn't have such absolute power in a family. In marriages, men and women should make decisions together. Kids should be involved in some of the discussions. However, as a society, we should teach kids to respect the experience of their elders. Young people can learn from the successes, problems, and failures of their parents. The trick is to listen. In the reading, the authors explained the Puritan method of parental control: delaying inheritance. That method wouldn't work today. However, parents should think about making things too easy for kids. Young adults should earn trust and independence.

Multiple Subjects

Writing sentences with more than one subject can help you say things more clearly and make your writing more interesting. For example, if you wanted to tell readers that three famous people have affected your life in a similar way, you could write three separate sentences:

> Helen Keller inspired me because she had a disability but still achieved so much. Franklin Delano Roosevelt inspired me because he had a disability but still achieved so much. Steven Hawking inspired me because he had a disability but still achieved so much.

Of course, you wouldn't want to be so repetitive in your writing. A better choice would be to create a sentence with multiple subjects.

> Helen Keller, Franklin Delano Roosevelt, and Steven Hawking inspired me because they had disabilities but still achieved so much.

Notice that the plural pronoun *they* had to be substituted for the singular pronouns, and *disability* had to become *disabilities*.

Notes

Punctuation Rule #1

Put commas between items in a series.

- See how commas were inserted between the names of Helen Keller, Franklin Delano Roosevelt, and Steven Hawking.

Here is another example:

- I bought eggs, milk and cheese at the store.
- (The comma before the *and* is optional with a list like this.)

Practice #5   Dating, Marriage, and Sex Education

For each set of sentences, write a new sentence that has multiple subjects. Remember to apply Punctuation Rule #1.

Example: Dating practices have been the focus in our health class for the last few weeks. Marriage has been the focus in our health class for the last few weeks. Sex education has been the focus in our health class for the last few weeks.

- Dating practices, marriage, and sex education have been the focus in our health class for the last few weeks.

Note: Verbs may change form when you create sentences with multiple subjects. For example, a verb like *has* would change to *have*.

1. In the 1600s, Puritan ministers spoke out against premarital sex. In the 1600s, the government spoke out against premarital sex. In the 1600s, parents spoke out against premarital sex.

2. Today, television influences our views on relationships. Today, music influences our views on relationships. Today, movies influence our views on relationships.

3. Education is an important part of preventing teen pregnancy. Open communication between parents and children is an important part of preventing teen pregnancy.

4. My grandparents' experience with dating was different than mine. My parents' experience with dating was different than mine.

5. After attending the training seminar, the principal had a better plan for dealing with sex education. After attending the training seminar, the school nurse had a better plan for dealing with sex education. After attending the training seminar, the teachers had a better plan for dealing with sex education.

Your Own Writing: Introduction to Subjects

Copy a paragraph from one of your journals, summaries, or responses.

- Underline verbs twice.

- Underline subjects once.

- If you don't have a sentence that uses an *–ing* word as a subject, revise one of your sentences or add a new sentence so that you have at least one sentence with an *–ing* word as the subject.

- You should also have at least one sentence that has more than one subject in it.

- Double-check what you have marked as verbs and subjects.

- Cross out prepositional phrases.

THE HARD-TO-FIND SUBJECT

Implied Subjects
Subjects in **There** *Sentences*
Subjects in Questions
Defining Subjects

In the last section, you learned that subjects are nouns or pronouns. Sometimes an *–ing* word can function as a noun and subject. You also learned that a sentence can have more than one subject but that no subject will be in a prepositional phrase.

This section will help you find subjects that may seem to be hidden in a sentence (or they may seem to not exist at all).

Implied Subjects

Look at the following sentences. The verbs are underlined twice.

<u>Study</u> these statistics. <u>Prepare</u> a report for the committee. <u>Be</u> prepared to explain the pay discrepancy. <u>Review</u> your ideas with the personnel director. <u>Present</u> your ideas at the next meeting.

In the paragraph above, who is supposed to do all the work? The sentences in the paragraph are called *command sentences*. **Command sentences** give someone work to do. They give directions. Command sentences do not have stated subjects: they have **implied** subjects. The implied subject is "you."

Notes

[You] <u>study</u> these statistics. [You] <u>prepare</u> a report for the committee. [You] <u>be</u> prepared to explain the pay discrepancy. [You] <u>review</u> your ideas with the personnel director. [You] <u>present</u> your ideas at the next meeting.

Practice #6   Equal Pay

In the following sentences, underline the verbs twice. Underline the subjects once. If the subject is implied, write *you* at the beginning of the sentence and underline the *you*.

Example: Review the punctuation rules before editing.

• [*You*] <u>Review</u> the punctuation rules before editing.

1. You should write a research paper on gender equality in the workplace.
2. Go to the Department of Labor's website.
3. You will find useful statistics.
4. Talk to our business professor.
5. She will give you some good articles to read.
6. Consider interviewing some men and women in your dad's corporation.
7. Check the college library for useful books.
8. Ask the librarian for assistance.
9. Remember to use the writing process.
10. Keep a good record of your sources.

Subjects in There Sentences

You may be used to sentences that start with the subject and have a verb shortly after the subject. A sentence that starts with *there* is a little different. In the following sentences, the subjects are underlined once and the verbs are underlined twice.

There <u>are</u> many <u>ways</u> to write an essay.

There <u>are</u>, however, a few key <u>steps</u>.

There <u>is</u> the planning <u>stage</u>.

As you may have noticed, *there* is never the subject. To help you find the subject in a sentence that begins with *there*, you may want to cross out *there*, infinitives, and prepositional phrases. (To review infinitives and prepositional phrases, see pages 76–78.)

~~There~~ <u>is</u> the crucial <u>step</u> ~~of rewriting~~ , too.

~~There~~ <u>are</u> <u>tutors</u>, <u>instructors</u>, and <u>books</u> ~~to help~~ you.

Practice #7   Essays and Reading

In the following sentences, underline the verbs twice and underline the subjects once. Cross out *there* and any infinitives and prepositional phrases you find.

1. There are four parts to an essay.
2. There are the introduction and the thesis.
3. There are body paragraphs.
4. There is also a conclusion.
5. There is a process for writing an essay.
6. There is also a process for reading.
7. There are the previewing and anticipating steps.
8. There is the reading and rereading step.
9. There is the think critically step.
10. There is the summarize step.

Read sentences 1–10 aloud from Practice #7. You'll notice how boring they sound. Part of the reason they sound boring is that they all begin in the same way (with *there*). Keep this in mind when writing your own essays; avoid starting all your sentences the same way. Also, *there* sentences are not as strong and clear as sentences that state their subjects more directly. Try to avoid writing *there* sentences.

Practice #8   Revising *There* Sentences

Revise sentences 1–10 in Practice #7 so that they don't start with *there*.

Example: There are many ways to write an essay.

- I know many ways to write an essay.

            or

- Essays can be written many different ways.

Note: There are usually many ways to revise a ***there*** sentence. You and your classmates will come up with different ways of revising sentences 1–10.

The Hard-to-Find Subject

The Hard-to-Find Subject

Notes

Subjects in Questions

You've seen that finding a subject in a sentence that begins with *there* can be a little tricky. Finding the subject in a question can be tricky too. Just remember that often the subject and verb won't be in their usual positions. For example, look at these questions. The verbs are underlined twice and the subjects are underlined once.

> <u>Did</u> <u>you</u> <u>read</u> Cox's essay?
> <u>Do</u> <u>you</u> <u>agree</u> with him?
> Which <u>experts</u> <u>believe</u> in love at first sight?

What happens to the verb in the first two questions? (Answer this question in the margin and share your response with your classmates.) To make finding the subject and verb easier, sometimes you can change a question into a statement. (Notice that the question word *which* is dropped in the third example.)

> <u>You</u> <u>did read</u> Cox's essay.
> <u>You</u> <u>do agree</u> with him.
> <u>Experts</u> <u>believe</u> in love at first sight.

Practice #9   Questions About Workplace Equality

In the following questions, underline the verbs twice and the subjects once. Change the questions into statements if you have any difficulty identifying the verb and subject. (Also, remember that you can use the test of time to find verbs, and you can use the "Who?" or "What?" question to find subjects.)

1. Why are male teachers paid more than female teachers in our district?
2. Where can I find a copy of the federal Equal Pay Act?
3. Why are men more willing to do the more dangerous jobs?
4. Why do social workers make less than probation officers?
5. Is a woman with kids less likely to devote herself to the job than a man with kids?
6. Did you read the statistics about women earning more college degrees than men?
7. How can we encourage more men to go to college?

8. Do we need a campaign to urge women to enter higher-paying fields?

9. Would you be good at negotiating higher pay for yourself?

10. Should we take action on this issue?

Defining Subjects

As you have learned, subjects can come in different forms, and they can show up in different places in sentences. Having a general understanding of how subjects work and where they can be in a sentence will help you gain better control of your writing. For example, you can ask yourself if you have clear, strong subjects, and you can choose to revise a *there* sentence to make your ideas clearer. Also, if you make subject-verb agreement errors in your essay, you'll need to rely on your knowledge of verbs and subjects as you learn to identify, fix, and avoid these errors. In this section, you will pull together all of your knowledge of subjects and create a summary of the information.

Practice #10   Defining Subjects
Part One:

Make a chart similar to the one that follows and use it to gather and record information about subjects. You may want to review the sentence work in Chapter 2 as you prepare your answers. (*Hint:* Since the last step of this practice exercise asks you to summarize using your own words, you should try to put your notes in your own words.)

What does a <u>subject</u> do?

What information do you have about <u>subjects</u> and the following?
nouns and pronouns

-*ing* words

Notes

prepositional phrases
there sentences
questions

What is an <u>implied subject?</u>

How many <u>subjects</u> can you have in a sentence?

Part Two:
Write a paragraph in which you summarize your knowledge of subjects. Be sure to use your own words.

Your Own Writing: The Hard-to-Find Subject

Choose a paragraph from one of your journals, summaries, or responses—preferably one you are currently working on. Copy the paragraph on a sheet of paper. Then underline all the verbs twice. After asking the "Who?" or "What?" questions, underline the subjects once.

After you've completed this part, show your work to a classmate and see if he or she thinks you've underlined all the subjects and verbs correctly. Show any questionable sentences to your instructor or tutor.

Examining the Writing Process

Main Topics

- Examining the writing process

- Communicating your ideas about advertisements and evil characters

- Identifying phrases and clauses in your sentences

- Achieving sentence variety with phrases and clauses

Peanuts

It was a dark and stormy night.

9-20

YOU KNOW WHAT'S WRONG WITH YOUR STORIES?

THEY LACK SUBTLETY

© 1985 United Feature Syndicate, Inc.

It was a sort of dark and kind of stormy night.

Washington Post Writer's Group, 1997

Notes

In the past, people often assumed that good writing was a matter of genetics—either you were born a Hemingway, or you weren't. Fortunately, good writing is not a result of special writing genes, nor is it a matter of knowing "the tricks." Good writing is largely the result of taking the right steps, of using an effective writing process.

You can think of this process as being similar to what you might do if you were preparing a presentation at work. The presentation doesn't simply appear. You must research your topic, gather information and props, plan the sequence of information, and perhaps write out a script.

Similarly, each writer must (and can) develop an effective writing process in order to produce effective essays. The assignments in this chapter will help you develop a writing process that works well for you.

THE STAGES OF AN EFFECTIVE WRITING PROCESS

The writing process can be broken into stages that you'll begin using in this chapter.

Discuss and Engage

You'll talk about the general topic and begin to get involved in the topic.

Read, Discuss, Think Critically

You'll read, discuss the readings, and think critically about the readings and how they relate to the writing assignment.

Explore the Writing Assignment

You'll carefully review the actual writing assignment and explore what kind of information should go into your essay. You may also take the time at this stage to outline and plan your essay.

Draft

You'll write a complete essay. The essay will probably be rough, so you'll have to work on the draft and improve it.

Revise

You'll change and improve the draft. You might add information, delete information, and move ideas around.

Edit

You'll work on sentence structure, usage, punctuation, and spelling. This is the "polishing" stage.

Points to Remember About the Writing Process

- The writing process stages will not always happen in this exact order. They may overlap, and some stages may need to be repeated.

- Approaching an essay assignment as a series of steps will actually make your task easier. You will be able to take your essay assignment one step at a time.

- All writers have some kind of writing process. Some processes are more effective than others and make writing easier, so it's important to refine your process until it works well for you.

Journal Assignment

Your Writing Process, Past and Future

In a sense, Snoopy, on page 119, uses some of the steps in the writing process. He rereads his work, and he revises (although perhaps not very effectively).

In your notebook, describe the writing process you have used until now. Consider some of the following questions:

- What do you do before you begin to write?
- Do you talk to anyone about your assignment?
- Do you handwrite your ideas on a notepad first?
- Do you compose on a word processor or computer?
- Do you usually write more than one draft?
- Are there certain steps that you must improve or add to your process? Explain.

Developing an Effective Writing Process

Analyzing your past writing process and thinking about how to improve your writing process are important activities. Of course, the next step is to begin *practicing* an effective writing process.

In this chapter, you will be offered three writing assignments. These assignments will help you begin to sharpen and refine your reading, writing, and critical thinking processes as you analyze some challenging subjects: advertising and the human character.

Writing Assignment #1: Analyzing Advertisements

In this assignment, you'll sharpen your critical thinking skills as you analyze a selection of advertisements. This analysis will require you to study the details of the ads so that you can draw conclusions about the ads and the motives of the advertisers.

Here, in brief, is the writing assignment that you are preparing for:

Write an essay in which you analyze one advertisement by discussing the strategies the advertiser is using to make the product "appeal" to buyers. Comment on how successful you think the advertisement is.

Keep this assignment in mind as you dig deeper into the issue of advertisements and prepare to write.

Save all the writing you do in preparation for your writing assignments. This writing will become your **process package**, a collection of work—including class notes, all brainstorming, an outline, a rough draft, and more. This process package will represent the writing process that takes you from initial ideas to a finished essay.

Discuss and Engage

Research shows that this is one of the stages of the writing process that some writers skip. These people jump into writing their papers before they discuss and think about the topic even though they would never consider making an important decision such as purchasing a new car without discussing their options with experts, friends, or family members. They would take the time to discuss the various makes and models (1998 Ford Explorer versus 2000 Jeep Grand Cherokee), extras (CD player, air conditioning, passenger air bags), and price before purchasing their vehicles. Otherwise, they might end up dissatisfied or even with a "lemon."

Discussion, planning, and critical thinking are also important when writers are given essay topics. Writers who discuss their topics with classmates, their instructor, a tutor, friends, or family members before writing are more satisfied with their papers than those who do not. In addition, these writers save time in the long run because they have taken time at the beginning to get to know the topic before they start to write.

Non Sequitur

Washington Post Writer's
Group, 1997

Activities

Discuss Advertisements

Discuss with your class advertisements that you remember and why you remember them.

- In what ways did the advertisements appeal to you?

- Do you remember some advertisements because they didn't appeal to you?

- Do you sometimes buy products because of the advertisements you've seen?

- Are advertisers always straightforward and honest in the way that they advertise?

Review the *Non Sequitur* cartoon.

- What product are the characters looking to sell?

- What tricks will they use?

- Why is this funny?

- Why does the second man say, "We?"

Get Involved!

With a classmate, visit AdAge.com's website, www.adage.com/century/ad_icons, to view "The Top 10 Advertising Icons of All Time." Take notes on the top 10 icons and bring your notes to class for discussion.

Notes

> ### *Journal Assignment*
>
> ### *Review Discussion*
>
> Think about your class discussion and write your thoughts about advertisements. This is an opportunity to express your thoughts privately and freely. (Refer back to your journal when you're ready to begin drafting your essay.)

Read, Discuss, Think Critically

In this stage, you gather information by reading material related to the topic. Inexperienced writers often worry that they do not have anything to say about an assigned topic. These writers need to realize (through discussions and journal writing) that they already know *something* about an assignment although they probably need more information on the subject (often gained through reading).

Returning to our analogy of buying a car, it would be wise to "read up" on the car you intend to buy before following through with the purchase. You may want to know, for example, what *Consumer Reports* or *Car and Driver* has to say about the car's performance, value, or gas mileage. Once you become knowledgeable on the subject, you will be better prepared to make a purchase. In the same way, the more you know about your writing topic, the better prepared you are to write about it.

Reading Assignment: The Advertisements

(The questions and suggestions that follow will help you continue to use some of the PARTS of the reading process.)

Preview   Quickly review the following advertisements and think about the kinds of readers the advertisers are trying to attract.

Anticipate   Next to each advertisement, write down a guess about what kind of magazine the advertisement might show up in. Can you name a specific magazine for each advertisement?

Read and Reread   Carefully study the details of the advertisements. Pay attention to the words, for they were carefully chosen by the advertisers. Also, note the objects and the people (their clothes, their postures, the expressions on their faces). Mark interesting parts or words in the advertisements and make notes about both the advertisement and who you think the intended audience might be. Do you want to change any of your earlier guesses about where each advertisement came from?

You promised to take care of me.

I don't understand the
"if I can afford it" part.

A wagging tail. A purr of delight. In return for those moments of love, you've promised to take care of your dog or cat.

And whether it's an ear infection, injury or a serious illness, there will come a time when your pet needs medical attention. When that day comes, Veterinary Pet Insurance will help you keep your promise to care.

Besides coverage for accidents and illness, we offer routine care coverage to help pay for an annual veterinary exam, vaccinations—even prescription flea control. And, you can use any veterinarian worldwide. In fact, 9 out of 10 veterinarians who recommend pet insurance recommend VPI. No wonder more and more pet owners depend on Veterinary Pet Insurance, the nation's oldest, largest and number one pet insurance plan.

Veterinary Pet Insurance: We'll help you keep your promise to protect your pet.

Avian and exotic pet coverage available; call for details.

Underwritten by: Veterinary Pet Insurance Co. (CA), Brea, CA; National Casualty Co. (Nat'l, Madison, WI. ©2002 Veterinary Pet Services Inc.

Protect your best friend.

It's easy, affordable
and the benefits can start with
your next veterinary visit.

Call 800-USA-PETS
(800-872-7387)
Or go to **petinsurance.com**

VETERINARY
PET INSURANCE
*Making the miracles of
veterinary medicine affordable*

Notes

Notes

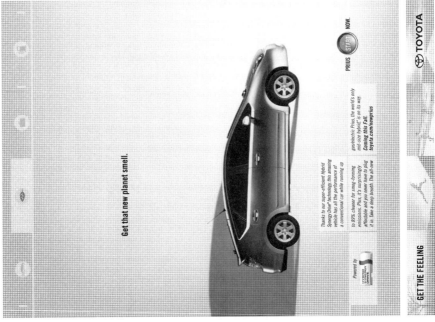

Activity   *Notes*

Discuss Selected Advertisements

In groups, discuss what you see in each advertisement. What sorts of words are used? What colors? What is (or is not) in the picture? If there are people, what do they look like? What sorts of expressions and clothes do they wear? How are the advertisers manipulating you? What kind of audience will respond best to the advertisement and want to buy the product? (Think about gender, age, ethnicity, economic status, and so on.) Are the advertisers relying on stereotypes? Explain. (Be sure to take notes during your class discussion.)

Get Involved!

Find an advertisement that would be interesting to analyze and bring it to class for discussion.

> **Journal Assignment**
>
> **Review Discussion**
>
> Think about your group discussion and review your notes and the advertisements. Now write down your thoughts. (Answer as many of the previous questions as you can, and add any other thoughts.) Exchange this journal with one or more classmates. When you read someone else's, simply say, "Thank you," when you return the journal to the author. Don't criticize or discuss.

Explore the Writing Assignment

At this stage, you and your classmates will carefully study the writing assignment. (No one wants to finish an assignment only to find out that he or she wrote "off topic.") It is at this point that you and your classmates can discuss how you might respond to the essay topic. What is the assignment asking? What kind of main point do you want to focus on? How will you prove your main point? Are you unclear about any facts? Talk with other people to help you think through the topic and help you make good choices as you begin writing.

Activities

Review the Writing Assignment

Here, again, is your writing assignment. Review it carefully before continuing. Underline the important terms in the assignment.

Write an essay in which you analyze one advertisement by discussing the strategies the advertiser is using to make the product "appeal" to buyers. Comment on how successful you think the advertisement is.

Notes

Choose an Advertisement

Choose an advertisement you would like to write about. (*Note:* It is acceptable to change your mind later about which advertisement to write about, but you will save yourself some time if you first carefully consider your choices.) Choose an advertisement that you find interesting and that has a number of features you want to think about and study.

Explore the Advertising Assignment

Explore the topic: Review and discuss the assignment with your classmates and consider these critical thinking questions.

1. What advertisement do you want to focus on? Why?

2. What sort of information needs to be in your essay? What doesn't?

3. What will you say? In what order will you state your points?

4. What kinds of details and explanations will you give? (Make notes as you do this.)

Analyze an Advertisement

Make a chart similar to the one that follows on a separate sheet of paper. To futher analyze your advertisement, list strategies and answer the questions provided.

Get Involved!

With a classmate, go to the following website to examine how women have been portrayed in cigarette advertisements: www.wclynx.com/ burntofferings/ adsvirginiaslims.html. Make a list of the strategies used by tobacco companies to make cigarette smoking appear appealing to women. Be ready to discuss these strategies in class.

Advertiser's strategies	How does the strategy work?	How effective is it?
1.		
2.		
3.		
4.		

Brainstorm   When you have read and thought about the topic, made notes, and discussed your ideas with classmates, you may want to let your thoughts flow freely on paper. This is called **freewriting,** which is one type of **brainstorming.** Let yourself write freely with no interruptions or worries about corrections. This can help you discover what points most interest you about a certain topic. The key is to let yourself write freely for as long as you can, even repeating ideas, because the ideas you repeat may be the ideas that most intrigue you. These are the ideas that might become the focus of your essay.

Activity

Brainstorming

Focusing on the current writing assignment and the advertisements you have been studying, write freely for as long as you can. Let your mind wander, but periodically look back at the assignment to remind yourself of what you will be writing an essay about. If you run out of ideas, look back at your class notes and reread what you've already written. Remember, it's okay to repeat yourself when you're freewriting.

Create Your Thesis Statement   The thesis is the sentence at the end of your introduction that expresses the main idea of your essay. In this sentence, you tell your reader precisely what you're planning to explain or prove in your essay and why it's important. Keep in mind that the thesis sentence should directly respond to the **essay assignment** (also known as the **essay prompt**). It may take a few attempts before you're able to create a sentence that clearly states your essay plan. In fact, as you develop your essay, you may need to return to your thesis to further refine it during the drafting or revising stages of the process. In creating your thesis, your goals should be to make sure your thesis clearly communicates what you'll explain or prove in your essay and why it's important. Writing a good thesis statement requires using your critical thinking skills as you decide what you'll focus on and what you'll explain or prove.

Activity

Creating a Thesis

Sometimes it's helpful to change the essay assignment, or prompt, into a question, if it isn't already a question. For example, your current essay topic is:

Notes

> Write an essay in which you analyze one advertisement by discussing the strategies the advertiser is using to make the product "appeal" to buyers. Comment on how successful you think the advertisement is.

If you turned this into a question, it might read like this:

> What strategies is the advertiser using to make the product appeal to buyers, and how successful is the advertisement?

Your answer to this question could become your thesis statement.

Now, focusing on the advertisement you have chosen, write down some possible answers to this question. Share your responses with classmates or a tutor. Work on polishing the sentence so that it clearly communicates your main idea. Remember that it's okay to come back later and improve your thesis statement.

Outline   Another helpful tool for writers is the **outline.** An outline can be a formal and thorough list of all the major and supporting points in an essay, or it can be a quick list of just the major points to be covered. The benefit in creating an outline is to make a plan for yourself so that you stay focused on your main idea and on ideas that directly support it. When creating an outline, think about what your major points will be and what order these points should be in. You'll need to use your critical thinking skills as you choose what to include in and what to leave out of your essay.

Some writers spend a lot of time perfecting their outlines—listing major points, supporting points, and details. These writers revise and perfect their outlines until the entire essay is just about written. Other writers start with a rough, quick outline—listing the thesis and topic sentences—and then begin drafting the essay, looking at the outline just to see if they are staying on track. These writers may drift away from their outlines and decide that drifting away is okay because the outlines weren't quite right for what they have decided to say. Some of these writers take the time to revise their outlines as a way of checking their drafts.

The goal with an outline is to make a plan first before diving into an essay. If you think about your thesis and what your major supporting points should be, you are more likely to stay on track and not get lost in many other related topics. Also, you can use an outline as a tool for sharing your ideas. That is, before writing an entire draft, you can test out your ideas by simply showing your outline to a reader and getting feedback.

Activity

Outline

Write down your thesis statement at the top of a page. Then make a list of supporting ideas. Again, you'll have to experiment and use your critical thinking skills as you decide what your major points should be. If you want to, add some notes under each major supporting point to remind yourself of the details you will use from the advertisement.

Share this outline with a classmate or tutor to see if you are responding clearly and directly to the writing assignment.

Draft

When you have discussed a topic, read about it, discussed related readings, thought critically about the topic and readings, and written an outline, it's time to begin drafting your essay.

Write a draft that you'll want to share with your classmates, a tutor, or your instructor. It should be complete—with an introduction, body, and conclusion. This complete draft will naturally be imperfect. You'll have opportunities later in your writing process to rearrange ideas, add ideas, or even take out some ideas if they don't fit. Keep your audience in mind as you write your draft, and repeat any earlier steps of your writing process as necessary. (For example, if you feel that midway through your essay you have run out of things to say, go back and look at the advertisement again, review your class notes, or talk to a classmate or tutor.)

Consider completing your draft on a computer so that you don't have to retype the entire essay after each improvement.

Activity

Draft Your Advertisement Essay

Draft your essay about the advertisement you selected. (Be sure to use the notes, charts, and outline you've made so far.) Remember that you're writing an essay to a reader who has never seen your advertisement before, so in

Notes

your introduction summarize what you see in your advertisement and what you believe the advertiser is trying to accomplish. In the body of your essay, support what you have said in your introduction by exposing the strategies the advertiser uses. Be specific. In your conclusion, comment on the effectiveness of the advertisement.

Activity

Study a Student Sample

The following is a student essay on one of the popular "Got Milk?" ads. Read the introductory paragraph closely. Underline the sentence that appears to be the thesis. (Remember the thesis tells the reader what the writer plans to explain or prove in her essay and why.) Then consider what you think is good about this student's introduction. Answer the questions that follow.

Got Milk?

1   The advertisement I chose to analyze is advertising the dairy product milk. It appeared in *Rolling Stone* magazine. The person who is promoting the product is the late-night talk show host Conan O'Brien. Conan is sitting at a desk in a classroom wearing blue jeans that are cuffed way up, high tops, and a striped T-shirt. He looks like he is portraying a little kid. He has a little kid innocent look on his face, and he is also wearing a milk mustache that goes along with the caption that reads under the picture, "Where's your mustache?" Next to the picture of Conan is a little paragraph that states why Conan likes to drink milk and how drinking milk can benefit a person. To convince people to buy milk in this advertisement, the advertiser successfully uses such tricks as colors, words, an eye-catching setting, and a celebrity.

2   The first trick the advertiser uses to get people to buy milk is a celebrity to promote the product. For anyone who watches late-night television, Conan O'Brien should look familiar. People who like him will read the advertisement, and maybe they will think that if Conan O'Brien drinks milk, they should too. If the advertiser had used an ordinary person in the advertisement, I don't think as many people would look at it because it would not catch their eye.

3   The advertiser uses words in this advertisement to draw people in. People see the short paragraph next to the familiar face of Conan O'Brien, and they want to read it. A person might figure that since it is a comedian advertising the product, whatever is written next to the picture will be funny. That is certainly true in this case. Most people would probably read the advertisement knowing they're in for a good laugh.

4   Another trick that the advertiser uses to convince people to buy milk in the advertisement is the use of colors. The advertisement contains an array of different colors. The shirt that Conan is wearing stands out because it is brighter than the colors in the background. The milk carton that is sitting on the desk really stands out because it is brighter than the colors in the background and is the only item in the picture that contains the color red. The advertiser wants the milk carton to stand out because that is exactly what is being advertised. The white milk mustache that Conan is wearing in the advertisement also stands out. This is the first thing a person would probably notice when looking at the ad.

5   The last trick the advertiser uses in the ad to get people to notice the product is the eye-catching setting. For anyone who went to grammar school, the setting should look very familiar. There is the huge blackboard, desks, and little chairs, all typical items a person would see in a classroom. The setting would catch the eye of a person because there is a grown man, Conan, dressed up like a little kid, sitting on a very small chair at a desk in a classroom. It looks funny and would not be something a person sees everyday in life.

6   Overall, I would say that the advertiser is very successful in convincing people to buy milk in this ad. The ad is very humorous along with informational. It's straight to the point, and I think the celebrity they chose to advertise their product was a good one.

—Jennifer Arch

There are many ways to introduce an essay, and Jennifer found a way that worked well for her. Respond to the following questions in your notebook and be prepared to discuss your responses with classmates.

Notes

1. What do you particularly like about this introduction? What good decisions did Jennifer make?

2. An introduction to an essay should tell you *what* the topic of the essay is and *why* the reader should read the essay. (What will the reader learn from reading the essay?) Can you find the *what* and *why* in this introduction? Underline the parts that you find, and then discuss them with your class.

3. An introduction usually has a thesis (a sentence that states the main idea). Do you see Jennifer's thesis? Where? Underline her thesis.

4. Now look at each of her body paragraphs. Explain how each of the body paragraphs (2–5) supports Jennifer's thesis.

Revise

Revising means *reseeing* what you have written and then *rewriting* it to make it better. It involves using your critical thinking skills to make choices and rearrange parts of your essay to help "make sense" of the topic. As you revise, you may need to add more information to help the reader see your point. Or you may need to delete information that does not fit. The revising stage overlaps with the previous stage because each time you revise (or rewrite), you'll end up with a new draft.

Take a moment now to look back at Jennifer's essay about the "Got Milk?" advertisement. Are there any suggestions you might make to help Jennifer improve her essay?

Points to Remember About Revision

- All writers need to revise. Revision is a normal and healthy part of the writing process.

- Effective revising requires the writer to think about audience and to use his or her critical thinking skills to decide what necessary changes need to be made.

- All writers need feedback on their work. Even professional writers have editors and friends comment on their work before publishing it. Be sure to share your writing with classmates and other readers.

- Effective writers take pride in their work, making it their own. This means that although they consider others' advice, they do not let others take over their work.

Activity

Share Your Writing

Find a classmate to work with. Read each other's essays and discuss the following questions in relation to each essay.

- Does your introduction tell *what* your essay is about and *why* your reader should read it?

- Have you given your reader enough details? Will he or she be able to "see" the advertisement in his or her mind?

- Have you told your reader what strategies the advertiser is using?

- Do you support your statements about the strategies with proof from the advertisements such as words or images?

- Have you clearly expressed how successful you feel the advertiser was in making the product appealing?

- Make a list of things you want to change in your essay. Start with the most important.

Begin revising your essay. Focus on one problem area at a time. Write more than one new draft. (Each time you revise, your essay will probably get better.)

Edit

When you have revised your paper to the point that you feel confident about its organization and development of ideas, then it's time to begin editing your essay. This is the stage where writers work on spelling, punctuation, and grammar to make sure their sentences are grammatically correct.

Activity

Edit Your Advertising Essay

When you feel your essay says everything you want it to (or when your deadline is nearing), then begin "polishing" it. (*Note:* Many writers feel that they could go on improving an essay forever—that's normal.) It's a good idea to have your teacher or tutor show you one area you need to work on (for example, making sure you've used complete sentences throughout). Have that person explain that type of error, and then focus your editing work on just that area. Also remember to check your spelling.

Notes

Writing Assignment #2: *Creating an Advertisement*

In this assignment, you'll create your own advertisement and analyze it. You'll exercise your critical thinking skills and practice your reading and writing processes as you consider your audience and your goals as an advertiser.

Here, in brief, is the writing assignment that you are preparing for:

Create an advertisement to promote a product of your choice. Then, write an essay in which you analyze your own advertisement.

Keep this assignment in mind as you dig deeper into the issue and prepare to write.

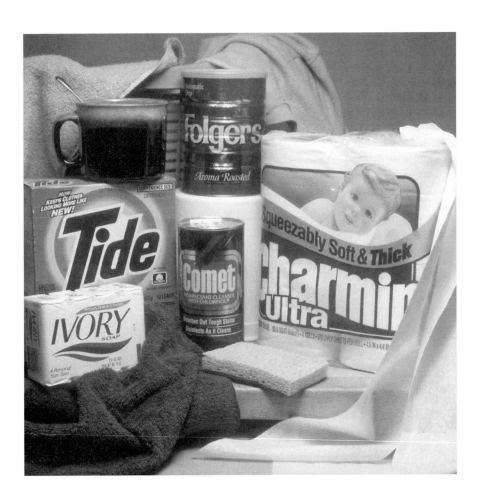

Discuss and Engage

Activity

Discuss Creating an Advertisement

Discuss with your classmates products you might want to sell and the types of people who would be interested in buying these products. (Think about selling your favorite cereal, perfume, shampoo, or car, for example.) Be specific. Also, discuss the ways to get the attention of different groups of people.

Journal Assignment
Products, Buyers, and Hooks

Think about products, buyers, and *hooks* (ways to grab consumer's attention). Write down some possible products you'd like to advertise. Describe the people you would be trying to attract with each product and how you might do that. Think about the people, props, colors, and words you might use. Write about more than one advertisement you could create. (This journal is for your eyes only.)

Read, Discuss, Think Critically

Remember that at this stage of your writing process you should gather more information and consider other people's thoughts on your subject.

Reading Assignment:
"When Advertising Offends: Another Look at Aunt Jemima"

(The questions and suggestions that follow will help you continue to use some of the PARTS of the reading process.)

Preview   Before you read, note when and where this essay was published. Read the title and introduction. Read and highlight the topic sentences.

Anticipate   What do you anticipate this essay will be about? Use the "Notes" column to record your thoughts.

Read and Reread   Read the essay quickly and mark unfamiliar words. Then reread the essay more slowly, interacting with the text by making comments in the "Notes" column and highlighting important points. Define unknown words.

When Advertising Offends: Another Look at Aunt Jemima

Based on Westerman (1989) and Simpson (1992)

by John J. Macionis

This essay comes from a college sociology textbook, *Sociology*.

1   Commercial advertisers want to sell products. However, some old ad campaigns are becoming counterproductive because they offend their audience by portraying categories of people in inaccurate and unfair ways.

2   A century ago, the vast majority of consumers in the United States were white people, and many were uneasy with growing racial and cultural diversity. Businesses commonly exploited this discomfort, depicting various categories of people in ways that were clearly condescending. In 1889, for example, a pancake mix first appeared featuring a servant mammy named "Aunt Jemima." Although somewhat modernized, this logo is widely used in the mass media, and the product continues to hold a commanding share of its market. Likewise, the hot cereal "Cream of Wheat" is still symbolized by the African-American chef Rastus, and "Uncle Ben" is familiar to millions of households as a brand name for rice. But to many people, use of such caricatures—which, after all, originally depicted the black slaves or servants of white people—is racially insensitive at best.

3   Changes in advertising have occurred in recent decades in all the mass media. The stereotypical Frito Bandito, long familiar to older television viewers, was abandoned in 1971 by Frito-Lay (a company, ironically, whose first product was a corn chip invented by a Latino living in San Antonio). The characterization of Latinos as bandits or outlaws, embodied in the bumbling cartoon figure of Frito Bandito, discredited an entire segment of the population. A host of other such images have also disappeared as businesses in the United States confront a new reality: the growing voice and financial power of minorities, who represent a market worth one-half trillion dollars a year. Taken together, Americans of African, Latino, and Asian descent represent 20 percent of the population and may constitute a national majority by the end of the next century. And, just as important, the share of the minority population that is affluent is steadily increasing.

4   Businesses are responding to the growing financial power of minorities. In the last ten years businesses have doubled their spending on advertising aimed at African Americans to about $1 billion annually. The results of this policy shift have been encouraging for the businesses involved—far higher sales—and pleasing to people who have historically found little to like in commercial advertising.

Questions for Critical Thought

"When Advertising Offends. . . ."

1. Find the thesis statement in this essay and underline it. What is the main point of this essay? Write it down in your own words.

2. What stereotypes are discussed in this essay?

3. It could be argued that advertisers must rely on stereotypes to some degree. Usually these stereotypes are harmless although obviously some stereotypes can be hurtful. Respond to this idea of "harmless" versus "hurtful" stereotypes.

4. When you write your advertisement, will you be relying on any stereotypes? Is this okay? Explain.

5. One of the stylistic strengths of this essay is the use of **transitions,** words that add **coherence** to the essay. *(In a coherent essay, all the ideas fit together and support the thesis.)* In paragraphs 1 and 2, you can find the following words that help the different ideas flow and fit together: *however, for example, although, likewise,* and *but.* Explain how the author used each transition to show how all the ideas fit together. (For example, how does *however* in the first paragraph help us move from the first sentence to the second? What does *however* tell us?) Discuss each of the five transitions mentioned above.

Journal Assignment

Ideas About Writing an Ad

Write your thoughts about writing an advertisement.

1. What is the hardest part about creating a good advertisement? What is the easiest part?

2. What products are you considering advertising, and how is the audience different for each one?

3. If the audience is large, how might you create your ad for an audience of a specific magazine?

4. What will attract each different audience?

   Exchange journals with a classmate, and when you've finished reading, say, "Thank you."

Explore the Writing Assignment

Here is a more detailed description of your writing assignment.

Create an advertisement to promote a product of your choice, and write an essay in which you analyze your advertisement. You may sketch the ad yourself or put together pictures from other advertisements. Be sure to make it clear in your sketch (or collage) what colors you would use, what the people would look like (expressions, clothes, posture, gender, ethnicity, age), and what props you would use. And, of course, write some interesting text to sell your product. Then, in your essay, describe the ad you have created, and explain what audience you are trying to attract and how you are trying to attract it. What strategies are you using?

Activity

Explore the Assignment

Discuss the following questions with your classmates.

1. What product will you sell?

2. What audience will you try to attract?

3. What strategies will you use?

Create Your Advertisement

Be thoughtful and creative as you design your advertisement. After you have created your advertisement, show it to friends and classmates and ask them what strategies they see you using. Are these effective strategies? Are your friends and classmates right? Do you need to change your advertisement at all?

Brainstorm   With your advertisement completed, it's time to begin the second part of your assignment. Focus now on the part that says, "Analyze your own advertisement." You may want to think of the prompt as a series of questions:

- How would you analyze your advertisement?
- What strategies are you using, and are your strategies effective?
- Who is in your audience?

Write freely and answer these questions, but don't feel limited to them. Remember that when you are brainstorming, you want to let your thoughts wander a bit.

Create Your Thesis   Use your brainstorm, readings, journal, and class notes to begin to experiment with thesis statements. You want to find a sentence that clearly explains what your essay will focus on and what you'll be explaining or proving in your essay.

Outline   When you've created a thesis statement you're satisfied with, begin listing ideas that will support your thesis statement. Decide what your main supporting points should be and create topic sentences that express these points. Consider the best way to organize your topic sentences. Can you use any transitions to help with coherence (*however, for example, likewise*)?

Draft

As you begin to draft your essay, refer to your outline, but feel free to vary from it if you need to. In the introduction, describe your advertisement, giving enough detail so that your audience will "see" your ad. Also, explain who your intended audience is and what you hope to accomplish with this advertisement. (Remember to give your reader a sense of what is coming and why your essay is worth reading.) In the body of your essay, support your introduction by explaining the strategies you have used in the ad. In your conclusion, explain what you hope the reader has learned from your essay.

Revise

Enter this stage with an open mind. Assume that you will find some weaknesses in your draft *and* that you will find ways to improve and strengthen your essay.

Activity

Share Your Writing

Work with a classmate and discuss the following questions as they relate to your essays.

- Do you have a thesis? Does your introduction tell *what* your essay is about and *why* your reader should read?

- Have you given your reader enough detail? Will he or she be able to "see" the advertisement in his or her mind?

- Have you told your reader what strategies you are using? Have you explained why you are using these particular strategies? Who is in your audience?

Notes

- Have you used any transitions to help your ideas flow? *(however, for example, likewise)*

Make a list of things you want to improve in your essay. Start with the most important.

Edit

Now begin "polishing" your essay. Carefully check for typing errors, spelling errors, and any other errors you tend to make. Also, review your essay for sentence variety. You may also want to consider these questions after completing the sentence work at the end of this chapter (pages 155–171).

- Have you used coordinators, transitions, and subordinators to add variety and to clarify relationships between ideas in your essay?
- Can you add useful information to your essay by including prepositional or participial phrases in some of your sentences?

Writing Assignment #3: *The Most Evil Character*

In this assignment, you'll examine the decisions people make and the values reflected by those decisions. You'll exercise your critical thinking skills and practice your reading and writing processes as you analyze the story that follows.

Here, in brief, is the writing assignment that you are preparing for:

Write an essay in which you analyze the story "The Most Evil Character" and determine who is the most evil of all the characters.

Keep this assignment in mind as you dig deeper into the topic and prepare to write.

Discuss and Engage

Activity

Making Decisions

Discuss with your classmates some decisions you've had to make recently. What were easy decisions? What were hard ones? Did any of these choices reflect your values? What do you value in people? What are important characteristics that you think people should have?

Notes

Journal Assignment

Review Class Discussion

Write down your answers to these questions: What do you value in people? What are important characteristics that you think people should have? You may also want to write down what your classmates said and what you thought about their comments. (This journal is for your eyes only. Refer back to this journal when you are getting ready to write your essay.)

Read, Discuss, Think Critically

Reading Assignment: *"The Most Evil Character"*

Preview   Note that this selection is not an essay. It is a fictional story used by teachers and students as a way to discuss people's values and decision-making skills. (The style of the writing here is, of course, different from that of academic essays.) Read the title and the first few sentences.

Anticipate   What do you anticipate this story will be about? Use the "Notes" column to record your thoughts.

Read and Reread   Read the story quickly and mark unfamiliar words. Then reread the story more slowly, interacting with the text by making comments in the "Notes" column and highlighting important points. Define unknown words.

The Most Evil Character
(author unknown)

1   Jack is in his third year of college and doing passing but below-average work. His mother has been insisting that he plan to enroll in law school and become an attorney, like his father. Angry at him for not receiving better grades, she has told him that under no circumstances will he get the car or the trip that he has been promised unless his average goes up one full grade. Although Jack has done slightly better work this term, he has been having trouble with his psychology course, especially with the term paper. Twice he has asked for a conference (not during office hours, the time of which conflicts with another class he cannot miss) with his teacher, but Professor Brown has told him that he is not being paid to run a private tutoring service. So Jack postpones writing the paper and finally puts it together hastily the night before it is due. Then Professor Brown calls him in

Notes

and tells him that the paper is disgraceful and that he has no chance of getting a passing grade or even an incomplete unless he submits a more acceptable essay by 9 a.m. the next day. Jack tries to explain his situation and his mother's demands, and he asks for some more time to revise the paper, but his teacher is inflexible and says, "You probably don't belong in college anyway." Since there is no way that Jack is going to be able to produce the revised essay on time, he decides to salvage the car and the trip by getting somebody to write it for him. He has heard about Victor, a recent graduate who always needs money. Victor agrees and, after some haggling about the fee, he writes an acceptable paper overnight. A few days after Professor Brown has accepted the paper and given Jack his grade, Jack gets a call from Victor, who says that, unless he gets double the original fee, he will reveal the entire transaction to Professor Brown and the dean. Jack does not have the money and cannot tell his parents.

Activities

Summarize the Story

Write a summary of "The Most Evil Character." What are the main points, the facts, and the names that you need to remember?

Who Is the Worst? The Best? Why?

Discuss the reading with your classmates. First, review the facts about what happened. (Refer to your summary.) Then begin discussing how the characters in the story rank. Who is the worst character, and why? Who is the best/most innocent character, and why? What does all of this suggest about your values?

Journal Assignment

Review Class Discussion

Immediately after your class discussion, write down your thoughts.

1. How do you feel about the characters in the story? Why?

2. How do your classmates feel? Why?

3. Did any of your classmates change your opinions? Did any of your classmates disagree with you?

4. How did your values influence your rating of the characters?

   Exchange journals with a classmate, and when you've finished reading, say, "Thank you."

Explore the Writing Assignment

Here is a more detailed description of your writing assignment.

> *Write an essay to a reader who has never read "The Most Evil Character."*
> *Briefly summarize for the reader what happens in the story. Then tell the*
> *reader what your judgment of the characters is. Who do you think is the most*
> *evil character, and who is the least evil? Where do the other characters rank?*
> *Also, explain why you have made these judgments.*

Activities

Explore the Assignment

Discuss with your classmates what kind of information you think you need
to put in your essay. Perhaps you want to make a list. What will your judgments be? How will you explain your judgments? What will come first in
your essay? Second?

Charting Your Thoughts

As a way of organizing your thoughts, make a chart similar to the one that
follows, and use it to gather information. Compare your chart with your
classmates'. (Keep in mind that it's not necessary for your charts to agree.)

Character	Deed	Judgment (Why?)
1.		
2.		
3.		
4.		

Character	Deed	Judgment (Why?)
5.		
6.		

Create Your Thesis   When you begin to work on your thesis for this assignment, review the writing assignment carefully and then ask yourself these questions: What do I want my audience to know after they have read my essay? What main point should stick in the reader's mind? You may want to summarize the assignment (in writing or out loud to a tutor) and explain what it is asking for. Summarizing and explaining will help you clarify what you must focus on with your thesis (and in your essay). Then experiment with sentences until you find one that would function well as a thesis statement.

Outline   Write your thesis statement at the top of a blank page and review, again, your writing assignment, notes, and chart. What major points should you cover in your essay to support your thesis? On a second piece of paper, make a list of possible points to cover. Use your critical thinking skills to decide which of these points should be made into topic sentences. Take your time in creating thoughtful topic sentences. Create an outline by writing these topic sentences beneath your thesis statement on the first page.

Draft

Refer to your outline as you begin drafting. In your introduction, you'll need to summarize the story for the reader and establish your position on who is the most evil character. In the body of your paper, you'll want to explain and prove why that person is the most evil. You'll also want to show how the other characters rank, and why. In your conclusion, discuss the values that you are supporting. Your goal is to complete an essay with an introduction, body paragraphs, and conclusion.

Activity

Study a Student Sample

The following is an introductory paragraph from a student's essay. Read it carefully and underline what you think works well. Then answer the questions that follow.

> "The Most Evil Character" is a story about a college student named Jack with mediocre grades who tries to live up to both his mother's and Professor Brown's expectations. With the help of Victor, a recent graduate who is constantly in need of money, Jack achieves his goal by less than honest means. We will now examine the characters from the most to the least evil.
>
> —*Miguel Viera*

1. What do you think Miguel did particularly well?
2. If a reader had never read "The Most Evil Character," would this introduction be clear? Why, or why not?
3. Does this writer have a clear thesis? If so, where?

Activity

Study a Student Sample

In the next student sample, you'll read the first body paragraph from another student's essay. (This student's thesis was "I intend to prove that Victor is 'The Most Evil Character' in this story." This thesis was the last sentence in the introduction.) Then answer the questions that follow.

> First body paragraph:
>
>   Jack's mom wanted him to become a lawyer, like his father. *Setting Limits*, by Robert J. MacKenzie, Ed.D., says that "the exploration is the most important part. . . . Teens need to try out new roles, new values and beliefs, new relationships and commitments." She did not give him that chance. Instead, she promised him a car and a trip to pursue the career of her choice. Because his grades were not commendable, she warned him that if he did not bring his average up one grade he would not receive the offering, and this became his first ultimatum.
>
> —*Keisha Harris*

1. This paragraph has a number of strengths. What do you think Keisha did well?

2. Study Keisha's paragraph. What is Keisha proving in this paragraph? Write your own topic sentence for this paragraph. (Remember, your topic sentence should show how this first body paragraph connects to the idea expressed in the thesis.)

Activity

Study a Student Sample

In the next student sample, you'll read a concluding paragraph from yet another student's essay. As you read it, think about what a conclusion should do and mark the parts of the conclusion that you like best. Then answer the questions that follow.

To wrap it all up, Jack by far is the evil person, in my opinion. He has created his own mess. He needs to stop and take a long look at his life, also his situation and fix it no matter what the outcome may be. Mom and Victor need to get real lives and stop the blackmail games. Professor Brown maybe could be a bit less open in his own personal opinion of his student's life outside of his classroom. As for dad and the dean they are just names thrown into a situation that they were not directly a part of.

—*Ruth Hathaway*

1. From reading this concluding paragraph, can you tell what Ruth's thesis probably was? If yes, write a thesis for her essay.

2. From this concluding paragraph, can you tell what Ruth's main supporting points might have been? Write topic sentences (in your own words) for body paragraphs that might work in her essay.

3. Will the conclusion in your essay be anything like Ruth's? Explain.

Revise

Use your critical thinking skills and find strengths and weaknesses in your own writing *before* you hear what others think. This will help you become an independent writer.

Then, when you do have a classmate or a tutor read your essay, listen carefully. But *you* make the decisions about what to change and what not to change. You are in control of your own writing.

Activity

Share Your Writing

Find a classmate to work with. Read each other's essays and discuss the following questions as they relate to your essays.

- What concerns do you have about your essay?

- Have you summarized the events of the story?

- Have you ranked the characters in order to show who is the *most* evil?

- Is it clear who the *least* evil character is?

- Do you support and explain your ideas?

- Do your ideas flow from one sentence to the next and from one paragraph to the next? Does each point clearly connect to the thesis?

- Does the essay contain an introduction, body paragraphs, and a conclusion?

Make a list of things you want to change in your essay. Start with the most important. Are there certain things that your instructor wants you to focus on when you revise?

Begin revising your essay. Focus on one problem area at a time. Write more than one new draft.

Edit

Now begin "polishing" your essay. Carefully check for typing errors, spelling errors, and any other errors you tend to make. Also, review your essay for sentence variety. You may also want to consider these questions after completing the sentence work at the end of this chapter (pages 155–171).

- Have you used coordinators, transitions, and subordinators to add variety and to clarify relationships between ideas in your essay?

- Can you add useful information to your essay by including prepositional or participial phrases in some of you sentences?

TIME TO REFLECT

> ### Journal Assignment
>
> ### Your Progress as a Writer, Reader, and Critical Thinker
>
> Reflect on the skills you have strengthened in this chapter. Write a journal entry in which you discuss
>
> - what you have learned in this chapter,
> - the skills you are improving,
> - the skills you feel need more work,
> - changes in your reading process, and
> - changes in your writing process.
>
> Also respond to this question: How have the writing assignments in this chapter sharpened your critical thinking skills?

SUMMARY OF CHAPTER 4

This chapter has focused on understanding and effectively using the stages of the writing process.

Discuss and engage

Read, discuss, and think critically

Explore the writing assignment

Draft

Revise

Edit

As you have studied advertisements, advertising strategies, and evil characters, you have

- used your reading, writing, and critical thinking skills, and
- seen the advantages of using an effective writing process.

Your tasks as a writer are easier when you approach writing as a process. In addition, your writing will be clearer, better organized, and more developed. Using the writing process effectively is key to writing well.

CLAUSES AND PHRASES

The Independent Clause
Using Coordinating Conjunctions
Punctuating Correctly with Coordinating Conjunctions
Using Semicolons and Transitions
The Dependent (or Subordinated) Clause
Punctuating Correctly with Dependent Clauses
Understanding Phrases
Prepositional Phrases
Participial Phrases

Thus far in *Connections*, you have focused on verbs and subjects—two key ingredients in sentences. Now, you'll turn your attention to two larger sentence units: the clause and the phrase.

Understanding clauses and phrases will help you avoid errors like run-on sentences. In addition, learning to use clauses and phrases effectively will help you add variety to your sentence structure. Good writing will have short sentences and long sentences. Short sentences can help you make powerful, direct statements, but too many short sentences will bore your reader and make your writing seem too simple. Long sentences can allow you to explain the complexity of an issue. They help you to show the relationships between ideas. Of course, too many long sentences might tire your reader and make your writing seem unbalanced. This chapter will help you create the right balance of short and long sentences in your essays.

The Independent Clause

A **clause** is a group of words with a subject and a verb. There are two kinds of clauses—independent and dependent. The **independent clause** can stand on its own and is the same thing as a complete sentence. (Remember, a *complete sentence* is a group of words with a subject and verb that expresses a complete idea.) Here are independent clauses with the subjects underlined once and verbs underlined twice.

Today, <u>we</u> <u>focused</u> on the writing process.

My <u>tutor</u> <u>helps</u> me with each step in the writing process.

<u>I</u> <u>like</u> to discuss my writing ideas with my spouse.

A simple independent clause can be very useful. If you have provided enough information and support, a simple sentence like "Jack is the most evil character" can make your point clearly and dramatically.

Using Coordinating Conjunctions

To add variety to your writing and to help show the relationships between your ideas, you can join two independent clauses and make one longer sentence. A **coordinating conjunction** is a word that can join independent clauses. (These words are also called *coordinators*.)

An *acronym* is a word that is created by using the first letters of other words. For example, you may have heard people say "ASAP" when they mean "as soon as possible." FANBOYS is an acronym also.

There are seven coordinating conjunctions, which you will study here briefly. You will get more practice with these in Chapter 8. You can remember them by remembering the acronym FANBOYS.

For   And   Nor   But   Or   Yet   So

When you want to join two independent clauses with one of the FANBOYS, you need to choose one that accurately expresses the relationship between the ideas you are joining.

For: expresses a relationship of *effect-cause*. The idea in the first sentence is the effect. The idea in the second sentence is the cause.

Joseph hurried to the store, <u>for</u> he desperately wanted the new home theater system.

And: expresses a relationship of *addition*. The idea in the first sentence is added to the idea in the second sentence.

The advertisement called the new CD/DVD home theater system the key to throwing a great party, <u>and</u> Joseph loved parties.

Nor: expresses a relationship of *negative addition*. The idea in the first sentence is negative, and it is added to a negative idea in the second sentence. (Notice that the subject and verb in the second independent clause are not in their usual order.)

Unfortunately, Joseph didn't actually have enough cash for the purchase, <u>nor</u> did he have any room left on his credit card.

But: expresses a relationship of opposition. The idea in the first sentence is in opposition to the idea in the second sentence.

He asked his roommate to loan him the money, <u>but</u> his roommate wouldn't do it.

Or: expresses a relationship of *alternatives*. The idea in the first sentence is one option. The idea in the second sentence is another option.

He could save up his money for the next few months, <u>or</u> he could call his parents for a loan.

Yet: expresses a relationship of opposition. The idea in the first sentence is in opposition to the idea in the second sentence.

The advertisement made the sound system seem so necessary, <u>yet</u> Joseph didn't want to go further into debt.

So: expresses a relationship of *cause-effect*. The idea in the first sentence causes the idea in the second sentence.

Joseph decided to save up for the home theater system, <u>so</u> he went to the bank and opened a savings account.

Punctuating Correctly with Coordinating Conjunctions

When you are using coordinating conjunctions to join independent sentences, remember the following rule.

Punctuation Rule #2

When you join independent clauses with a coordinating conjunction, you need to put a comma after the first independent clause.

- She spent a lot of time thinking about shopping, for she was a slave to advertising.
- My kids don't watch much television, yet they still seem to know about all the newest toys and sugared cereals.

Sometimes writers choose to begin sentences with coordinators. This adds a slight emphasis to the sentence that begins with the coordinator:

Cassidy doesn't go shopping much. And she particularly dislikes people who constantly talk about shopping.

Practice #1 Creating an Advertisement

On a separate piece of paper, join the independent clauses below using carefully chosen coordinators (FANBOYS.) Remember to put a comma after the first independent clause. (Don't use the same coordinator twice.)

Example: I have never analyzed an advertisement before.
I do not know much about creating an advertisement.

- I have never analyzed an advertisement, nor do I know much about creating an advertisement.

Notes

Remember that when you use *nor* to join independent clauses, the subject and verb will not be in their usual positions. Also, the negative word in the second sentence must be dropped. In the example, *not* has been dropped.

Clauses and Phrases

Notes

1. My mom loaned me a bunch of magazines. I want to study how advertisers manipulate their audiences.
2. In class, we made a great list of products to advertise. I can only choose one.
3. Advertising baby strollers could be interesting. I may choose to advertise briefcases for women.
4. For a stroller advertisement, pastel colors would be best. I would emphasize safety and beauty with my words.
5. Most briefcases are okay for either gender. I think I could create an advertisement that women would be especially drawn to.
6. The briefcase advertisement shouldn't be too feminine. It should not be sexy.
7. The stroller advertisement might be more fun. I think I will choose that one.

Using Semicolons and Transitions

Another way to join independent clauses is to use a semicolon. A semicolon is as strong as a period. Use a semicolon when the ideas in each independent clause are closely related.

> I studied the advertisement carefully; I was preparing to analyze it.
>
> Sheila is an artist; she loved creating her advertisement.

You can also use a transition with a semicolon. A transition is a word or phrase that helps show the relationship between two ideas. It acts like a bridge between independent sentences. Transitions like *however, therefore,* and *then* cannot join independent clauses with a comma like coordinators do, but you can use them with semicolons. Note that the semicolon separates the sentences and a comma follows the transition. You are actually combining two punctuation rules when you use transitions in this manner.

> The advertisement was directed at women; *however,* I think men will pay attention too.
>
> He clearly stated his goal for the advertising campaign; *therefore,* the staff knew exactly how to proceed.

Punctuation Rule #3

You may use a semicolon to separate two complete sentences.

- Three people at the advertising agency worked on the ad; they liked bouncing ideas off of one another.

Punctuation Rule #4

Follow an introductory word or phrase with a comma.

- <u>Then,</u> they got together to exchange their ideas.

Note: Punctuation Rules 3 and 4 are both applied when you join two complete sentences with a semicolon and transition.

- The three people on the project drafted their own ads; <u>then,</u> they got together to exchange their ideas.

Common transitions:

<u>also, furthermore, next, similarly, in addition, likewise</u>: *express addition of similar ideas*

<u>consequently, therefore, thus, as a result</u>: *express cause-effect*

<u>however, otherwise, on the other hand, in contrast</u>: *express opposition*

<u>then, next, finally, now, first, second, third</u>: *express time*

<u>for example, such as, for instance</u>: *tells the reader an example is coming*

Practice #2   Advertising (and Transitions)

On a separate piece of paper, create the sentences described below.

Example: Join these sentences with a semicolon.

The advertisement used bold colors and the words "dynamic" and "successful." It would appeal to people seeking power and prestige.

- The advertisement used bold colors and the words "dynamic" and "successful"; it would appeal to people seeking power and prestige.

Notes

1. Join these sentences with a semicolon.

   The advertising staff discovered that the target audience watched a lot of prime-time television. They decided to use television stars to promote the product.

2. Join these sentences with a semicolon.

   Baby food manufacturers like to advertise in women's magazines. Mothers buy more baby food than other people do.

3. Join these sentences with a semicolon and one of these transitions: *therefore, however,* or *then.*

   The perfume manufacturer wanted women to believe that the new fragrance would make them sexier. The advertisement showed a beautiful half-naked woman in bed.

4. Join these sentences with a semicolon and one of these transitions: *therefore, however,* or *then.*

   The advertising firm did a phone survey. The staff had a better idea about who is interested in the product.

5. Join these sentences with a semicolon and one of these transitions: *on the other hand, similarly,* or *consequently.*

   Harrison loved creating advertisements. Samantha felt there was something dishonest about the whole business.

6. Join these sentences with a semicolon and one of these transitions: *similarly, in contrast,* or *consequently.*

   I wanted to encourage people to spend more money on diamond engagement rings. My advertisement suggests that spending more money means your love is deeper.

7. Join these two sentences with a semicolon and one of these transitions: *therefore, similarly,* or *then.*

   I really enjoyed searching for just the right words for my advertisement. My classmate, Tim, loved experimenting with color and props.

The Dependent (or Subordinated) Clause

The **dependent** or **subordinated clause** is a group of words that contains a subject and verb but cannot stand on its own. It is *not* a complete sentence.

When <u>Cecilia</u> <u>looked</u> at the advertisement.

Even though <u>I</u> <u>read</u> magazines frequently.

Because <u>Neil</u> <u>believed</u> every advertisement.

The words *when, even though,* and *because* change the independent clauses into dependent clauses. If you read the dependent clauses carefully aloud, you will hear how they sound "unfinished."

Subordinators are words that can attach to independent clauses and make them dependent (or subordinated). Here is a list of subordinators:

although

because

even though

if

since

though

when

while

You cannot use a dependent clause by itself. A dependent clause standing alone is called a **fragment,** or an incomplete sentence. However, joined to independent clauses, dependent clauses can be very useful because they allow you to express complex ideas and the relationships between those ideas.

When will allow you to tell your reader that two ideas are connected by time.

<u>When I studied the words more closely</u>, I could see how the advertiser was trying to manipulate me.

Since allows you to express a cause-and-effect relationship or a time relationship.

<u>Since I had so many ideas for this essay</u>, I had to spend a lot of time planning and organizing my thoughts. (cause and effect)

I haven't written an essay <u>since I was a senior in high school</u>. (time)

While allows you to express a relationship of opposition or of time.

<u>While I have never relied on outlines</u>, I actually found one helpful with this assignment. (opposition)

<u>While listening to the class discussion</u>, I got some good ideas for my own essay. (time)

Clauses and Phrases

Notes

Even though, *though*, and *although* allow you to tell your reader that one idea is the opposite of another.

> <u>Even though my target audience is male sports fans</u>, I believe that women will like my ad also.

Because allows you to tell your reader that the ideas have a cause-and-effect relationship.

> <u>Because my tutor said I was trying to cover too much in my second paragraph</u>, I decided to break that paragraph into two.

If allows you to tell your reader that the ideas have a conditional relationship.

> You might discover more ideas to write about <u>if you start by discussing your assignment with your tutor</u>.

Punctuating Correctly with Dependent Clauses

There are two punctuation rules to remember with dependent clauses.

Punctuation Rule #5

When you begin a sentence with a subordinated or dependent clause, you must put a comma after the subordinated (or dependent) clause.

- <u>Because I didn't have enough to say about the bicycle ad</u>, I decided to write about the jewelry ad.

Punctuation Rule #6

If the subordinated clause comes after the independent clause, you do not need a comma.

- I decided to write about the jewelry ad <u>because I didn't have enough to say about the bicycle ad</u>.

Practice #3   Advertising (and Dependent Clauses)

On a separate piece of paper, join the sentences with an appropriate subordinator from the following list.

[Clauses and Phrases — vertical side tab]

- In some sentences, put the dependent clause first. In other sentences, put the dependent clause second.
- Underline the dependent clause.
- Do not use a subordinator more than once.
- Don't forget to use commas when necessary.

although

because

even though

if

since

though

when

while

Example: You don't start your essay soon. You won't finish in time!

- <u>If you don't start your essay soon</u>, you won't finish in time!

1. My classmates gave me some good suggestions. I asked for their advice on my essay.
2. I thought the advertisement was very effective. It skillfully played on my emotions.
3. I decided to take some art classes. My new goal was to go into advertising.
4. I took notes. I watched the advertisements on television.
5. Martha was afraid of public speaking. She did a really good job presenting her advertisement to the class.
6. You don't draw well. You can create a collage by cutting items out of magazines.
7. Music would make my advertisement so much better. We're supposed to focus on print ads, not on television or radio ads.

Practice #4   **Creating Sentences with Clauses**

On a separate piece of paper, create original sentences that fit the descriptions below.

- Your sentences must be on the same topic as your current reading or writing assignment.

Clauses and Phrases

Notes

1. Create one sentence for each coordinating conjunction. (You'll be creating seven different sentences.)

2. Create one sentence using a semicolon.

3. Create one sentence using a semicolon and a transition word or phrase.

4. Create a sentence that has an independent clause and a subordinated clause that begins with *if*. Put the subordinated clause first and underline it. (Remember to use a comma.)

5. Create a sentence that has an independent clause and a subordinated clause that begins with *because*. Put the subordinated clause second and underline it. (Remember, do not use a comma when the subordinated clause comes second.)

Understanding Phrases

A **phrase** is a group of words that is missing a subject, a verb, or both. Phrases are very useful to writers because they allow writers to insert critical pieces of information into sentences. Phrases are one key to writing longer, more sophisticated, more expressive sentences. Understanding phrases is also important in avoiding sentence fragments.

Here are some examples of phrases—groups of words missing one or more sentence ingredients:

worrying about his grade

on his chemistry test

for her parents' approval

embarrassed by the scandal

at the prestigious college

from the cameras

If a writer were to use one of these phrases by itself, the writer would be creating a fragment. However, these phrases can be inserted into independent clauses, creating nicely shaped, sophisticated sentences that will add variety and interest to an essay:

<u>Worrying about his grade</u>, Kyle decides to cheat <u>on his chemistry test.</u>

Susan was desperate <u>for her parents' approval.</u>

Embarrassed by the scandal, the students at the prestigious college   *Notes*
hid their faces from the cameras.

Prepositional Phrases

A *prepositional phrase* is a group of words made up of a preposition
and its object. A *preposition* is a word that suggests position, location,
direction, condition, or time. An *object* is the noun that follows the
preposition. Sometimes a prepositional phrase will include descriptive
information too (between the preposition and the object). In these examples, the preposition is underlined once and the object is underlined
twice:

at the college

in the overcrowded, noisy classroom (note that *overcrowded* and
noisy describe the object)

after much thought (*much* describes the object)

There is neither a subject nor a verb in a prepositional phrase. Prepositional phrases, however, are very useful because they add information to sentences and often help the writer avoid unnecessary
repetition. These sentences, for example, suffer from unnecessary repetition:

The movie addressed the issue. The movie was on HBO. The issue
of cheating was the topic. The cheating was on college campuses.

This is a better sentence that uses prepositional phrases (prepositional
phrases are underlined):

The movie on HBO addressed the issue of cheating on college
campuses.

Practice #5   **Cheaters**

Add the prepositional phrases to each sentence to make longer, more
complex sentences. Underline the prepositional phrases in your new
sentences.

Example:

Many students accept cheating.

as a normal part

of college

Notes

- Many students accept cheating <u>as a normal part</u> of college.
  1. Some are worried.

     of my friends

     about getting

     into the best graduate schools
  2. To keep up, they think that they must cheat too.

     with their dishonest classmates
  3. A news commentator said our public officials are partly to blame because they often cheat.

     on television
  4. Lately, many CEOs have been found guilty.

     of major companies

     of cheating
  5. However, I keep hearing the old saying, "Two wrongs don't make a right."

     from my childhood
  6. I'm afraid.

     of the long-term effects

     of such widespread cheating
  7. What can we look forward to if many make it?

     of our future doctors, lawyers, military officers, and professors

     through school

     by cheating

Participial Phrases

A **participial phrase** consists of a present or past participle and the words attached to that participle. (Participial phrases can include prepositional phrases.)

Present participles end in *–ing:*

talking

focusing

questioning

hoping

Here are those same present participles in participial phrases: *Notes*

talking to my classmates

focusing intently

questioning their ideas

hoping for a better future

Past participles usually end in *–ed,* but sometimes they have an irregular form:

concerned

written (irregular)

questioned

chosen (irregular)

Here are those same past participles in participial phrases:

concerned by the new study

written clearly

questioned by my peers

chosen by the voters

Participial phrases can add interesting information to sentences and often help the writer express ideas with fewer sentences. In this section, you'll focus on participial phrases that describe nouns. Consider the following sentences:

I was talking to my classmates. I learned that they don't approve of cheating.

Callie was focusing intently on her exam. She didn't notice her classmate looking at her answers.

The dean is concerned about cheating. The dean buys a new antiplagiarism software program.

I was questioned by my peers. I felt ashamed of my actions.

The following revised sentences are more interesting and would add nice sentence structure variety to an essay:

<u>Talking to my classmates</u>, I learned that they don't approve of cheating.

<u>Focusing intently on her exam,</u> Callie didn't notice her classmate looking at her answers.

<u>Concerned about cheating</u>, the dean buys a new antiplagiarism software program.

<u>Questioned by my peers</u>, I felt ashamed of my actions.

Clauses and Phrases

Notes   Although participial phrases can be used in a number of positions in sentences, in this chapter, you'll focus on participial phrases that begin sentences. Note that in the following examples the participial phrases describe a noun that immediately follows. The participial phrase has a single underline. The noun has a double underline. *(Hint:* This is the sentence pattern to follow: Participial phrase, noun + verb + completing information.)

> <u>Working all night</u>, <u>Frieda</u> finished her essay.
>
> <u>Taking his time with the revision,</u> <u>Tom</u> created a persuasive analysis.
>
> <u>Irritated by the noise,</u> the <u>student</u> moved to a different part of the library.

Punctuating Correctly with Participial Phrases

A participial phrase that comes at the beginning of a sentence is also called an introductory phrase. When you begin a sentence with such a phrase, remember the following rule.

Punctuation Rule #4 (Review)
Follow an introductory word or phrase with a comma.

* <u>Working all night,</u> Frieda finished her essay.

Practice #6   The Most Evil Character
* Underline the participial phrases that are describing nouns.
* Use a double underline to mark the nouns each phrase describes.

(You may find infinitives and prepositional phrases within the participial phrases.)

Example: Determined to do well on the assignment, Jess sought the help of a tutor.
* <u>Determined to do well on the assignment,</u> <u>Jess</u> sought the help of a tutor.

  1. Hoping for the car and the trip, Jack paid someone else to write his essay.
  2. Wanting more money, Victor blackmailed Jack.

3. Angered by Jack's lack of effort, the professor had little sympathy for Jack.

4. Asked to analyze each character, the student made a chart describing their actions and motives.

5. Looking for more information, the student listened carefully to the class discussion.

Practice #7   Using Participial Phrases

On a separate piece of paper, write new sentences that include the participial phrases given. (Hint: Place the participial phrases at the beginning of the new sentences.)

Example: Oscar knew he had to pay closer attention to creating a clear thesis and useful topic sentences.

Reflecting on the instructor's comments on the previous essay

- Reflecting on the instructor's comments on the previous essay, Oscar knew he had to pay closer attention to creating a clear thesis and useful topic sentences.

1. James decided who the most evil character is.
   Considering his own morals and values carefully

2. Sam asked some classmates to get together for a study session.
   Finding it difficult to get started on the essay

3. Veronica spent double her usual amount of time editing her essay.
   Wanting to show some significant improvement

4. Francesca changed her major to philosophy.
   Realizing her love for philosophical discussions

5. Lyle decided to go play a game of hoop.
   Tired of thinking and writing

6. Charise did some independent research.
   Determined to liven up her paper

7. The professor spoke up against the antiplagiarism software.
   Worried that the school would be sending a message of no trust

Notes

8. Elise found some areas in her essay that needed to be more fully developed.

Reading her essay aloud.

Practice #8   Creating Sentences with Phrases

Part One: Create five original sentences that have prepositional phrases in them.

- The sentences must connect to the topics of your current reading and writing assignments.
- Underline the prepositional phrases.

Part Two: Create five original sentences that begin with participial phrases.

- The sentences must connect to the topics of your current reading and writing assignments.
- Underline the participial phrases.

(*Hint:* This is the sentence pattern to follow: participial phrase, noun + verb + completing information.)

Your Own Writing: Clauses and Phrases

Review one of the journals, summaries, or essays you have written and look at the sentence structure.

- How many of your sentences are short? How many are long? Highlight the short sentences.
- Have you expressed complex ideas by joining independent clauses with coordinators, semicolons, or transition words with semicolons? Circle coordinators, semicolons, and transition words.
- Have you used any subordinators? Circle subordinators.
- Have you used any prepositional phrases? Underline the prepositional phrases.
- Do any of your sentences begin with participial phrases? Underline any participial phrases that start sentences.

Rewrite a few sentences from the journal, summary, or essay that you have selected, improving the variety in your sentence structure. Use coordinators, subordinators, transition words, semicolons, prepositional phrases, and participial phrases. You may even decide to add new information. Here are some of the coordinators, subordinators, and transitions you can choose from:

<u>Coordinators</u>: for, and, nor, but, or, yet, so

<u>Subordinators</u>: if, since, while, though, although, even though, because, when

<u>Transitions</u>: therefore, however, then, on the other hand, similarly, in contrast, consequently

Highlight the improved sentences in the revised version of your journal, summary, or essay (or paragraph from an essay).

Clauses and Phrases

SECTION II

Employing the Connections

This section offers you four chapters, each devoted to a different contemporary theme. In each chapter, you'll read about the topic and be guided through productive reading, writing, and critical thinking processes as you create essays that communicate your thoughts on these themes.

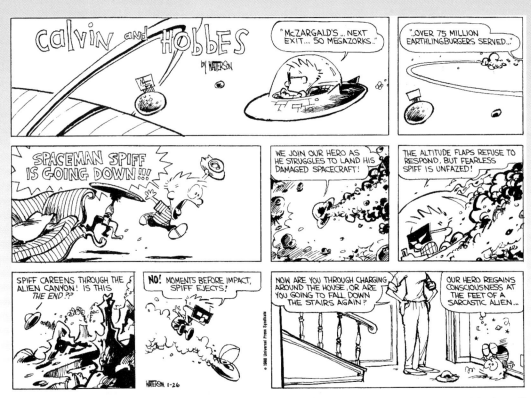

Writing About Heroes

Main Topics

- Focusing your writing

- Communicating your ideas about heroes

- Using pronouns effectively

- Understanding parallel structure

The Essential Calvin & Hobbes Treasury, Andrews & McMeel (Universal)

One of the first things readers expect from academic paragraphs and essays is for the writing to be **focused**. When we speak, we often wander from one topic to another. That's acceptable in speech. (Consider the stand-up comedian who can begin talking about his mother-in-law and end up talking about car repair.) However, in academic writing, your audience expects you to choose a subject and stay focused on it. This requires you to think critically about your topic and your own writing. Every writer must make choices about what to say and how to say it so that the audience doesn't get distracted from the main message. In this chapter, you'll explore the topic of heroes and then write a focused definition and essay about a hero. You'll get practice focusing your writing as you write an essay on the heroic qualities of the person you choose.

FOCUSING YOUR WRITING

Imagine that your photography instructor asks you to photograph one person in a crowd of people. He wants you to study a crowd and choose one face that interests you. You go downtown during the weekday lunch hour and watch people as they go to lunch, do their shopping, and so on. Then, after you make your choice, you take a close-up photograph, making sure that this person's face is in perfect focus. Everyone around this person is blurry.

Photo courtesy of Milenko Vlaisavljevic.

Writing an essay is similar to this type of photography. You are given a topic (a crowd), you explore your options (the many faces), and then, using your critical thinking skills, you choose one manageable, interesting point to make (the best face). Finally, you write your essay about that point only, leaving out all distracting information. (One person is in focus and all the rest are blurry.) This kind of focus helps your reader stay interested and understand what you want to explain or prove.

Focusing the Paragraph

A **focused paragraph** will have a clear, informative topic sentence that tells the reader what the main idea of the paragraph is. This sentence should not be too broad or too narrow. That is, it must be broad enough to express an idea worth developing in a paragraph, but it shouldn't be so broad that the reader has a hard time telling where your writing is going next.

The sentences that follow the topic sentence are called the body of the paragraph, and these sentences will clearly support the topic sentence. This support can be in the form of examples, statistics, details, explanations, comparisons, or other forms of evidence. In addition, a paragraph may have a wrap-up sentence that closes the paragraph by summarizing points made or restating the main idea.

All of the sentences in the well-focused paragraph must stick to and support the main idea in the topic sentence. To achieve this clear focus, good writers use the writing process: they brainstorm, draft, and revise. Throughout the process, they make choices. For example, if a student who has been reading about and discussing heroes in class wants to write a paragraph on why a particular athlete is a hero, he may need to write down a list of ideas and many trial topic sentences before finding a main idea he is comfortable with. After he has a topic sentence (a main idea), he drafts the paragraph and makes choices about which ideas support his topic sentence the best. When he adds information that strengthens the paragraph and takes out information that doesn't, he is revising effectively and improving the focus of the paragraph.

Activity

Miguel's Focused Paragraph

Read the following paragraph.

(This is the third paragraph in an essay about Roberto Clemente. The second paragraph focused on how well Clemente played baseball and on his dedication to the sport.)

> In the same manner that Roberto played baseball with all his heart and soul, he also gave to all those who were less fortunate than him. In Puerto Rico he had a baseball clinic where he donated all of the equipment and spent much of his off-time teaching children the fundamentals of baseball. Roberto also donated large amounts of money to children's charity. He understood how much he meant to children and people in general, took his role as a leader of youth very seriously, and always held himself to a higher standard.
>
> —*Miguel Viera*

1. Write *T.S.* next to the topic sentence. Highlight the part of the sentence that announces what this paragraph will focus on.

2. Write *S* next to specific pieces of support in the body of the paragraph that stay focused on the topic sentence. Note how the topic sentence and specific pieces of support work together to create a focused paragraph.

3. Why would the following topic sentence be *less* effective for Miguel's paragraph?

   Roberto Clemente had other good qualities.

Focusing the Essay

A **focused essay** relies on a thoughtful thesis statement: the sentence at the end of the introduction that announces the main idea of the essay. A writer must read, discuss, think, brainstorm, draft, and revise to find the thesis statement that expresses a focused idea worth developing. Sometimes a writer must return to earlier steps in the writing process to find a good, focused thesis. For example, a writer might be in the middle of writing an essay when she realizes that part of her essay doesn't seem to support her thesis. If this happens, the writer must use her critical thinking skills and make some choices. Should the thesis be changed? Should certain ideas she has written down be left out of the essay? Perhaps she needs to go back and take another look at her brainstorm and outline. The writer must stay sensitive to the reader's need for focus.

Notes

Notes

Of course, the thesis isn't the only part of the essay that is important to focus. The topic sentence of each body paragraph and each piece of support should clearly relate to the thesis. Good topic sentences in a focused essay often repeat key terms from the thesis and always announce a major point that directly supports the thesis.

Activities

A Focused Outline: Malcolm X

Consider this outline for a well-focused essay on a hero.

Thesis: Malcolm X is a hero to me because of the strength he showed in his fight to improve his life and the lives of others.

Topic sentence for body paragraph #1: First of all, he had the strength to turn away from the life of street crime he knew so well and become a respectable citizen.

Supporting information—explain:
He had been involved in crime for a long time.
His friends were all criminals.
He had to turn his back on everything he knew well.
He reached out to family and religion.

Topic sentence for body paragraph #2: Malcolm X also drew on great inner strength when he taught himself to read and write in prison.

Supporting information—explain:
He read and copied the entire dictionary.
He read many, many books.
He studied late at night (broke curfew).

Topic sentence for body paragraph #3: After deepening his understanding of his Muslim religion, Malcolm X showed great strength as he moved away from separatist beliefs and fought to create a peaceful, multiracial community.

Supporting information—explain:
He traveled to Mecca.
He learned the truth about his religion.
He courageously changed his views about separating blacks and whites.

Topic sentence for body paragraph #4: Finally, I admire Malcolm X's strength and determination to help the black race.

Supporting information—explain:

His life revolved around politics.
He didn't work to get rich.
He spoke honestly.

Topic sentence for conclusion: Overall, I see Malcolm X as a hero because he showed such strength as he evolved from a poor, uneducated criminal to a leader of people.

1. Highlight the key words in the thesis statement that tell the reader what the essay will be about.

2. Highlight the words in each topic sentence that show that the topic sentence connects directly to the thesis.

Checking the Focus: "My Dad"

Study the thesis and notes that follow.

Thesis: My father is a hero in our neighborhood.

The thief who stole my friend's car was caught by an alert neighbor.
My uncle, who lives down the street, had his house broken into three times before the neighborhood watch program began. Since we started the program, he hasn't had a single problem.
My father became an important man in our neighborhood when he organized a neighborhood watch program and helped reduce crime in the neighborhood.
He helped clean up all the broken glass, old newspapers, and tires that littered the neighborhood.
He took charge because my brother got hurt playing in the empty lot next door.
We walked door-to-door, talked to people about the way our neighborhood looks, and organized a clean-up day.
Also, my father made our neighborhood a more attractive place to live.
My dad is an outstanding golfer, and he plays basketball too.

1. Which of the sentences here might make good topic sentences for an essay that focuses on the thesis statement the student wrote?

2. Which sentences might act as support to which topic sentences?

3. Which of the ideas don't connect clearly to the thesis?

4. Rewrite the sentences showing how you might group them to create an outline for an essay.

Notes

Points to Remember About Focus

As you work through this chapter and think about focusing your writing, remember these points:

- When you first start the writing process, let your mind wander and explore many different ideas.
- Spend plenty of time brainstorming, reviewing readings, and talking to classmates before you choose a focus for your essay.
- Allow yourself to change the focus of your essay if your thesis isn't working for you.
- When you revise, think critically about what you've written. Do your words communicate a focused idea to the reader?

INVESTIGATING HEROES

This section of the chapter is the beginning of your writing process. You'll discuss heroes. Then you'll read about heroes and discuss the readings. Toward the middle of the chapter, you'll find three writing assignments and support and advice as you complete the writing process.

Discuss and Engage

We've all heard about superheroes—Batman, Superman, Wonder Woman, Spiderman, the Power Rangers, even Underdog. These characters have certain human qualities that we admire and think of as heroic. However, they also have superhuman abilities, such as X-ray vision, which help them perform heroic feats. Film heroes also have extraordinary qualities—sometimes to the point of being superhuman. Think about, for example, a film hero's ability to fight off five attackers, dodge hundreds of bullets, and jump out a window just before a bomb explodes (and look good while doing it). Although you'll be writing about real-life heroes in this chapter, let's consider for a moment what we love about superheroes and film heroes.

Journal Assignment

Calvin and Hobbes

In the *Calvin and Hobbes* comic strip on page 174, Calvin pretends to be a superhero named Spiff. Study the comic strip and think about the qualities Spiff seems to have. What heroic qualities has Calvin's imagination created?

Activities

Superheroes

Discuss with your classmates what you admire about various superheroes.
Create a chart similar to the one below to record your class discussion
notes. Then answer the class discussion questions.

Superhero	Heroic or Admirable Qualities	Superhuman Abilities
Superman		

1. What heroic or admirable qualities do these heroes share?

2. How do their superhuman abilities differ from their heroic qualities?

3. In your opinion, why do we enjoy our superheroes?

   (*Note:* Remember to take notes during class discussion.)

Film Heroes

Before we move on to "real-life" heroes, think about film heroes. Most people love to watch men and women in films who act, look, and live like heroes. Take a few minutes to consider this kind of hero.

   Discuss with your classmates some of your favorite film heroes. Who
are they? In what films do they perform? What makes them heroes? Do film
heroes look and act a certain way? How are film heroes different from real-
life heroes? Explain. (Be sure to take notes.)

Real-Life Heroes   Studying superheroes and film heroes helps us begin
thinking about heroes and what makes a hero, but what about "real-
life" heroes? These include the famous (public) heroes as well as the private (personal) heroes (individuals who act in remarkable ways). Do
they share certain qualities? What do public and private heroes have in
common?

   As you begin to define heroes, consider what these students had to
say about them.

Notes

A hero is a person who has shared or done some good deeds in a country or in the world. Heroes may risk their lives and some even die for their own fellow men. They're often written about and remembered through history.

—*Diony Fernandez*

A hero can be any person on this planet, who, without ever thinking about it, goes to the rescue of his fellow man. I'd like to think that each of us has been a hero at one time or another in our lives, and didn't even realize it. A hero is a person who is sensitive to the feelings of others, and receives the pleasurable satisfaction of being able to help as their reward. A hero is that one person who wasn't noticed, recognized, or sometimes even thanked. The real hero receives his or her rewards within because they don't want to be known as a hero.

—*Maria Gonzales*

A hero is a person that goes above and beyond what any normal person can do. It's a person that works for what he or she believes in and helps others to be better people in society.

—*Doris Maysonet*

Activities

Identifying the Characteristics of Public Heroes

If you ask a group of people to list their favorite heroes, certain names keep showing up. Consider the names that follow.

Maya Angelou	Serena Williams
Cesar Chavez	Mother Teresa
Eleanor Roosevelt	Rosa Parks
Marie Curie	Bill Gates
Albert Einstein	Harriet Tubman
Mahatma Gandhi	George Washington
Michael Jordan	Tiger Woods
Martin Luther King, Jr.	

Get Involved!
The reading "Who Is Great?" in Section III offers information about many "great" people, some of whom might also be considered heroes.(See pages 414–418.) Come to class prepared to discuss what you've discovered.

Now, discuss with your classmates what you admire about some of these public heroes. Create a chart similar to the one that follows and list some names and admirable qualities. Then respond in your notebook to the questions after the chart.

Public Heroes	Heroic or Admirable Qualities

Notes

Get Involved!
Bring a superhero comic book to class and explain what heroic qualities the characters have.

1. What heroic qualities do these famous people share?

2. What kinds of heroic acts have these famous people performed?

3. What are the differences between a hero and a "normal" person?

4. Are there less obvious heroes among us in society, people who don't perform dramatic acts of bravery but who could still be considered heroes? Explain.

5. How would you define the term *hero?*

Identifying the Characteristics of Private or Personal Heroes

Think about people who aren't famous but who are considered heroes. The New York City firefighters are a good example. They risked (and many lost) their lives helping innocent victims escape the World Trade Center disaster of September 11, 2001. They've become famous following the disaster, but before September 11, they were performing heroic deeds without much notoriety. There are many other people who could be called heroes for their acts of strength and courage. Perhaps you know of a private citizen who has acted heroically.

Discuss with your classmates what you admire about private citizens who exhibit heroic qualities. Create a chart similar to the one below and list some names and heroic or admirable qualities these people possess. Then respond in your notebook to the questions after the chart.

Personal Heroes	Heroic or Admirable Qualities

Notes

1. What heroic qualities do the private citizens on your list share?

2. What kinds of heroic acts have these people performed?

3. What are the differences between a private citizen we might call a hero and a "normal" person?

4. Add to your definition of the term hero to account for the private citizen you might consider a personal hero.

Journal Assignment

Reviewing Your Hero Discussions

Write about your class discussions. Were there any important heroes left out of your discussions? Write about the heroes and heroic qualities that interest you most. Also, write about any heroes in your own life or in your community.

Activity

Definition Paragraph

Write a focused paragraph in which you define a hero. Your topic sentence should announce the focus of your paragraph, and all of your body sentences should support this topic sentence. Remember to use the writing process (brainstorm, make choices, plan, draft, revise, edit). Keep this paragraph. You might want to include all or part of it in your essay.

Get Involved!

Rent and watch the film *Schindler's List* (1993) starring Liam Neeson, Ben Kingsley, and Ralph Fiennes and directed by Steven Spielberg. In your next class meeting, share your reactions to the film and discuss what it has to say about heroes as well as the Holocaust.

Writing Assignment #1: *Paying Tribute to a Personal Hero*

Here, in brief, is the writing assignment that you are preparing for.

Write an essay in which you define what a hero is and then prove that an individual person you know is a hero. Focus on only one person, and focus on only those qualities that make him or her a hero. Consider including information you find through talking to family members or friends who know or have known the individual.

Keep this assignment in mind as you proceed to dig deeper into the issue of heroes and prepare to write.

Read, Discuss, Think Critically

This section of the chapter offers a personal essay written about a family member, a hero of World War II. The author of the essay describes her uncle and the qualities and actions that made him a hero.

Reading Assignment: *"A Hero in My Family"*

Preview   Read the title and the first two paragraphs, which serve as the introduction. Read and highlight topic sentences.

Anticipate   What do you anticipate this essay will be about? Use the "Notes" column to record your thoughts.

Read and Reread   Read the essay once quickly, marking unknown terms. Then reread the essay, responding to ideas in the "Notes" column and highlighting important points. Define unknown words.

A Hero in My Family
by Megan Burroughs

(with permission from Elaine Roberts and Geoffrey Burroughs)

Megan Burroughs is a college English instructor and writer. This essay was written specifically for this textbook.

1   My girls, ages 2, 2, and 5, love Mulan, the lead character in Disney's film *Mulan.* A young Chinese girl, Mulan pretends to be a boy and, to the horror of her family, dresses as a soldier and runs off to fight the Huns in her father's place. To bring honor to her family, Mulan is supposed to be a traditional Chinese young lady—feminine, quiet, beautiful, and skilled in womanly tasks like serving tea and cooking. Mulan, however, is outspoken, athletic, and headstrong. She has her own ideas, and she pursues them against many odds. Compared to some of the other "heroes" my girls have taken a liking to—Batgirl, Snow White, and Sleeping Beauty—I like Mulan quite a bit. I consider her to be a positive role model.

2   Yet, the girls know (especially my 5-year-old) that Mulan is "pretend," and as Dennis Denenberg, a professor of education at Millersville University of Pennsylvania points out, children need real heroes—people, not fictional characters. My girls should learn about other heroes, people who have lived, accomplished great deeds, and made our world a better place. My girls need human footsteps to follow in. I have found a soldier in our own family whom I will tell the girls about someday when they put

down their Mulan weapons (wrapping paper tubes) long enough to listen. I can't swear that I have a complete picture of this hero. I can't swear that the early parts of the story haven't been embellished over the years. He is a legend in my family, and as such, he has reached a level of perfection in my memory. And yet all the early pieces of the story seem to lead so naturally to the end of the story (which I know is true) that I will confidently tell my girls this story of Uncle Spencer, a real hero in our family.

3   Early signs that Uncle Spencer might have the characteristics of a hero began to show when Spencer was just a boy. Spencer was a handsome, athletic leader among the boys in the neighborhood. He, 16 years older than my father, organized games for the boys to play—from soldiers to football. He was charismatic and the other kids loved him; they accepted him as a leader. As he grew older, he continued to shine as he completed college and pursued a law degree. My father once wrote in a poem about Spencer: "He was the first born son, / The scion of a family of lawyers, / Soon to graduate from Hastings / . . . He had the power to help us."

4   However, beyond having the personality and the intelligence to lead and succeed, Uncle Spencer had the integrity and sensitivity of a hero. As well-liked as he was, as busy as he was, he was also kind and thoughtful. My father also wrote: "He was also the brother ever there, / Who sensed a child's confusion. / A brother who could stop for "soldiers" / On the Sunday of his wedding to Elaine." I know this meant a lot to my dad. His brother was going to leave home to fight in World War II within a few weeks, and it was the day of his wedding. But Uncle Spencer put all that aside to share some time with his little brother and play "soldiers." My father wrote: "He had room for me. / It was never, 'I'm sorry, not right now.' / What I said was heard. / What I was told I understood." This is a man my father looked up to. This is a person my girls could look up to.

5   His integrity, leadership skills, and selflessness formed the foundation to Spencer's character, and in his final minutes he became a bona fide hero not only to my family but to other families and the nation as well. I cannot tell the story of his end any better than his commanding officer did in a letter to Spencer's wife. So, to you, reader, I submit the letter that tells how Uncle Spencer died a hero at age 25.

June 9, 1945

Dear Mrs. Burroughs:

6   It is with a heavy and saddened heart that I undertake to tell you of the death of your husband in action aboard this vessel last May twenty-seven. You have my utmost and sincerest sympathy in your bereavement. We

who are left to serve on are doing so with saddened spirits and a real feeling of loss. Every officer and man of this vessel is with me in the knowledge that we have lost a very dear friend and comrade, that you have lost a loving and devoted husband, and that our country has lost an admirable, able, and brave officer.

7   Sunday, May twenty-seven, had begun as a fine day for us, though we knew that enemy action might come at any moment. During the afternoon we received our mail, including packages of books and phonograph records for Spencer. After having admired the books and listened to the records we were called to general quarters as enemy planes were sighted.

8   Spencer was at his battle station supervising the firing of our after guns when an enemy plane loaded with explosives dived at us in a suicide dive. Though it was a dark night the guns gave a good account of themselves and the plane was forced to change its course and approach from astern. This put the whole burden of our defense on Spencer's gun. The men on the gun, inspired and encouraged by your husband, courageously kept up a heavy and effective fire despite the fact that the enemy plane was diving upon them at utmost speed.

9   When the plane was almost upon us their fire succeeded in detonating the bombs it carried, thus destroying the plane. The courage of your husband in facing this attack saved the lives of many, many of his shipmates, but cost him his own. He was struck in the temple by shrapnel from the exploding plane and was killed instantly. The Medical Officer and I were at his side almost immediately, but he passed away quietly and without suffering. A great sense of loss descended upon us at that moment, and will remain with us whose lives he saved until the time we can no longer feel loss or pain.

10   Spencer was buried with military honors on an Eastward slope of the military cemetery in this area. Close by is the grave of one of our men who perished with him. Had it not been for the unflinching courage of your husband in the performance of his duty those two graves might well have been twenty.

11   With this letter I send my prayer for the Divine to ease your grief and grant peace to your heart.

Sincerely,

John O. Harper

Questions for Critical Thought

"A Hero in My Family"

1. Burroughs doesn't come right out and list the qualities of a hero, but she does mention a number of specific qualities she considers to be heroic. Review the entire essay carefully and identify the heroic qualities Burroughs mentions. Do you think her Uncle Spencer is a hero? Why, or why not?

2. In this chapter, you've studied how thesis statements and topic sentences can help focus an essay. Write down Burroughs's thesis and topic sentences. Do they work well as tools for focus? Would you change or improve any of these sentences? If so, explain what you might change and why.

3. Identify any signs you can find that Burroughs is aware of her audience.

4. Burroughs includes interesting details in this essay that help support her ideas. (**Detail** is specific information that helps you understand ideas and perhaps paints a picture in your head.) Choose two details that help you understand and enjoy her essay.

5. In your own words, what is Burroughs's purpose in writing this essay? Who is her audience?

Journal Assignment

Personal Heroes

Write down your thoughts about heroes in general. Then write about one or two more personal heroes in a bit more detail. Why do they interest you? What impresses you about them? Exchange your journal with classmates, and when you are done reading your classmates' work, simply say, "Thank you" when returning their journals.

Explore the Writing Assignment

Here, again, is the writing assignment that you are preparing for.

Write an essay in which you define what a hero is and then prove that an individual person you know is a hero. Focus on only one person, and focus on only those qualities that make him or her a hero. Consider including information you find through talking to family members or friends who know or have known the individual.

It's important to explore your options before planning or drafting. The first topic you think of for an essay may not be the best. If you take the time to explore your options, you may find a topic that is even more interesting or worthwhile than the first one that popped into your head. You'll be putting considerable time into writing this essay, so give yourself the chance to find a personal hero to write about who truly interests you. (Be sure to choose a personal hero—not a public hero. You'll write about public heroes later in the chapter.)

Brainstorm   Spend 10 to 20 minutes and write freely about individuals you know personally or have heard about who have performed heroic deeds. Write as much as you can about each hero. If there is a person you are interested in but don't know much about, write down questions you have about that person. Also write down where you can go to find some answers. (Consider interviewing other family members or friends who may have known the person and the heroic deed.) When you have finished brainstorming, write down the name of the person you think you will write about and explain why you have chosen to focus on this person.

Gather Information About Heroes   Find some information on the person you have chosen. You may already have information (from personal experience or from listening to family stories over the years). If you don't have enough information, go to those who knew this person and ask for the basic facts (date of birth, place of birth, education, accomplishments, and date of death—if applicable). Then identify the admirable qualities and actions that make you consider this person a hero. Take notes as you speak to family and friends. If you quote a sentence or two from someone you interviewed, practice your quoting skills. (See pages 479–483 for information on using quotations in your essay.)

Think Critically About Your Choice of a Hero   Do you still want to write your essay about the person you chose? Why, or why not? Why is the person you've chosen considered a hero? If you have decided *not* to write about the person, you should go back and look at your brainstorm. Then talk to your instructor or a tutor. Think about why your first choice turned out to be unsatisfactory. Then make a new choice and find information on this new person.

Narrow Your Brainstorm   Once you have chosen your personal hero and gathered some basic information, you should write freely for approximately 30 minutes about anything connected to this person. Don't use your critical thinking skills at this point. Let your mind wander and don't worry about what you write. A good brainstorm is long and full of many different ideas. Some of the ideas will prove useful and others will not, but now is not the time to make those choices.

Notes

When you have finished your brainstorm, use your critical thinking skills and highlight the ideas that seem most likely to prove that the person you've chosen to write about is a hero.

Consider Your Audience   Before you actually begin thinking about your thesis or outline, you should consider who is in your audience and what they want to know. Thinking about your audience will help you begin to focus your thoughts and determine what must be included in your essay.

Activities

Audience

In small groups, ask each other the following questions.

1. What do you know about my hero?

2. What would you like to know about my hero?

3. Do you think the person I have chosen is a hero?

When you have answers to these questions, write down your own description of a larger audience. Who is in your audience? What do they know and not know about the hero you have chosen? Will you have to persuade your readers that your hero is, indeed, a hero? Assume that your audience extends beyond your classroom. What kinds of information about heroes in general do you want to share with this larger audience? What specific information about your hero seems important?

Speak Your Mind

Share your responses to the following prompts with a classmate. (Be sure to make notes so that you can use them when you outline and draft your essay.)

1. My definition of a hero is . . .

2. The person I have chosen as a hero has the following characteristics (he or she doesn't have to have all the characteristics in the hero definition) . . .

3. The main points I should cover in my essay are . . .

4. I probably don't need to mention the following information in my essay:

Create Your Thesis   Remember that a thesis statement is the sentence that expresses the main idea of your essay. It usually comes at the end of your introduction, and everything else in the essay should connect to and support this thesis. Obviously, it is an important element in your essay. You'll want to experiment with different ways of expressing your main idea. While you are experimenting with the thesis statement, you'll find that you are thinking critically about exactly what you want to prove in your essay.

Review the writing assignment, your brainstorm, activities, and class notes and write a thesis statement for your essay. You may need to write a few thesis statements before you create one that expresses your ideas well. Share your thesis statement with your classmates, tutor, and instructor. Ask them what they expect your essay to be about. Think critically about what they say and about your own reaction to your thesis statement. Is it too broad? Too narrow? Your thesis should give your reader a clear sense of where your essay is going and why.

Outline   After revising and polishing your thesis statement, copy it down on a clean piece of paper and experiment with possible topic sentences for your essay. (*Note:* For a well-focused essay, your topic sentences must clearly support your thesis.) Be careful of topic sentences that give facts rather than state the main idea of a paragraph. For example, a topic sentence that says, "He was born in 1852," does not give the reader a good sense of what that paragraph will be about. Such a sentence also does not show how the paragraph will support the idea that "he" is a hero. Your topic sentences will probably each focus on a different heroic quality you see in your hero.

Revise your topic sentences until they seem clear and effective. List them beneath your thesis statement. You may also want to list a few pieces of support under each topic sentence to remind yourself of the type of information that will go into the body of each paragraph. Share this outline with classmates, a tutor, or your instructor. Can your reader(s) tell what your essay will be about? Does everything connect to your thesis?

Feel free to change and revise your outline at any time during your writing process. The outline should be a guide, not something that forces you to state something you are no longer satisfied with.

Notes

Draft

At this stage of the writing process, you want to create a complete essay (introduction, body, and conclusion). However, remember that this is a work in progress, and you should not try to make the draft perfect. Striving for perfection at this stage will probably just make you worry about every word you put on paper. You will have the chance to revise later. In fact, you, like many writers, may write many drafts—each one better than the previous one.

When you are ready to draft your essay, remember that you should assume that your reading audience doesn't know very much, if anything, about the hero you are focusing on, so it's your job to provide important information about this person and why he or she is a hero. Your introduction should define heroes and generally explain why the person you selected is considered a hero. In your body paragraphs, describe in more detail the different heroic qualities your personal hero possesses. In your conclusion, tell your reader what you've learned from writing this essay and what you want the reader to learn from it.

Revise

This is the stage in the writing process in which you change and improve your draft. As you complete this stage, you may find that you actually produce a number of drafts. It is important to have someone review your work and respond to your ideas. Don't worry about sentence corrections yet. Put your energy into improving the *focus, development,* and *organization* of your essay.

Activity

Share Your Writing

Find a classmate to work with. Discuss the following questions as they relate to your essay.

- Do you have a clear definition of what a hero is?

- Do you focus on just one person in your essay?

- Do you focus on only those qualities that make your person a hero? (For example, you might remember your mother making great lemon meringue pies when you were a kid, but you wouldn't mention that in your essay because it doesn't explain why she is a hero.)

- Is there enough specific evidence that this person is a hero? Do you have enough facts? Do you need to find out more about this person?

- Check the coherence of your essay. Will your reader see how each piece of information connects to your point that this person is a hero?

Edit

Now is the time to work on polishing your sentences. The goal is to make your ideas clear and to project a professional image so that your reader will respect your work.

Read your essay aloud and look (and listen) for awkward spots and typographical errors.

Review your essay again, slowly, sentence by sentence, and consider the following:

- Are there any errors that you tend to repeat? Focus on them one at a time.

- Is there a certain area your instructor wants you to focus on?

You may also want to consider these questions after completing the sentence work at the end of the chapter.

- Are you using pronouns to improve the flow and coherence of your essay without overusing them?

- Do your pronouns agreee in number with their antecedents?

Now begin "polishing" your essay. Carefully check for typing errors, spelling errors, and any other errors you tend to make. Also, review your essay for sentence variety.

- Can you use coordinators, transitions, or subordinators to add variety and clarify the relationships between the ideas in your essay?

- Can you add useful information to your essay by including prepositional or participial phrases in some of your sentences?

- Are there any misspelled words? Use spell check on your computer, or get out your dictionary and look up any words you are uncertain about. Do this early enough so that if you need it, you can get help from a tutor or instructor.

Notes

Specific words to be aware of in this assignment include the following:

- hero/heroes (notice that the singular form doesn't have an *e* on the end),
- the name of your hero, and
- the names of places and events (like your hero's birthplace, and so on).

Have you quoted any sources (relatives or friends you interviewed)? If so, be sure to identify the source and place direct quotations in quotation marks. (See "Using Outside Sources" on pages 479–483 for review.)

Writing Assignment #2: Honoring Our Public Heroes

Here, in brief, is the writing assignment that you are preparing for.

Write an essay about a heroic public figure. Focus on only one person, and focus on only those qualities that make him or her a hero. Prove to your audience why and how that person fits the definition of "hero." Be sure to include information you find through research.

Keep this assignment in mind as you proceed to dig deeper into the issue of heroes and prepare to write.

Read, Discuss, Think Critically

Get Involved!

Two more essays on heroes appear in Supplemental Readings: "How One Woman Became the Voice of Her People" is about Aung San Suu Kyi's leadership in the Burmese struggle for democracy (pages 409–414); "Who Is Great?" explains how we evaluate those we consider great (pages 414–418). Read one or both essays and come to class prepared to discuss what you've learned.

Two additional readings about heroes follow. The author of the first essay looks at many different kinds of heroes and discusses the role of heroes in our lives. The author of the later essay discusses a specific hero and the qualities and actions that made this person a hero.

Reading Assignment:
"Move Over, Barney: Make Way for Some Real Heroes"

Preview   This is a long essay. Begin previewing and reading when you have enough time to read the entire essay without being interrupted. Read the title and the first two paragraphs. Read and highlight topic sentences.

Anticipate   What do you think this essay will be about? Use the "Notes" column to record your response.

Read and Reread   Read the entire essay, marking unknown terms and interesting points. Then reread more slowly and use the

"Notes" column to interact with the essay. Use your dictionary to define unknown words.

Move Over, Barney: Make Way for Some Real Heroes
by Dennis Denenberg

This essay was published in the *American Educator*, a magazine published by the American Federation of Teachers, a labor union. Dennis Denenberg is a full professor of education at Millersville University of Pennsylvania. He and Lorraine Roscoe are the authors of *Hooray for Heroes* (Scarecrow Press, 1994), an annotated guide to children's books and activities about outstanding men and women, and *50 American Heroes Every Kid Should Meet!* (Millbrook Press, 2001).

1   William Penn was an obsession for Elaine Peden, the *Philadelphia Inquirer Magazine* reported in 1991. Peden had devoted enormous time and energy to promoting recognition of Pennsylvania's founder. In 1984, she had persuaded Congress to extend honorary United States citizenship to both Penn and his wife, Hannah. But her successes in bringing Penn into the consciousness of Americans had been soured for her by disappointments. When she visited the restored William Penn statue on top of Philadelphia's City Hall, she expected to see again in the waiting areas the seventy-five paintings of events in the life of the Penns done by high school students. Instead she found a blowup of the Phillie Phanatic, the cartoonish mascot of the city's professional baseball team. The city's founder was out: The city's newest fantasy figure was in.

2   The situation is not much better at our country's official museum. Recently, the Smithsonian Institution's National Museum of American History published a new brochure to guide kids through the museum. It is written around the Charles Schulz figures, with their pictures everywhere. So there's Snoopy leading our kids around our national history museum—instead of Sacagawea who led Lewis and Clark across our nation!

3   We continually think we have to "dumb down" things to amuse kids. Well, we don't have to. We can challenge them to think, and most of them will love it and rise to the occasion. Our national history museum exists to teach us about our history, and while pop culture is a part of it, it should not dominate the turf. Harriet Tubman risked her life to lead more than 300 slaves to freedom—imagine the exciting trail she could lead kids on through the museum. Instead, there's Lucy entertaining the kids, and probably boring them, too.

4   Classrooms and homes around the United States resemble that Smithsonian brochure and the Philadelphia City Hall waiting area. Pictures of great people have given way to fantasy creatures. At one time many—if not most—public school classrooms in America displayed

Notes

portraits of George Washington and Abraham Lincoln. Today, if such portraits appear at all, it is usually for a two-week period in February, during Presidents Day commemorations. In their place, Garfield (the cat, not the president), Michelangelo and Leonardo (the turtles, not the artists), and of course, Walt Disney's Mickey Mouse and his numerous compatriots hold prominent positions. They, not great women and men, are the figures young people see repeatedly—and come to think of as "heroes."

5   I have visited hundreds of classrooms over the past twenty years. I have talked with teachers, observed displays, and examined curriculum materials, and I have become aware of how fantasy figures compete with real-life heroes for students' attention. Often, the fantasy ones are winning.

6   Cartoon and other fantasy characters pervade children's lives. Little Mermaids and big Beasts adorn the clothing kids wear and the lunch pails they carry. Think of kids in the world today. A little girl gets up in the morning. Her head probably rested on an Aladdin pillowcase. She goes down to breakfast and eats cereal from a box with a cartoon character on it, then gets dressed in a T-shirt with Bugs Bunny on it, picks up her Garfield lunch pail, and heads off to school where there is a bulletin board with cartoon figures on it.

7   Teachers and parents choose such materials so frequently, they tell me, because they believe these figures have motivational value. Cartoon mice and ducks are familiar. "They can be comforting to kids," parents and teachers say.

8   Perhaps fantasy characters motivate and comfort. But junk food motivates and comforts, too. Like junk food, popular fantasy and cartoon characters are sweet, enticing to the eye—and empty of real value. Like junk food, they displace what is more important. They fill kids up. The kids no longer hunger for the nourishment they need to become healthy, fully mature adults.

9   Is it any wonder that teenagers become hooked on the next level of fad fantasy figures—the super-rich athletes and popular culture rock and entertainment stars. Their presence in the media is everywhere, with entire cable channels devoted to the icons of music and athletics. So the Barney T-shirts eventually become Smashing Pumpkins shirts, Power Ranger backpacks become Dennis Rodman gym bags, and the very innocent Little Mermaid poster in a child's bedroom is replaced by a nearly life-sized one of Madonna (and not the religious one!). Think about it: It's an easy transition from the fantasy world of Spiderman for kids to the unreal world of Michael Jackson for teenagers.

10   The over-presence of fantasy characters in our culture and in our schools and homes contributes, I am convinced, to a confusion for our children and adolescents about the value of real-life human accomplish-

ments. It is not surprising, I think, that when in 1991, a Harrisburg-area school district asked its fifth to twelfth graders to name people they most admired, the teenagers chose rock stars, athletes, and television personalities, people who often seem to be larger than life. Other than Nelson Mandela, no famous people from any other field of endeavor were mentioned. No great artists, inventors, humanitarians, political leaders, composers, scientists, doctors—none were mentioned by the 1,150 students.

11   Likewise, when the Scripps-Howard newspaper chain asked a representative sample of twenty-five- to forty-five-year-olds to write a two-page essay about their favorite hero, there were a lot of blank pages; 60 percent of the group said they have no personal heroes.

12   I frequently am asked to give presentations on why heroes are important for children. I sometimes begin by putting on the familiar Mickey Mouse ears, and I lead my adult audience in a rousing rendition of the "Mickey Mouse club" song. Almost everyone knows the words. Then I switch to a colonial hat and recite a portion of the Patrick Henry speech that ends with a very famous line (or at least what once was a very famous line). I leave it to the audience to finish the speech, but few can. The comparison with the Mickey Mouse song leads to a spirited discussion of what has happened to real heroes in our culture.

13   "Look around," I say to my audiences. "You're surrounded by people. Count thirty people, yourself among them. One of that thirty would probably have polio if it weren't for Jonas Salk. That's how prevalent polio was. But when Salk died two years ago, we as a nation hardly took notice. Certainly, few young people have any sense of how that great doctor saved their generation from a crippling disease."

14   Have we lost a generation of people who don't have heroes, who don't know what a hero is or don't understand what a positive influence a hero can be in a person's life?

15   A hero is an individual who can serve as an example. He or she has the ability to persevere, to overcome the hurdles that impede others' lives. While this intangible quality of greatness appears almost magical, it is indeed most human. And it is precisely because of that humanness that some individuals attain heroic stature. They are of us, but are clearly different.

16   We look to heroes and heroines for inspiration. Through their achievements, we see humankind more positively. They make us feel good. They make us feel proud. For some of us they become definite role models, and our lives follow a different direction because of their influence. For others, while the effect may be less dramatic, it is of no less import, for these heroes make us think in new ways. Their successes and failures lead us to ponder our own actions and inactions. By learning about *their* lives, *our* lives become enriched.

Notes

17   Molly Pitcher saw what had to be done and did it. Women had a defined role in the war; they were a vital support to the fighting colonials. But when her husband was wounded, and the cannon needed to be fired, she knew what she had to do. Molly Pitcher was, and is, a heroine, and her story deserves to be told and retold. Neither a great statesman or soldier, she was an ordinary person who performed an extraordinary deed.

18   Michelangelo spent a lifetime at his craft, leaving the world a legacy of magnificent paintings and sculptures. His hard work was a daily reaffirmation of his belief in a human's creative potential. Through toil, he produced artistic monuments that have continued to inspire generations.

19   This world has had (and still has) many Molly Pitchers and Michelangeloes, people who set examples that inspire others. Some had only a fleeting moment of glory in a rather normal life, but oh, what a moment. Others led a life of longer-lasting glory and had a more sustained impact on humankind. All were individuals who, through their achievements, made positive contributions.

20   Where are the heroines and heroes for children today? They are everywhere! They are the figures from our past, some in the historical limelight, others still in the shadows. They are the men and women of the present, struggling to overcome personal and societal problems to build a better world.

21   Indeed they are everywhere, but most children know so very few of them. Quite simply, in our schools and in our homes, we have removed these great people from our focus. They have become "persona non grata" instead of persons of importance. The greats are still around; they have merely been removed from everyone's view.

22   "Once upon a time . . ." kids had heroes, and lots of them. Some of these great individuals were real (Lincoln, et al.); others were legendary (such as Paul Bunyan and Casey Jones); still others, like Hercules, were of a different realm altogether. Most of them were male and white, as if heroics somehow knew gender and racial lines of distinction. Frequently, kids pretended to be these heroes or at the very least their followers. Since not every boy could be King Arthur, the others could be Knights of the Round Table. Yes, it was clearly better to be the King, but even as a knight, one got to slay a dragon now and then. All—kings and knights—were capable of great deeds!

23   These heroes seemed to be everywhere. They were part of the curriculum, so textbooks and other reading materials (even the classic comic books) provided details of their adventures. The movies portrayed details of their adventures. The movies portrayed them in action, adding

an exciting visual dimension. Heroes truly came alive for kids, who not only learned about them but, often, learned values from them.

24   Whether or not "the Father of Our Country" ever did chop down a cherry tree is not a question of significant historical importance. What is telling is that for generations the story helped children understand the meaning of honesty. Even heroes had faults, but they were moral enough to admit their errors.

25   The inclusion of heroes in schools served dual purposes. In addition to learning about specific great individuals, students also were exposed to the ethical nature of those persons. The presence of heroes provided a focus for children's dreams and wishes, and those heroes were cloaked in mantles of virtuous behavior.

26   As the advertising industry grew, however, heroes became displaced persons and virtually disappeared from children's views. Through the wonders of the mass media, a whole new array of characters became a daily part of American culture. Cartoon creatures and company advertising mascots existed for many decades, but not until the advent of megacommunications did they intrude into everyone's lives in a seemingly unending manner. Billboards, print ads, television and radio programs, commercials, videotapes, and many other avenues provide ads "ad infinitum." Even while relaxing on the beach, one's attention is pulled skyward to read the fly-by advertisements.

27   The issue is not so much that they have joined the ranks of known figures, it is rather that they have totally replaced real heroes for children. Today the role models are often whatever the latest commercial fad creatures happen to be. Once the new character catches the public's attention, the merchandising machine marches on. The T-shirts, buttons, books, book bags, greeting cards, games and toys, trading cards, movies, and, of course, television series all follow in rapid succession. The presence of the latest sensation dominates the child's world. Consciousness leads to demands for the newest marketable item bearing the creature's image. And everywhere—in the child's mind, in the home, and in the classroom—the character assumes a new status of heroic proportions. It's out with Ben Franklin entirely; here comes the Mouse!

28   I think parents and teachers should replace many of these fantasy characters with *real* heroes, real-life women and men. We should "de-mouse" (to start with the most successful cartoon character of all time) not only the classroom, but our homes, as well. We should offer people of significance equal space and time.

29   For what I like to call a "De-mousing Starter's List," I would choose people whom I think American children should know. We need to show our children that heroes come from both sexes, every race, every ethnic

One individual who has resisted the commercialization of his creation is Bill Watterson, famous for his brilliant *Calvin and Hobbes* strip. Now retired from drawing the strip (because he felt his ideas were becoming redundant), Mr. Watterson did something unheard of in the fad business. How many stuffed Hobbes tigers do you see in the store? How many *Calvin and Hobbes* backpacks? T-shirts? bed sheets? juice glasses? and so on and so on . . . . None! Because Mr. Watterson believes fantasy figures belong on the comic page, not in every aspect of our children's lives. Hooray for a real hero—Bill Watterson, to whom principles are more important than money. [Denenberg's note.]

Notes

Get Involved!

Go to Time.com to read about "The Most Important People of the 20th Century," located at www.time.com/ time/time100/. While at the site, click on the Time 100 Game: Place the Face. See how many important figures and heroes you recognize. Be ready to discuss some of these people when you return to class.

background, and every field of human endeavor. Young people need to encounter images of Thomas Edison, Jane Addams, George C. Marshall, and Cal Ripken, Jr. They need to come in contact with Lech Walesa and Mother Teresa, with Stephen Hawking and Rosa Parks. They should learn about the real Michelangelo instead of knowing only his modern-day amphibian namesake. . . .

30   Let me emphasize that in the efforts to bring great people to the attention of children, balance and focus must be watchwords. Flooding the classroom, school, or home with dozens of pictures of famous people may have little effect. I would be selective and concentrate on a few people at a time, so that a genuine understanding and appreciation can be established. And I would focus on the essence of the individual's contribution to humanity, not the minutia that so often ends up obscuring a hero's greatness.

31   Balanced, focused attention to significant people may mean that even Walt Disney becomes a hero. We should, perhaps, give time and space to the cartoonist whose studio has helped create such an unbalanced attention to fantasy creatures.

32   No doubt many parents and teachers have already taken up the cause. It is time for the rest of us to return great individuals to the pedestals they deserve. Young people need to see that humans can and do make a difference. Children can learn that they too are capable of reshaping life in a positive way. By reintroducing heroes to children, parents and teachers can show them that there are real people worthy of recognition and emulation.

Questions for Critical Thought

"Move Over, Barney. . . ."

1. a. Denenberg says cartoon figures are taking over and replacing real-life heroes. What examples does he give that cartoon figures are everywhere in children's lives?

    b. How does including examples help a writer prove his or her point?

2. a. In Paragraph 8, Denenberg chooses to make a comparison between cartoon figures and junk food. Explain what he is saying here. Do you agree?

    b. Think about the comparison between cartoon figures and junk food. How do comparisons help a writer explain ideas?

3. In Paragraph 9, Denenberg says that as children get older, they trade in their childish heroes for other pop heroes. What doesn't

Denenberg like about kids having Dennis Rodman or Madonna   *Notes*
(or other popular figures) as their heroes?

4. Why is it important for kids to know about the other kinds of heroes Denenberg mentions at the end of Paragraph 10 (artists, inventors, humanitarians, political leaders, composers, scientists, and
   doctors)?

5. In Paragraph 16, Denenberg says, "We look to heroes and heroines
   for inspiration." He also says, "For some of us they become definite role models, and our lives follow a different direction because
   of their influence." Can you think of a hero who has influenced
   you or anyone you know? How has that hero been an influence?

6. Does Denenberg want to completely get rid of cartoon heroes?
   Give proof from the essay to support your answer.

7. The last word in this essay is *emulation*. What does this word
   mean? (If you are unsure of the meaning, first try to figure out the
   meaning by using context clues. Then use a dictionary. See "Building Your Vocabulary" in Section IV to review *context clues*.)

8. *Emulation* and *emulate* are key words when discussing heroes. Put
   each word into a sentence of your own. (Consider using these
   words in your essay about heroes.)

9. a. Who is Denenberg's audience?

   b. What is his purpose? (What does he hope his audience will learn
      from his essay?)

   c. Denenberg's essay is well focused even though it doesn't have a
      stated thesis. Create a thesis that expresses Denenberg's main idea.

Reading Assignment:
"Rosa Parks Joins Children's Wall of Heroes"

Preview   Read the title, the information about the author, and
where the essay was published. Read the first few paragraphs.

Anticipate   What do you anticipate this essay will be about? Record
your response in the "Notes" column.

Read and Reread   Because this essay is written by a journalist and
was published in a newspaper, we can guess that it will be written in
journalistic style. This style and the relatively short length of the essay suggest that you will be able to read this essay fairly quickly and

easily. (Consider reading it all the way through once before marking anything.) When rereading, define terms and use the "Notes" column.

Rosa Parks Joins Children's Wall of Heroes
by Sandy Banks

Sandy Banks is a *Los Angeles Times* columnist. This essay was published in the editorial section of the *Sacramento Bee* on April 23, 1998.

1   You would have thought I'd announced a meeting with one of the Spice Girls, from the reaction I got at home.

2   "I can't believe you get to meet her, in person."

3   "Please, please, Mom, can I go with you?"

4   And, to a friend, "You won't believe who my mom is taking us to meet."

5   The object of their excitement wasn't a rock diva or movie star. It was an elderly woman—hardly bigger than my oldest child—who rolled toward us in a wheelchair, climbed out carefully and adjusted her pillbox hat before extending a soft brown hand to each of my daughters.

6   "So pleased to meet you," she said, asking each girl her name, gazing straight into their shining eyes. "I'm Mrs. Rosa Parks."

7   I don't recall that I even knew her name as a child, although she's known the world over now as the mother of the civil rights movement.

8   The Rev. Martin Luther King Jr. was the reigning hero of the movement-in-progress when I was growing up in the 1950s and 1960s. But it is Rosa Parks who ignited the indignation of the masses 43 years ago with her simple act of defiance aboard a Montgomery, Ala., bus.

9   Then a middle-age seamstress, Parks was tired from eight hours on her feet when she boarded the bus that would take her home from work. Blacks were banned from the first four rows, so she settled in the middle section, which could be occupied by either whites or blacks. But segregationist Jim Crow laws dictated that if a white passenger needed a seat, all the black people seated in those middle rows had to get up and move, so that no white person would have to sit next to a black passenger.

10   That day, though, as whites filled the bus, Parks merely sighed, slid closer to the window to make room on her seat and told the driver, "I am not going to move."

11   Police were called, and Parks was arrested. She was bailed out of jail by a local civil rights activist, who then enlisted a young minister—26-year-old King—to help organize a boycott of the city's bus line.

12 The yearlong boycott—which ended when the U.S. Supreme Court ruled that Montgomery's bus segregation laws were unconstitutional— garnered Parks a place in history but cost her her job and forced her and her husband, Raymond, to move north to Detroit to rebuild their lives.

13 It also made her an international symbol of courage, whose influence reaches to the children of today.

14 I suppose we were too close to the moment when I was growing up to appreciate the import of what she did. History only becomes historic when you can stand back and view it through the prism of time.

15 It is different for my daughters—who learn about our struggle for civil rights as they celebrate Martin Luther King's birthday and study Black History Month in their mostly white schools.

16 And it is Rosa Parks who represents to them all that was good about that tumultuous period of our country's history—with an act so straightforward that even my first-grader can understand: A tired woman on a bus, who simply decided not to get pushed around anymore; whose refusal to stand struck a blow for fairness and freedom, and spoke volumes about courage and righteousness and faith.

17 There is a majesty in that looming larger for my children than all they have learned about marches on Washington and Supreme Court decisions—mighty events, but beyond their grasp.

18 It's an overly simplistic view of history, I know—reducing it to one moment, one woman. But I don't mind.

19 It is enough to see my daughters glowing with pride, as I snap their photo standing next to this small, brave, 85-year-old woman from their history books.

20 And to know that Puff Daddy, Leonardo DiCaprio and the Spice Girls have to move over. They're about to be bumped by a new face on the bedroom wall.

Notes

Questions for Critical Thought

"Rosa Parks Joins. . . ."

1. Try to put yourself in Rosa Parks's place on that bus. Think about how she was feeling as she sat down and the many different emotions she must have gone through as she decided to stay in her seat and deal with the consequences. Describe how you think she might have felt as she sat down, as she spoke to the bus driver, and as she was arrested. Describe how you think she felt when she lost her job and had to move.

2. In what ways is Rosa Parks a hero?

3. Banks seems to think like Denenberg: they're both glad to see popular figures "move over" to make room for other heroes. Why would Banks rather have a poster of Rosa Parks on the wall than, say, a poster of the Spice Girls or Leonardo DiCaprio?

4. Because Banks's essay is not written in academic form, she doesn't have an introductory paragraph with a thesis statement at the end. Review her essay and find sentences that come close to expressing the main idea of the essay. Can you find a sentence that expresses the overall focus of the essay? Explain.

Journal Assignment

Heroes

Write down your thoughts about public heroes in general. Do any particular people come to mind? In what ways do they interest or impress you? Exchange your journal with classmates, and when you are done reading your classmates' work, simply say, "Thank you" when returning their journals.

Explore the Writing Assignment

Here, again, is the writing assignment that you are preparing for.

Write an essay about a heroic public figure. Focus on only one person, and focus on only those qualities that make him or her a hero. Prove to your audience why and how that person fits the definition of "hero." Be sure to include information you find through research.

Now it's time to explore your options even further. As you've probably discovered, the first topic you think of for an essay may not be the best. When you take the time to explore your options, you often find a topic that is even better than the first. Because you'll be putting considerable time into writing this essay, be sure to select a public hero you really want to know more about. (Be sure to keep source notes throughout the writing process so that you'll be able to cite your sources easily when you write your essay.)

Brainstorm   Spend ten to 20 minutes writing freely about as many public heroes as you can think of. Refer to the list on page 182 to help you get started. Also, refer to your class notes and the readings in this chapter. What do you know about each hero? Write down the questions you would like to have answered about each hero. If there is a person you are interested in but don't know much about, write down questions you have about that person. When you have finished brainstorming, evaluate the names that have come up. Narrow the list to the person you most admire. Write down why you admire this person.

Gather Information About Heroes   Locate information on the person you have chosen. You may already have information (from essays in this book, materials at home, or readings from your instructor). However, if you don't have enough information, go to the library (or the Internet) and research this person. Find out the basic facts (date of birth, place of birth, education, accomplishments, and date of death—if applicable). Then identify the heroic qualities and actions that make this person a hero. Take notes and record your source information (author, title, and source). Use your own words. Do not copy your research sources. If you find a sentence or two in a source that is worth quoting, practice your quotation skills. (See pages 479–483 for help in using outside sources.)

Think Critically About Your Choice of a Hero   Evaluate why the person you researched is considered a hero. If you have decided *not* to write about the person you researched, you should return to your brainstorm, select another candidate from your list, and then research that person. You may want to talk to your instructor or a tutor. Think about why your first choice turned out to be unsatisfactory. Then make a new choice and find information on this new person.

Narrow Your Brainstorm   Once you have chosen a hero and gathered some basic information, freewrite for 30 minutes on your hero. Don't use your critical thinking skills at this point. Let your mind wander and don't worry about what you write. Some of the ideas will prove useful, and others will not, but now is not the time to make those choices.

When you have finished your brainstorm, go back, use your critical thinking skills, and highlight the ideas that seem most promising to you.

Notes

Consider Your Audience   Before drafting your thesis or outline, you should consider who is in your audience and what they want to know. Thinking about your audience will help you begin to focus your thoughts and determine what must be included in your essay.

Activities

Audience

In small groups, ask each other the following questions.

1. What do you know about my hero?

2. What would you like to know about my hero?

3. Do you think the person I have chosen is a hero?

When you have answers to these questions, write down your own description of a larger audience. Who is in your audience? What do they know and not know about the hero you have chosen? Will you have to persuade your readers that your public hero is, indeed, a hero? Assume that your audience extends beyond your classroom. What kinds of information about heroes in general do you want to share with this larger audience? What specific information about your hero seems important? What distinguishes your hero from other public figures?

Speak Your Mind

Share your responses to the following prompts with a classmate. (Be sure to make notes so that you can use them when you outline and draft your essay.)

1. My definition of a hero is . . .

2. The person I have chosen as a public hero has the following characteristics (he or she doesn't have to have all the characteristics in the hero definition) . . .

3. The main points I should cover in my essay are . . .

4. I probably don't need to mention the following information in my essay:

Create Your Thesis   Your thesis statement is the sentence that expresses the main idea of your essay. As you've learned, it usually comes at the end of your introduction. The body paragraphs of the essay should connect to and support this thesis. To create a successful thesis, you'll want to experiment with different ways of stating your main idea. While you are experimenting with the thesis statement, you'll find that you are thinking critically about exactly what you want to prove in your essay.

Notes

Review the writing assignment, your brainstorm, activities, and class notes and write a thesis statement for your essay. You may need to write a few thesis statements before you develop the statement that best expresses who your hero is and why. Share your thesis statement with your classmates, tutor, and instructor. Ask them what they expect your essay to be about. Think critically about what they say and about your own reaction to your thesis statement. Is it too broad? Too narrow? Your thesis should give your reader a clear sense of where your essay is going and why.

Outline   After revising and polishing your thesis statement, copy it down on a clean piece of paper and experiment with possible topic sentences for your essay. (*Note:* For a well-focused essay, your topic sentences must clearly support your thesis.) Be careful of topic sentences that give facts rather than state the main idea of a paragraph. For example, a topic sentence that says, "He was born in 1852," does not give the reader a good sense of what that paragraph will be about. Such a sentence also does not show how the paragraph will support the idea that "he" is a hero. Your topic sentences will probably each focus on a different heroic quality you see in your hero.

Revise your topic sentences until they seem clear and effective. List them beneath your thesis statement. Also list a few pieces of support under each topic sentence to remind yourself of the type of information that will go into the body of each paragraph. Outside information would fit well in the body of your essay. (To avoid plagiarism, be sure to use quotation marks around words taken directly from sources and always include in your essay where you found the information.)

Share this outline with classmates, a tutor, or your instructor. Can your reader(s) tell what your essay will be about? Does everything connect to your thesis?

Feel free to change and revise your outline at any time during your writing process. The outline should be a guide, not something that forces you to state something you are no longer satisfied with.

Notes

Draft

Now it's time to write a complete draft of your essay (introduction, body, and conclusion). Since this is a work in progress, you don't have to make the draft perfect. Remember that you will have the chance to revise later. In fact, you, like most writers, will write many drafts, each showing improvement over the previous one.

As you write, you should assume that your readers have probably heard of the public hero you've chosen, though they may not know many details about the hero's deeds. So it's your job to provide important information about this person and why he or she is a hero. Your introduction should define public heroes and generally explain why the person you selected is considered a hero. In your body paragraphs, describe in more detail the different heroic qualities the hero you've chosen possesses. You may want to turn to "Using Outside Sources" on pages 479–483 for some pointers on presenting quotations. That section also reminds you that most quotations need to be followed by an explanation so that your reader understands the quotation and its relationship to your main point. In your conclusion, tell your reader what you've learned from writing this essay and what you want the reader to learn from it.

Revise

This is the stage in the writing process in which you change and improve your draft. As you complete this stage, you may find that you actually produce a number of drafts. It is important to have someone review your work and respond to your ideas. Don't worry about sentence corrections yet. Put your energy into improving the *focus, development*, and *organization* of your essay.

Activity

Share Your Writing

Find a classmate to work with. Discuss the following questions as they relate to your essay.

- Do you have a clear definition of what a public hero is?

- Do you focus on just one person in your essay?

- Do you focus on only those qualities that make your person a hero? (For example, George Washington may have been an excellent card player, but you wouldn't mention that in the essay because it doesn't explain why he is a hero.)

- Is there enough specific evidence that this person is a hero? Do you have enough facts? Do you need to do more research?

- Check the coherence of your essay. Will your reader see how each piece of information connects to your point that this person is a hero?

Edit

Now that you've revised your essay and have cited sources correctly, it's time to work on polishing your sentences. The goal is to make your ideas clear and to project a professional image so that your reader will respect your work.

Read your essay aloud and look (and listen) for awkward spots and typographical errors.

Review your essay again, slowly, sentence by sentence, and consider the following:

- Are there any errors that you tend to repeat? Focus on them one at a time.
- Is there a certain area your instructor wants you to focus on?

You may also want to consider these questions after completing the sentence work at the end of the chapter.

- Are you using pronouns to improve the flow and coherence of your essay without overusing them?
- Do your pronouns agree in number with their antecedents?

Now begin "polishing" your essay. Carefully check for typing errors, spelling errors, and any other errors you tend to make. Also, review your essay for sentence variety.

- Can you use coordinators, transitions, or subordinators to add variety and clarify the relationships between the ideas in your essay?
- Can you add useful information to your essay by including prepositional or participial phrases in some of your sentences?
- Are there any misspelled words? Use spell check on your computer, or get out your dictionary and look up any words you are uncertain about. Do this early enough so that if you need it, you can get help from a tutor or instructor.

Notes
Specific words to be aware of in this assignment include the following:

- hero/heroes (notice that the singular form doesn't have an *e* on the end),
- the name of your hero, and
- the names of places and events (like your hero's birthplace, and so on).

Are you using outside sources correctly? (See "Using Outside Sources" pages 479–483 for examples.)

Writing Assignment #3: Analyzing a Film, Hero

In the next assignment, you'll study a film called *Hero*, which does not offer the typical Hollywood hero. The realistic story in this film will challenge you as you analyze the characters. Here, in brief, is the writing assignment that you are preparing for:

Write an essay in which you argue that Bernie LaPlante is a hero, or write an essay in which you argue that John Bubber is a hero. Focus on only one of these men and only on those events in the film that connect to the issue of heroism.

Keep this assignment in mind as you dig deeper into the film and prepare to write.

View, Discuss, Think Critically

As you view the film, take notes. You should view the film more than once. You should also discuss the film and share your notes with classmates.

View the film *Hero*, directed by Stephen Frears, 1992, with

Dustin Hoffman as Bernie LaPlante,

Geena Davis as Gale Gayley, and

Andy Garcia as John Bubber.

Questions for Critical Thought

Hero

1. Which of the two main characters (LaPlante or Bubber) looks more like a typical hero? Do heroes look a certain way?

2. Does a hero have to want to perform a heroic task in order to be called a hero? What if he or she does it by accident or unwillingly?

3. Was John Bubber a hero? What heroic acts did he perform? Why? When? How? In what ways was John Bubber not a hero? What unheroic acts did he perform? Why? When? How?

4. Was Bernie LaPlante a hero? What heroic acts did he perform? Why? When? How? In what ways was Bernie LaPlante not a hero? What unheroic acts did he perform? Why? When? How?

5. Discuss the following quotes from the movie. Do you agree or disagree with them? Why?

John Bubber (when he first hears Bernie LaPlante's story): "A lot of people would say that's what heroism is—stupidity. Doing something that if you thought about it, you wouldn't do it if it's not in your interest."

John Bubber (near the end of the movie): "I think we're all heroes if you catch us at the right moment. We all have something noble and decent in us trying to get out, and we're all less than heroic at other times."

Journal Assignment

The Hero(es) in Hero

Review "Activity—Film Heroes" on page 181 and your notes about heroes. You may also want to look again at the readings earlier in this chapter. Write your thoughts about this film. Specifically, think about LaPlante and Bubber and their heroic and nonheroic qualities. Exchange your journal with classmates, and when you are done reading your classmates' work, simply say, "Thank you" when returning their journals.

Explore the Writing Assignment

Take a moment to review Writing Assignment #3.

Write an essay in which you argue that Bernie LaPlante is a hero, or write an essay in which you argue that John Bubber is a hero. Focus on only one of these men and only on those events in the film that connect to the issue of heroism.

To make a good choice between the two writing topics, take time to explore where each topic might lead you.

Notes

Activity

Explore the Topics

Discuss the following questions with your classmates.

1. What is your definition of a hero?

2. Which of these qualities does LaPlante have? What proof do you have from the film?

3. Which of these qualities does Bubber have? What proof do you have from the film?

4. What nonheroic qualities does each character appear to have? Can each character still be considered a hero?

5. Whom do you think you'll write about, and why?

6. What main points will you include in your essay? (Remember, it's okay to admit that your hero is not perfect. He can still be a hero.)

Brainstorm   Drawing on your notes from class discussions and the film, write freely and explore your thoughts on each character. Write down all the ideas that come to your mind. Don't censor your thoughts.

Gather Information   Consider looking up reviews and/or critiques of the film in communication or film journals. Because this is a limited search, you should ask your librarian, instructor, or tutor for help on finding such journals. If you come across information during your search that you would like to use in your essay, be sure to record source information and place quotation marks around any material that is quoted directly.

Consider Your Audience   With this assignment, you can assume that your audience has seen the film *Hero* but probably doesn't remember it well. Before you begin planning or drafting your essay, think about your audience's needs. Write down a list of basic information that will remind your audience of the **plot line** of the film. (The plot line is a concise summary that tells the reader about the major events and actions in a film.)

Also, write down what you think your audience might expect in an essay about a film hero. Will you surprise your audience in any way? Will you have to persuade your audience to believe in any of your ideas?

Create Your Thesis   Remember, the thesis statement is the sentence
that comes last in your introductory paragraph. It tells your readers
what you'll be explaining, discussing, or proving in your essay. It is important for you to shape this sentence carefully.

Review the writing assignment and your brainstorm, activities, and
class notes, and begin experimenting with possible thesis statements.
Write several thesis statements as you search for one that expresses
your idea well. Share your thesis statement with a reader and ask him
or her what he or she expects you to discuss in your essay. Think critically about what your reader says and about your own reaction to
your thesis statement. Is it too broad? Too narrow? (A thesis statement
that is too broad might not get the reader focused specifically on your
chosen hero, or it might not get the reader focused on the idea that this
character is a hero. A thesis statement that is too narrow might focus
on just one heroic quality rather than on the larger point that the character you have chosen is indeed a hero.)

Outline   After revising and polishing your thesis statement, copy it on
a clean piece of paper, and experiment with possible topic sentences for
your essay. Create topic sentences that focus on separate heroic qualities.

Work on your topic sentences until they seem clear and effective.
List them beneath your thesis statement. You may also want to list a
few pieces of support under each topic sentence to remind yourself
of the type of information that will go into the body of each paragraph. If you are using a quotation, place quotation marks around it
and note the source information. (See "Using Outside Information"
on pages 479–483 for information on using quotes and recording
source information.)

Share this outline with classmates, a tutor, or your instructor. Can
your reader(s) tell what your essay will be about? Does everything connect to your thesis?

Feel free to alter your outline at any time during the writing process.
The outline should be a guide, not something that forces you to state
something you are no longer satisfied with.

Draft

At this stage of the writing process, you want to create a complete essay (introduction, body, and conclusion). Remember that you must allow yourself to write without too many interruptions. Accept that this

first draft may not be perfect. Relax and focus on ideas. Review all of your notes. You may even want to review the film again. Remind yourself that the first goal is to get a complete draft done. Then you can go back and improve and polish.

Your introduction should introduce the basic plot line of the movie and your definition of a hero. Your thesis should give your reader a clear sense of what you will prove in your essay and why the reader should read it. In your body paragraphs, offer the most interesting detailed information you can from the film (or from outside sources) that shows why the character you have chosen is indeed a hero. Remember, each paragraph should focus on one point at a time: use topic sentences to help you with this. You may need to include quotes from the movie to help you explain and prove your points. See "Using Outside Sources" on pages 479–483 for ways to incorporate quotations smoothly and effectively. In your conclusion, tell your reader what you've learned from writing this essay and what you want the reader to learn. (*Note:* You don't have to actually say, "I have learned . . . and you should have learned. . . ." Find other ways to state your message.)

Revise

This is your opportunity to look objectively at your essay and consider its strengths and weaknesses. This is also a time to get another reader's response to your work. When you have identified some areas that you think need work, approach revising one step at a time. Make a list of revision tasks and prioritize it.

Activity

Share Your Writing

Find a classmate to work with. Discuss the following questions as they relate to your essays.

- Do you have a clear definition of a hero?

- Have you clearly and quickly summarized the plot of the movie? (Too much information will bore the reader, and too little will leave the reader confused.)

- Do you focus on just one hero from the film?

Notes

- Do you focus on the most important information from the film?

- Is your essay coherent? Do all the paragraphs clearly connect back to your thesis? Check your topic sentences.

Edit

Now is the time to work on polishing your sentences. The goal is to make your ideas clear and to project a professional image so that your reader will respect your work.

Read your essay aloud and look (and listen) for awkward spots and typographical errors.

Review your essay again, slowly, sentence by sentence, and consider the following:

- Are there any errors that you tend to repeat? Focus on them one at a time.

- Is there a certain area your instructor wants you to focus on?

You may also want to consider these questions after completing the sentence work at the end of the chapter.

- Are you using pronouns to improve the flow and coherence of your essay without overusing them?

- Do your pronouns agree in number with their antecedents?

Now begin "polishing" your essay. Carefully check for typing errors, spelling errors, and any other errors you tend to make. Also, review your essay for sentence variety.

- Can you use coordinators, transitions, or subordinators to add variety and clarify the relationships between the ideas in your essay?

- Can you add useful information to your essay by including prepositional or participial phrases in some of your sentences?

- Are there any misspelled words? Use spell check on your computer, or get out your dictionary and look up any words you are uncertain about. Do this early enough so that if you need it, you can get help from a tutor or instructor.

Specific words to be aware of in this assignment include the following:

- hero/heroes (notice that the singular form doesn't have an *e* on the end),

- the name of your hero, and
- the names of places and events (like your hero's birthplace, and so on).

  Have you cited outside sources correctly? (See pages 479–483 for review.)

TIME TO REFLECT

> ### *Journal Assignment*
>
> ### *Your Progress as a Writer, Reader, and Critical Thinker*
>
> Write in your journal your reflection on any or all of the following:
>
> - Have your reading and writing processes continued to change and improve? Explain.
> - What reading and writing skills do you feel really good about?
> - What skills are you most concerned about?
> - Are you using any of the tutoring resources on campus?

SUMMARY OF CHAPTER 5

In this chapter, you have studied the role of *focus* in effective writing. You have

- considered how topic sentences and thesis statements help writers focus their writing,
- seen how important critical thinking is in creating a focused piece of writing, and
- practiced your ability to focus your thoughts on paper while you communicated your own ideas about what makes a hero and who is a hero.

PRONOUNS

Identifying Pronouns
Identifying Antecedents
Avoiding Unclear Pronoun References
Avoiding Pronoun Disagreement and Sexist Language

A **pronoun** is a word that can be used instead of a noun in a sentence. (Remember, a noun is a person, place, thing, or idea: *Jim, store, chair, happiness.*) Knowing about pronouns gives you more options when you write because you won't have to use the same nouns over and over. You'll be able to use pronouns in their place. This section will help you identify and then use pronouns correctly (avoiding such errors as pronoun disagreement and sexist language). In addition, you'll study **synonyms** (words that have similar meanings), which can also help you add variety to your writing.

Identifying Pronouns

Pronouns come in five different forms: subject, object, possessive, relative/interrogative, and indefinite.

Subject form	I, he, she, it, they, we, you
Object form	me, him, her, it, them, us, you
Possessive form	my/mine, his, her/hers, its, their/theirs, our/ours, your/yours
Relative/Interrogative form	who, that, which
Indefinite form	somebody/someone, everybody/everyone, each, neither, either, anybody/anyone

In the following sentences, pronouns are underlined.

I (subject form) asked him (object form) if I (subject form) could borrow his (possessive form) copy of Malcolm X's autobiography.

After reading her (possessive form) suggestions on my (possessive form) draft, I (subject form) realized that Samantha was a pretty good critic.

Jackie was a nurse who (relative form) gave her (possessive form) heart to her (possessive form) patients.

Everybody (indefinite form) can learn from her (possessive form) dedication.

Notes

Practice #1   Molly Pitcher

Read the following passage aloud. Then, reread the passage and put boxes around the pronouns you find. (The paragraph comes from "Move Over, Barney.")

Molly Pitcher saw what had to be done and did it. Women had a defined role in the war; they were a vital support to the fighting colonials. But when her husband was wounded, and the cannon needed to be fired, she knew what she had to do. Molly Pitcher was, and is, a heroine, and her story deserves to be told and retold. Neither a great statesman or soldier, she was an ordinary person who performed an extraordinary deed.

1. Cross out every *she* in the passage that refers to Molly Pitcher and write in *Molly Pitcher*. Also cross out every *her* and write in *Molly Pitcher's*.
2. Read the paragraph aloud the way you have rewritten it. How does the paragraph sound without using *she* or *her*?

As you can see (and hear), pronouns are important so that writing doesn't become repetitive.

Identifying Antecedents

An **antecedent** is the noun a pronoun refers to. It is important for pronouns to have clear antecedents so that the reader knows to whom you are referring. Think of an *antecedent* as an "ancestor" (someone who came before you). Pronouns must have *antecedents* just as people must have *ancestors*. In the following sentences, the pronouns are boxed and the arrows point to the antecedents.

My father first showed an interest in caring for animals when he was only 5 years old.

The children all cheered when they saw Mickey Mouse.

In the paragraph that follows, the pronouns are boxed and there are arrows going from the pronouns to the antecedent. (The paragraph comes from "Move Over, Barney.")

Notes

Michelangelo spent a lifetime at [his] craft, leaving the world a legacy of magnificent paintings and sculptures. [His] hard work was a daily reaffirmation of [his] belief in a human's creative potential. Through toil, [he] produced artistic monuments that have continued to inspire generations.

Practice #2   Heroes

In the sentences below, put boxes around the pronouns and draw arrows to the antecedents. Notice how the pronoun/antecedent relationship helps us see the connection between different sentences. This improves the flow and coherence of the writing. (The sentences come from "Move Over, Barney" and "Rosa Parks Joins Children's Wall of Heroes.")

1. Where are the heroines and heroes for children today? They are everywhere! They are the figures from our past, some in the historical limelight, others still in the shadows. They are the men and women of the present, struggling to overcome personal and societal problems to build a better world. (Par. 20, "Move Over, Barney")

2. These heroes seemed to be everywhere. They were part of the curriculum, so textbooks and other reading materials (even the classic comic books) provided details of their adventures. The movies portrayed details of their adventures. The movies portrayed them in action, adding an exciting visual dimension. Heroes truly came alive for kids, who not only learned about them but, often, learned values from them. (Par. 23, "Move Over, Barney")

3. Police were called, and Parks was arrested. She was bailed out of jail by a local civil rights activist, who then enlisted a young minister—26-year-old King—to help organize a boycott of the city's bus line. (Par. 11, "Rosa Parks. . . .")

Remember, a *coherent* piece of writing has ideas and sentences that fit together smoothly and logically.

Avoiding Unclear Pronoun References

If a pronoun does not have a clear antecedent, an instructor may use the phrase "unclear pronoun reference." There are a few exceptions. For example, when you use pronouns like "I," "everyone," and "anyone,"

Notes

an antecedent is not necessary because your reader will not be confused by these pronouns. This sentence, however, suffers from an unclear pronoun reference:

> My father and my classmate both liked my hero essay. However, he said I should remove a few details that seemed more distracting than helpful.

Who suggested the change? The father or the classmate? In this situation, the writer needs to make the antecedent clear. The writer might do this without repeating words. For example, if it is the father that made the suggestion, the writer can use a synonym like "dad" instead. A word is a *synonym* of another if it means basically the same thing. Here is the revision:

> My father and my classmate both liked my hero essay. However, Dad said I should remove a few details that seemed more distracting than helpful.

Here's another example of an unclear pronoun reference:

> After my brother finished boot camp, my dad visited him at the base. He was so happy about this.

Who does *he* refer to? The brother or the father? And what does *this* refer to? Finishing boot camp or visiting? Here is one way of revising the sentence:

> After my brother finished boot camp, my dad visited him at the base. Dad was so proud of my brother and so pleased to see him.

Or

> After my brother finished boot camp, my dad visited him at the base. My brother was thrilled to see my dad.

Obviously, these two ways of revising result in sentences that express very different ideas. It is up to the writer to provide clear antecedents (clear pronoun references) so that the reader will understand the writer's point. So, keep in mind that you must be careful that pronouns refer directly to clear antecedents. In addition, don't use *this* to refer to complex ideas or events.

Practice #3   Oprah, A Modern Hero
The following paragraph has some unclear pronouns and some unnecessary repetition.

- Read the paragraph aloud and listen for unclear pronouns and repetition.
- Read the additional directions that follow the paragraph.

- On a separate piece of paper, rewrite the paragraph using pronouns and synonyms to make this paragraph clearer and less repetitive.
- Read the paragraph aloud again and notice the improvement in flow when the pronouns are clear and there is less repetition.

One of the most obvious signs that Oprah is a modern hero is her charitable acts. Oprah frequently gives guests on Oprah's show great gifts like pajamas, books, cameras, and even trips to Disneyland. More importantly, Oprah started the Angel Network to which people donated their spare change. With a viewing audience as large as Oprah's, Oprah collected millions of dollars and used the money for scholarships for underprivileged kids. On Oprah's own, Oprah has given hundreds of thousands of dollars to colleges and students. In a country where celebrities make so much money and yet we still have people living in poverty, I admire Oprah for this.

- Replace repetitive nouns with appropriate pronouns.
- Use "the Queen of Daytime" as a synonym for Oprah once.
- Be sure to replace the "this" in the last sentence with a word or phrase that makes the meaning of the paragraph clear. Remember, writers shouldn't use *this* to refer to complex ideas or events. (You and your classmates will probably come up with different solutions and slightly different ideas of how the paragraph should end. That's okay. Discuss your ideas.)

Avoiding Pronoun Disagreement and Sexist Language

Pronouns must have clear antecedents, and the pronouns must agree in number with those antecedents. If the antecedent is singular, the pronoun must be singular. If the antecedent is plural, the pronoun must be plural. Note that "indefinite" pronouns are always singular.

Singular Pronouns	Plural Pronouns
He, she, it	We, they
My, mine, his, hers	Their, theirs
Somebody, someone, everybody, everyone, each, neither, either, anybody, anyone	

The antecedents and pronouns are marked in the following sentences.

> I consider <u>Harriet Tubman</u> a hero. She took great risks to help other people.

> The underground <u>railroad</u> Tubman created was not really underground; it was really just a series of complex routes and "safe houses" that brought the slaves to freedom.

> <u>All of the slaves</u> that took the underground railroad were successful. They made it to the North, and from there they could go to Canada.

An easy error to make is using *they* when the antecedent is *singular:*

> A *person* doesn't have to be perfect to be a hero. *They* are human.

The antecedent to *they* in the example is *person. Person* is singular; *they* doesn't work because *they* is plural. Instead, the writer should use *he, she,* or *he or she.* Traditionally, writers have used *he* or *him* when the gender of the person is unknown. However, this can seem sexist:

> An effective social worker needs to enjoy his vacation time to avoid getting burned out.

It isn't accurate to suggest that all social workers are men. To make your antecedents and pronouns agree in number *and* avoid sexist language, consider these solutions.

- Change the antecedent to plural and then use the plural pronouns *they* or *their.*

  > Effective social workers need to enjoy their vacation time to avoid getting burned out.

- Keep the singular antecedent and use *he or she* or *his or her.*

  > An effective social worker needs to enjoy his or her vacation time to avoid getting burned out.

Occasionally, you may find that you want a singular antecedent and pronoun to make your idea clear and persuasive. In the following paragraph, using *he or she* would make the paragraph awkward and wordy because *he or she* would have to be stated so many times. Changing the antecedents and pronouns to the plural would be okay, but using a singular pronoun might make the paragraph seem less vague and more interesting. In such a case, the writer would choose either the female pronoun or the male pronoun and then stick with it.

> A teacher who wants to make a difference in students' lives must continue to learn, change, and grow. The teacher needs to take classes and attend seminars to learn new approaches to learning be-

cause researchers are always gathering new information. Updating <u>her</u> knowledge is, of course, only the first step for the dedicated teacher. <u>She</u> will have to use this knowledge by changing <u>her</u> approaches and updating <u>her</u> teaching materials. Such a teacher will have greater empathy for <u>her</u> students as they struggle to learn, for <u>she</u> will be struggling and growing right along with them.

Notes

Practice #4   Heroes and Pronouns

The following sentences have pronoun agreement problems. On a separate piece of paper, rewrite these sentences and make the changes described.

Example: A <u>person</u> who wants to be a firefighter needs to consider how <u>they</u> deal with high-pressure situations. (Revise the sentence so that both the antecedent and pronoun are plural.)

- People who want to be firefighters need to consider how they deal with high-pressure situations. (Notice that more than just the antecedent had to be changed in this sentence. *Wants* changed to *want*, *firefighter* changed to *firefighters*, and *needs* changed to *need*. Make all necessary changes in the exercises that follow.)

1. A <u>hero</u> may go unnoticed. <u>They</u> might do wonderful things that don't make headlines. (Revise the sentences so that both the antecedent and the pronoun are plural.)

2. You may know a <u>person</u> who has helped change your neighborhood. <u>They</u> may have started a neighborhood watch program, or perhaps <u>they</u> look out for the kids in the neighborhood who have parents who work all day. (Revise the sentences so that both the antecedent and the pronouns are singular. Use *he or she* as your pronouns.)

3. This type of <u>person</u> may sacrifice many hours of <u>their</u> own time in order to keep your neighborhood happy and safe. (Revise the sentences so that both the antecedent and the pronoun are singular. Use *her* as your pronoun.)

4. <u>Someone</u> found my wallet. <u>They</u> dropped it off at my house with a note that said, "Have a nice day." (Revise the sentences so that both the antecedent and the pronoun are singular. Use *he or she* as pronouns.)

5. A <u>volunteer</u> at the animal shelter will need to be tender and strong. <u>They</u> need to care about animals but also be prepared for the sad truth that some of the animals will not survive. (Revise the sentences so that both the antecedent and the pronoun are plural.)

6. A person who volunteers their time to help clean up oil spills or other environmental hazards is a hero in my book. (Find the antecedent and pronoun that don't agree in number. Decide if they should both be plural or singular and then make the corrections.)

7. Anybody who understands this computer accounting system would be an asset to our volunteer organization. They could really help us clean up this bookkeeping mess. (Find the antecedent and pronoun that don't agree in number. Decide if they should both be plural or singular and then make the corrections.)

8. A doctor who flies to foreign countries to donate their time and help suffering people should be recognized as a hero. (Find the antecedent and pronoun that don't agree in number. Decide if they should both be plural or singular and then make the corrections.)

9. I would like to meet a politician who focuses on what their constituents want instead of what the special interest groups want. (Find the antecedent and pronoun that don't agree in number. Decide if they should both be plural or singular and then make the corrections.)

10. I don't think a person is a hero if they do a good deed only to be noticed and praised. (Find the antecedent and pronoun that don't agree in number. Decide if they should both be plural or singular and then make the corrections.)

Practice #5   Creating Sentences with Pronouns
Create the sentences described below.

1. Write a sentence that has an antecedent and *he* to refer to that antecedent. (Draw an arrow from *he* to the antecedent.)

2. Write a sentence that has an antecedent and *she* to refer to that antecedent. (Draw an arrow from *she* to the antecedent.)

3. Write a sentence that uses *a person* as the antecedent and has a pronoun that refers to *a person*. (Draw an arrow from the pronoun to the antecedent.)

4. Write a sentence that has an antecedent and *they* to refer to that antecedent. (Draw an arrow from *they* to the antecedent.)

Parallelism

Your Own Writing: Pronouns

Copy down some of your notes about heroes (perhaps a journal or an answer to a reading question). Underline all the pronouns that you use. Check your use of pronouns. Correct any errors you find. Use pronouns and synonyms to add clarity and variety and to improve coherence. Share your revisions with your class.

PARALLELISM
Understanding and Identifying Parallel Structure
Creating Parallelism

Certain sentence structures are easier for readers to read, and these structures deliver your message more clearly. This section focuses on one such structure—*parallel structure*.

Understanding and Identifying Parallel Structure

Parallel structure is having two or more items in a sentence in similar grammatical form. For example, having a list of three *–ing* adjectives in your sentence demonstrates parallel structure. Having two infinitives in your sentence would also demonstrate parallel structure. The parallel items in the following sentence are all verb phrases.

> The students were <u>discussing the general qualities of heroes</u>, <u>listing these qualities</u>, and <u>creating a definition of heroes</u>.

The parallel items in the following sentence are all *–ing* words working as subjects (gerunds).

> <u>Protecting lives</u>, <u>serving others</u>, and <u>donating money</u> are all ways that a person might become a hero.

The parallel items in this sentence are all adjectives.

> The film was <u>inspiring</u>, <u>frightening</u>, and <u>exciting</u>.

The parallel items in this sentence are all infinitives. The *to* is only stated once, but it works with all of the underlined words (*to help animals, to run in charity races, to donate money.*)

> Caroline loved <u>to help animals</u>, <u>run in charity races</u>, and <u>donate money</u>.

Notes

Practice #6   Beginning My Hero Essay

Underline the words or phrases that are parallel (similar in grammatical form). Use separate underlines for each item.

Example: The assignment requires that I define heroism, focus on one person, and prove that person is a hero.

• The assignment requires that I <u>define heroism</u>, <u>focus on one person</u>, and <u>prove that person is a hero</u>.

1. I discussed the assignment with my tutor, went to the library to do research, and started the draft.
2. My classmates said I need to make the introduction more interesting, supply more facts, and sharpen my topic sentences.
3. I had thought about writing about Jimmy Carter because he is still building houses for the poor, guiding political discussions in foreign countries, and promoting the idea of peace.
4. I think I can find more information on the Internet, at the public library, and in my grandfather's collection of history books.
5. When I edit, I have to watch out for run-ons, comma splices, and fragments.

Creating Parallelism

When you are editing your writing, read your work aloud. Listen for awkward places and look for groups of words that you think should be parallel in form. Keep in mind that the parallel items must be similar in form but not necessarily in "size." That is, you might have three adjectives in a list; two might be single-word adjectives and one might be a multiword adjective phrase:

My father is <u>strong</u>, <u>adventurous</u>, and <u>committed to protecting the environment</u>.

The underlined items in this sentence are parallel even though one item is longer than the others.

The following examples show how to create parallel structures in the editing stage of the writing process. This first sentence does *not* have parallel structure. Look closely at the underlined parts.

Parallelism

Our group's mission is <u>to feed</u>, <u>house</u>, and <u>educating the homeless</u>. *Notes*
The first two underlined items are infinitives:

Our group's mission is *to feed*.

Our group's mission is *to house*.

The last underlined item, *educating*, is a present participle. It ruins the parallel structure the writer started with. To make all items parallel, the writer could make the following revision:

Our group's mission is to <u>feed</u>, <u>house</u>, and <u>educate the homeless</u>.

As noted earlier, it is okay for the last underlined part to be longer than the first two. All three items are now infinitives: *to feed*, *to house*, *to educate*.

Now, consider this sentence that also does *not* have parallel structure.

She wrote an essay <u>defining heroism</u> and <u>to prove that Rosa Parks is a hero</u>.

The first part that is underlined is an adjective phrase. The second part is an infinitive phrase. To create parallelism, the writer could make both parts adjective phrases:

She wrote an essay <u>defining heroism</u> and <u>proving that Rosa Parks is a hero</u>.

You may have noticed that parallel items can share a lead-in word. For example, you don't have to repeat the *to* with infinitive phrases.

Jillian plans <u>to watch the film again</u>, <u>to take careful notes</u>, and <u>to discuss her ideas with her husband</u>.

You can write the *to* just once.

Jillian plans <u>to watch the film again</u>, <u>take careful notes</u>, and <u>discuss her ideas with her husband</u>.

Another point to keep in mind is that each item in a parallel list must fit smoothly with the words that come before the list. For example, the parallel items in the following list are all nouns (working as objects of the preposition *in*), but they *don't all fit* with the beginning of the sentence.

I found some great information <u>in the school library</u>, <u>the public library</u>, and <u>the Internet</u>.

You can say *in the school library* and *in the public library*. However, you can't say *in the Internet*. In this case, you would have to include the correct preposition before each noun.

I found some great information <u>in the school library</u>, <u>in the public library</u>, and <u>on the Internet</u>.

Parallelism

Notes

Practice #7   Creating Parallel Items in a List

Make the items in each group parallel in form. Discuss different solutions with classmates.

Example: drafting, revising, to edit

- drafting, revising, editing

1. on the Internet, in the encyclopedia, the new biography
2. discussing, explanation, analysis
3. escape, to succeed, hide
4. introducing, developing, conclusion
5. defining the word, to analyze his actions
6. fighting in wars, protecting U.S. citizens, to volunteer time
7. dynamic, going on adventures, brave
8. making choices, to be objective, to delete unnecessary information
9. in the newspaper, television, in the movie
10. frightening, forcefully, excite

Practice #8   Creating Parallelism in Sentences

On a separate piece of paper, rewrite the following sentences, correcting the parallelism error that is underlined.

Example: Before her famous arrest, Rosa Parks worked as a seamstress and <u>serving as secretary for the NAACP.</u>

- Before her famous arrest, Rosa Parks worked as a seamstress and served as secretary for the NAACP.

1. Aung San Suu Kyi is a caring mother, a skilled politician, and <u>supports only nonviolent action.</u>
2. Don Quixote is a fictional hero who fights windmills that he thinks are giants and <u>battling flocks of sheep that he thinks are armies.</u>
3. In my film class, we discussed how some heroes from films made in the 1950s were actually racist and <u>had sexist beliefs.</u>
4. In my hero essay, I need to define heroism, <u>applying this definition to one hero</u>, and stay focused on just the heroic qualities.

5. Carl has done a good job introducing his essay, stating a clear thesis, and <u>has stayed focused on his main points</u>.

6. Determined to choose an unusual hero, I searched the Internet, scoured the bookshelves at the college library, and <u>was asking my parents and grandparents for their suggestions</u>.

7. My goal with this essay is to improve my focus, devote more time to revising, and <u>editing carefully</u>.

8. <u>To participate in class discussions</u>, brainstorming, and planning have helped me come up with a good topic and stay focused on my topic.

9. To learn more about Gandhi, I watched a film, studied a few encyclopedia articles, and <u>was looking at Internet articles</u>.

10. My great grandfather helped feed, clothe, and <u>was hiding slaves</u>.

Practice #9   Adding a Parallel Item

On a separate piece of paper, rewrite the following sentences inserting parallel items. (You will be inserting single words or phrases. Do not insert independent clauses.)

• Underline each parallel item in each sentence.

• Compare your answers with your classmates' answers. Discuss the differences.

Example: Not intending to eavesdrop, Clara listened to the single dad next door talking on the phone and _____ to someone that he didn't have any money for Christmas this year.

• Not intending to eavesdrop, Clara listened to the single dad next door <u>talking</u> on the phone and <u>explaining</u> to someone that he didn't have any money for Christmas this year. (The words *lamenting* or *complaining* would have also worked. In fact, there are a number of ways to complete this sentence.)

1. After hearing the conversation, Clara felt depressed and _____.

2. The young children deserved to _____ toys and enjoy the holiday season.

3. On a limited budget herself, Clara knew that she could only buy a few decorations and _____.

4. She decided to _____ a few neighbors, _____ some money, and surprise the little family.

5. Every neighbor she spoke with responded with joy and _____.

6. Making a detailed plan for decorating, the neighbors planned to buy Christmas lights, a tree, and _____.

7. Next they divided up the tasks of shopping for presents, _____ the house, and _____ the presents.

8. The family was thrilled when they returned home one day to find their house decorated with lights and their porch _____ with presents.

9. To top off the surprise, the neighbors came over with freshly baked _____ and homemade _____.

10. Later that evening the father said to Clara, "You are my hero for _____ of us and _____ so much time and energy to give my kids a Christmas they will never forget."

Practice #10   Sentence Combining and Parallelism

Parallel structures can help you avoid repetition. In the following exercises, cross out the words that don't need to be repeated and then create one sophisticated sentence using the joining word in parentheses. (Remember, Punctuation Rule #1 states that you must put commas between items in a series. See page 111 for a review of Punctuation Rule #1.)

Example:

A hero should be selfless.
A hero should be honest.
A hero should be courageous.(and)

- A hero should be selfless.
- ~~A hero should be~~ honest.
- ~~A hero should be~~ courageous.(and)
- A hero should be selfless, honest, and courageous.

1. Did you define heroism?

   Did you explain how your hero fits the definition?

   Did you provide details and examples? (and)

2. I discussed his childhood.

   I discussed his teen years.

   I discussed his adult years. (and)

3. Sheila found my introduction interesting.

   Sheila found my conclusion boring. (but)

4. The tutor asked me to clarify my definition of hero.

   The tutor asked me to add a few more examples.

   The tutor asked me to leave out the quote in Paragraph four. (and)

5. I hate deleting ideas from my draft.

   I know that it is necessary. (but)

6. Parents should teach their kids the importance of volunteering.

   Parents should teach their kids the importance of speaking up for the underprivileged.

   Parents should teach their kids the importance of protecting the young. (and)

7. My children must call their grandparents once a week.

   My children must complete one community service project a year.

   My children must donate 10 percent of their weekly allowance to charity. (and)

8. Does a person become a hero on purpose?

   Does a person become a hero by chance?

   Does a person become a hero through fate? (or)

9. In the film *Hero*, Bernie LaPlante is funny.

   In the film *Hero*, Bernie LaPlante is not very likeable. (but)

10. Can a person be heroic once?

    Can a person be nonheroic the rest of the time? (but)

Practice #11 Create Original Parallelism

Create five sentences that demonstrate your knowledge of parallelism. (The sentences can each be on a different topic.) Underline each parallel item in each sentence.

Parallelism

Your Own Writing: Parallelism

Study a piece of your writing and find places where parallel structure could make your ideas easier to read and understand. Pay close attention to any sentences that have two or more items in a series. Revise this piece of writing (adding parallel structures) and be prepared to share this piece with your class.

Writing About Television

Main Topics

- Developing your writing

- Evaluating the effects of television

- Creating more expressive sentences with adjectives, adverbs, and prepositional phrases

MARGULIES
©1998 THE RECORD
www.bergen.com/margulies

"So, like, what do you do here the other 51 weeks of the year?"

Sacramento Bee, May 3, 1998, Forum: 5.

Notes

Essay assignments, like blueprints, are designed to guide students in developing their essays. An assignment outlines a basic plan for completing an essay, but it's up to the student to take that plan and build upon it. In the same way that a building contractor transforms blueprints into a building, a writer focuses on the plan, organizes the development of the project, and then moves the project through different levels of development until it reaches completion.

Development is the process of moving from a basic idea to a fully expressive, well-supported main idea that communicates to a specific audience for a specific purpose. Although you have been practicing some forms of development through the lists, charts, journals, workshop questions, and essays you've written in earlier chapters, this chapter will teach you specific strategies for further developing your essay ideas as you write about the effects of television upon the family.

DEVELOPING YOUR WRITING

When writing a paper, it's possible to follow an assignment and give just enough information to prove the thesis. This kind of a paper usually leaves the reader wanting more. A developed essay, however, offers more than just the facts. It interests, persuades, enlightens, informs, or delights the reader because of the choices made by the writer, choices that enrich the writing and compel the reader to read. Such writing may contain a single, detailed, thoughtful example, or it might contain a layering of several examples, depending on the point the writer wants to make. The developed piece of writing also has a strong voice, one that says, "Listen to me. I have something important to say." In developing a piece of writing, the writer anticipates the reader's needs, supplies enough evidence to prove the main point, and expresses her opinion in a distinct voice.

As you have written your essays, you have been practicing several forms of essay development already. If you *analyzed* advertisements to explain how a particular ad worked, you practiced a form of development. Whenever you have *added examples* to support your paragraphs in your essays, you have practiced another form of development. As you began to *include your own opinion* and *explain your position* on an issue such as privacy and technology, you developed your essay. In *using and citing sources,* you practiced development. In fact, wherever you have added examples, made comparisons, offered research data, or shared personal experience that related directly to your thesis, you have developed your writing.

Examining Developed Paragraphs

In a developed paragraph, the writer includes evidence, analysis, and detail that support the topic sentence and enrich the paragraph discussion. Sometimes examples appear layered as the writer builds upon the paragraph's main idea. This kind of paragraph communicates the main idea to the audience through precise examples, careful wording, and clear structure. In the examples that follow, you will see how three writers constructed well-developed paragraphs.

> Television is the most popular of the popular media. Indeed, if Nielsen research and other studies are correct, there are few things that Americans do more than they watch television. On average, each household has a TV on almost fifty hours a week. Forty percent of households eat dinner with the set on. Individually, Americans watch an average of thirty hours a week. We begin peering at TV through the bars of cribs and continue looking at it through the cataracts of old age.
>
> —*Joshua Meyrowitz, from "Television: The Shared Arena"*

You may have noticed that Meyrowitz's paragraph isn't long, yet it includes enough interesting information and focused support to prove his topic sentence—"Television is the most popular of the popular media." Though a well-developed piece of writing is usually longer than an undeveloped piece, the term *development* doesn't necessarily suggest length. It refers more to the choices made by the writer that enrich his writing and help prove the main idea.

One choice Meyrowitz made is to follow his topic sentence with statistics that will make the reader stop and think. It's shocking, for instance, to think that in the average household, the television is on almost 50 hours a week. That means that the television runs longer than most people's work week. Before the reader has a chance to react to this fact, Meyrowitz offers a second, even more sobering, fact to reinforce the first. On the average, most individuals watch 30 hours of television per week. If statistics alone are not enough to convince you that television is the most popular form of media, the writer takes another approach, employing a creative example to make his point when he concludes that most people begin watching television as babies and continue watching into old age. If you take a moment to reflect on this idea in terms of hours of viewing over a lifetime, then you would probably have to agree with Meyrowitz that television is more popular than any other of the popular media. Indeed, Meyrowitz makes a powerful statement about television by backing his topic sentence with statistics and a creative example.

Here is the second well-developed paragraph.

> TV is one of the things that brings us together as a nation. Thanks to television, the Super Bowl has become our greatest national spectacle, watched in at least 40 million homes. (By contrast, Ross Perot's first "town meeting," which was wildly successful compared to other political broadcasts, was watched in only 11 million homes.) Such peak moments generated mind-boggling revenues. Advertisements during the 1993 Super Bowl, which NBC sold out a month before kickoff, cost in the neighborhood of $28,000 per second. Nevertheless, because virtually the entire nation assembles to watch this single game in January, advertisers such as Pepsi, Budweiser, and Gillette gladly ante up, and others have found it a perfect showcase for major new products. It was during Super Bowl XVIII in January 1984 that Apple introduced the world to the Macintosh personal computer. (The Los Angeles Raiders beat the Washington Redskins, 38 to 9.)
>
> —*Douglas Gomery, from "As the Dial Turns"*

Gomery, like Meyrowitz, proves his main idea by layering statistics and examples, each more powerful than the previous. For one thing, the writer has anticipated his reader's need to know who's made money off the Super Bowl (not only networks but also powerful companies—Pepsi, Budweiser, Gillette, and Apple Computer). Notice, too, that Gomery has placed the score of Super Bowl 1984 in parentheses. Could his point be that the game itself took a back seat to the advertising? Certainly Gomery proves that the Super Bowl generates lots of money for advertisers, but he also makes the more subtle point that such an emphasis on advertising deemphasizes the game.

Here is the third effectively developed paragraph.

> One of the most ambitious and conclusive studies (conducted by Dr. Leonard D. Eron and others) examined a group at ages 8, 19, and 30 in a semirural county of New York State. The findings: the more frequently the participants watched TV at age 8, the more serious were the crimes they were convicted of by age 30; the more aggressive was their behavior when drinking; and the harsher was the punishment they inflicted on their own children. Essentially the same results emerged when the researchers examined another large group of youths for three years in a suburb of Chicago. And when they replicated the experiment in Australia, Finland, Israel, and Poland, the outcome was unchanged: as Dr. Eron states it, "There can no longer be any doubt that heavy exposure to televised vi-

olence is one of the causes of aggressive behavior, crime, and violence in society. The evidence comes from both the laboratory and real-life studies. Television violence affects youngsters of all ages, of both genders, at all socioeconomic levels, and all levels of intelligence."

—Neil Hickey, from "How Much Violence?" TV Guide,
August 22, 1992

Reprinted with permission from TV Guide. © 1992 TV Guide
Magazine Group, Inc.

TV Guide is a registered trademark of TV Guide Magazine
Group, Inc.

Hickey also uses the technique of layering in his paragraph on television violence. Rather than sharing just one study on violence, Hickey uses study after study to make Dr. Eron's point "that heavy exposure to televised violence is one of the causes of aggressive behavior, crime, and violence in society." You may have noticed that Hickey has inverted the typical paragraph form here as well. In this paragraph, he begins with evidence and ends with his paragraph point.

Activity

Examining Developed Paragraphs

Think about the ways in which Meyrowitz, Gomery, and Hickey developed their paragraphs about television.

1. Read each paragraph a second time.

2. In the "Notes" column, label the topic sentence(s) in each as well as the types of support (such as statistics, examples, and studies) used to prove each paragraph idea.

3. Write what you have learned about development from Meyrowitz's, Gomery's, and Hickey's paragraphs. Think about their use of precise examples, careful wording, and clear structure. At this point, how would you define *development*?

Using the Questions for Development

Writers interested in developing their paragraph (or essay) ideas fully often rely on a series of questions known as the **Questions for Development.** These common questions simply help remind writers to make sure they've answered all the reader's questions in their paragraphs (or essays). The questions are listed here for you to refer to as you write and revise.

WHO?   Who is involved?

Who is affected?

Who is interested?

Who is my audience?

Who believes this?

Who said this?

WHAT?   What happened?

What are the main issues?

What else does my reader need to know?

What can I explain further?

WHEN?   When did it happen?

When is it a problem?

When will it occur again?

When will it be resolved?

WHERE? Where did it occur?

Where were the participants?

WHY?   Why is the issue important?

Why did it happen this way?

Why should you or I care?

Why should my audience care?

HOW?   How did it happen?

How does it work?

How can the problem be resolved?

Asking these questions helps writers make sure they have fully explained, explored, and supported their paragraph ideas (or essay ideas). You may apply these Questions for Development at any stage of the writing process.

Activity

Your Favorite Television Series

Using the Questions for Development, describe your favorite television program in a paragraph (or two). Your goal is to develop your paragraph, making it so interesting that your reader will want to watch the program. Be sure to tell when

it's on, who's in it, what happens in a typical episode, where it's set (location),   *Notes*
why you like it, how you first heard about it, and why you began to watch it.

1. Rather than beginning your paragraph with the typical—"My favorite program is . . ."—spend a few minutes creating a topic sentence that will draw the reader's interest. Consider the following beginnings:

   - For those who love drama, [name of show] is worth watching.
   - Looking for excitement and intrigue? Then you must see [name of show] . . .
   - Consistently funny, [name of show] . . .

2. As you support your topic sentence, you should try to anticipate your reader's questions and answer them fully.

3. Ask a classmate to read your paragraph(s) and identify any of the Questions for Development that haven't yet been answered.

4. Revise your paragraph, being sure to supply any missing information.

Examining a Developed Essay

Like the developed paragraph, the developed essay includes evidence, analysis, and detail that help support the main idea and enrich the discussion. But what makes the developed essay different from the developed paragraph is that it addresses a number of significant points. Each of these significant points will be found in well-developed paragraphs that support the overriding idea or thesis of the essay.

In developing the essay, the writer uses the same writing process practiced in the previous chapters. Naturally the writer would spend time brainstorming. Then, after discussion and research, she would begin narrowing the field of topics to a single topic of interest. From there, she would create a thesis for her essay and then a list of ideas to support that thesis. The most important of these ideas will be developed into body paragraphs when she drafts the essay.

After determining which ideas could be developed into paragraphs to support her thesis, she would consider which examples, studies, statistics, experiences, and other forms of evidence would best support these body paragraphs. As she drafted her essay, she would strive to achieve a balance of evidence and discussion in each of the body paragraphs. For example, if she included a quotation by an expert, she would follow that quotation with a sentence or two of explanation to help the reader understand the expert's opinion *and* to reinforce the

Notes   particular paragraph idea. In doing so, she would also be reinforcing the thesis of the essay. As she built well-developed paragraphs that support the thesis of her essay, she would achieve a well-developed essay containing a balance of evidence, carefully selected detail, and discussion.

Activity

Study a Developed Essay

In the essay that follows, writer Nancy Signorielli has balanced evidence and explanation in her discussion of television roles for women. Read the essay carefully once, marking unknown words.

Gender Role Images on Television
by Nancy Signorielli

Signorielli, a media researcher, writes frequently about television and its effects on the family. The following excerpt is from a longer essay, "Television, the Portrayal of Women, and Children's Attitudes."

1   For the past twenty years, in study after study, men have outnumbered women by two or three to one in prime-time dramatic programming. Women are likely to be younger than men; tend to be cast in traditional and stereotypical roles. . . . This is not to say that "liberated" or nontraditional women do not appear on television; it is just that these images are not found consistently. Naturally, most people can easily cite five, six, or more examples of women who are not stereotyped and most of the research examining nonstereotyped roles has focused upon a small number of programs. Consequently, it is easy to forget that the majority of female characters in prime time are found in more traditional roles.

2   Overall, occupational portrayals on television are varied but stereotyped. Women's employment possibilities are somewhat limited, with clerical work the most common job. Television does not recognize adequately that women can successfully mix marriage, homemaking, and raising children, with careers. Rather, programs in which married women work outside the home (e.g., Claire Huxtable on *Cosby*) often focus on the character's home-related role rather than her work persona. Nor does the television world adequately acknowledge the importance of homemaking and raising children. As in the real world, on television the woman who stays home has less status than the one who has a career.

3   Content analyses on seventeen week-long annual samples of prime-time network dramatic programs, conducted as part of the

Cultural Indicators project, sheds some light on the traditional and stereotypical ways in which characters are portrayed. Women are seen less often than men and in many respects may be considered as less important. When women do appear, they usually are younger than the men; they are also more attractive and nurturing; more often seen in the context of romantic interests, home, or family; and are more likely to be victimized. Women are somewhat more likely than men to be married, and if they are married, they usually are not employed outside the home. Only 26% of the women who are employed outside the home are also married or have been married. This schism is not perpetuated for male characters.

4 Women who are employed outside the home are usually cast in traditional female occupations—nurses, secretaries, waitresses, and teachers. Nevertheless, the world of television does not always accurately reflect women's work roles. There are a number of occupations in the U.S. labor force where women outnumber the men, but in the television world, due to the general overabundance of men, the men outnumber the women. These include teachers and restaurant workers.

5 Men, on the other hand, are presented as older. They tend to be more powerful and potent than women and proportionately fewer are presented as married. Significantly more men are employed outside the home, and they usually work in high prestige and traditionally masculine occupations such as doctors, lawyers, police, and other higher status and higher paying jobs. Moreover, among married male characters, about three quarters are employed and one quarter are either not working or their employment status is unknown. Among women, the pattern is reversed—only three out of ten married female characters are also employed, a finding quite different from the "real world," in which more than half of all married women are employed. Thus, the image conveyed by prime-time television is that women, especially if married, should stay home and leave the world of work to men. . . .

1. Reread the essay. Define any unknown terms. Now highlight the thesis in the opening paragraph. In your notebook, write a sentence or two explaining what Signorielli plans to prove in her essay.

2. Now move through Paragraphs 2–5 and highlight topic sentences. In your notebook, explain what Signorielli shows in each paragraph. Then explain how each paragraph helps support the thesis.

3. In your notebook, list the kinds of support Signorielli uses to develop each paragraph idea.

Notes

4. In which paragraph does Signorielli offer the best balance of evidence and discussion? Explain how evidence and discussion develop that paragraph point.

5. Which paragraph contains the most effective detail? Explain how the detail helps develop that paragraph point.

6. Based on what you've learned in this segment of the chapter, how would you describe a well-developed essay?

DEVELOPING THE FOCUSED ESSAY

As you focus and develop your essays in this chapter, you will continue to engage in the same productive writing-reading-critical thinking process you have been practicing. Before you write, you'll read, discuss, think critically, brainstorm, research, and observe. You'll spend time gathering information, examining research, and analyzing studies. You'll think about personal experiences. In fact, having some of this material early in the process helps you consider your options and gives you a pool of information and research from which to draw support when developing your essay idea. Once you have determined your essay's focus, you'll begin the process of organizing and thinking critically about what information to include when developing your essay.

Points to Remember About Development

- Explore ideas and then narrow your focus before worrying about development. An idea is only worth developing if it is focused.
- Construct a thesis for your essay and decide what main points you'll need to address in body paragraphs in order to sufficiently support your thesis.
- Use examples, studies, statistics, experiences, and other forms of evidence to develop paragraphs and support the thesis of your essay.
- Include *only* the pieces of evidence that help you develop paragraph ideas and support the thesis of your essay.
- Create a balance between examples and discussion in your paragraphs.
- Include your own opinion and analysis of research, ideas, and issues.
- Include creative sentences and examples that help develop ideas.
- Use the Questions for Development to help you fully develop ideas.

INVESTIGATING THE EFFECTS OF TELEVISION

Most Americans living today grew up with a television in the home. In fact, 99 out of 100 American families own at least one television set, and many families own two or more. As a result of cable, some Americans have access to as many as 200 stations on a daily basis. And in most households, the television is on for the better part of the day. Can so much exposure to television be good for us?

Discuss and Engage

Many experts are concerned over the possible negative effects of television on children and the family. Some believe that television has taken over families, stripping them of valuable time they once spent reading or interacting with each other. Others warn that children are being exposed to too much violence and sex via the screen. However, other experts assert that television can have a positive impact if used as an educational tool or if monitored by responsible parents.

Journal Assignment

TV vs. Books

The cartoonist expects you to look at the picture, read the caption (or question) under the cartoon, and then look for clues in the drawing that help you understand the humor and message of the cartoon. In writing, describe the cartoon on page 233 for someone who hasn't seen it and explain your reaction to it.

- What can you say about the two characters? What do they look like? What are they doing?
- What important clues help the audience understand the cartoonist's message?
- Can you explain the cartoonist's humor? Why is the cartoon funny?

Journal Assignment

TV Yesterday and Today

Thinking back to your childhood, you can probably remember watching a favorite program. Perhaps you grew up watching *The Brady Bunch* or *The Cosby Show*. Or maybe as a young child you watched *Sesame Street* or *Mister Rogers' Neighborhood*.

Notes

1. Describe your early television viewing experiences. What programs did you watch as a child? Why? Describe your favorite program. Who starred in it? Where was it set? What happened during a typical episode?

2. Overall, do you believe you were influenced in a positive way by your early experiences watching television? Explain. Do you think your viewing experiences as a child had a negative effect? Explain. (If you didn't watch television as a youngster, explain what other activities took its place and their effects on you.)

3. Now describe your current television viewing experiences. What programs are you drawn to now? Why? Describe your favorite program.

4. In general, in what ways has television changed since your childhood? Are these changes positive or negative? Explain. (This journal is for your eyes only. Refer back to it when you begin to write your television essay.)

Writing Assignment #1: *The Effects of Television*

Here, in brief, is the writing assignment you are preparing for.

Write an essay in which you argue for or against Marie Winn's view of television and its effect on children and the family.

Read, Discuss, Think Critically

This section of the chapter offers you a single reading. It's a lengthy excerpt from a book, so plan your reading time well. The reading is organized with eight subheadings that have been numbered and appear in boldface print.

Reading Assignment: *"The Trouble with Television"*

Preview   Read the title, introductory material, and the eight subheadings in bold.

Anticipate   What do you anticipate this excerpt will be about? Use the "Notes" column to record your thoughts.

Read and Reread   Read the entire excerpt, being careful to highlight unknown terms and interesting points. Then reread more slowly and write your responses in the "Notes" column. Mark important points and define unknown terms.

The Trouble with Television
by Marie Winn

Marie Winn, mother of two and author of *Unplugging the Plug-In Drug*, is known for her concern over television and its effect on the family. In this chapter from her book, she argues there are "eight significant ways" television affects children and families. She suggests that all families try a "No-TV Week" to break the TV habit.

Most Parents Worry About TV—But Not for the Right Reasons

My parents don't think I should watch as much TV as I do. They think a lot of the programs I watch are meaningless.

—*Fifth grader, P.S. 84, No-TV Week*

1   Of all the wonders of modern technology that have transformed family life during the last century, television stands alone as a universal source of parental anxiety. Few parents worry about how the electric light or the automobile or the telephone might alter their children's development. But most parents do worry about TV.

2   Parents worry most of all about the programs their children watch. If only these weren't so violent, so sexually explicit, so cynical, so *unsuitable*, if only they were more innocent, more educational, more *worthwhile*.

3   Imagine what would happen if suddenly, by some miracle, the only programs available on all channels at all hours of day and night were delightful, worthwhile shows that children love and parents wholeheartedly approve. Would this eliminate the nagging anxiety about television that troubles so many parents today?

4   For most families, the answer is no. After all, if programs were the only problem, there would be an obvious solution: turn the set off. The fact that parents leave the sets on even when they are distressed about programs reveals that television serves a number of purposes that have nothing to do with the programs on the screen.

5   Great numbers of parents today see television as a way to make child-rearing less burdensome. In the absence of Mother's Helper (a widely used nineteenth-century patent medicine that contained a hefty dose of the narcotic laudanum), there is nothing that keeps children out of trouble as reliably as "plugging them in."

6   Television serves families in other ways: as a time-filler ("You have nothing to do? Go watch TV"), a tranquilizer ("When the kids come home from school they're so keyed up that they need to watch for a while to simmer down"), a problem solver ("Kids, stop fighting. It's time for your program"), a procrastination device ("I'll just watch one more program before I do my homework"), a punishment ("If you don't stop teasing your little sister, no TV for a week"), and a reward ("If you get an

Get Involved!

Read the essay "Why We Tuned Out" by Karen Springen on pages 431–433 in Supplemental Readings. Report back to your classmates about the choices Springen has made. Share your reaction to Springen's approach.

Notes

A on your composition you can watch an extra hour of TV"). For parents and children alike it serves as an avoidance mechanism ("I can't discuss that now—I'm watching my program"), a substitute friend ("I need the TV on for company"), and an escape mechanism ("I'll turn on the TV and try to forget my worries").

7   Most families recognize the wonderful services that television has to offer. Few, however, are aware that there are eight significant ways television wields a negative influence on children and family life:

1. TV Keeps Families from Doing Other Things

The primary danger of the television screen lies not so much in the behavior it produces— although there is danger there—as in the behavior it prevents: the talks, the games, the family festivities and arguments through which much of the child's learning takes place and through which his character is formed. Turning on the television set can turn off the process that transforms children into people.[1]

8   Urie Bronfenbrenner's words to a conference of educators almost two decades ago focus on what sociologists call the "reduction effects" of television—its power to preempt and often eliminate a whole range of other activities and experiences. While it is easy to see that for a child who watches 32 hours of television each week, the reduction effects are significant—obviously that child would be spending 32 hours doing *something* else if there were no television available—Bronfenbrenner's view remains an uncommon and even an eccentric one.

9   Today the prevailing focus remains on improving programs rather than on reducing the amount of time children view. Perhaps parents have come to depend so deeply on television that they are afraid even to contemplate the idea that something might be wrong with their use of television, not merely with the programs on the air.

2. TV Is a Hidden Competitor for All Other Activities

Now that I couldn't watch TV I thought of other things to do. I read all the books that I had classified as "boring" and discovered how good they really were.
                                                                    —*Sixth grader, Marshall, Missouri, Turn-Off*

10   Almost everybody knows that there are better, more fulfilling things for a family to do than watch television. And yet, if viewing statistics are to be believed, most families spend most of their family time together in front of the flickering screen.

11   Some social critics believe that television has come to dominate family life because today's parents are too selfish and narcissistic to put in the effort that reading aloud or playing games or even just talking to

---

[1]Urie Bronfenbrenner, "Who Cares for America's Children?" Address presented at the Conference of the National Association for the Education of Young Children, 1970.

each other would require. But this harsh judgment doesn't take into consideration the extraordinary power of television. In reality, many parents crave a richer family life and are eager to work at achieving this goal. The trouble is that their children seem to reject all those fine family alternatives in favor of television.

12   To be sure, the fact that children are likely to choose watching television over having a story read aloud to them, or playing with the stamp collection, or going out for a walk in the park does not mean that watching television is actually more entertaining or gratifying than any of these activities. It does mean, however, that watching television is easier.

13   In most families, television is always there as an easy and safe competitor. When another activity is proposed, it had better be really special; otherwise it is in danger of being rejected. The parents who have unsuccessfully proposed a game or a story end up feeling rejected as well. They are unaware that television is still affecting their children's enjoyment of other activities, even when the set is off.

14   Reading aloud is a good example of how this competition factor works. Virtually every child expert hails reading aloud as a delightful family pastime. Educators encourage it as an important way for parents to help their children develop a love for reading and improve their reading skills. Too often, however, the fantasy of the happy family gathered around to listen to a story is replaced by a different reality: "Hey kids, I've got a great book to read aloud. How about it?" says the parent. "Not now, Dad, we want to watch 'The Cosby Show,'" say the kids.

15   It is for this reason that one of the most important *Don'ts* suggested by Jim Trelease in his valuable guide *The Read-Aloud Handbook* is the following:

> Don't try to compete with television. If you say, "Which do you want, a story or TV?" they will usually choose the latter. That is like saying to a 9-year-old, "Which do you want, vegetables or a donut?" Since *you* are the adult, *you* choose. "The television goes off at eight-thirty in this house. If you want a story before bed, that's fine. If not, that's fine too. But no television after eight-thirty." But don't let books appear to be responsible for depriving children of viewing time.[2]

3. TV Allows Kids to Grow Up Less Civilized

The Turn-Off showed us parents that we can say "no" without so many objections from the kids.

—*Mother, Buffalo, New York, Great TV Turn-Off*

16   It would be a mistake to assume that the basic childrearing philosophy of parents of the past was stricter than that of parents today.

---

[2]Jim Trelease, *The Read-Aloud Handbook* (Penguin, 1985.)

Notes

American parents, in fact, have always had a tendency to be more egalitarian in their family life than, say, European parents. For confirmation, one has only to read the accounts of eighteenth- or nineteenth-century European travelers who comment on the freedom and audacity of American children as compared to their European counterparts. Why then do parents today seem far less in control of their children than parents not only of the distant past but even of a mere generation ago? Television has surely played a part in the change.

17   Today's parents universally use television to keep their children occupied when they have work to do or when they need a break from child care. They can hardly imagine how parents survived before television. Yet parents did survive in the years before TV. Without television, they simply had to use different survival strategies to be able to cook dinner, talk on the telephone, clean house, or do whatever work needed to be done in peace.

18   Most of these strategies fell into the category social scientists refer to as "socialization"—the civilizing process that transforms small creatures intent upon the speedy gratification of their own instinctive needs and desires into successful members of a society in which those individual needs and desires must often be left ungratified, at least temporarily, for the good of the group.

19   What were these "socialization" strategies parents used to use? Generally, they went something like this: "Mommy's got to cook dinner now (make a phone call, talk to Mrs. Jones, etc.). Here are some blocks (some clay, a pair of blunt scissors and a magazine, etc.). Now you have to be a good girl and play by yourself for a while and not interrupt Mommy." Nothing very complicated.

20   But in order to succeed, a certain firmness was absolutely necessary, and parents knew it, even if asserting authority was not their preferred way of dealing with children. They knew they had to work steadily at "training" their child to behave in ways that allowed them to do those normal things that needed to be done. Actually, achieving this goal was not terribly difficult. It took a little effort to set up certain patterns—perhaps a few days or a week of patient but firm insistence that the child behave in certain ways at certain times. But parents of the past didn't agonize about whether this was going to be psychologically damaging. They simply had no choice. Certain things simply *had to be done,* and so parents stood their ground against children's natural struggle to gain attention and have their own way.

21   Obviously it is easier to get a break from child care by setting the child in front of the television set than to teach the child to play alone for certain periods of time. In the first case, the child is immediately amused (or hypnotized) by the program, and the parent has time to

pursue other activities. Accustoming children to play alone, on the other hand, requires day-after-day perseverance, and neither parent nor child enjoys the process very much.

22   But there is an inevitable price to pay when a parent never has to be firm and authoritative, never has to use that "I mean business" tone of voice: socialization, that crucial process so necessary for the child's future as a successful member of a family, a school, a community, and a nation is accomplished less completely. A very different kind of relationship between parent and child is established, one in which the parent has little control over the child's behavior.

23   The consequences of a large-scale reduction in child socialization are not hard to see in contemporary society: an increased number of parents who feel helpless and out of control of their children's lives and behavior, who haven't established the parental authority that might protect their children from involvement in such dangerous activities as drug experimentation, or from the physical and emotional consequences of precocious sexual relationships.

4. Television Takes the Place of Play

I always used to turn the TV on for my 2 1/2-year-old son Alexander in the morning. Then I noticed during No-TV week that he played in a different way all morning. He seemed less irritable—in a better mood—everything was entirely different. I realized it wasn't Alexander who wanted to watch TV—it was I who needed to turn it on for him.

—Parent, P.S. 84, New York City, No-TV Week

24   Once small children become able to concentrate on television and make some sense of it—usually around the end of their second year of life—it's not hard to understand why parents eagerly set their children before the flickering screen: taking care of toddlers is hard! The desperate and tired parent can't imagine *not* taking advantage of this marvelous new way to get a break. In consequence, before they are three years old, the opportunities of active play and exploration are hugely diminished for a great number of children—to be replaced by the hypnotic gratification of television viewing.

25   Yet many parents overlook an important fact: children who are suddenly able to sustain attention for more than a few minutes on the TV screen have clearly moved into a new stage of cognitive development—their ability to concentrate on TV is a sign of it. There are therefore many other new activities, far more developmentally valuable, that the child is now ready for. These are the simple forms of play that most small children enjoyed in the pre-television era: cutting and pasting, coloring and drawing, building with blocks, playing games of make-believe with toy soldiers or animals or dolls. But the parent who begins to fill in the

child's time with television at this point is unlikely to discover these other potential capabilities.

26   It requires a bit of effort to establish new play routines—more effort, certainly, than plunking a child in front of a television screen, but not really a great deal. It requires a bit of patience to get the child accustomed to a new kind of play—play on his own—but again, not a very great deal. It also demands some firmness and perseverance. And a small amount of equipment (art materials, blocks, etc.), most of it cheap, if not free, and easily available.

27   But the benefits for both parent and child of *not* taking the easiest way out at this point by using television to ease the inevitable child-care burdens will vastly outweigh the temporary difficulties parents face in filling children's time with less passive activities. For the parent, the need for a bit more firmness leads to an easier, more controlled parent-child relationship. For the child, those play routines established in early childhood will develop into lifelong interests and hobbies, while the skills acquired in the course of play lead to a sense of accomplishment that could never have been achieved if the child had spent those hours "watching" instead of "doing."

5. TV Makes Children Less Resourceful

> *Tuesday I got home from school and didn't get to watch any of those old reruns that I've seen a hundred times before. I did my homework right after school, then I practiced my clarinet and guitar.*
>
> —*High school student, Richmond, Indiana, Turn-Off*

28   Many parents who welcome the idea of turning off the TV and spending more time with the family are still worried that without TV they would constantly be on call as entertainers for their children. Though they *want* to play games and read aloud to their children, the idea of having to replace television minute-for-minute with worthwhile family activities is daunting. They remember thinking up all sorts of things to do when they were kids. But their own kids seem different, less resourceful, somehow. When there's nothing to do, these parents observe regretfully, their kids seem unable to come up with anything to do besides turning on the TV.

29   One father, for example, says, "When I was a kid, we were always thinking up things to do, projects and games. We certainly never whined to our parents, 'I have nothing to do!'" He compares this with his own children today: "They're simply lazy. If someone doesn't entertain them, they'll happily sit there watching TV all day."

30   There is one word for this father's disappointment: unfair. It is as if he were disappointed in them for not reading Greek though they have never studied the language. He deplores his children's lack of inventiveness, as if the ability to play were something innate that his children are missing. In

fact, while the *tendency* to play is built into the human species, the actual *ability* to play—to imagine, to invent, to elaborate on reality in a playful way—and the ability to gain fulfillment from it, these are skills that have to be learned and developed.

31   Such disappointment, however, is not only unjust, it is also destructive. Sensing their parents' disappointment, children come to believe that they are, indeed, lacking something, and that this makes them less worthy of admiration and respect. Giving children the opportunity to develop new resources, to enlarge their horizons and discover the pleasures of doing things on their own is, on the other hand, a way to help children develop a confident feeling about themselves as capable and interesting people.

32   It is, of course, ironic that many parents avoid a TV Turn-Off out of fear that their children won't know what to do with themselves in the absence of television. It is television watching itself that has allowed them to grow up without learning how to be resourceful and television watching that keeps them from developing those skills that would enable them to fill in their empty time enjoyably.

6. TV Has a Negative Effect on Children's Physical Fitness

Dear Diary:

Today instead of TV I did exercises. I kicked my legs 50 times and jumped up and down 50 times. Then I took a bath. Then I cut papers and drew. Then I did knitting five times. It did not turn out so good.

—Fifth grader, P.S. 84, No-TV Week

33   Not long ago a study that attracted wide notice in the popular press found a direct relationship between the incidence of obesity in children and time spent viewing television. For the 6–11 age group, "children who watched more television experienced a greater prevalence of obesity, or superobesity, than children watching less television. No significant differences existed between obese, superobese, and nonobese children with respect to the number of friends, their ability to get along with friends, or time spent with friends, alone, listening to the radio, reading, or in leisure time activities," wrote the researchers. As for teenagers, only ten percent of those teenagers who watched TV an hour or less a day were obese as compared to twenty percent of those who watched more than five hours daily. With most other variables eliminated, why should this be? The researchers provided a commonsense explanation: Dedicated TV watchers are fatter because they eat more and exercise less while glued to the tube.[3]

---

[3]W. H. Dietz and S. L. Gortmaker, "Do We Fatten Our Children at the Television Set? Obesity and Television Viewing in Children and Adolescents." *Pediatrics* 75 (1985: 807–12).

7. TV Has a Negative Effect on Children's School Achievement

One day my class was getting ready to have a science test. There was nothing to do during the Turn-Off Week so I studied instead. I got S–, a good grade. My parents were proud of me.

—Fourth grader, Marshall, Missouri, Turn-Off

34   It is difficult if not impossible to prove that excessive television viewing has a direct negative effect on young children's cognitive development, though by using cautionary phrases such as "TV will turn your brain to mush" parents often express an instinctive belief that this is true.

35   Nevertheless an impressive number of research studies demonstrate beyond any reasonable doubt that excessive television viewing has an adverse effect on children's achievement in school. One study, for instance, shows that younger children who watch more TV have lower scores in reading and overall achievement tests than those who watch less TV.[4]

36   Another large-scale study, conducted when television was first introduced as a mass medium in Japan, found that as families acquired television sets children showed a decline in both reading skills and homework time.

37   But it does not require costly research projects to demonstrate that television viewing affects children's school work adversely. Interviews with teachers who have participated in TV Turn-Offs provide confirmation as well.

38   Almost without exception, these teachers testify that the quality of homework brought into class during the No-TV period was substantially better. As a fifth grade teacher noted: "There was a real difference in the homework I was getting during No-TV Week. Kids who usually do a good job on homework did a terrific job. Some kids who rarely hand in assignments on time now brought in surprisingly good and thorough work. When I brought this to the class's attention during discussion time they said, 'Well, there was nothing else to do!'"

8. Television Watching May Be a Serious Addiction

Every time I walked through the living room I longed to sit down, relax, and watch dumb reruns on TV. I think I was suffering from TV withdrawal symptoms. After a few days, though, I was used to doing other things with my time.

—Tenth grader, Marshall, Missouri, Turn-Off

39   A lot of people who have nothing but bad things to say about TV, calling it the "idiot box" and the "boob tube," nevertheless spend quite a lot of their free time watching television. People are often apologetic, even shamefaced about their television viewing, saying things like, "I

---

[4]S. G. Burton, J. M. Calonico, and D. R. McSeveney, "Effects of Preschool Television Watching on First-Grade Children." *Journal of Communication* 29, no. 3 (1979): 164–70).

only watch the news," or "I only turn the set on for company," or "I only watch when I'm too tired to do anything else" to explain the sizable number of hours they devote to TV.

Notes

40   In addition to anxiety about their own viewing patterns, many parents recognize that their children watch too much television and that it is having an adverse effect on their development and yet they don't take any effective action to change the situation.

41   Why is there so much confusion, ambivalence, and self-deception connected with television viewing? One explanation is that great numbers of television viewers are to some degree addicted to the *experience* of watching television. The confusion and ambivalence they reveal about television may then be recognized as typical reactions of an addict unwilling to face an addiction or unable to get rid of it.

42   Most people find it hard to consider television viewing a serious addiction. Addictions to tobacco or alcohol, after all, are known to cause life-threatening diseases—lung cancer or cirrhosis of the liver. Drug addiction leads to dangerous behavioral aberrations—violence and crime. Meanwhile, the worst physiological consequences of television addiction seem to be a possible decline in overall physical fitness, and an increased incidence of obesity.

43   It is in its psychosocial consequences, especially its effects on relationships and family life, that television watching may be as damaging as chemical addiction. We all know the terrible toll alcoholism or drug addiction takes on the families of addicts. Is it possible that television watching has a similarly destructive potential for family life?

44   Most of us are at least dimly aware of the addictive power of television through our own experiences with the medium: our compulsive involvement with the tube too often keeps us from talking to each other, from doing things together, from working and learning and getting involved in community affairs. The hours we spend viewing prove to be curiously unfulfilling. We end up feeling depressed, though the program we've been watching was a comedy. And we cannot seem to turn the set off, or even not turn it on in the first place. Doesn't this sound like an addiction?

Questions for Critical Thought

"The Trouble with Television"

1. What main points does Winn make to support her view that television has a negative effect on the family?

2. Winn has developed each of her points over several paragraphs (except for point 6, which has been developed in a single paragraph). Which of her points appears best developed? Why? List the evidence,

Notes

examples, and details she used to support this point. What other forms of support could she have used to make her point even better?

3. Which of Winn's points appears less developed or weaker than the others? What kinds of evidence might help to prove these points?

4. Which of her points do you agree with most? Explain why. What evidence does she use to help prove this point? Are there other forms of support that she could have used to strengthen her argument?

5. Which of her points do you disagree with most? Explain why. What evidence does she use to help prove this point? How might you *rebut* (argue against) the point?

6. Examine Winn's use of outside sources in Paragraphs 8 and 15. How did she integrate her sources in each case?

7. Identify Winn's audience. To whom is she speaking in the piece? What is her purpose for writing?

8. How does your own view of television compare to Winn's?

Get Involved!

Watch a child's TV program. Make notes. What channel did the program appear on? What is the title of the program? What do you think the intended age group is? What positive and negative qualities did you see in the program? Report back to your class.

Journal Assignment

Considering Winn's View

Think about the concerns Winn has raised regarding television and its effect on children and families. Think about your own television viewing habits as well as the habits of those in your family. Write a response in the form of a letter to Winn telling her, overall, what you think of her ideas and suggestions. Exchange your journal with a classmate or two. After reading someone else's journal, just say, "Thank You," when you return it.

Explore the Writing Assignment

Here, again, is the writing assignment you are preparing for.

*Write an essay in which you argue **for** or **against** Marie Winn's view of television and its effect on children and the family.*

Activities

Summary and Response

One method of exploring is to look more closely at each of Winn's arguments. In the activity that follows, you'll utilize your summary and response skills as you address Winn's arguments one at a time. Complete this activity on a separate sheet.

Summary of Introduction

1. TV Keeps Families from Doing Other Things
    (List main points.)

Do you agree or disagree that TV keeps families from doing other things?
How? Why? Use examples from your own experience to develop your response.

2. TV Is a Hidden Competitor for All Other Activities
    (List main points.)

Do you agree or disagree that TV is a hidden competitor? If so, in what
ways does it compete? Whom or what does TV compete with?

3. TV Allows Kids to Grow Up Less Civilized
    (List main points.)

Do you agree or disagree that kids who watch TV grow up less civilized?
Offer specific examples to support your response.

4. Television Takes the Place of Play
    (List main points.)

Do you agree or disagree that TV takes the place of play? What kinds of activities does TV interfere with? Discuss specific observations you've made.

5. TV Makes Children Less Resourceful
    (List main points.)

Do you agree or disagree that children lose their resourcefulness because of
TV? What evidence do you have to support your point?

6. TV Has a Negative Effect on Children's Physical Fitness
    (List main points.)

Do you agree or disagree that TV takes the place of physical activity and
causes children's fitness to suffer? Offer specific examples to prove your point.

7. TV Has a Negative Effect on Children's School Achievement
    (List main points.)

Do you agree or disagree that children's achievement falls short because of
television? If so, in what areas? How? Why? What evidence does Winn use
to support this point?

8. Television Watching May Be a Serious Addiction
    (List main points.)

What does it mean to be addicted to something? Do you agree or disagree
that people may become addicted to TV?

Discuss your views with classmates.

Observing Children's Viewing Habits

To further explore the topic, conduct an observation and record data on the viewing habits of children and families you know.

Over a period of three to five days, observe a child's television habits. Apply your Questions for Development. Who is the child? What are the child's viewing habits? When does the child watch television most? Least? Where does the child sit while viewing? Does the child appear to enjoy TV? How does the child behave while viewing? Why does the child view TV? Do any of Winn's concerns appear to hold true?

Interviewing Families

To gather additional information on families' viewing habits, conduct interviews with parents.

Using the Questions for Development, compose a set of interview questions that addresses Winn's concerns. Interview three to five parents from different families. Note where similarities and differences occur in their viewing habits.

Sample Questions:

- When do you watch television most? Least?

- How many hours do you (and your family) watch television daily/weekly?

- Do you monitor your children's viewing habits? When? Why? How? Which programs, if any, are off-limits?

- What do you see as the positive aspects of television?

- What are the negative aspects of television?

Be careful to keep your source information (who says what) in case you want to cite any of the adults as sources in your essay.

Brainstorm   Write freely about Marie Winn's concerns and other possible effects of television on children and the family. Don't worry about deciding which side of the issue you are on right now. Although Winn asserts there are "eight significant ways" that television affects the family, you should not argue for or against all eight points. Instead, write on two or three of the issues that interest you most. It might help to review your summary/response sheets to see which of the arguments you found most important. Also review your journals and your activities.

When you have finished writing, review your brainstorm and decide which side you want to take on the issue(s). Highlight the parts of
your brainstorm you think might be useful when writing your essay.

Consider Your Audience   Imagine your audience as a group of concerned parents. It might help to visualize the PTA at a local elementary
school. Which of Winn's concerns about television, children, and the
family would you discuss with them? What might be some of their concerns? How would you address the concerns of those who disagree
with your view? Direct your argument toward those who might be
swayed by your discussion. Make a list of things to keep in mind when
writing for your audience.

Create Your Thesis   Your thesis should reflect that you have narrowed
the scope of your essay to focus on two or three of Winn's arguments.
Also note that you are being asked to argue *for or against* Winn. It is
okay to agree with some of her points and disagree with others. Your
position should be clearly stated in your thesis. Experiment with thesis
statements until you find one that expresses your position and what
you intend to focus on in your essay.

Outline   With your thesis in mind, list the two or three points that you
intend to argue in your essay. Under each point, note the kind of support you will use to develop your idea. You should also consider what
your opponent (the person on the other side) might say about each
point and how you would respond. At this point, you might draft a
rough outline that shows how you will organize all of this information.
  Here are some ways for you to consider organizing your arguments:

- Offer least important ideas first and most important ideas last.
- Present least interesting ideas first and most interesting ideas last.
- Alternate your views and your opponent's views.
- Present all of your opponent's views (divided into different para-
  graphs), then all of your views (divided into different paragraphs).

Draft

Using your summary/response sheets, your notes, the reading, your brainstorm, and your outline as guides, begin drafting your essay. In your in-

Notes

troduction you should introduce the two or three most important issues raised by Winn and tell whether you agree or disagree with them. Remember, it is okay to agree with some of her points but not with others. In your body paragraphs, address these points one at a time, explaining and supporting your position with examples, personal experience, research, and discussion. Also, be sure to address your opponent's concerns. In your conclusion, remind your reader where you stand in regard to Winn's opinions.

Revise

Activity

Share Your Writing

As you work with a classmate, consider the following:

- Have you established your position in the introduction? Remember that your task is to show that you either agree or disagree with Winn. (Or maybe you've decided to agree with some of her points but not with them all.)

- Can your reader see your organizational pattern? Have you addressed the arguments one at a time? Is it clear which paragraphs contain pro or con arguments?

Here is an example of a topic sentence for a **pro argument** (an argument in favor of):

> In her article, Winn argues that television keeps families from doing things together, and I agree.
>
> —*Allison Baxter,*
> *student writer*

Here is an example of topic sentences for a **con argument** (an argument against):

> Marie Winn said that television could become an addiction, which could be compared to a drug addiction. I strongly disagree.
>
> —*Lynita Harris,*
> *student writer*

- Have you developed/supported your ideas fully? Use any of the Questions for Development that help.

Copyright © 2004 by Pearson Education, Inc.

WHO?	Who is involved?	*Notes*
	Who is affected?	
	Who is interested?	
	Who is my audience?	
	Who believes this?	
	Who said this?	
WHAT?	What happened?	
	What are the main issues?	
	What else does my reader need to know?	
	What can I explain further?	
WHEN?	When did it happen?	
	When is it a problem?	
	When will it occur again?	
	When will it be resolved?	
WHERE?	Where did it occur?	
	Where were the participants?	
WHY?	Why is the issue important?	
	Why did it happen this way?	
	Why should you or I care?	
	Why should my audience care?	
HOW?	How did it happen?	
	How does it work?	
	How can the problem be resolved?	

- Have you included examples or personal experience to support your ideas?

Review the following paragraph to see how one student effectively used personal experience to develop a body paragraph idea.

In her article Winn argues that television keeps families from doing things together, and I agree. Just recently, I realized that the big square box has kept me from doing things with my own children. For example, on our way home from school, my oldest son would ask me to play Monopoly with him after dinner, and of course I would agree to play. Some time after dinner, he would come to me with the board, and remind me that I had said I would play the game with him, but most of the time I would say, "Not right now. My show is on," and I would ask if we could play a little later. When he returned again with the game, I would say, "It's too late to play tonight. We will play to-morrow evening, I promise." This was very painful for my son,

Notes

> and I did have every intention of playing with him. I just got too involved in that mindless box.
>
> —*Allison Baxter,*
> *student writer*

You may also want to consider these questions after completing the sentence work at the end of the chapter (pages 274–288).

- Have you used concessions—*though, although,* or *even though*—when you need to make one argument appear more important or stronger than another?

Example of a concession:

> Although I agree with most of Winn's article, I don't agree that TV has a negative effect on a child's academic achievement.
>
> —*Parris Ray,*
> *student writer*

- Have you used transitions to move the reader smoothly from one idea to the next and to provide **cohesion** (unity) throughout your essay?

In addition, address the following questions about using sources in your essay.

- Have you integrated and identified your own research findings in your essay?

- Have you included publication information for sources? Have you cited sources correctly? (See "Using Outside Sources," pages 479–483.)

Note: If you have any concerns about your essay at this stage of the writing process, be sure to talk them over with your instructor or a tutor.

Activity

Study a Student Sample

Read the student essay below and prepare to discuss it with your classmates.

The Strength of Television

According to the article, "Attention Span—How TV Produces Overstimulated, Underactive Kids" in the *Sacramento Bee*, "The average U.S. household has 2.24 television sets, and the television is on an average of 6 hours, 47 minutes daily in those homes." That's a lot of TV. But do parents really know the negative influence that it has on children and family life? Marie Winn, the author of *Unplugging the Plug-In Drug* and a mother of two, has argued in her book that there are "eight significant ways" television affects children and families. I am for Winn's views on television and its effect on children and parents. In the following paragraphs I will discuss three of the more interesting points out of the eight that Winn talks about in her book.

First, I believe that TV has a negative effect on children's school achievement. I agree with Winn when she said, "It is difficult if not impossible to prove that excessive television viewing has a direct negative effect on young children's cognitive development." She is saying that there is no exact reason why television has a direct negative effect on the minds of young children, but there have been recent studies that help support her point. For example, in Japan, a large-scale study has found that as families acquired television sets, children showed a decline in both reading skills and time spent on homework. Low reading skills may be the result of watching TV rather than reading or writing. Also, less time spent on homework may result in the lack of understanding of future assignments; therefore, a child may receive low test and quiz grades. In my opinion when a child is at school, that means there is no television. No television means that more time would be spent doing their homework. If they are at home, that means there is television. Where television is present, there is a chance of it being turned on and viewed while in the process of doing homework or studying.

Next, I firmly agree with Winn when she argues that television has a negative effect on children's physical fitness. Researchers in a recent study found that dedicated TV watchers are overweight because they eat more and exercise less while glued to the tube. In a class lecture, my instructor Ms. Johnson quoted this statistic, "More than 60 percent of TV ads are for sugared cereal, candy, fatty foods, and toys." These kinds of products grab the attention of young children; the mixture of unhealthy foods and television may be a harmful combination. Most of the time when a child is watching television they are plopped right in front of the TV on the floor or the couch. In this situation, no physical activity is occurring. There may be a good chance that the child is eating a snack or drinking while watching television. I doubt that the child is eating a healthy snack or drink. I believe this is where the parents need to step in. The parents can feed their children healthy snacks like fruits or vegetables while the kids watch TV. Also, the parents can set up times when a child needs to exercise before or after watching television.

Finally, I strongly agree that television can be very addictive if children are exposed at a young age. An addiction is a compulsive need for and use of a habit-forming substance (i.e., drugs, nicotine, alcohol, etc.). In this case, television is the "habit-forming substance." In point 8, Winn put it best when she said, "The great numbers of television viewers are to some degree addicted to the experience of watching television." I believe that the addiction to television may not be as harmful as drugs or alcohol, but it will affect you as you get older. I also believe that if kids are heavily exposed to television at a young age for prolonged amounts of time, then they too may become addicted. Then as they get older they won't know that they're addicted, and they will find it harder to go without television. In Chapter 6 of *Connections: Writing, Reading, and Critical Thinking* by Boeck and Rainey, the authors quote Joshua Meyrowitz, who says, "On average, each household has a TV on almost fifty hours a week. Forty percent of households eat dinner with the set on. Individually, Americans watch an average of thirty hours a week" (from "Television: The Shared Arena"). This means most children spend more time watching TV than they spend in school. Again, this is where I believe that the parents should take action. Besides worrying too much on the content of television, they should limit the amount of time a child watches TV. Limiting the amount of television being watched would lessen the chance of a possible uncontrollable addiction.

In conclusion, I find Winn's views to be strong and straightforward. The key to not letting the television take over the family is to establish clear communication between the children and parents. I feel that if a parent takes control of the situation (in this case, television), problems would be less likely to occur. Also, if parents regulate their children at a young age, then as the child gets older he or she may be less involved with the television.

—*Paul Gregorio,*
student writer

Apply the same questions for revision that you applied to your own draft.

1. What is the writer's position? How many of Winn's points has the writer addressed?

2. What are the main points the writer makes in the essay? Is it clear which paragraphs contain pro or con arguments?

3. What kinds of support has the writer used to develop his main points? Are there any additional questions the writer might have addressed? (See page 259 for a list of the Questions for Development.)

4. Has the writer used a concession in his essay? Identify where a concession might be used effectively in this essay. (See pages 277–279 for information on concessions.)

5. Has the writer used transitions to move the reader smoothly from one idea to the next through the essay? Are there any places where a transition might provide more cohesion?

6. Has the writer included research in his essay? Has publication information been provided for sources? Have sources been cited correctly? Highlight an example.

7. If this writer were part of your workshop gr_____ would you offer his essay? Are there _____ you would like to make?

Edit

Now begin "polishing" your essay. Read your essay _____ _____ _or typing errors, spelling errors, and any other errors you _____ make. After completing the sentence work at the end of this chapter, consider these questions:

- Have you used subordinators, concessions, and transitions to create clear bridges between opposing ideas?

- Have you punctuated correctly when using subordinators, concessions, and transitions?

If you work with a tutor, ask the tutor to tell you how many (if any) and what types of errors you have made so that you can correct them.

Writing Assignment #2: Television: Good, Bad, or Tolerable?

Here, in brief, is the writing assignment you are preparing for.

Write an essay in which you discuss objectively the negative and positive effects of television. Come to a conclusion about what, if anything, should be done to minimize the negative effects of television and maximize the positive.

Read, Discuss, Think Critically

In this section, you'll read an essay in opposition to Marie Winn's "The Trouble with Television." Reconsider the issue of television and its effects as you read the article that follows.

Reading Assignment: "How TV Influences Your Kids"

Preview   Review the title and pay close attention to the prereading information after the title. Note the author's preparation for writing such an article.

Anticipate   What do you think this article will be about? Use the "Notes" column to record your response.

Read and Reread   Read the entire essay quickly, being careful to mark unknown terms. Then reread it slowly. Take your time in writing notes or reactions in the "Notes" column and in highlighting or underlining important ideas. Define unknown terms.

How TV Influences Your Kids
by Daniel R. Anderson

Daniel R. Anderson, "How TV Influences Your Kids," *TV Guide*, March 3, 1990. Reprinted with permission from TV Guide. © 1990 TV Guide Magazine Group, Inc. TV Guide is a registered trademark of the TV Guide Magazine Group, Inc.

Daniel R. Anderson is a professor of psychology at the University of Massachusetts at Amherst. Anderson and his graduate student assistant, Patricia Collins, reviewed 165 studies on the effects of TV on the development of children.

1   A few months ago, when she was twenty-three months old, Sarah started to watch TV. "She *cries* when *Mister Rogers' Neighborhood* goes off the air," her mother wrote me. "The first time she saw it, she sat quietly with me and watched the whole show. She talked about it for the rest of the day."

2   Children typically begin paying consistent attention to a few television programs at about age two. If Sarah continues to be a typical American child, she will spend about thirty percent of her waking hours in front of a TV, watching a wider range of programs as she matures. In terms of sheer

Get Involved!

"Guilt Free TV" by Daniel McGinn also argues that TV can be good for children. Read the article (which appears in Supplemental Readings, pages 424–430) and make a list of the positive effects of TV. Be ready to discuss and challenge this list in class.

exposure, television has the potential to be a major influence on Sarah's, and most children's, development. In recent years, researchers have begun to clarify the nature of that influence. The news is both good and bad.

3   The good news is that, contrary to a widespread theory, TV doesn't transform children into mindless "vidiots." The theory first gained popularity in the 1970s when social critics began to write that television mesmerizes young children by its rapid scene changes. A consequence, so these critics believe, is that children watch TV mindlessly and passively, with little thought and reflection. And they believe the long-term effects are worse: a short attention span and a diminished intellect.

4   But the theory has a flaw. It's been based mostly on anecdotes, never convincingly proved. And more than 100 studies on TV and children's attention span, comprehension and intellectual development have largely discredited it. In other words, there is no consistent evidence that TV makes children mentally passive, shortens their attention span, reduces their interest in education or otherwise impairs their ability to think. In fact, researchers are finding that young children aren't mesmerized by TV. Children seem to pay the greatest attention when they are most mentally involved with the program. The studies also show that young children tend to ignore or reject programs that they don't understand.

5   Sarah's TV viewing illustrates this. She now enjoys watching many children's TV shows, her mother reports, but not all. When a science program directed at older kids comes on, Sarah asks her mother, "'Change? Change TV?' She doesn't just turn away," her mother wrote. "She's insistent we get rid of that program."

6   The fact that children actively think about television indicates that television can be an effective tool for education, an idea supported by a great deal of research. For twenty years PBS's *Sesame Street* has helped preschoolers learn elementary reading and arithmetic, and *Mister Rogers' Neighborhood,* also on public TV, has helped them deal with emotions and self-control. The potential of television for teaching children is beginning to be demonstrated with such science programs as *3-2-1 Contact* and the math program *Square One TV,* both on PBS.

7   Despite the lack of evidence that TV impairs intellectual development, many educators blamed TV when national achievement-test scores declined. While it is true that heavy viewers have lower achievement scores, studies suggest that heavy TV viewing is more a symptom of poor achievement than a cause. Poor achievers tend to come from disrupted families or have parents who fail to provide intellectually stimulating activities. Such families tend to be heavy TV viewers.

8   Unfortunately, much of what kids watch is intended for adults and may not be limited or interpreted by their parents. When it comes to adult-

Notes

Get Involved!
Go online to the Children's Television Workshop website (www.ctw.org) to examine the supplemental activities available to children who watch *Sesame Street.* What types of activities appear on the site? Which appear to be more educational? Which appear to be less educational? Take notes and be prepared to discuss your findings in class.

oriented TV, young children take in the information but jumble up the meaning. Consider my conversation with six-year-old Sebastian. He had just seen a commercial in which a young couple sitting on the grass share a sumptuous lunch in front of their new Mercedes. When asked what the ad meant, Sebastian answered unhesitatingly, "They want you to buy picnics!"

9   Sebastian's misunderstanding was benign and amusing. Less amusing is the realization that uncontrolled TV viewing can expose a child to large doses of violence, antisocial values and sexual imagery. To the adult, this fare may have entertainment value. A given violent program may even deliver the implicit message that criminals get punished, so crime doesn't pay. The problem is that the child may see the violence of the crime and the criminal's glamorous lifestyle but not make the connection between those things and the criminal's subsequent downfall.

10   We know a lot about the effects of television violence. Studies suggest that TV has a role in producing aggressive play and real-life violence. Children who watch a lot of TV violence are described by other children as more aggressive. And some long-term studies find that viewing violent programming contributes to later aggressive behavior. Some of the most disturbing incidents occurred in 1973 after the movie *Fuzz* was aired. Apparently reenacting scenes in which youths set homeless people on fire, teenagers in Boston and Miami fatally burned two people.

11   Most researchers who study the effects of TV violence suggest that children are not equally susceptible to its influence. If parents are loving and discourage aggressive behavior, their children are unlikely to be influenced. But if parents are unavailable or permissive of violence, children are more likely to be influenced.

12   For many children from broken homes and poor neighborhoods, television may be the only window to the world outside. At its worst, television provides these children images of violence and crime associated with wealth and glamour. At its best, television provides these children with knowledge of positive alternatives in life and gives them hope.

13   Sarah, who just began watching TV, has loving parents who will monitor and limit her viewing. They will discuss programs with her and instill social values that will enable her to evaluate the things she experiences from TV. TV won't be her only entertainment and learning resource. For Sarah, TV will provide positive education and wholesome entertainment.

Questions for Critical Thought

"How TV Influences Your Kids"

1. Overall, what main point does Anderson make about television and its influence on children?

2. How does Anderson's view differ from Winn's? On what points does Anderson disagree with Winn?

3. What negative effects of television is Anderson concerned about? List them. Do you agree or disagree? Why?

4. What does Anderson see as the benefits of television? List them. Do you agree or disagree? Why?

5. Identify Anderson's audience. To whom is he speaking? What is his purpose for writing? How does Anderson's purpose differ from Winn's?

6. What kinds of support does Anderson use to develop his points in Paragraphs 6 and 10? Are there other forms of support that he could have used to make any of his points stronger?

7. How does the story of 23-month-old Sarah and her viewing habits work to provide cohesion in this article?

8. How does your own view of television compare to Anderson's?

Journal Assignment

Considering Anderson's View

Just as you wrote to Winn earlier in the chapter, take time now to write a letter to Anderson letting him know whether you support and agree with his views or not. Consider your own viewing habits as well as what you've discovered about the viewing habits of others. Exchange your journal with a classmate, and when you've finished reading, say, "Thank you."

Explore the Writing Assignment

Here, again, is your writing assignment. Review it carefully before continuing. Underline the important terms in the assignment.

> Write an essay in which you discuss **objectively** the negative and positive effects of television. Come to a conclusion about what, if anything, should be done to minimize the negative effects of television and maximize the positive.

Activities

Charting the Negatives and Positives of Television

An effective way to generate, develop, and organize ideas is to complete charts on the negatives and positives of television. This will help you separate the arguments and reasons on both sides of the issue. Refer back to Anderson's article first, then to Winn's. On the first chart, list negative effects on the left, then support, proof, and examples on the right. On the second chart, list positive effects on the left, then support, proof, and examples on the right.

Negative Effects of TV	
Negative Effects Watching violence on TV can lead to violent behavior.	**Sources/Proof/Examples** In 1973, after the movie *Fuzz* was shown on TV, kids actually set some homeless people on fire; two died (from Anderson's article, "How TV Influences Your Kids," Par. 10).
Use additional pages as necessary.	
Positive Effects of TV	
Positive Points	**Sources/Proof/Examples**
Use additional pages as necessary.	

Look for Information at the Library and on the Internet

N o t e s

To further explore the topic, look for information on the effects of television.

1. Go to the library to find books and articles on the issue of television and its effect on children and the family. Here are some titles to get you started:

> Chen, Milton. *The Smart Parent's Guide to Kids' TV.*
> Davis, Bennett. *Television and Families.*
> Gitlin, Todd. *Inside Primetime.*
> Minow, Newton N. *Making Television Safe for Kids.*
> Signorielli, Nancy. *Sourcebook on Children and Television.*
> Winn, Marie. *The Plug-In Drug.*
> Winn, Marie. *Unplugging the Plug-In Drug.*

Note: You don't need to read the entire book to get information on the effects of television. Look in the table of contents at the beginning of the book for chapters that appear to be about the effects of television on children and the family. Also, refer to the index in the back of the text. Look up words such as *children, effects, family, education,* or *violence* to find specific sections that focus on these important issues. Apply the Questions for Development to what you read.

As you read sections from these books, be sure to take notes and write down source information—author, title, page numbers, and publication information. Then add new information to your positive and negative effects charts. (See pages 479–483 for more information on using outside sources.)

2. Spend some time on the Internet. Look for articles on "television and violence," "television and effects," or "television and children." (Ask a librarian for help if you have any trouble locating sources.) Apply the Questions for Development to what you read.

As you conduct your research, be sure to take notes and write down source information—author, title, web address, and the date on which you retrieved the information. Add any new information to your positive and negative effects charts. (See pages 479–483 for more information on using outside sources.)

Get Involved!

Go online to read the article by Dr. Peter Niewman, "Doctor Says Kids Should Watch More TV" (www.childrennow.org/ newsroom/news-03/ cam-ra-03-31-03.htm). Return to class prepared to discuss with classmates whether you agree or disagree with the doctor's advice.

Brainstorm   Write freely about the positive and negative effects of television. Use this as an opportunity to look at both sides. Review both Anderson's and Winn's pieces. Also, go back to your lists of the

Notes   negative and positive effects of television and respond to the most important points on each list.

When you are done writing, review your brainstorm. Because you'll present a balanced paper showing both the positives and negatives, focus on only two or three of the most important points for each side. Highlight these points for now.

Consider Your Audience   Imagine you are presenting an objective discussion to a group of concerned parents, teachers, and other members of the community. Whereas some would argue that television has a negative influence on children, others would point to the positive programming television has to offer. What might be some of the difficulties you'd face in fairly presenting both sides of the issue?

Create Your Thesis   Review the writing assignment. Note that the assignment asks that you present the negative and positive effects objectively. This means you should create a thesis that will allow you to present both sides of the issue. Your thesis should also show that you'll limit your discussion to the most important positive and negative effects.

Outline   Think about how you might organize the points you have highlighted in a way that will allow you to present both sides fairly. Draft an outline or make a list of the arguments you'll be presenting. Under each point, note the kind of support you'll use to develop your idea. Here are some options for organizing your essay effectively:

- Offer least important ideas first and most important ideas last.
- Present least interesting ideas first and most interesting ideas last.
- Alternate positive and negative effects.
- Present all positive effects (divided into different paragraphs), then all negative effects (divided into different paragraphs).

Draft

Using your positive effects and negative effects lists, your notes, your own library or Internet sources, Anderson's and Winn's articles, your brainstorm, and your outline, begin writing your essay. Your introduc-

tion should explain the basic conflicts between those who believe TV is
a negative influence and those who believe the opposite. In your body
paragraphs, present each side's concerns, but include only one main
concern per paragraph. Be sure to develop each point with support in
the form of evidence, details, examples, and discussion. In your conclusion, let your reader know what you believe should be done to minimize the negative and maximize the positive effects of television.

Notes

Revise

Activity

Share Your Writing

As you work with a classmate, think about the following:

- Have you presented a fair discussion with both sides represented?

- Can your reader see your organizational pattern? Have you addressed
  the arguments one at a time? Is it clear which paragraphs show negative effects and which show positive ones?

- Have you developed your ideas fully? Apply any of these Questions
  for Development that help.

Note: Some questions have been altered so that they are specific to this
assignment.

WHO?	Who is involved?
	Who is affected?
	Who is interested?
	Who is my audience?
	Who believes or says TV is a negative influence?
	Who believes or says TV is a positive influence?
WHAT?	What happened?
	What are the main arguments raised by Anderson?
	What are the main arguments raised by Winn?
	What else does my reader need to know?
	What can I explain further?
WHEN?	When is TV a problem?
	When is TV a benefit?
	When will the issues involving TV be resolved?
WHERE?	Where did the problem occur?
	Where were the participants?

Notes

WHY?	Why is the issue important?
	Why did it happen?
	Why should you or I care?
	Why should my audience care?
HOW?	How did it happen?
	How does it work?
	How can the problem be resolved?

You may also want to consider these questions after completing the sentence work at the end of the chapter (pages 274–288).

- Have you used transitions to move the reader smoothly from one idea to the next and to provide cohesion through your essay?
- Have you used concessions—*though, although, even though*—when you need to make one argument appear more important or stronger than another?

In addition, address the following questions about using sources in your essay.

- Have you brought in your own research findings?
- Have you included publication information for sources? Have you cited sources correctly? (See pages 479–483, "Using Outside Sources.")

Note: If you have any concerns about your essay at this stage of the writing process, be sure to talk them over with your instructor or a tutor.

Edit

Now begin "polishing" your essay. Read your essay aloud and check for typing errors, spelling errors, and any other errors you tend to make. After completing the sentence work at the end of this chapter, consider these questions:

- Have you used subordinators, concessions, and transitions to create clear bridges between opposing ideas?
- Have you punctuated correctly when using subordinators, concessions, and transitions?

If you work with a tutor, ask the tutor to tell you how many (if any) and what types of errors you have made so that you can correct them.

TIME TO REFLECT

> ### *Journal Assignment*
>
> ### *Your Progress as a Writer, Reader, and Critical Thinker*
>
> Think about what you've learned about development in this chapter. Write a journal entry explaining what you've learned. You may want to think about these questions before you write.
>
> - What should writers keep in mind when developing their paragraph or essay ideas?
> - How do the Questions for Development help writers fully develop their ideas?
> - What have you learned about developing a discussion or argument?

SUMMARY OF CHAPTER 6

In this chapter, you've strengthened your essay writing skills as you've practiced

- exploring ideas and then narrowing your focus to identify a thesis worth developing;

- selecting only the most significant main points to address in body paragraphs;

- relying on examples, studies, statistics, experiences, and other forms of evidence to develop paragraphs and support the thesis of your essay;

- including *only* the pieces of evidence that help you develop paragraph ideas and support the thesis of your essay;

- achieving a healthy balance between examples and discussion in your paragraphs;

- expressing your own opinion and analysis of research, ideas, and issues; and

- using the Questions for Development to help you fully develop ideas.

Notes

SUBORDINATORS, CONCESSIONS, AND TRANSITIONS

Reviewing Subordinators
Punctuating Correctly with Subordinators
Recognizing Emphasis
Making Concessions
Transitions
Punctuating Correctly with Transitions
Transitions that Interrupt Sentences
Punctuating Correctly with Interrupting Transitions

In this chapter, you're exploring different ideas about television and its effects on children and the family. In one writing assignment, you're asked to argue. In another, you're asked to compare the negative effects of television to the positive. Thus, one of your challenges in this chapter is to discuss opposing ideas in a smooth, clear manner. You need to create bridges that explain the relationship between ideas.

There are many ways to create these bridges. This chapter will focus on two ways. The first method requires you to use a select group of subordinators that allow you to make concessions. The second method for moving smoothly from one idea to another requires that you use transitions.

See Chapter 4 for a complete review of subordinators

Reviewing Subordinators

In this section, you'll learn how to handle opposing ideas by using a group of subordinators that express opposition, and you'll learn how to place a subordinator in just the right place to make your position clearer and stronger.

Remember, the following subordinators express opposition:

although
even though
though
while
whereas

When you are discussing viewpoints that are different from one another—maybe even the opposite of one another—you can use these subordinators to build bridges between the ideas. The following sentences might be confusing with no bridge between them:

Obesity is linked to television viewing. The cause-effect relationship between the two is not a strong one.

These sentences read more smoothly when a subordinator attaches to one of them, creating a dependent clause and warning the reader that the two ideas are in contrast to one another.

<u>Although</u> obesity is linked to television viewing, the cause-effect relationship between the two is not a strong one.

The subordinator can also go between the two sentences.

Obesity is linked to television viewing <u>although</u> the cause-effect relationship between the two is not a strong one.

Punctuating Correctly with Subordinators

In Chapter 4, you learned that there are two punctuation rules that apply to subordinated clauses. Remember that when a subordinator attaches to an independent clause (a sentence), the independent clause becomes dependent:

I learned quite a bit from Winn's essay. (independent clause)

<u>Although</u> I learned quite a bit from Winn's essay . . . (dependent clause)

The point about resourcefulness was excellent. (independent clause)

<u>Even though</u> the point about resourcefulness was excellent . . . (dependent clause)

To create a complete sentence, the dependent clause must attach to an independent clause:

Although I learned quite a bit from Winn's essay, I disagreed with four important points.

<u>Even though</u> the point about resourcefulness was excellent, I have serious objections to Winn's points about obesity and addiction.

How you punctuate a sentence with a dependent and independent clause depends on where the dependent clause is. Review these rules from Chapter 4:

Punctuation Rule #5 (Review)

When you begin a sentence with a subordinated or dependent clause, you must put a comma after the subordinated (or dependent) clause.

- <u>Although</u> I learned quite a bit from Winn's essay, I disagreed with four important points.

Notes

> ## Punctuation Rule #6 (Review)
>
> ### If the subordinated clause comes after the independent clause, you do not need a comma.
>
> • I disagreed with four important points <u>although</u> I learned quite a bit from Winn's essay.

Recognizing Emphasis

So where should you place your subordinator? Does it matter which sentence it attaches to? Yes! It does matter. Where you place your subordinator is very important because one clause (and the idea in that clause) will get more emphasis than the other, so keep the following point in mind:

> When a sentence consists of a subordinated clause and an independent clause, the idea in the independent clause will come across with more emphasis. The subordinated clause is considered the weaker clause with the weaker idea.

Consider the following sentence (the independent clause is underlined):

> Although some kids might behave differently after watching violence on television, <u>most kids will not be affected</u>.

The writer is emphasizing that *most kids will not be affected*. In the next sentence, the writer is emphasizing possible dangers of violent television:

> Although most kids will not be affected, <u>some kids might behave differently after watching violence on television</u>.

Or

> <u>Some kids might behave differently after watching violence on television</u> although most kids will not be affected.

Practice #1   Emphasizing and Punctuating
In the following sentences,

• underline the independent clause—the independent clause expresses the idea that is being emphasized; and

• check the punctuation, adding a comma when necessary.

Example: Although I liked Anderson's calm, no-nonsense tone I felt he needed more serious research to back up his points.

- Although I liked Anderson's calm, no-nonsense tone, <u>I felt he needed more serious research to back up his points</u>. (Notice the comma after the dependent clause.)

1. Even though I know I can't and shouldn't shelter my children from popular culture I limit their television viewing time in the hope that they won't emulate what they see on television.

2. Although my son prefers the violent cartoons he also enjoys educational shows like *The Magic School Bus*.

3. Television can teach kids basic school skills and even show them a variety of careers though television sometimes glamorizes criminal lifestyles.

4. I believe that the key to health and happiness is balance whereas my spouse tends to be more extreme.

5. I think the kids should be able to watch two hours of television a day while my spouse thinks that there should be no television until the weekend.

Making Concessions

Using subordinators to show emphasis is particularly helpful when you are writing an argumentative essay. These subordinators allow you to *make a concession* while still emphasizing your own point. **Making a concession** means that you acknowledge the other side's position. For example, assume that a writer is arguing in favor of turning the television off. In a desire to put forth a reasonable and educated tone, the writer wants to acknowledge that the opposition has some reasonable arguments. However, the writer wants to maintain an emphasis on his own points. The subordinators *although*, *though*, *even though*, and *while* are particularly good for such a situation.

Examine the following sentences. The writer has placed the subordinator next to the ideas he wants to deemphasize.

Although I understand that kids might learn from educational television programs, <u>there are other, better ways to learn that don't carry the dangers of television viewing</u>.

Subordinators, Concessions, and Transitions

Notes

Even though most kids probably recognize the "unreality" of television, <u>adults can't always tell how children are interpreting what they see and hear.</u>

Concessions are quite powerful when writing argumentative essays. The following exercises will give you some practice in manipulating subordinated clauses in order to show emphasis and make concessions.

Practice #2   Making Concessions

On a separate piece of paper, join the sentences below using the following subordinators: although, even though, though, and while. Use each subordinator at least once. Check your punctuation.

1. For the moment, assume that you support a No-TV Week. Placing your subordinators carefully, join the sentences and emphasize your position.

   a. One week of no television may not change everyone's perspective about television. It may wake up some kids and parents and result in some really wonderful changes for those families.

   b. My kids had a great time rediscovering old games and toys. The first few days without a television were pretty rough.

2. Now, assume that you do <u>not</u> support a No-TV Week. Placing your subordinator carefully, join the sentences so that you are expressing a concession, but still emphasizing your own position.

   a. I don't believe that it is necessary to turn off the television for a whole week. I do think we could cut back a bit.

   b. There are some kids who watch too much television. I think most kids at our school have too much homework and extracurricular activities to watch much television.

3. Assume that you want to argue that television has a negative effect on how kids perform at school. Placing your subordinator carefully, join the sentences so that you are expressing a concession, but still emphasizing your own position.

   a. Some kids respond well to educational television programs. I think even educational programs teach kids to be passive learners.

4. Assume that you want to express your support of educational television. Placing your subordinator carefully, join the sentences so that you are expressing a concession, but still emphasizing your own position.

   a. Some people will claim that television is not a good teacher. My child resisted learning her ABCs from me but loved the lessons on PBS.

5. Assume that you want to argue that television does not affect a child's resourcefulness. Placing your subordinator carefully, join the sentences so that you are expressing a concession, but still emphasizing your own position.

   a. My nephews have learned games and created their own craft projects after watching a preteen show on PBS. Winn says that television makes children less resourceful.

   b. A few may just stare at the screen and seem to get little benefit. The kids I observed had interesting things to talk about after watching their favorite shows.

Practice #3   Create Concessions

Choose from the following list of subordinators and create the sentences described in the exercises:

although

even though

though

while

Example: Create a sentence that supports one of Winn's eight points and makes a concession to those who don't agree with Winn.

• While it may be difficult at first to see television viewing as an addiction similar to alcoholism, I think Winn makes a strong case for labeling excessive viewing as an addiction.

1. Create a sentence that supports one of Winn's eight points and makes a concession to those who don't agree with Winn.

Notes

2. Create a sentence that supports another one of Winn's eight points and makes a concession to those who don't agree with Winn.

3. Create a sentence that argues against one of Winn's eight points and makes a concession to those who do agree with Winn.

4. Create a sentence that argues against another one of Winn's eight points and makes a concession to those who do agree with Winn.

Transitions

Transitions are another valuable tool when building bridges between ideas. Consider how odd these sentences sound together:

> Mr. Beazer wasn't sure his wife would approve of the movie he rented for the children because it had some bad language in it. He loved the unpredictable plot line and message at the end.

Now consider how these sentences sound when they have a transition acting as a bridge between them:

> Mr. Beazer wasn't sure his wife would approve of the movie he rented for the children because it had some bad language in it; however, he loved the unpredictable plot line and message at the end.

The *however* warns the reader that an *opposite* idea is coming. The writer is acknowledging two opposing ideas.

Here's another example. Without a transition, the following sentences might appear to be a list of unrelated ideas.

> I think kids today spend too much time watching television. I think kids rely on high-tech toys instead of their own imaginations for fun.

In the following sentences, the relationship between the ideas is much clearer. The transition tells the reader that a *similar* idea is coming. Note that the transition comes at the beginning of a sentence.

> I think kids today spend too much time watching television. <u>Similarly</u>, I think kids rely on high-tech toys instead of their own imaginations for fun.

Here is a list of transitions and their meanings:

> *also, furthermore, next, similarly, in addition, likewise:* express addition of similar ideas
>
> *consequently, therefore, thus, as a result:* express cause-effect

however, otherwise, on the other hand, in contrast: express opposites
then, next, finally, now, first, second, third: express time
for example, such as, for instance: introduce an example

Notes

Practice #4   Identify the Transitions

In the following sentences, underline the transitions you find.

Example: I asked the question three times. Finally, she gave me an answer.

- I asked the question three times. <u>Finally,</u> she gave me an answer.

1. He didn't want to use television as a babysitter; however, he couldn't think of a better alternative.
2. The mother didn't limit the amount of television the children watched. Furthermore, she let them watch any programs they wanted.
3. My son's grades were dropping. Consequently, I took away his television privileges for a week.
4. I interviewed three children in my neighborhood; then, I interviewed their parents and day care providers.
5. I was surprised by what the preschool teacher said. For example, she said that she encourages parents to have their children watch *Sesame Street.*

Punctuating Correctly with Transitions

Unlike subordinators, transitions do not change independent clauses into dependent clauses. As a result, even if you add a transition to create a bridge between sentences, you still have to punctuate the sentences as two independent clauses. You have two options: you can use a period or a semicolon.

Option #1

Put a period between the two sentences and a comma after the transition word.

I think we need clearer guidelines for how much television the children can watch. <u>Furthermore,</u> we need to set rules for using the computer.

Notes

Option #2

Put a semicolon between the two sentences and a comma after the transition word.

I think we need clearer guidelines for how much television the children can watch; <u>furthermore,</u> we need to set rules for using the computer.

Review these punctuation rules from Chapter 4.

Punctuation Rule #3 (Review)

You may use a semicolon to separate two complete sentences.

- The television broke; I turned to my dusty bookshelf to find a source of entertainment.

Punctuation Rule #4 (Review)

Follow an introductory word or phrase with a comma.

- Consequently, I watch only cable channels.

Note: Punctuation Rules 3 and 4 are both applied when you join two complete sentences with a semicolon and transition.

- I despise commercial interruptions; consequently, I watch only cable channels.

Practice #5   Using Transitions

On a separate piece of paper, rewrite the sentences, adding the transitions as directed.

Example: I used to think that I couldn't live without television. You can imagine my fear when I moved to a dorm room with no TV! (Use *thus* with a semicolon and a comma between the two sentences.)

- I used to think that I couldn't live without television; thus, you can imagine my fear when I moved to a dorm room with no TV!

1. Kyle thought Winn was right about the link between obesity and television. He felt that her theory about television being an addiction was a little nutty. (Use *however* with a semicolon and a comma between the two sentences.)

2. I did some further research into the effects of television on children. I created strict rules for television watching at my house. (Use *then* with a semicolon and a comma between the two sentences.)

3. I realized I was watching over 50 hours of television a week. I set a goal to spend at least five hours a week exercising and five more hours reading novels. (Use *consequently* with a semicolon and a comma between the two sentences.)

4. First, I did some research on the Internet. I went to the college library. (Use *next* and a comma to begin the second sentence.)

5. The researcher shared her notes with us. She loaned us some of her videotapes. (Use *furthermore* and a comma to begin the second sentence.)

6. The article came from a tabloid that is known for poor journalism. I don't think you should give it much attention. (Choose a transition from the following list that most clearly expresses the relationship between these two sentences: *however, therefore,* or *for instance.* Use the transition word with a semicolon and a comma to join the two sentences.)

7. I don't want my children watching television all day. I don't want them focused on video games or the computer. (Choose a transition from the following list that most clearly expresses the relationship between these two sentences: *otherwise, therefore,* or *likewise.* Use the transition word with a semicolon and a comma to join the two sentences.)

8. My grandkids were glued to the video screen in the minivan. They didn't even notice the amazing cliffs and waterfalls we drove by. (Choose a transition from the following list that most clearly expresses the relationship between these two sentences: *similarly, for instance,* or *as a result.* Use the transition word and a comma to begin the second sentence.)

9. First, I made notes about the cartoons the kids were watching. I observed how they behaved immediately following the cartoons. (Choose a transition from the following list that most clearly expresses the relationship between these two sentences: *second, however,* or *consequently.* Use the transition word and a comma to begin the second sentence.)

Subordinators, Concessions, and Transitions

Notes

10. My daughter used to drive me crazy by asking for everything she saw advertised on television. I told her she could only watch PBS. (Choose a transition that clearly expresses the relationship between these two sentences. Choose to join the sentences by using a semicolon and comma, or choose to keep the sentences separate.)

Transitions that Interrupt Sentences

Thus far you have learned that you can place transitions at the beginning of independent clauses to create a link between ideas. To add variety to your sentence structure, you can also *interrupt* a single sentence with a transition. Study the examples that follow.

> I always enjoyed reading. My brother, <u>however</u>, was hooked on television at an early age.
>
> The children were participating in a no-television week. Their afternoon playtime, <u>therefore</u>, changed.
>
> The kids discovered all sorts of old toys. Jason, <u>for example</u>, found his old Monopoly game.

Interrupting a sentence with a transition word can add variety to your style while also helping you to strengthen the coherence of your essay.

Punctuating Correctly with Interrupting Transitions

Punctuation Rule #7

If you interrupt a single sentence with a transition word, you must put a comma before and after the transition word.

- The kids were entranced by the documentary on volcanoes. I, therefore, extended their usual television time.
- Bob's classmates weren't persuaded by his arguments. Bob, consequently, decided to do a little more research.

Practice #6   Using Interrupting Transitions

- Read these sentence pairs carefully.
- Insert an appropriate transition word or phrase in the second sentence in each pair. Read each sentence aloud to make sure that you have made the best choice.

- Use each of these transitions once:
  similarly
  therefore
  however
  consequently
  on the other hand

1. My spouse argues that a limited amount of television watching is

   okay.

   I, _____, want to throw out the set.

2. During the No-TV Week, the teachers saw that the students were

   doing better work on take-home assignments.

   The parents, _____, found that the kids com-

   pleted their chores more quickly.

3. I realized I hadn't played any sports with my kids in months.

   All of us decided, _____, to begin playing tennis at

   least one evening every week.

4. Sandy always had the television turned on.

   Her new roommate, _____, accused Sandy of being

   addicted to television.

5. According to Anderson, kids in happy, supportive homes proba-

   bly won't be affected by violence on television.

Subordinators, Concessions, and Transitions

Notes

Kids from unhappy, dysfunctional homes, _____,

might be more influenced by the violence.

Practice #7   More Practice with Interrupting Transitions

Interrupt the second sentence in each pair with a transition word. Write your new sentence on a separate piece of paper. Choose from the following list of transitions. (Use each transition once.)

furthermore	*finally*
on the other hand	*for example*
however	*consequently*
therefore	*for instance*

Example: Everyone in class had an opinion.
The class discussion was excellent.

• The class discussion, <u>consequently</u>, was excellent.

Hint: The interrupting transition word often fits most smoothly right after the subject and before the verb.

1. I wanted to paint a picture in my reader's mind. I focused on using my five senses to find details that would intrigue the reader.

2. My classmate said I used some great quotes. The quotes needed to be explained.

3. I think that if you involve your kids in fun after-school activities, they won't even think about turning on the television. My kids are so busy with soccer, piano, and homework that they don't even mention television during the week.

4. I knew one example wasn't enough to make readers take my side. I found two more examples to use in that paragraph.

5. Every student in the workshop group told Cassandra that she shouldn't try to argue against all of Winn's points. Cassandra selected two of the more complex points to argue.

6. I really enjoyed interviewing parents in my neighborhood. One of my classmates found it really hard to ask people questions.

7. I agree with Anderson that children do think while watching television. My son will talk to the television when watching *Blue's Clues*.

8. I watch television to learn about gardening, cooking, decorating, and even fixing my plumbing. Television offers me an easy mental escape at the end of a stressful day.

Practice #8   Creating Sentences with Transitions

Create original sentences according to the directions that follow. (Your sentences should connect to the topic of television. Some of these sentences might even end up in your essay.)

1. Write two original sentences. The second should start with "similarly."
2. Write two original sentences. Connect the sentences using a semicolon, a comma, and the transition phrase "next."
3. Write two original sentences. The second should start with "also."
4. Write two original sentences. Connect the sentences using a semicolon, a comma, and the transition "then."
5. Write two original sentences. The second should start with "likewise."

Practice #9   Creating Sentences with Interrupting Transitions

Create original sentences according to the directions that follow. (Your sentences should connect to the topic of television. Some of these sentences might even end up in your essay.)

1. Write two original sentences. Interrupt the second sentence with "however."
2. Write two original sentences. Interrupt the second sentence with "therefore."
3. Write two original sentences. Interrupt the second sentence with "on the other hand."
4. Write two original sentences. Interrupt the second sentence with "consequently."
5. Write two original sentences. Interrupt the second sentence with "furthermore."

Notes

Your Own Writing: Concessions and Transitions

Copy one paragraph from a journal or essay in which you are arguing a point. Look for places where a concession would help you maintain a reasonable tone while making your point stand out. Add the concession sentence.

Copy another paragraph from a journal or essay. Improve the coherence of your writing by building bridges with transition words.

- Put a transition at the beginning of a sentence,
- use a transition and a semicolon to connect two sentences, or
- interrupt a sentence with a transition.

CHAPTER

7

Writing About Technology

Main Topics

- Organizing your writing

- Communicating your ideas about technology

- Using adjectives, adjective phrases, adverbs, and prepositional phrases to make your sentences more expressive

Hi and Lois

Chance Brown 1999
King Features Syndicate
Sacramento Bee 4/16/99

At work and in college, you may find yourself swimming in data, facts, observations, and ideas. As a writer, reader, and critical thinker, you'll need strategies to organize this information so that you can make sense of it and utilize it. In this chapter, you'll concentrate on understanding and using different methods of *organizing* all the data, facts, observations, and ideas that you choose to communicate.

ORGANIZING YOUR WRITING

One way to think about organization is to remember that as a writer you are similar to a guide leading someone who temporarily doesn't see well. You want to make your reader's journey as smooth as possible (no bumps, cliffs, or wrong turns—unless carefully planned for dramatic effect), so you must *organize* what you say. Of course, you already organize ideas every day: when you explain to someone how to get to a specific file on your computer, when you summarize last night's great movie plot, or when you explain to your child why dishwashing detergent doesn't work in the clothes washer, you organize. In each case, you organize your thoughts to communicate clearly and quickly.

In this chapter, the organizing and communicating will not happen quite so quickly because you will be creating more formal responses to the complex topics about technology and high-tech surveillance. You will be presented with many ideas and opinions about the advantages and disadvantages of technology in general and the advantages and disadvantages of high-tech surveillance specifically. It will be your job to use your critical thinking skills, to carefully consider and sort through different ideas and opinions, to form your own opinion, and to focus and organize your ideas as you create a clearly written essay.

Organizing the Paragraph

In an organized paragraph, the writer states the main idea in the topic sentence. Then the writer offers detail and support that usually grow more specific and/or more important. A writer must also include an explanation of the details and supporting ideas. Paragraphs sometimes end with a wrap-up sentence that reminds the reader of the main point of the paragraph. Most paragraphs follow this general pattern:

- Main idea

- Increasingly specific and/or increasingly important details and support

- Wrap-up explanation

For example, consider the following body paragraph from a student's essay on the advantages of having Internet access in high school. The topic sentence announces the paragraph's main idea. The second sentence emphasizes the importance of the main idea. The writer then gives a specific example and explains the significance of this example. Finally, the writer wraps up the paragraph with a note of explanation that also emphasizes the importance of the main idea.

> Obtaining other people's views may be limited in a small city or town, but with the Internet, students can communicate with other students from all over the world. This can lead to the understanding of others' views and opinions. For example, students who take French can enhance their skills by writing to someone in France. A student is not only learning the language but can learn about the culture from someone with first-hand experience, instead of what may be in an outdated book. All of this knowledge will lead our children to a better understanding of the world.
>
> —*Stacy Michel*

main idea and explanation

specific example and explanation

concluding explanation that emphasizes importance of point

However, some paragraphs have other, distinct patterns. Here are some other **patterns of organization** that you use every day for speaking, thinking, and writing:

- Least important ideas first, most important ideas last

- Least interesting ideas first, most interesting ideas last

- (time) First idea or event that occurred, second, third, and so on

Occasionally these patterns overlap. That is, a writer might organize his ideas by a time pattern (telling what happened first, second, and so on), *and* he might have in mind that he is organizing his ideas according to importance. (The first event was least important to him, and the last event was most important to him.)

When revising a paragraph, a writer needs to think critically about organization and perhaps experiment with the order a bit. The writer must also make sure that the reader can see the logical organization of ideas. The writer can help the reader by using transitions that show the

For additional information about transitions, see pages 280–288.

Notes

relationships between ideas. For example, if the writer wants to show that the ideas in her paragraph go from the least important idea to the most important idea, she might use any of these transition phrases:

- significantly
- more importantly
- of most importance

If the writer wants to show that the ideas in her paragraph move from the first thing that happened to the second thing that happened and so on, she might use any of these transition words:

- first
- second
- next
- then
- last
- finally

There are many different words and phrases writers can use to organize their thoughts and keep the reader on track. Consider how the following words help to explain the relationships between ideas.

<u>To show that a similar idea follows</u>

- also
- in addition
- similarly
- furthermore
- in fact (also adds emphasis)

<u>To show that an example follows</u>

- for example
- for instance

<u>To show that an opposite idea follows</u>

- in contrast
- otherwise
- however

<u>To show that one idea has "caused" another</u>

- consequently
- as a result
- therefore

Activities

Study an Organized Paragraph

Carefully read the paragraph that follows.

> I am concerned that entertainment technology—television, CD players, Nintendo, computers—has led families to spend less quality time together. I don't know any families who spend time together creatively: dancing, singing, painting, or drawing. Similarly, I don't know any families who regularly play Monopoly or other board games. In fact, I can only think of one family I know that sits down together for dinner every day with no television blaring in the background. Quality time together is crucial so that adults can teach children social and communication skills. Perhaps more importantly, this time together shows that the parents care for the children and want to spend time with the children. Children gain much of their self-esteem from time spent with their families. I think that we need to watch our use of technology more carefully. What good is technology if it destroys the fabric of our families?

1. In the margins, mark the topic sentence (TS), the examples (Exam), and explanations (Explan).

2. Highlight or circle any transitions you find, and think about what relationships these words are expressing.

3. What organizational pattern (or patterns) is the writer using?

Organize These Thoughts

Read the following topic sentence and list of supporting ideas for a single paragraph. The sentences have been mixed up and are in no order. Study the information and then decide what order the sentences should be in. (You may want to review the patterns of organization.) Referring to the earlier list of transitions, find transition words and phrases that would help build bridges between the ideas in the paragraph, and rewrite the sentences so that you have an organized paragraph with transition words that help the reader understand how all the ideas fit together. Write your version of the paragraph and compare it to the paragraphs your classmates create.

Hint: There may be more than one way to organize the sentences logically. There are many different transitions to choose from.

Topic Sentence: I rely on modern technology to maintain my family ties.

Notes

> Since she and I both have fax machines at work, sometimes I'll fax Mom a letter I received from someone else in the family.
>
> My company has set up the day care rooms with cameras that are linked to our computers at work so that I can look in on my kids any time during the day.
>
> That way we can keep up on family news.
>
> I am in regular e-mail contact with two cousins, an aunt and uncle, and all three of my sisters.
>
> I rely on the computer even more.
>
> The phone is important to me so that I can call my mom in Alaska once a month.
>
> I use the computer to check in on my kids at the day care center.
>
> E-mail saves me a lot of money on long-distance bills, and it's so quick!
>
> Now I can check to see if my kids are having fun and if they are being treated well.
>
> I love technology.

Organizing the Essay

The same principles for organizing a paragraph apply to organizing an essay. That is, the ideas in an essay, like the ideas in a paragraph, must be in a thoughtful, logical order. In addition, essays rely on transitions just as paragraphs do.

The organized essay has a clear thesis and topic sentences that relate to that thesis. Often the topic sentences will begin with transition words that explain to the reader why the paragraphs have been organized in a certain pattern. The patterns listed for paragraphs also work with essays. Here, again, are those patterns and some additional patterns:

- Least important ideas first, most important ideas last
- Least interesting ideas first, most interesting ideas last
- (time) First idea or event that occurred, second, third, and so on
- (comparison of two subjects) One point about subject X, a related point about subject Y, another point about subject X, a related point about subject Y, and so on

- (comparison of two subjects) All points about subject X (divided into different paragraphs) and then all points about subject Y (divided into different paragraphs)

Activity

Study an Organized Essay

The following essay comes from *Sociology*, a textbook. Read the essay carefully once, marking any unknown words.

Modernization and Women: A Report from Rural Bangladesh
by John J. Macionis

This excerpt appeared in Macionis's textbook, *Sociology*, 5th edition, 1995.

1   In global perspective, gender inequality is greatest where people are poorest. Economic development, then, weakens traditional male domination and gives women opportunities to work outside the home. Birth control emancipates women from a continual routine of childbearing, allowing them to benefit from schooling and to earn more in the paid work force.

2   Even as living standards rise, however, economic development has drawbacks for women. Investigating a poor, rural district of Bangladesh, Sultana Alam (1985) reports that women confront several new problems as a result of modernization.

3   First, economic opportunity draws men from rural areas to cities in search of work, leaving women and children to fend for themselves. Men sometimes sell their land and simply abandon their wives, who are left with nothing but their children.

4   Second, the eroding strength of the family and neighborhood leaves women who are deserted in this way with few sources of assistance. The same holds true for women who become single through divorce or the death of a spouse. In the past, Alam reports, kin or neighbors readily took in a Bangladeshi woman who found herself alone. Today, as Bangladesh struggles to advance economically, the number of poor households headed by women is increasing. Rather than enhancing women's autonomy, Alam argues, this spirit of individualism has actually reduced the social standing of women.

5   Third, economic development—as well as the growing influence of Western movies and mass media—undermine women's traditional roles as wives, sisters, and mothers while redefining women as objects of men's sexual attention. The cultural emphasis on sexuality that is familiar to us now encourages men in poor societies to desert aging spouses for women who are younger and more physically attractive. The same emphasis contributes to the world's rising tide of prostitution. . . .

6   Modernization, then, does not affect men and women in the same ways. In the long run, the evidence suggests, modernization does give the sexes more equal standing. In the short run, however, the economic position of many women actually declines, and women are also forced to contend with new problems that were virtually unknown in traditional societies.

1. Reread the essay more carefully. Mark the thesis and topic sentences. Define any unknown terms. Note that the first *two* paragraphs act as the introduction to the essay.

2. Mark all transition words and phrases you find (at the beginning of paragraphs and within paragraphs).

3. Note in the margins the organizational pattern the author has used to put his paragraphs in order. Note also how individual sentences relate to one another. For example, look for transitional words or phrases that tell you the author is connecting opposite ideas.

4. In your own words, what is the writer's main point in this essay?

One Approach to Organization

Just as there are many different ways that writers brainstorm, gather information, and draft essays, there are also many different ways to organize information for an essay. In this chapter, you will practice one approach that utilizes index cards. When you reach the point in your writing process when you are ready to outline the ideas of your essay, you'll write down one point per index card, label the card, and perhaps even color code the card. Then you'll be able to arrange the cards in different orders until you find an organizational pattern that fits with what you want to say. Here are some examples of how you can create the cards for an essay about the advantages and disadvantages of technology.

(front of card)

> *Advantage*
>
> Television can be used by teachers to teach classes to people who can't get to the college or training center in person.

(back of card)

> Personal experience

(front of card)

> *Disadvantage*
>
> Television has encouraged the idea that women are sex objects.

(back of card)

> Personal experience and Macionis, "Modernization and Women: A Report from Rural Bangladesh," Paragraph 5

Cards for the work in this chapter should be labeled as *Advantage* or *Disadvantage* since both writing assignments in the chapter deal with advantages and disadvantages of technology. You may even want to color code your cards—one color for advantage cards and another color for disadvantage cards. Use your own words when making these

Notes

notes. On the front of each card, you'll have just one idea. On the back of the card, you'll write down where you got the information. If the information comes from a reading, you'll have to write down the author's name, the title of the reading, and the paragraph number. Then you'll be able to go back and read more about an idea if you need to, and you'll have your source information ready when you begin writing your essay.

You may find that some cards have ideas that will become topic sentences. Other cards will have ideas that belong in the bodies of paragraphs. The key is to write just one idea per card. Then you can easily move the ideas around until you have found the best way to group them and organize them.

At the outline stage of your writing process, feel free to make many cards because this way you'll have many ideas to choose from as you prepare to write your essay, and it's easy to set aside a card that you decide doesn't fit. (Keep all the cards you make in this chapter. If you are assigned both essays from this chapter, some of your cards may be needed twice.)

Points to Remember About Organization

- Although only five organizational patterns have been described so far, there are more than just five ways to organize ideas in an essay, and some of the patterns mentioned here can be combined. (You'll be introduced to more patterns later in the chapter.)
- Use a pattern that makes sense to you and that seems to fit with what you want to say.
- Stick to your pattern. Your reader will have an easier time understanding your ideas if you have a clear pattern of organization and if you stick to your pattern. Your reader will enjoy the smooth path you create.
- Use transitions to help guide your reader.

INVESTIGATING TECHNOLOGY

Now that you have begun to think about the skill of organizing, you'll begin your writing process. You'll discuss technology and the many ways our lives have been affected by it. You'll have quite a bit of information to consider and sort through. Later in this chapter, you will find two writing assignments and step-by-step guidelines as you complete your writing process.

Discuss and Engage

Technology is a broad term encompassing anything that science has created, usually relating to industry and commercial items. In other words, technological advances include the creation of the telephone, the microwave oven, the home computer, and the compact disc player. Technology is also responsible for changing how we shower, store food, and travel from place to place. With so many items to consider, it's no wonder that people find much to praise about technology and much to criticize.

Get Involved!

If you are new to the Internet, find out where you can log on to the Internet on your college campus. With a classmate or by yourself, spend one hour visiting Internet sites. Seek assistance from a librarian or computer lab technician if possible. Make notes about which sites you visited and your reaction to the Internet in general. Share your experience with your classmates and instructor. (These notes might also prove helpful with the first writing assignment in this chapter.)

> ### *Journal Assignment*
>
> #### *Technology at Home*
>
> Reread the comic strip on the preview page of this chapter. What does the teenage son mean when he says, "I liked it better when *I* was the only one who knew how to use the computer!" What does his statement suggest about the place of technology in the home today? What positive and negative points are being made about technology?

Activity

Technology Inventory

1. Working with a classmate, make an inventory of how technology affects your daily life. That is, make a list of mechanical devices that you use to get through your day. You may want to begin your list by thinking about how you start your day. For example, do you rely on an alarm clock to get up in the morning? Do you use the Internet at work or at home? (You won't be able to list *every* technological device that touches you. Concentrate on creating a thoughtful list.)

2. After you have listed many items technology has produced, highlight those items on your list that are the most technologically advanced. (Which items have been created most recently and seem to be the most sophisticated?)

Notes

3. Which of the highlighted items do you most value? Which seem to clearly make your life better? Are there any items that seem to negatively affect your quality of life? Can an item both increase and decrease your quality of life? Explain.

Journal Assignment

Advantages and Disadvantages of Technology

Review your class notes on technology. Write freely about technology. What do you find most promising about current technological advances? What worries you the most about technology? Have your classmates said anything in class discussions that surprised you or that you disagreed with? Explain. (This journal is for your eyes only. Refer back to this journal when you are getting ready to write your essay.)

Writing Assignment #1: Discussing Technology in Our Lives

Here, in brief, is the writing assignment you are preparing for.

Write an essay in which you discuss some of the advantages and disadvantages of technology in your life.

Read, Discuss, Think Critically

This section of the chapter offers you a reading about the advantages, disadvantages, and limitations of technology. The reading is a college student's essay that was published in a magazine.

Reading Assignment: "Stop the Clock"

Preview   Read the first two paragraphs.

Anticipate   What do you anticipate this essay will be about? Use the "Notes" column to record your response.

Read and Reread   Read the entire essay, marking unknown terms and interesting points. Then reread more slowly and use the "Notes" column to interact with the essay. Mark important points and define unknown terms.

Stop the Clock

by Amy Wu

This article first appeared in *Newsweek* magazine, January 22, 1996.

1   My aunt tends to her house as if it were her child. The rooms are spotless, the windows squeak, the kitchen counter is so shiny that I can see my reflection and the floors are so finely waxed that my sister and I sometimes slide across in socks and pretend that we are skating.

2   Smells of soy sauce, scallions and red bean soup drift from the kitchen whenever I visit. The hum of the washing machine lulls me to sleep. In season, there are roses in the garden, and vases hold flowers arranged like those in a painting. My aunt enjoys keeping house, although she's wealthy enough to hire someone to do it. I'm a failure at housework. I've chosen to be inept and unlearn what my aunt has spent so much time perfecting. At 13, I avoided domestic chores as my contribution to the women's movement. Up to now, I've thought there were more important things to do. I am a member of a generation that is very concerned with saving time but often unaware of why we're doing it. Like many, I'm nervous and jittery without a wristwatch and a daily planner. I am one of a growing number of students who are completing college in three years instead of four—cramming credits in the summer. We're living life on fast-forward without a pause button.

3   In my freshman year, my roommates and I survived on Chinese takeout, express pizzas and taco take-home dinners. We ate lunch while walking to class. Every day seemed an endless picnic as we ate with plastic utensils and paper plates. It was fast and easy—no washing up. My girlfriends and I talked about our mothers and grandmothers, models of domesticity, and pitied them. We didn't see the benefits of staying at home, ironing clothes and making spaghetti sauce when canned sauces were almost as good and cleaning services were so convenient. A nearby store even sold throwaway underwear. "Save time," the package read. "No laundry."

4   We baked brownies in ten minutes in the microwave and ate the frosting from the can because we were too impatient to wait for the brownies to cool. For a while we thought about chipping in and buying a funky contraption that makes toast, coffee and eggs. All you had to do was put in the raw ingredients the night before and wake up to the smell of sizzling eggs, crispy toast and rich coffee. My aunt was silent when I told her about plastic utensils, microwave meals and disposable underwear. "It's a waste of money," she finally said. I was angry as I stared at

Notes

her perfect garden, freshly ironed laundry and handmade curtains. "Well, you're wasting your time," I said defensively. But I wasn't so sure.

5   It seems that all the kids I know are timesaving addicts. Everyone on campus prefers e-mail to snail mail. The art of letter writing is long gone. I know classmates who have forgotten how to write in script, and print like five-year-olds. More of us are listening to books instead of reading them. My roommate last year jogged while plugged in. She told me she'd listened to John Grisham's *The Client*. "You mean read," I corrected. "I didn't read a word," she said with pride.

6   My nearsighted friends opt for throwaway contacts and think the usual lenses are tedious. A roommate prefers a sleeping bag so she doesn't have to make her bed. Instead of going to the library to do re-search we cruise the Internet and log on to the Library of Congress.

7   Schoolkids take trips to the White House via Internet and Mosaic. I heard that one school even considered canceling the eighth-grade Washington trip, a traditional rite of passage, because it's so easy to visit the capital on the Information Highway. I remember how excited my eighth-grade classmates and I were about being away from home for the first time. We stayed up late, ate Oreos in bed and roamed around the Lincoln Memorial, unsupervised by adults.

8   It isn't as if we're using the time we save for worthwhile pursuits like volunteering at a soup kitchen. Most of my friends spend the extra min-utes watching TV, listening to stereos, shopping, hanging out, chatting on the phone or snoozing.

9   When I visited my aunt last summer, I saw how happy she was after baking bread or a cake, how proud she seemed whenever she made a salad with her homegrown tomatoes and cucumbers. Why bother when there are ready-made salads, ready-peeled and -cut fruit and five-minute frosting?

10   Once, when I went shopping with her, she bought ingredients to make a birthday cake for her daughter. I pointed to a lavish-looking cake covered with pink roses. "Why don't you just buy one," I asked. "A cake is more than a cake," she replied. "It's the giving of energy, the thought behind it. You'll grow to understand."

11   Slowly, I am beginning to appreciate why my aunt takes pleasure in cooking for her family, why the woman down the street made her daughter's wedding gown instead of opting for Vera Wang, why the old man next door spends so much time tending his garden. He offered me a bag of his fresh-grown tomatoes. "They're good," he said. "Not like the ones at the supermarket." He was right.

12   Not long ago, I spent a day making a meal for my family. As the pasta boiled and the red peppers sizzled, I wrote a letter to my cousin in Canada.

At first the pen felt strange, then reassuring. I hand-washed my favorite skirt and made chocolate cake for my younger sister's 13th birthday. It took great self-control not to slather on the icing before the cake cooled.

13   That night I grinned as my father and sister dug into the pasta, then the cake, licking their lips in appreciation. It had been a long time since I'd felt so proud. A week later my cousin called and thanked me for my letter, the first handwritten correspondence she'd received in two years.

14   Sure, my generation has all the technological advances at our fingertips. We're computer-savvy, and we have more time. But what are we really saving it for? In the end, we may lose more than we've gained by forgetting the important things in life.

Questions for Critical Thought

"Stop the Clock"

1. Wu's personal essay doesn't follow traditional academic essay style. For example, she doesn't have a thesis statement at the end of the introduction. Review her entire essay and, in your own words, write down Wu's main point (her implied thesis).

2. What does Wu mean in Paragraph 2 when she says she was making her "contribution to the women's movement"?

3. Study how Wu has organized her essay. In the margins, note the place where she mentions timesaving conveniences in a positive, or at least neutral, light. Now note in the margins the places where she hints that she is no longer satisfied with her fast-paced life. Where does the essay begin to really focus on the positive aspects of living more slowly?

4. One of the strengths of Wu's essay is the number of interesting and vivid pieces of detail. Select a few of your favorite pieces of detail from her essay and explain why these details are so effective.

5. Wu mentions a number of timesaving devices that she and her friends have relied on. List those devices and highlight the ones that most clearly connect to recent technology.

6. What timesaving devices do you use? How do you spend the time you "save"? (Review Wu's Paragraph 8.)

7. Review Paragraphs 10 and 14. Do you have any old-fashioned domestic interests (like baking or gardening)? What do you think are the important things in life? How should you spend your time? Can technology help you do this? Explain.

Notes

Journal Assignment

Technology in Modern Life

Reflect on the two technology paragraphs on pages 291 and 293, the paragraph you organized on pages 293–294, the essay "Modernization and Women: A Report from Rural Bangladesh" on pages 295–296, the essay "Stop the Clock" on pages 301–303, and your class discussions so far. Then consider this quotation: "By his very success in inventing labor-saving devices, modern man has manufactured an abyss of boredom that only the privileged class in earlier civilizations have ever fathomed" (Lewis Mumford, *The Conduct of Life,* 1951). What ideas in the readings, class discussions, and this quotation do you most strongly support? What ideas do you want to argue with? Exchange journals with a classmate, and when you've finished reading, say, "Thank you."

Explore the Writing Assignment

Here, again, is your writing assignment. Review it carefully before continuing. Underline the important terms in the assignment.

Write an essay in which you discuss some of the advantages and disadvantages of technology in your life.

Brainstorm   Write freely in response to the writing assignment. Explore the many different advantages and disadvantages of technology that you read about and discussed in class. Let your mind wander, and let yourself repeat ideas that keep coming to your mind. When you have completed a lengthy, thoughtful brainstorm, go back and highlight any promising ideas for your essay. Pay attention to ideas that you repeatedly came back to.

Consider Your Audience   Your audience will be familiar with most technological advances, but if you are interested in discussing lesser-known technological devices, think about what kind of background information you should give your audience. Also, do you expect your audience to agree with everything you say? Do you expect some disagreement? What will your audience expect from an interesting, thoughtful essay? Make a list of things to keep in mind when writing for your audience.

Create Your Thesis   Review the writing assignment. Note that the assignment uses the word *some*. This means that you are not expected to write about every technological advance you can think of. Choose advantages and disadvantages that most interest you and that connect logically to one another. For example, you may want to focus on technological advances in the area of entertainment or in the areas of housekeeping or work. Your thesis should show that you have carefully narrowed the scope of your essay. Also note that the writing assignment asks for both advantages *and* disadvantages. You should cover both in your thesis and essay. Experiment with thesis statements until you find one that expresses what you want to focus on in your essay.

Notes

Outline   Keeping your thesis in mind, carefully review your notes and readings. Write down on index cards the technological advantages and disadvantages you think you should cover in your essay. You may want to review the section on index cards at the beginning of the chapter. (Remember, only one idea per card.)

Review your cards and think about how you might organize your ideas. You'll probably find cards that you don't know what to do with or cards that you simply aren't interested in. Get rid of these cards—or at least set them aside. You should only work with the cards that are most interesting to you and that fit your general message. (You are working on your focus skills when you do this.)

Experiment with different ways to organize your cards. Plan on discussing only one technological advantage or disadvantage per paragraph. Of course, it is possible that you'll have more than one index card per advantage or disadvantage. For example, you might have two or three index cards dealing with the advantages of e-mail. In that case, you'd want to group these cards together as one paragraph and experiment with how the ideas in that paragraph should be organized. You'd also want to experiment with where you'll place that paragraph in your essay.

When you think you have a pretty good idea of which index cards you'll use and the order you'll put them in, get together with a small group of classmates and show them what you've decided. Explain your choices. You may find that you need to make some changes, and you may get some new ideas from listening to how your classmates are organizing their cards.

Notes

Draft

Using your notecards as a guideline, draft your essay. In your introduction, prepare your audience to read about technology and the advantages and disadvantages you have been thinking about. In the body of your essay, discuss one advantage or disadvantage in each paragraph. In your conclusion, discuss what you and your reader should have learned from your essay.

Revise

Activity

Share Your Writing

Find a classmate to work with. Read each other's essays. Then discuss the following questions as they apply to each essay.

- Have you chosen a reasonable number of points to cover?
- Do you cover just one advantage or disadvantage per paragraph?
- Do you offer interesting support and explanations in each paragraph?
- Is the organization of your points logical?
- Do you use transitions to help your reader? Do you need more? Fewer?

Edit

You may want to review earlier, graded essays to see what, if any, sentence errors you tend to repeat. Then carefully review your technology essay and look for any of these errors.

Read your essay aloud, listening for awkward spots and looking for typographical errors. You may want to have a friend read your essay aloud to you. Sometimes it's easier to find mistakes this way.

Additional ideas for editing:

- Carefully review your essay for spelling errors.
- Note that *Internet* is always capitalized. (*World Wide Web* is capitalized also.)

You may also want to consider these questions after completing the sentence work at the end of this chapter (pages 324–337).

- Have you used adjectives, adjective phrases, adverbs, and prepositional phrases to make your writing clearer and more descriptive?
Mark each adjective, adverb, and prepositional phrase in your essay. Would your essay be more interesting and clearer with more
of them?

Writing Assignment #2:
The Advantages and Disadvantages of High-Tech Surveillance

Here, in brief, is the writing assignment you are preparing for.

*Do you see more advantages or disadvantages in the types of high-tech surveil-
lance mentioned in "Big Brother Logs On"? Describe in detail the disadvantages
and advantages that most intrigue you. (Note: It is possible to write an essay in
which you say that you see an equal number of advantages and disadvantages.)*

Read, Discuss, Think Critically

This section of the chapter offers you one lengthy reading about the
advantages and disadvantages of high-tech surveillance. You may find
this reading to be challenging due to its length, terminology, and so-
phistication. Plan your reading time well, allowing yourself time to
read it once just to get the general idea and then again to really understand the information.

Reading Assignment: "Big Brother Logs On"

Preview   Read the title, introductory material, subheadings, and
the topic sentences. And review the following definitions and explanations to get a preview of some of the most important terms in
the essay:

Ubiquitous (an adjective you will see many times in this essay)
means widespread, constantly present.

Ubiquitous surveillance refers to cameras or other tools that
other people can use to watch you all the time.

George Orwell's 1984 and *Big Brother*: George Orwell's book
1984 (published in 1949) is a novel that explores what it would
be like if the government could watch us constantly, control our
actions, and rewrite history. Big Brother was the name in the
book for the government or people who were always watching.
Occasionally in this essay you will see Orwell's name made into

Notes

the adjective *Orwellian*. An Orwellian society would be a society that is very similar to the one described in *1984*.

Algorithm and *biometric* are also terms repeated many times in this essay. An algorithm is a step-by-step procedure that must be repeated again and again. This term is often used in connection to computers and mathematics. Biometric refers to a study of the body. For example, one biometric tool studies people's faces to see if they match any of the pictures of criminals in a computer database.

Anticipate   What do you think the article will be about? Use the "Notes" column to record your response.

Read and Reread   Read the entire essay quickly, marking unknown terms. Then reread more slowly and use the "Notes" column to interact with the essay. Mark important points and define unknown terms.

Big Brother Logs On
by Ivan Amato

This article first appeared in *Technology Review*, September 2001.

Is privacy a right or a privilege? Recent developments in surveillance technology are calling the concept of privacy into question, as cameras invade our streets and software records our facial expressions while we shop. Is our loss of privacy inevitable?

1   The door to paranoia opens benignly—and early. Just think of Santa. He knows when you are sleeping. He knows when you're awake. He knows if you've been bad or good, for goodness' sake. And he knows these things all the time, even though you can't see him. Millions of kids all over the world happily and wholeheartedly believe in ubiquitous surveillance as a de facto piece of the annual Christmas present-getting machine. Parents just shake their heads in adoring wonder.

2   But those same parents might be shocked to learn how short the journey is from the pleasant surveillance fantasy of Santa to the freedom-squashing invasion of Big Brother. In the world detailed by George Orwell in the novel *1984*, surveillance cameras follow every move a person makes, and the slightest misstep, or apparent misstep, summons the authorities. Now, similarly, police departments, government agencies, banks, merchants, amusement parks, sports arenas, nanny-watching

homeowners, swimming-pool operators, and employers are deploying cameras, pattern recognition algorithms, databases of information, and biometric tools that when taken as a whole can be combined into automated surveillance networks able to track just about anyone, just about anywhere.

3   While none of us is under 24-hour surveillance yet, the writing is on the wall. As Scott McNealy, CEO of Sun Microsystems, starkly told reporters in 1999, "You already have zero privacy. Get over it." The techno-entrepreneurs who are developing and marketing these tools anticipate good things to come, such as reduced crime rates in urban environments, computer interfaces that will read eye movements and navigate the Web for you, and fingerprint or facial recognition systems and other biometric technologies that guarantee your identity and eliminate the need for passwords, PIN numbers and access cards—even identifying potential terrorists before they can strike.

4   But privacy advocates paint a far dimmer picture of this same future, accepting its reality while questioning whether it can be managed responsibly. "The technology is developing at the speed of light, but the privacy laws to protect us are back in the Stone Age," says Barry Steinhardt, associate director of the American Civil Liberties Union, which is among several groups that have tried, so far almost universally unsuccessfully, to introduce legislation aimed at protecting privacy. "We may not end up with an Orwellian society run by malevolent dictators, but it will be a surveillance society where none of the detail of our daily lives will escape notice and where much of that detail will be recorded."

The Fifth Utility

5   In many ways, the drama of pervasive surveillance is being played out first in Orwell's native land, the United Kingdom, which operates more closed-circuit cameras per capita than any other country in the world. This very public surveillance began in 1986 on an industrial estate near the town of King's Lynn, approximately 100 kilometers north of London. Prior to the installation of three video cameras, a total of 58 crimes had been reported on the estate. None was reported over the next two years. In 1995, buoyed by that success, the government made matching grants available to other cities and towns that wanted to install public surveillance cameras—and things took off from there.

6   Most of these closed-circuit TV systems are installed in business districts or shopping centers by British Telecommunications, the national phone network, and jointly operated and managed by law enforcement

Notes

Get Involved!

Read the excerpt of *1984* in Supplemental Readings (pages 439–441). Report back to your class about your reading.

and private industry. In addition, some townships are using BT to hook up video telephony, a technology that allows transmission of video images via telephone lines—but in a monitor-friendly network that provides officials quick and easy remote access to the images. On another front, the U.K. Home Office, the government department responsible for internal affairs in England and Wales, is starting construction of what promises to be the world's biggest road and vehicle surveillance network, a comprehensive system of cameras, vehicle and driver databases, and microwave and phone-based communications links that will be able to identify and track the movements of vehicles nearly nationwide. All told, the country's electronic eyes are becoming so prevalent that Stephen Graham of the Centre for Urban Technology at the University of Newcastle upon Tyne has dubbed them a "fifth utility," joining water, gas, electric and telephones.

7   The United States and many other parts of the developed world are not far behind in video surveillance. Just look at the cameras looking at you. They're in ATMs, banks, stores, casinos, lobbies, hallways, desktops, and along highways, main streets and even side streets. And those are the cameras you can see. Companies like All Security Systems of Miami, FL, advertise Clock Cameras, Exit Sign Cameras, Smoke Detector Cameras, and Covert Tie and Button Cams, as well as Nanny Cams and other easily hidden eyes, some of which send video signals wirelessly to a recorder located elsewhere.

8   But cameras seem relatively benign when compared to new technology being developed and deployed. Until recently, closed-circuit systems have fed video signals to monitors, which human beings had to watch in real time, or sent the images to recording media for storage. Now, however, the job of spotting suspicious people and behavior in this stream of electronic imagery is becoming automatic, with computers programmed with special algorithms for matching video pixel patterns to stored patterns associated with criminals or criminal actions— and the machines themselves passing initial judgment on whether a behavior is normal.

9   For example, last January at the Super Bowl in Tampa, FL, law enforcement agencies, without announcement, deployed a face recognition system from Viisage Technology of Littleton, MA. Cameras snapped face shots of fans entering the stadium. Computers instantly extracted a minimal set of features from each captured face, a so-called eigenface, and then compared the eigenfaces to those of criminals, stored in a database. The system purportedly found 19 possible matches, although no one was arrested as a result of the test. Less than six months later, in mid-July, Tampa police sparked public protests after deploying a face

recognition system from Visionics, of Jersey City, NJ, to scan city sidewalks for suspected criminals and runaways.

10   And this is just the beginning of the technology being piloted and prototyped to watch you—and judge your behavior. Beginning in 1997, the U.S. Defense Advanced Research Projects Agency (DARPA) funded some 20 projects under a three-year program called Video Surveillance and Monitoring. That effort has just gathered new momentum under a $50 million follow-up program known as Human ID at a Distance. The aim is to determine if it's feasible to identify specific individuals at distances up to 150 meters.

11   Under the program, researchers at Carnegie Mellon University in Pittsburgh are investigating whether a remote sensing technique known as "hyperspectral imaging"—a technology typically used by satellites to find minerals or peer through military camouflage—can be adapted for identifying specific human beings by measuring the color spectrum emitted by their skin. Skin absorbs, reflects and emits distinct patterns of color, and those patterns are specific enough to individual people to serve as spectral signatures. Such systems already work. But according to Robert Collins, a computer scientist at Carnegie Mellon's Robotics Institute, the process currently requires a person to sit stiffly in a chair as a sensor sweeps through hundreds of emitted wavelengths over a period of about five seconds. "Ideally, what will happen is we'll find some small group of wavelengths that we can use to distinguish people," explains Collins. That could reduce the scan time to a fraction of a second.

12   Another approach being developed involves a video-based network of sensors that would automatically measure such characteristics as leg length and waist width to provide, as Collins says, "the measurements you give to a tailor." The idea here, he says, is that those numbers should be able to serve as a kind of body fingerprint for identifying specific individuals.

13   There is no shortage of cleverness when it comes to building the surveillance state. At the Georgia Institute of Technology, scientists are developing sensor riddled "smart floors" that can identify people by the "force profiles" of their walking feet. Meanwhile, Princeton, NJ–based Sarnoff is working toward an antiterrorist technique that uses a special camera to identify individuals from a hundred meters off by the patterns of color, striation and speckles in their irises. This isn't easy, since the iris and its elements move so quickly relative to a distant camera that the technical task bears some resemblance to "tracking a ballistic missile," says Norman Winarsky, president of nVention, Sarnoff's venture technology company. Still, the technology is coming.

Get Involved!

Rent the movie *Gattaca,* directed by Andrew Niccol, 1997. Explain to your class how this film connects to the topics in this essay.

Notes

Get Involved!

Rent the movie *Minority Report,* directed by Steven Spielberg, 2002. Take notes during the movie and then report to your class about the different types of high-tech surveillance you see in the movie and what you think their advantages and disadvantages are.

---

14   Beyond identity is intention—and there are technologies in the works for divining that as well. IBM has introduced a software product called BlueEyes *(see "Behind BlueEyes"* TR *May 2001)* that's currently in use at retail stores to record customers' facial expressions and eye movements, tracking the effectiveness of in-store promotions. And psychologist Jeffrey Cohn of Carnegie Mellon's Robotics Institute and colleagues have been trying to teach machines an even more precise way to detect facial expressions.

15   From video signals, the Carnegie Mellon system detects and tracks both invariant aspects of a face, such as the distance between the eyes, and transient ones, like skin furrows and smile wrinkles. This raw data is then reclassified as representing elemental actions of the face. Finally, a neural network correlates combinations of these measurable units to actual expressions. While this falls short of robotic detection of human intentions, many facial expressions reflect human emotions, such as fear, happiness or rage, which, in turn, often serve as visible signs of intentions.

16   Cohn points out that this particular work is just part of the team's more encompassing "goal of developing computer systems that can detect human activity, recognize the people involved, understand their behavior, and respond appropriately." In short, the effort could help lead to the kind of ubiquitous surveillance system that can automatically scan collective human activity for signs of anything from heart-attack-inducing Type-A behavior to sexual harassment to daydreaming at the wheel to homicidal rage.

The Good, the Bad and the Well-Intentioned

17   The list of emerging technological wonders goes on and on, which is why many observers argue it's no longer a question of whether ubiquitous surveillance will be applied, but under what guidelines it will operate—and to what end.

18   "Like most powerful technologies, total surveillance will almost certainly bring both good and bad things into life," says James Wayman, a former National Security Agency contractor who now directs human identification research at San Jose State University in California. Specifically, he notes, it will combine laudable benefits in convenience and public safety with a potentially lamentable erosion of privacy.

19   These contradictory values often trigger vigorous debate over whether it will all be worth it. The glass-half-full crowd contends that the very infrastructure of surveillance that conjures fears of Big Brother will actually make life easier and safer for most people. Consider the benefits of the "computer-aided drowning detection and prevention" system that Boulogne, France–based Poseidon Technologies has installed in

nine swimming pools in France, England, the Netherlands and Canada. In these systems, a collection of overhead and in-pool cameras relentlessly monitors pool activity. The video signals feed into a central processor running a machine perception algorithm that can effectively spot when active nonwater objects, such as swimmers, become still for more than a few seconds. When that happens, a red alarm light flashes at a poolside laptop workstation and lifeguards are alerted via waterproof pagers. Last November, a Poseidon system at the Jean Blanchet Aquatic Center in Ancenis, Loire-Atlantique, France, alerted lifeguards in time to rescue a swimmer on the verge of drowning. Pulled from the water unconscious, the swimmer walked away from a hospital the next day.

20   Similarly, when cell phones and other mobile gadgetry start coming embedded with Global Positioning System transponders, it will be possible to pinpoint the carrier and quickly come to his or her aid, if necessary. Such transponders are already built into many new cars *(see "The Commuter Computer" TR June 2001)*. A click of a button or the triggering of an air bag sends a call to a service center, where agents can then direct emergency personnel to the vehicle, even if the occupants are unconscious. A public ubiquitous surveillance system could also enhance safety by noticing, for example, if a car hits you or if large, unauthorized crowds start congregating around an accident or altercation. As with the car rescue systems, a person's plight could be recognized and help dispatched almost instantly, sort of how air bags are now immediately deployed on impact.

21   And not many argue about surveillance's ability to deter crime. Recent British government reports cite closed circuit TV as a major reason for declining crime rates. After these systems were put in place, the town of Berwick reported that burglaries fell by 69 percent; in Northampton overall crime decreased by 57 percent; and in Glasgow, Scotland, crime slumped by 68 percent. Public reaction in England has been mixed, but many embrace the technology. "I am prepared to exchange a small/negligible amount of privacy loss so I don't have to be caught up in yet another bomb blast/bomb scare," wrote one London computer programmer in an online discussion of the technology.

22   Do the developers of this controversial technology weigh the pros and cons of their creations? Robert Collins of Carnegie Mellon concedes that much of the work that might fall into the surveillance category conjures an Orwellian quease, but he joins a veritable chorus of colleagues who say it's not their station to be gatekeepers looking out for how the technology ultimately is used. "We who are working on this are not so interested in applying it to surveillance and Big Brother stuff," Collins says. "We're making computers that can interact with people better."

Notes

Get Involved!

Go online and retrieve the article noted here in Paragraph 20 (www.technologyreview. com/articles/buder. 0601.asp). After reading the article, report to your class and summarize the main points of the article.

Indeed, Collins notes that he and his colleagues are motivated by the notion of "pervasive computing," in which the technoenvironment becomes aware of its human occupants so that computers and other gadgets can adjust to human needs. The way it is now, he says, humans have to accommodate the limitations of machines.

23   Jonathon Philips, manager of DARPA's Human ID at a Distance program, puts it another way: "We develop the technology. The policy and how you implement them is not my province."

24   So who is watching the gate? Well, the courts are slowly getting involved. A U.S. Supreme Court decision last June determined that in the absence of a search warrant, the government's use of a thermal imaging device to monitor heat coming off the walls of a suspected marijuana grower's private residence in Florence, OR, violated the Fourth Amendment prohibition against "unreasonable searches and seizures." The ruling could have far-reaching consequences for how new, more powerful surveillance technologies can be deployed. Overall, however, the responsibility of surveillance technology management and regulation is up for grabs in the United States, even as the technology proliferates. And so whether society goes Orwellian or not could well hinge on how responsibly the databases, biometric details and all the rest are managed and protected. After all, notes the ACLU's Steinhardt, it's a small step from a technological advance to a technology abuse.

25   Take the fact that the faces of a large portion of the driving population are becoming digitized by motor vehicles agencies and placed into databases, says Steinhardt. It isn't much of a stretch to extend the system to a Big Brother–like nationwide identification and tracking network. Or consider that the Electoral Commission of Uganda has retained Viisage Technology to implement a "turnkey face recognition system" capable of enrolling 10 million voter registrants within 60 days. By generating a database containing the faceprint of every one of the country's registered voters—and combining it with algorithms able to scour all 10 million images within six seconds to find a match—the commission hopes to reduce voter registration fraud. But once such a database is compiled, notes John Woodward, a former CIA operations officer who managed spies in several Asian countries and who's now an analyst with the Rand Corporation, it could be employed for tracking and apprehending known or suspected political foes. Woodward calls that "function creep."

26   Function creep is where things get really dicey for privacy advocates. Several grass-roots efforts now under way seek to rein in surveillance technology through more responsible privacy legislation. The Privacy Coalition, a nonpartisan collection of consumer, civil liberties, labor and family-based groups, is trying to get federal and state lawmakers to

commit to its "Privacy Pledge," which contains, among other things, a vow to develop independent oversight of public surveillance technology and limit the collection of personal data. And several organizations, including the AFL-CIO, Communications Workers of America, 9to5, National Association of Working Women and the United Auto Workers, are supporting legislation to restrict electronic monitoring of employees. As Steinhardt declares, "We can't leave this to systems designers or the marketplace."

27   In spite of these broad efforts, a number of factors, not the least of which is disagreement in Washington about what form such legislation should take, are making it difficult to put words into action. Last year Congress debated the Notice of Electronic Monitoring Act, which would have required companies to notify employees if they were being watched. Although that legislation died in committee, it will probably resurface again this year. As far as individual state laws are concerned, only Connecticut requires employers to tell employees if they are being monitored.

28   Which leads to the question of what exactly constitutes "private" activity. As former spymaster Woodward observes, a total-surveillance society will not actually expose individuals that much more than ordinary public circulation does now. "Once you leave your house and enter public spaces," he says, "just about everyone you can see can see you right back." In other words, you do not walk around most of the day with an expectation of privacy. Your face is not private, so if a camera sees you, it's no big deal. What's more, asks Woodward, even if rich and powerful entities, such as the government or mega-corporations, had sole access to a system capable of watching everyone all of the time, why would they bother? "The bottom line is that most of us are very boring. We flatter ourselves to think that someone is building a multibillion-dollar system to watch us," he says.

29   Even if public opinion does manage to slow down the deployment of surveillance infrastructure, no one involved in the debate thinks it will stop some form of Big Brother from arriving eventually. In his 1998 book *The Transparent Society,* which is well known in the privacy advocacy community, science fiction author and technology watcher David Brin argues that society inevitably will have to choose between two versions of ubiquitous surveillance: in one, only the rich and powerful use and control the system to their own advantage; in the second, more democratic future, the watchers can also be watched. Brin concedes that the latter version would mean everybody's laundry hung out in public view, but the transparency would at least be mutual. Rent a porn video and your wife knows it; but if she drives to your best buddy's house four times a week while you're at the office, you'll know that also.

Get Involved!

Find a copy of Brin's novel *The Transparent Society* in a library or bookstore. Read the first chapter and report to your class. What is the book about? Is it interesting or not? Why?

Notes

Get Involved!

Visit www.tecnology review.com and click on opinions/forums to read and participate in online discussions about technology. Report back to your class about your experience.

30   Whether or not the coming era of total surveillance fits neatly into one of Brin's scenarios will be determined by a complex equation encompassing technological development and the decisions that local, state and federal governments choose to make. The question largely boils down to this: is privacy a right or a privilege? Most Americans assume it is a right, as in our "right to privacy." But the truth of the matter is that privacy isn't guaranteed by the Constitution. It is implied, certainly, but not assured. This subtle difference is being tested right now, within our own neighborhoods and workplaces.

Questions for Critical Thought

"Big Brother Logs On"

1. Amato has a strong vocabulary that helps make his writing both accurate and interesting. In your vocabulary notebook, define the following words (through context clues and by using the dictionary).

   deploying, Para. 2
   malevolent, Para. 4
   per capita, Para. 5
   buoyed, Para. 5
   benign, Para. 8
   feasible, Para. 10
   divining, Para. 14
   invariant, Para. 15
   transient, Para. 15
   laudable, Para. 18
   lamentable, Para. 18
   conjures, Para. 19
   proliferates, Para. 24
   foes, Para. 25
   rein in, Para. 26

2. How does Amato's introduction draw you into the essay? Why is it an effective introduction?

3. Amato has quite a bit of information to give his readers. He carefully planned how he would group and organize his information, and his topic sentences are critical tools for showing the reader this organizational structure. Pick out four topic sentences that seem strong. Remember that a strong topic sentence will explain what the main point of the paragraph will be, and it may have a word or

phrase that explains why the paragraph is located in that spot of the essay. (The word or phrase, called a *transition*, will point out how the paragraph connects directly to the paragraph before or the paragraph after.) Copy down these strong topic sentences and explain why you chose them.

4. What do the last two sentences in Paragraph 8 mean?

5. In Paragraph 6, surveillance cameras are called the "the fifth utility." What does this mean? (What are the other four utilities?) What is your reaction to surveillance cameras becoming the fifth utility?

6. In Paragraph 20, the author notes that public cameras could alert police if "unauthorized crowds start congregating around an accident or altercation." Why would this be helpful? In what other situations might large crowds congregate? Would you always want police to be alerted? Explain.

7. Amato describes a number of advantages and disadvantages to high-tech surveillance. What are two advantages that interest you? What are two disadvantages that interest you?

8. In Paragraph 25, Amato notes that Uganda has begun to use "face prints." What problem does the author see with this technology in Uganda? Why might someone argue that the citizens of some third world countries have more to fear from high-tech surveillance?

9. How would you feel if all, or most, of your day was monitored by cameras and sensors? Explain.

10. Writers often use their titles to give their readers immediate hints about their main point. What is the main point of this reading and how does the title of this piece connect to the main point?

Journal Assignment

Big Brother: Friend or Foe?

Since September 11th, 2001, many people in the United States are fearful of terrorist attacks. In addition, some people are concerned about growing crime rates and bizarre, horrifying crimes like the shootings at Columbine High School and the sniper attacks in Virginia and Maryland. Do you fear for your safety on a regular basis? Do you think you would feel better if we had constant high-tech surveillance in public places? Do you think you would be actually safer? Do you worry about your privacy? After reading someone else's journal, just say, "Thank you," when you return it.

Explore the Writing Assignment

Here, again, is your writing assignment. Review it carefully before continuing. Underline the important terms in the assignment.

Do you see more advantages or disadvantages in the types of high-tech surveillance mentioned in "Big Brother Logs On"? Discuss in detail the disadvantages and advantages that most intrigue you. (Note: It is possible to write an essay in which you say that you see an equal number of advantages and disadvantages.)

Activities

Find Out Who Is Watching You

Choose one or both of the activities below. You may want to work in groups of two or three.

- Choose two or three public places to visit in your city. You could choose from any of these places: grocery store, bank, library, airport, mall, government building, a newly built school, or a clothing or record store. Observe how you are being observed. Are there cameras? (Are the cameras obvious or hidden or disguised?) Metal detectors? One-way mirrors? Do you have to show ID? Are there other methods of surveillance being used? Report your observations to your class.

- Interview a business owner or manager, or interview someone who is in charge of security at a business or office. Prepare some questions ahead of time. Sample questions: What are the security concerns of this business/office? What kinds of high-tech security do you currently use? What might you use in the future? (You might have to describe the types of high-tech surveillance you read about in Amato's essay.) You will want to prepare questions that are appropriate for the business/office and person you are visiting. Report your findings to your class.

Round-Table Discussion

Amato gave you many technical terms and many reasons why people both support and fear high-tech surveillance. As a way of becoming more familiar with the terminology, the different types of high-tech surveillance, and their advantages and disadvantages, you will have a round-table discussion with your classmates. A round-table discussion is an approach that many companies use to understand an issue, problem, or goal. Each participant must come with both information and questions. Follow the preparation steps carefully, and you'll have a great discussion, and you'll find that writing the essay becomes much easier.

1. First, working as a class, make a list of all the types of high-tech sur-veillance tools mentioned in "Big Brother Logs On" and agree on a name for each type. For example, the surveillance technique in Para-graph 12 could be called "body measure." Some of the high-tech tools already have names, like BlueEyes in Paragraph 14.

2. Use the index card system described on pages 296–298 to record what you have learned about high-tech security. Begin by writing the name of one type of high-tech security on a card. (Make a note next to the name about which paragraph of Amato's essay you found it in.) On the back of the card, write one advantage or disadvantage with this type of high-tech security. You might repeat—in your own words—what you read in the essay, or you might jot down your own idea. (If you write about an advantage or disadvantage that you found in the essay, be sure to write down the source of the informa-tion. Did it come from Amato or someone else? If someone else, record his or her name and title or job. What paragraph?) You'll prob-ably want to create more than one card for each type of high-tech security. Most types of security have both advantages and disadvan-tages. Continue to create cards for each type of high-tech security mentioned in the essay.

3. On a separate piece of paper, make a list of questions you have about high-tech security and/or your writing assignment. Do you under-stand, basically, how each type of high-tech security works? (You do not have to be an expert, but you do need to have a reasonable un-derstanding of how the technology works and in what places and why it might be used.)

4. During your round-table discussion, each student should have a chance to share a card and a question. You will need someone to keep track of ideas on a chalkboard or white board. Each student, of course, will need to keep his or her own notes, copying down what is said, what is written on the board, and any comments or questions he or she has.

Notes

Brainstorm   Write freely about high-tech security. Review the essay and your critical thinking answers. Think about what you observed in person. Review your round-table notes. Also, you may want to imag-ine yourself in an Orwellian world. What would it be like to be watched constantly? How would you feel? Would your behavior change? Is that okay? What are some of the advantages to high-tech se-curity? What are some of the disadvantages?

Notes   When you are done writing, review your brainstorm and decide which advantages and disadvantages you want to focus on. Highlight the parts of your brainstorm that you think might be useful when writing your essay.

Consider Your Audience   Imagine a general audience for this essay—the citizens of the United States, or even an international audience. Write down what most people already know about high-tech security. How do you think they feel about high-tech security? Now, consider what your audience probably doesn't know about high-tech surveillance. Make notes about the crucial types of information you will need to give your audience.

Create Your Thesis   In your own words, what must you do in your essay? Review the writing assignment. Experiment with thesis statements until you find one that clearly explains your focus.

Outline   Keeping your thesis in mind, carefully review your notes and readings. Although you completed some index cards in preparation for your round-table discussion, you will now need to create a complete set of cards that represents the ideas you will cover in your essay. You may want to review the section on index cards on pages 296–298. When you have all your cards filled out, review your cards and think about how to organize your ideas. Keep in mind that it is okay to discard some of the cards if the ideas on them don't seem to fit smoothly with your other ideas or if the ideas just don't interest you.

Experiment with different ways to organize your cards. (*Note:* One index card does not necessarily equal one paragraph. A paragraph can be built around one or more index cards.) Since the assignment asks you to state if you see more advantages or disadvantages, you may not have an equal number of paragraphs for disadvantages and advantages—unless you state in your thesis that you see an equal number of advantages and disadvantages. If you are saying there are more advantages than disadvantages, you may want to name and explain a few key disadvantages early in your essay and then focus on the most interesting advantages later in your essay. Obviously, this can work the other way around too. (First discuss the few advantages and then discuss more disadvantages.)

It is also possible that you will want to organize your paragraphs by particular criteria. For example, if you want to focus on public versus private high-tech security, you could try this organizational approach:

- Advantages to having high-tech security on public streets (one or more paragraphs)
- Disadvantages to having high-tech security on public streets (one or more paragraphs)
- Advantages to having high-tech security in our homes (one or more paragraphs)
- Disadvantages to having high-tech security in our homes (one or more paragraphs)

To avoid creating an underdeveloped essay, it is important that you discuss only one advantage or disadvantage per paragraph. Also keep in mind what you learned in Chapter 6 about concessions (pages 277–279). You can't reasonably state that there are absolutely no advantages or state that there are absolutely no disadvantages. So, as you plan your outline, be sure to make room for each side.

When you have a pretty good idea of which index cards you'll use, how you'll group your ideas into paragraphs, and how you'll order your paragraphs, get together with a small group of classmates and show them what you've decided. Explain your choices. You may find that you need to make some changes, and you may get some new ideas from listening to how your classmates are organizing their cards.

Draft

Using your cards as a guide, begin drafting your essay. Your introduction should explain what your topic is and why it's important. (Remember that your audience includes people who may know very little about high-tech security.) In your body paragraphs, discuss the points you have selected. Give interesting examples that come from your imagination or personal experience. Description will work well in this essay, so consider how you might paint a picture in your reader's mind using adjectives, adverbs, and prepositional phrases. In your conclusion, tell your reader what you intended to accomplish in this essay.

Notes

Revise

Activity

Share Your Writing

Find a classmate to work with. Read each other's essays, and discuss the following questions as they relate to both essays.

- Have you discussed both advantages and disadvantages?

- Are you trying to cover more than one disadvantage or advantage in any of your paragraphs?

- Have you explained the terminology?

- Is there enough information and detail so that your reader will see your point of view? Have you used quotes from Amato's essay? Should you?

- Have you mentioned where you got your information? (See pages 479–483 for a review of how to cite sources.)

- Can your classmate understand and describe your organizational pattern? Can you make any improvements? Have you used transitions?

- What has your instructor been telling you to work on? Do you have any questions about this essay and the skills your instructor wants you to work on?

- What questions do you have about your essay? What are your greatest concerns?

Edit

Pay special attention to errors that you tend to repeat, and focus on one at a time. Also, does your instructor have a certain area he or she wants you to focus on?

Additional ideas for editing:

- Note that *Internet* is always capitalized. (*World Wide Web* is capitalized also.)

- Can you use any new vocabulary words in your essay?

You may also want to consider the following question after completing the sentence work at the end of the chapter (pages 324–337).

- Are you using adjectives, adverbs, and prepositional phrases to add detail and interest to your writing?

TIME TO REFLECT

> ### *Journal Assignment*
>
> ### *Your Progress as a Writer, Reader, and Critical Thinker*
>
> As you look back over the chapter, consider carefully what you have learned about organization.
>
> - What should writers remember about organizing an essay well?
> - What do you think you most benefited from in this chapter? And what did you do best in your essay(s)?
> - As a reader, what skills did you sharpen in this chapter? Do these skills relate to organization?
> - How is organizing an essay a critical thinking challenge?

SUMMARY OF CHAPTER 7

In Chapter 7, you have

- seen that organization is one key to keeping your readers interested and helping them understand and, perhaps, be persuaded by your ideas;
- learned that thinking critically about organization patterns, choosing a logical pattern, and sticking to that pattern is important in creating a well-written essay; and
- learned to use transitions to build bridges between ideas to help your readers see your organizational structure.

Notes

CREATING EXPRESSIVE SENTENCES

Examining the Kernel Sentence
Creating More Meaningful Sentences
Using Adjectives to Improve Sentences
Using –ing Adjective Phrases to Improve Sentences
Using Have Form Adjectives to Improve Sentences
Using Adverbs to Improve Sentences
Using Prepositional Phrases to Improve Sentences

In this section, you will focus on making your sentences more descriptive and thereby more accurate and expressive. You will study adjectives, adverbs, and prepositional phrases and complete many sentence combining exercises that help you move from simple sentences to colorful, interesting, more sophisticated sentences.

Examining the Kernel Sentence

First, let's look at the *kernel sentence*. The **kernel sentence** is the basic subject and predicate of a simple sentence. In the following examples, subjects are underlined once and predicates are underlined twice.

 a. The television is on.
 b. The child watches the monsters and bears.
 c. The child enjoys the songs and the stories.
 d. The parents watch the show, too.
 e. The parents and child discuss the program.

Read sentences a–e aloud. Imagine that this is a paragraph from an essay. Most readers would find these sentences (and the essay) choppy and boring.

Creating More Meaningful Sentences

So how do writers make their sentences and essays more interesting? How do writers pack in more meaning? Experienced writers do a number of different things to make their writing come alive:

- They use adjectives to describe the nouns in their sentences.
- They use adverbs to describe the action in their sentences.
- They use prepositional phrases to add more meaning to their sentences.

- They **embed** (or insert) phrases in their sentences to include more information.

Notes

- They combine short, simple sentences to create longer, more interesting sentences.

You'll begin practicing all these methods for creating interesting sentences in this chapter.

Using Adjectives to Improve Sentences

Adjectives are words that describe nouns. (Remember: *Nouns* are people, places, things, or ideas.) In the following examples, the adjectives are highlighted and the arrows point to the nouns they describe:

The young children want to watch their favorite television program.

The tired parents hope the educational program will interest the rambunctious kids.

Rambunctious means noisy and active

Practice #1   Class Discussion of Adjectives

As a class, list some adjectives on the chalkboard. If you are unsure if a word is an adjective, see if you can use it before a noun in a sentence. Be sure to list some adjectives that you might use in an essay about technology.

Practice #2   Revisiting the Kernel Sentences

Below, you are given kernel sentences a–e again. Complete the work described in 1–3.

   a. The television is on.

   b. The child watches the monsters and bears.

   c. The child enjoys the songs and stories.

   d. The parents watch the show, too.

   e. The parents and child discuss the program.

1. Highlight the nouns you see in the kernel sentences. These are the words that you will make more interesting by using adjectives.

2. In small groups, rewrite sentences a–e, adding adjectives that make the sentences more interesting. (Do not use adverbs or prepositional phrases yet. You'll work with those later.)

Here is one way to improve sentence a:

Creating Expressive Sentences

- The new, expensive television is on.

Note: In the new version of sentence a, there are two adjectives that describe *television*, so there must be a comma between the two adjectives. Review Punctuation Rule #1.

3. Share your sentences with your class.

Punctuation Rule #1 (Review)

Separate items in a series with commas.

Examples:
- The hot, delicious food is on the table.
- He is tall, skinny, and handsome.

The last comma before *and* is optional.

Practice #3   Reading Amato

In the following exercises, the "K" sentence will be your kernel sentence. The sentences below this kernel sentence will have information (in this case, adjectives that are highlighted) that you should add into the kernel sentence. Combine the sentences and use correct punctuation. (The new sentences you write in exercises 1–14 can be written as three paragraphs: 1–6, 7–10, and 11–14.)
Examples:

K: I cannot watch television programs at my grandparents' house.

The television programs are violent .

The television programs are sexy .

- I cannot watch violent, sexy television programs at my grandparents' house.

K: They watch only programs on PBS.

The programs are educational .

- They watch only educational programs on PBS.

1. K: Ivan Amato wrote an essay called "Big Brother Logs On."
   The essay is lengthy .

When completing #1, remember the *a/an rule*. Use *a* before words that start with consonant sounds and *an* before words that start with vowel sounds.

2. K: With essays that have points, it is useful to first read just the introduction, subheadings, and conclusion.

   The essays are long .

   The points are many .

3. K: Then when the experienced reader has time, she can read through the essay quickly.

   The time is ample .

   The essay is complete .

4. K: While reading, she should underline words.

   The words are unfamiliar .

5. K: Some of the words in Amato's essay are "laudable," "lamentable," and "conjures."

   The words are difficult .

6. K: These are words to learn and use, but the reader doesn't have to look up their meanings when she first sees them.

   These words are important .

   The reader is efficient .

   [end of first paragraph]

7. K: After taking these steps, the reader might want to set goals for a rereading.

   The rereading should be careful .

8. K: For example, the reader might decide to reread and take notes on just the first points.

   The points are four .

9. K: This time, she could look up words and highlight points.

   The words are unfamiliar .

   The points are significant .

10. K: Then, the next day, the reader could tackle the points.

    The reader is smart .

    The points are remaining .

    [end of second paragraph]

11. K: Additionally, the reader might write a summary about the essay.

    The summary is short .

12. K: Also, she should find an opportunity to discuss and respond to the points in Amato's essay.

Notes

The points are [key] .

13. K: She might do this in class, with a study group, or with a tutor.

The tutor is [helpful] .

14. K: Breaking up tasks into pieces is a study strategy.

The tasks are [long] .

The pieces are [manageable] .

The study strategy is [good] .

Using -ing *Adjective Phrases to Improve Sentences*

An *-ing* word (a present participle) cannot be a verb without a helper, and if the *-ing* word is not working as a verb, it could be acting as either a noun or an adjective. Let's review how *-ing* words function as adjectives.

Examples of *-ing words* (present participles) working as adjectives:

The [ringing] phone grates on my nerves.

The [flashing] light shows that the camera is on.

The [laughing] man dances for the so-called hidden camera.

Notice that in the sentences above, the single *-ing word* goes *before* the noun it describes.

Examples of *-ing phrases* (present participle phrases) working as adjectives:

The phone [ringing in the next office] grates on my nerves.

The children [dancing the tango] are tired.

The light [flashing in the upper corner] shows that the camera is on.

The man [laughing loudly] dances for the so-called hidden camera.

Notice that in the sentences above, the *-ing phrase* goes *after* the noun it describes.

Practice #4   War Time

Combine the following choppy sentences to create descriptive, sophisticated sentences. (You'll be adding regular adjectives and -ing adjectives into the kernel sentences.) In the first four sentences, the adjectives that you should add into the kernel sentences are highlighted. Remember to punctuate your sentences correctly. (The new sentences you create in exercises 1–13 can be written as a paragraph.) It is 1944. There are few forms of technological entertainment. Kids find other ways to fill their time.

1. K: The boys are hurrying off to play in the lot.

   The boys are laughing .

   The lot is vacant .

2. K: The boys are the kids there.

   The boys are carrying the shoe boxes of toy soldiers .

   The kids are first .

3. K: The sun warms their backs as they carefully divide up the toy soldiers, cannons, and materials.

   The sun is shining down on them .

   The toy soldiers are made of lead .

   The cannons are sturdy .

   The materials are for building .

4. K: The boy digs his trenches and carefully places his soldiers.

   The boy is freckled .

   The boy is working quietly .

   His soldiers are small .

   His soldiers are serious .

5. K: He thinks carefully about his strategy.

   His strategy is for war.

6. K: By lunch time, a battlefield is ready.

   The battlefield is enormous.

   (Remember: Use "an" before words that start with a vowel sound.)

7. K: The boys break for lunch.

   The boys are hungry.

8. K: Then, with the sun on the men, the battle begins.

   The sun is hot.

   The sun is beating down.

   The men are young.

   The battle is raging.

9. K: The boys test their strategies.

   The boys are yelling.

   The boys are arguing.

10. K: Plans must be altered and sacrifices made.

    The sacrifices are hard.

When completing items 4, 9, and 11, remember Punctuation Rule #1.

Creating Expressive Sentences

11. K: The boy launches one attack.
    The boy is freckled.
    The attack is final.
    The attack is violent.
12. K: His planning has paid off.
    His planning was extensive.
13. K: The boy yells, "Victory!"
    The boy is freckled.
    The boy is raising his arms in triumph.

Using Have Form *Adjectives to Improve Sentences*

There is another verb form that can act as an adjective: the *have form* of a verb. Usually the **have form** of a verb is the base form plus *-ed*. (The **base form** is the form you find listed first in the dictionary.) If the have form is used with a helper verb, then the have form is being used as a verb. However, without the helper verb, the have form can be an adjective.

base forms	have forms
experience	experienced
supervise	supervised
walk	walked
look	looked

Sometimes the have form is *irregular* (doesn't follow the normal pattern of adding *-ed*).

base forms	have forms
show	shown
see	seen
sing	sung
buy	bought

(For more examples, see the Chart of Irregular Verbs on pages 499–500.)

If you are ever unsure about verb forms, you can look up the base form in the dictionary. After the base form, you'll find the past-tense form, the have form, and finally the *-ing* form. If the past-tense and have forms are the same, the dictionary will only list that form once.

In the following sentences, have form verbs are in phrases that are acting as adjective phrases. The have form verbs are underlined and the adjective phrases are highlighted.

The program <u>shown</u> late at night is meant for adults.

The violence <u>seen</u> on that program is graphic.

Notes

(See "Using the Dictionary," page 452, for more information about how dictionaries are set up.)

Practice #5 Artist at Work

Now try some more sentence combining that uses all the types of adjectives we have discussed (regular adjectives, *-ing* adjectives, have form adjectives.) (The new sentences you write in exercises 1–9 can be written as a paragraph.)

1. K: The girl's cousin sits in front of the television.

   The cousin is playing a video game.

   (*Hint:* Put the adjective phrase *playing a video game* at the beginning of the sentence and put a comma after it. You've now used an adjective phrase as an introductory phrase.)

2. K: The girl leaves the room and sits at the kitchen table.

   The girl is bored.

   The girl is unused to playing video games.

   The kitchen table is cluttered.

3. K: After moving the muffin, the coffee, and the newspaper her grandmother left behind, she takes out her paper and begins to create a spaceship.

   The muffin is half-eaten.

   The coffee is cold.

   Her paper is for drawing.

4. K: She is only 7 years old, but she is an artist.

   The artist is experienced.

5. K: The girl in the kitchen draws the shell of the ship.

   The girl is concentrating.

   The kitchen is quiet.

Creating Expressive Sentences

Notes

The shell is exterior.

(*Hint*: Put *concentrating* at the beginning of the sentence and put a comma after it. You've now used an adjective as an introductory word to a sentence.)

6. K: However, she doesn't stop with the exterior.

The exterior is simple.

7. K: She draws another view of the ship.

The view of the ship is showing the interior control panels.

The interior control panels are complicated.

8. K: She carefully details the buttons and switches.

The buttons and switches are many.

9. K: She gazes up at the sky and imagines soaring away.

She is finished.

The sky is clear.

(*Hint*: Start your sentence with the adjective *finished* and put a comma after it.)

Practice #6   **Creating Sentences with Adjectives**

Create three sentences that might show up in an essay about technology. Make sure that each sentence uses adjectives that help add vivid detail and meaning. Underline the adjectives in your sentences.

Using Adverbs to Improve Sentences

Adverbs are words that describe verbs, adjectives, other adverbs, and whole groups of words. Often (but not always), adverbs end in *-ly*. Adverbs usually explain *where, when, how, why*, or *to what extent*. In the following sentences, the adverbs are highlighted and the arrows show which words the adverbs describe:

One father sadly complains about the television.

He says his child watches TV constantly .

The child listens intently to the television but not to his father.

Practice #7   **Class Discussion of Adverbs**

List some adverbs on the board. If you are unsure if a word can be used as an adverb, try putting it into a sentence and discussing it with your classmates. Be sure to put some adverbs on the board that you might use in an essay on technology.

Practice #8   Adding Adverbs

In the following exercises, combine sentences using adverbs to add meaning. The words that are (or will become) adverbs are highlighted.

1. K: The 8-year-old boy and his dad watch a situation comedy on television.
   They watch quietly .

2. K: Although the program is funny, it does mention gangs.
   Most of the program is funny.
   (*Hint*: Change *most* into an adverb by adding *ly*. Put the new adverb before the adjective *funny*.)

3. K: After the program, the dad listens to his son's views on gangs.
   The dad listens carefully .

4. K: The father is surprised to find out that his son learned something about gangs from television.
   The surprise is pleasant .
   (*Hint*: Change *pleasant* into an adverb by adding *ly*. Put the new adverb before the verb *surprised*.)

Practice #9   Thinking About High-Tech Security

In the following exercises, combine sentences using adjectives and adverbs to add meaning. (You may have to change an adjective into an adverb when combining sentences.)

1. K: Ivan Amato doesn't believe that Americans should try to stop advances.
   Amato's beliefs are clear.
   The advances are technological.
   (*Hint*: Change *clear* into an adverb and put it before *doesn't believe*.)

2. K: ACLU's Steinhardt says an advance can change into an abuse.
   The advance is technological.
   The change can be easy.
   The abuse is technological.
   (*Hint*: Change *easy* into an adverb and put it before *change*.)

3. K: In 1999, Scott McNealy, CEO of Sun Microsystems, told reporters, "You already have zero privacy. Get over it."
   His statement was blunt.
   (*Hint*: Change *blunt* into an adverb and put it before *told*.)

Remember the *a/an rule.* Use *a* before words that start with a consonant sound. Use *an* before words that start with a vowel sound.

Creating Expressive Sentences

4. K: John Woodward, employed by the CIA, argues that no one wants to watch each of us.

   Woodward is a former employee of the CIA.

   The watching is constant.

   (*Hint*: Change *former* into an adverb and place it before *employed*. Change *constant* into an adverb and place it at the end of the sentence.)

5. K: I am a person, but I am also a person who doesn't want Big Brother peering at me.

   I am a person who abides by the law.

   I enjoy my privacy.

   Big Brother seems suspicious.

   (*Hint*: Change *abides by the law* into the adjective *law-abiding*. Change *privacy* into an adjective and place before the second *person*. Change *suspicious* into an adverb and place after *peering*.)

6. K: The man argues that we should support the city's plan to install cameras on streets.

   The man is leading the neighborhood watch meeting.

   The argument is persuasive.

   The plan is new.

   The streets are public.

   (*Hint*: Change *persuasive* into an adverb.)

7. K: My classmate explained the similarities between Orwell's novel and the movie.

   The similarities were interesting.

   The similarities were frightening.

   The movie was released.

   The release was recent.

   (*Hint*: Change *recent* into an adverb.)

8. K: I make faces into the ATM camera.

   I am hoping to make some security person laugh.

   I make the faces on purpose.

   The faces are strange.

   (*Hint*: Place the *–ing* adjective phrase that begins with *hoping* at the beginning of your new sentence. Put a comma after the phrase. Change *purpose* into an adverb.)

9. K: If we spend amounts of time and money on security, will we ignore the causes of crime and terrorism?

   The amounts are excessive.

   The causes are root.

10. K: In an effort to keep her safe, the parents made their daughter wear the device.

    The parents were reluctant to take this action.

    The device was for tracking.

    (*Hint*: Change *reluctant* into an adverb.)

Practice #10   Creating Sentences with Adverbs

Create three sentences that might show up in an essay about technology. Use adverbs to create more meaning and detail. Underline the adverbs you have added.

Using Prepositional Phrases to Improve Sentences

A prepositional phrase, as you studied in Chapter 4, is a phrase made up of a preposition and its object. These phrases can add significant information to sentences, making the sentences far more compelling. In the following sentences, the prepositional phrases are bracketed:

[In his essay "Big Brother Logs On,"] Ivan Amato discusses his concerns [about high-tech surveillance.]

He writes [about face recognition, iris scanning, and hidden cameras] and how we will all be affected [by these tools.]

Practice #11   Class Discussion of Prepositional Phrases

List some prepositional phrases on the chalkboard that might show up in an essay about technology.

Practice #12   Adding Prepositional Phrases

Combine the following sentences, using prepositional phrases to create more interesting sentences. The prepositional phrases that should be added to the kernel sentences are bracketed.

1. K: When I write, I always research the issue.

   I write [about controversial issues].

I research [at the library].

2. K: I go to find articles.

I go [to the computers].

The articles are [from magazines and newspapers].

3. K: Last week, the librarian helped me find information.

The information was [for my essay].

My essay is [about security] [at airports].

Practice #13   **Instructor Big Bird**

Combine the following sentences, using prepositional phrases, adjectives, and adverbs to add greater detail and meaning. (The new sentences you write in exercises 1–9 can be written as two paragraphs: 1–4 and 5–9.)

1. K: The mother sang the ABC song.

   She sang happily.

2. K: The child just smiled.

   The child was small.

   The child was sweet.

3. K: The mother asked the child to sing.

   The mother was patient.

   The singing was with her.

4. K: But the child laughed and pointed and said, "You!"

   The child only laughed.

   The pointing was at her mom.

   [end of first paragraph]

5. K: Later, the child watched *Sesame Street*.

   It was later in the morning.

6. K: When Big Bird began to sing the ABC song and dance around, the child sang too.

   Big Bird danced happily.

7. K: The child tripped, but she was trying.

   The tripping was over the l-m-n-o-p sequence.

   The trying was at least.

8. K: The mother listened and smiled.

   The listening was to her child.

The child was struggling.

The struggling was with the ABC song.

9. K: The child would learn.

The learning would be easy.

The learning is with the help.

The help is of Big Bird.

(*Hint*: Change *easy* into an adverb.)

Practice #14   Creating Sentences with Prepositional Phrases

Write three sentences that you might use in an essay about television. Use some prepositional phrases in these practice sentences. Underline the prepositional phrases you use.

Your Own Writing: Creating Expressive Sentences

Study a piece of your writing (a journal or a paragraph from an essay). Underline any adjectives, adverbs, and prepositional phrases you find. Revise the piece adding adjectives, adverbs, and prepositional phrases to make your sentences more descriptive and expressive. Underline all adjectives, adverbs, and prepositional phrases in your revised work.

Creating Expressive Sentences

Writing About Music and Poetry

Main Topics

- Inferring and analyzing in your essays

- Communicating your interpretations of song lyrics and poems

- Combining sentences with coordinators and subordinators

Mutts

Sacramento Bee. March 7, 1996, E:6.

On the job and in college, you'll frequently use your analysis and inference skills. These critical thinking skills require you to break down something complex into smaller pieces (**analyze**) and figure out meaning by studying these pieces (**infer**). You analyze and infer frequently throughout your day. For instance, if you ask a friend to drive you to the library, and your friend heaves a big sigh and says, "Oh, I guess I could if I have to," you automatically *analyze* the sigh and the words "guess" and "have to," and you *infer* that even though your friend said he would drive you, he doesn't really want to.

In other situations, analyzing and inferring can be more challenging. In a laboratory, for example, a scientist might analyze large bodies of data and infer information about how a particular cancer is caused, or a businessperson might study a product or market and infer information about how to best sell the product. In college, a history student might analyze the events leading to World War I and infer information about the cause of the war, or a literature student might analyze a novel and infer meaning from the text as part of the course work. In this chapter, you'll strengthen your analytical and inferential skills as you think about music lyrics and poetry, two forms of communication that often need to be studied in depth in order to be fully understood and appreciated.

Notes

ANALYSIS AND INFERENCE IN YOUR WRITING

As you may have guessed, all the essays you've been writing have required you to analyze and infer. You may have studied advertisements and inferred information about the types of audiences the ads were aimed at. You may have analyzed information about people and determined whether or not they qualified as heroes. You may have also analyzed the advantages and disadvantages of television and technology. Academic writing assignments generally require this kind of critical thinking, since studying information and discovering relationships, causes, effects, advantages, and disadvantages are at the core of college work. In this chapter, you'll take a closer look at what you've been doing in your essays and further sharpen your analytical skills.

Analyzing and Inferring in Your Essays

When you wrote your earlier essays, you took large topics (advertising, heroes, television, technology), broke them down into smaller pieces

Notes

(one ad, one heroic person, a few advantages or disadvantages of television or technology), analyzed key facts, and inferred information. For example, if you wrote about advertising, you selected one ad to study closely and broke that down into smaller pieces to look at colors, words, people, and props. In fact, if there were people in the ad, you looked even more closely and studied their age, ethnicity, expressions, clothing, posture, and so on. From this information, you inferred the advertiser's message and who the advertiser was trying to attract with the ad.

Breaking down large topics into smaller pieces is what analytical and inferential thinking is all about. The structure of an academic essay is perfect for this kind of work. The thesis allows you to state a main idea, and the paragraphs allow you to discuss pieces of that main idea one at a time. To do this well, a writer must utilize an effective writing process that allows her to explore, learn, divide things into smaller pieces, and think critically. Brainstorming, discussing, reading, outlining, drafting, revising, and editing make such exploration and learning possible.

Analyzing and Inferring in Your Paragraphs

As you've read, academic essays are structured perfectly for analytical writing. The paragraph, in particular, offers an effective structure for analysis and inference. The topic sentence allows the writer to state one specific point that supports the thesis of the essay. Then the writer can offer detailed support gathered through reading, discussion, and critical thinking. Finally, the writer can explain her support and show how it indeed supports the topic sentence.

Activity

Study These Data and This Analytical Paragraph

Here are some statistics that were published in the *World Almanac and Book of Facts,* 1998.

Sales of Recorded Music and Music Videos, by Genre and Format, 1992–1996
Source: Recording Industry Assn. of America, Washington, D.C.

Breakdown by percentage of all recorded music sold

Genre	1992	1993	1994	1995	1996
Rock	31.6	30.2	35.1	33.5	32.6

Genre	1992	1993	1994	1995	1996
Country	17.4	18.7	16.3	16.7	14.7
Urban Contemp.	9.8	10.6	9.6	11.3	12.1
Pop	11.5	11.9	10.3	10.1	9.3
Rap	8.6	9.2	7.9	6.7	8.9
Gospel	2.8	3.2	3.3	3.1	4.3
Classical	3.7	3.3	3.7	2.9	3.4
Jazz	3.8	3.1	3.0	3.0	3.3
Oldies	0.8	1.0	0.8	1.0	0.8
Soundtracks	0.7	0.7	1.0	0.9	0.8
New Age	1.2	1.0	1.0	0.7	0.7
Children's	0.5	0.4	0.4	0.5	0.7
Other	5.4	4.6	5.3	7.0	5.2

Format	1992	1993	1994	1995	1996
Compact disc (CD)	46.5	51.1	58.4	65.0	68.4
Cassette	43.6	38.0	32.1	25.1	19.3
LP	1.3	0.3	0.8	0.5	0.6
Singles (all types)	7.5	9.2	7.4	7.5	9.3
Music video	1.0	1.3	0.8	0.9	1.0

Note: Totals may not equal 100 percent because of "Don't know/no answer" responses to survey.

Notes

The following paragraph was written after careful analytical study of those statistics.

From studying the data available, I have concluded that compact discs now outsell cassettes to such a degree that we should reduce our cassette stock considerably. I have analyzed the statistics available from the years 1992–1996 and have found that compact discs and cassettes pretty much shared the market equally in 1992, but by 1996, the market heavily favored compact discs. Specifically, in 1992, 46.5 percent of music products sold in music stores in this country were in the form of compact discs, and 43.6 percent of music products sold were in the form of cassettes. However, in 1996, 68.4 percent of sales were in compact discs and only 19.3 percent were in cassettes. Our store still carries almost as many cassettes as compact discs. These statistics show that we need to move forward with the times. We should have perhaps only 15 percent of our stock in the form of cassettes, and I would recommend phasing cassettes out completely within the next five years.

1. Which statistics in the almanac did this writer pay closest attention to? Highlight the statistics he used.

2. Highlight the topic sentence of this paragraph. What is this writer promising to write about? Explain his purpose in your own words.

3. Put a box around the part of the paragraph that contains the specific support for the main idea.

4. After offering specific support, this writer explains the support and then wraps up the paragraph by making a recommendation. Put "E" next to the lines of the paragraph that *explain* the support, and put "R" next to the lines that express this writer's *recommendation*.

5. Describe in your own words the different parts of this analytical paragraph.

Analyzing Music Lyrics and Poetry

Music and poetry are both covered in this chapter because they are similar in many ways. They are both creative expressions that have the ability to go beyond the boundaries of gender, ethnicity, and class to appeal to just about everyone. Although most people have favorite songs or poems, people won't always agree on how to interpret these songs or poems—which leads to interesting discussions and excellent analytical brain work.

The key difference between a song lyric and a poem is, of course, that one is set to music and the other isn't. However, many poems do have a rhythm of their own, and some poems end up being put to music. If you have never enjoyed studying poetry, but love music, you might find that many of the things you love about music—its ability to paint pictures in your mind, its ability to make you feel certain emotions, and its ability to help you escape everyday life—are also in poems.

This section of the text will offer you some basic information about lyrics and poems. You'll learn a few terms that will help you when you begin to analyze specific pieces.

Form   The words in lyrics and poems sometimes rhyme, but often they do not. Sometimes poems will follow a specific, formal rhythmic pattern called **meter**. Other times, poems, like lyrics without their musical notes, will have an inconsistent rhythm or no rhythm.

Paragraphs in music lyrics and poems are called **stanzas**. Stanzas can be long or short, and, much like the paragraphs in journalistic writing, they generally don't have topic sentences.

Language   Because lyricists (people who write music lyrics) and poets are interested in creating images and feelings, and because they generally don't insist on only one interpretation of their work, they don't write in complete, detailed sentences. (You'll find that capital letters and periods aren't used like they are in academic writing.) Lyricists and poets choose their language very carefully, finding words that will create the message, image, or feeling they are aiming for. When analyzing lyrics and poems, you'll want to pay attention to the vocabulary. Is the writer using slang? Is the language formal? Is it the language of a child? Of a parent? Of a lover? Of a sister? What types of words are being used?

Lyricists and poets also use **figurative language** to compare things—helping to paint an image in the reader's mind. "She cried like a baby" is an example of figurative language. The person, "she," is not really a baby, but the writer is saying she cried like one—painting the image of loud, constant crying in our minds. Sometimes the word "like" is left out: "The moon, a silver platter in the sky, lit our way." The moon isn't really a silver serving dish. The writer is simply saying it's similar in appearance to a "platter."

Effect   By choosing to use certain words and figurative language, the writer is sending a message to her audience. She is creating a specific image in the reader's mind and a certain mood in the reader's heart. For example, if a writer uses words like *unrippled water, glassy reflection, grass warm and still,* she may be trying to create images of summer at a lake. She may also be creating a quiet, calm, peaceful mood. If she adds that "the lake was a lonely child waiting for summer visitors to return," she is continuing these images by using figurative language and suggesting that the lake sits still and quiet—perhaps even sadly—like a lonely child might, waiting for the excitement and commotion of friends. The writer's message in these lines might be that there is beauty and peace in anticipating the summer. Both the quiet and the excitement can be admired.

Responding and Interpreting   Because lyricists and poets don't fully explain and develop their ideas the way essayists do, it's often difficult to be absolutely certain what a song or poem means. Many people find this uncertainty to be the magical part of lyrics and poetry. Each person hearing or reading the lyric or poem will create images in his own mind based on his own experiences. However, although there is usually

Notes

room for more than one interpretation, your formal analytical essay must be based on a careful study of the vocabulary and the figurative language. The interpretation you offer in your essay must be something you can carefully and thoughtfully defend by offering specific support from the song or poem itself.

Discussing   Discussing the lyrics and poems with classmates will help you increase your understanding of the pieces because other people will see things and make connections that you may miss. You and your classmates can help one another by listening to each other's responses and respectfully challenging each other to provide proof and support for each interpretation.

How One Reader Analyzed and Responded to a Poem   The handwritten notes here represent one student's personal and class notes about a poem written by Langston Hughes, a poet who lived from 1902 to 1967. A major African American voice in the field of literature, Hughes frequently wrote using vocabulary that represented southern speech and a rhythm similar to blues or jazz music. This poem, like many of his, explores the southern African American experience of migrating north. It was also put to music and can be considered both a poem and a song. Look at how one reader studied and responded to the poem by listening to class discussion and analyzing the language carefully.

Evenin' Air Blues

Langston Hughes

Notes from class

southern style vocab.

Folks, I come up North
Cause they told me
de North was fine.
I come up North
Cause they told me de North was fine.
Been up here six months—
I'm about to lose my mind.

southern style vocab.

This mornin' for breakfast
I chawed de mornin' air.
This mornin' for breakfast
Chawed de mornin' air.
But this evenin' for supper,
I got evenin' air to spare.

My notes

suggests he used to live in the South.

Repeats, creates a rhythm.

Things have not gone well.

Is he hungry? No money? No job?

He has spirit and humor.

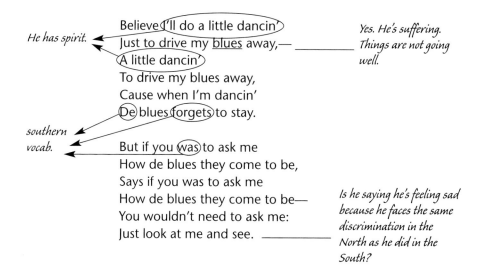

Notes

He has spirit.

Believe I'll do a little dancin'
Just to drive my <u>blues</u> away,— _____
A little dancin'
To drive my blues away,
Cause when I'm dancin'
De blues forgets to stay.

Yes. He's suffering. Things are not going well.

southern vocab.

But if you was to ask me
How de blues they come to be,
Says if you was to ask me
How de blues they come to be—
You wouldn't need to ask me:
Just look at me and see. _____

Is he saying he's feeling sad because he faces the same discrimination in the North as he did in the South?

My Informal Response to "Evenin' Air Blues"

I think this is a beautiful "song" about an African American man's struggle to make a life for himself after he has moved from the South to the North. It seems to me that he had high hopes when he moved:"I come up North/Cause they told me de North was fine." But now he says, "I'm about to lose my mind." I don't think he has any money or job because he doesn't have anything to eat: "I chawed de mornin' air." (My instructor said that line referred to eating and was written in a southern dialect.) Oh, and one of my classmates pointed out the beauty of this poem: the speaker's spirit. Instead of crying and complaining, the speaker dances! Wow. This poem is both painful and beautiful.

How One Reader Analyzed a Song in an Essay

The following essay is a student analysis of "Silent Legacy" by Melissa Etheridge from the CD *Yes I Am*. (The song appears on pages 356–358.) As you read the student paper, note how the student has examined what she terms "clues" that reveal the speaker's struggle between resigning herself to her parents' expectations and accepting who she is.

A Silent Legacy

The song "Silent Legacy" appearing on Melissa Etheridge's CD *Yes I Am* caught my attention because of the title as well as the deep lyrics. The title "Silent Legacy" is part of the refrain, which is repeated through the song. "Silent Legacy" in this song refers to a secret inheritance. After reading the lyrics, I feel the speaker is uncovering her true feelings about her hidden sexuality.

My first clue was found in stanza #3. This stanza focused on a teen dealing with feelings pertaining to her sexuality that she cannot control. I understand this when I read that she is "craving for affection." But to come back into her parent's home, she has to deny her sexual feelings: "Deny all that you feel/And they will bring you home again." Because most parents talk to their children about sex, I feel that the song must deal with something other than a heterosexual relationship. And since some groups condemn homosexuality, I thought this song was about homosexuality.

My second clue was found in stanza #5. It talks about the teen entering puberty and not knowing how she would feel. I got this from the lines, "Your body is alive/But no one told you what you'd feel." The parents have had a hard time dealing with the fact that their daughter is having homosexual feelings. I get this from the line, "they cover it with shame." Because her parents cannot understand what their daughter is going through, she feels nothing but anger toward them. This became clear to me when the speaker suggests that the more the parents try to cover her feelings with shame, these feelings turn to rage.

My last clue comes from stanza #6. This teen is depressed and caught up in emotions about her sexuality. To her, there is no way out. I got this from the refrain, "as you pray in your darkness/For wings to set you free/You are bound to your silent legacy." She is desperately searching for help to find a solution; this is from the lines, "You are digging for the answers/Until your fingers bleed." Also, the parents are trying to use religion to make her feel bad enough to deny her feelings and to make her feel ashamed about what she feels. I got that from the lines, "They feed you guilt/To keep you humble keep you low/Some man and myth they made up/A thousand years ago." I truly feel that the speaker's parents were probably quoting scripture to her because of the last line.

The song deals with a teenage girl stuck in her emotions about her sexuality. It is a song directed at parents so that they'll listen and not be so close-minded about sexuality. It's also a song to fellow sufferers who may not feel accepted because of their sexuality.

I believe this song was important for Melissa Etheridge to write because at one time she went through what she is singing about. According to barnes&noble.com, Etheridge recently wrote a book titled *The Truth Is . . .*, which is a biography of her life in which she discusses openly her own "coming out." Her "coming out" has enabled her to become an advocate for gays and lesbians.

Whether Etheridge was talking about herself or someone else, this song shares deep emotion and hope and sends a message to parents about teens caught between the love of their parents and the love of their own lives.

> —*Melody Bruley,*
> *student writer*

Activity

Analyze the Student Sample

1. Highlight the main idea or thesis the writer has intended to make in her essay.

2. How does Bruley organize her ideas in this essay? Would you organize anything differently?

3. Bruley includes quotations from the song, but she doesn't stop there. She explains what she sees in the quotations. Pick one instance where she does this particularly well. Explain your choice. Can you think of additional points that could be made to support her thesis?

4. Do you agree with Bruley's interpretation of the song? If so, explain why. If not, what do you believe the song is about? What clues would you present to help support your interpretation?

Points to Remember About Analyzing Lyrics and Poems

- Respond honestly. Discuss lyrics and poems with others.
- Divide the lyric or poem into small pieces (lines and words), and study these pieces. Use your critical thinking skills and look carefully at vocabulary and figurative language.
- When writing an essay, have clear topic sentences that connect to the thesis and that cover one piece of the lyric or poem at a time.
- Use examples from the lyric or poem to support the points you make. Include particular vocabulary words and figurative language.
- Explain your support.

Notes

Writing Assignment #1: Analyzing Music Lyrics

In this assignment, you'll strengthen your ability to analyze and infer as you study music lyrics. This analysis requires you to study the details of the lyrics so that you can draw conclusions about what the songs mean.

Here, in brief, is the writing assignment you are preparing for.

Write an essay about one of the songs in this book or a song you have chosen and reviewed with your instructor. In your essay, summarize what you think the song is about. Then choose a couple of the most interesting parts to support your point and show that you have read the lyrics carefully and have good reasons for your interpretation.

Keep this assignment in mind as you begin to analyze music lyrics.

Discuss and Engage

Activities

Analyze the Mutts *Cartoon*

Analyze the cartoon on page 338 and answer the questions that follow.

1. Describe what is happening in the first frame of the cartoon. (What does the musical note represent? What does "SQUAWK KRAW EEEE" represent?)

2. In the second frame, why didn't the cartoonist write any words? What is going on between the two birds?

3. Why did the cartoonist choose the words "Man" and "digs"? What do these words mean to you?

4. Can you infer anything about the birds by the way they look?

5. What is the cartoonist's message?

Your Experiences with Music

Discuss with your classmates the types of music you like. Which songs do you like the most, and why? Are there people in your class who listen carefully to lyrics in songs? What do they look for in good lyrics? Are you always sure what a song means?

Get Involved!

Go online to www.lyrics.com and find lyrics that would be interesting and challenging to analyze. Bring the lyrics to two or three songs to class and share them with your classmates.

> ### *Journal Assignment*
>
> #### *Thoughts About Song Lyrics*
>
> Write about song lyrics and how you and your classmates react to them. Write down some of your favorite lyrics and explain why they are important to you. Also, write about some lyrics that you have heard or read, but haven't enjoyed. Why didn't you like these lyrics? (This is for your eyes only. Refer back to this journal when you are getting ready to write your essay on music.)

Read, Discuss, Think Critically

This section of the chapter offers you the lyrics to five songs, in a variety of styles: classic rock (John Lennon), country (Randy Travis), mellow rock (Bonnie Raitt and Melissa Etheridge), and alternative rock (Alanis Morissette). Notice that the title of the song is given first, then the name of the performer and album.

Reading Assignment: "Imagine"

Preview   Read the title and the first two stanzas.

Anticipate   What do you think this song will be about? What kind of mood or message do you think it has? Use the "Notes" column to record your thoughts.

Read and Reread   Quickly read the lyrics one time, marking unknown terms. Then reread more slowly and use the "Notes" column to record images and meanings that come to mind. Also write down any questions you have. Define unknown terms. Finally, listen to the song or read it aloud.

Imagine
John Lennon

Imagine

1   Imagine there's no heaven
It's easy if you try
No hell below us

Notes

Above us only sky
Imagine all the people
living for today. . . .

2   Imagine there's no countries
It isn't hard to do
Nothing to kill or die for
And no religion too
Imagine all the people
living life in peace. . . .

3   You may say I'm a dreamer
But I'm not the only one
I hope someday you'll join us
And the world will be as one.

4   Imagine no possessions
I wonder if you can
No need for greed or hunger
A brotherhood of man
Imagine all the people
Sharing all the world. . . .

5   You may say I'm a dreamer
but I'm not the only one
I hope some day you'll join us
And the world will live as one.

Questions for Critical Thought

"Imagine"

1. What is your general reaction to this song? How does it make you feel? What words and images in the lyrics support your reaction?

2. Summarize what you think each stanza is about.

3. Lennon uses the term "imagine" frequently. Why is the repetition of this word necessary?

4. What do you think is the general message of this song?

5. Does any particular line or image in the song make you reconsider the way you or others live their lives? Explain.

Reading Assignment: *"Old 8 x 10"*   Notes

Preview   Read the title and the first two stanzas.

Anticipate   What do you think this song will be about? What kind of mood or message do you think it has? Write down your thoughts in the "Notes" column.

Read and Reread   Quickly read the lyrics one time, marking unknown terms. Then reread more slowly and use the "Notes" column to record images and meanings that come to mind. Also write down any questions you have. Define unknown terms. Finally, listen to the song or read it aloud.

Old 8 x 10

Randy Travis

Old 8 x 10

1   Well I know it ain't much
      But it's all that I have since she's gone
      One black and white memory of the only love I've ever known
      One moment in time when we were together
      A page from the past to haunt me forever
      A constant reminder that hearts heal much slower than bones

2   Now my whole world's in one 8 x 10
      With four metal walls holding it in
      Through one plate-glass window
      'Neath the blanket of dust
      Stands an 8 x 10 picture of us
      I wish I'd have told her
      What I felt inside
      Back when her sweet love was flowing like wine
      I wish she would come back and love me again
      The way that she loved me
      In that old 8 x 10

3   Now the silence is deafening
      As the day turns to dark
      Her presence gets stronger with each beat of my heart
      I pretend that she's here and we've made a new start

Notes

And for a moment
She's back in my arms

4 Now my whole world's in one 8 x 10
With four metal walls holding it in
Through one plate-glass window
'Neath the blanket of dust
Stands an 8 x 10 picture of us
There's an 8 x 10 picture of us

Questions for Critical Thought

"Old 8 x 10"

1. What does the title tell you about the song? What does it make you think of?

2. What do the following lines refer to?

   "One black and white memory of the only love I've ever known"

   "One moment in time when we were together"

   "Now my whole world's in one 8 x 10"

   What is he singing about? (What is "black and white"? What "moment in time" is he referring to? What is the 8 x 10?) (He is using figurative language here.)

3. He also sings about "four metal walls holding it in" and "one plate-glass window." What are these walls? What is this window? (He is using figurative language here.)

4. What is the general feeling of the song? What image do you have of the speaker in the lyrics? What can you say about him, his life, and his home? What details in the lyrics support your reactions?

5. Do any of the lines or images in these lyrics remind you of yourself or your life? Explain.

Reading Assignment: "Tangled and Dark"

Preview Read the title and the first two stanzas.

Anticipate What do you think this song will be about? What kind of mood or message do you think it has? Use the "Notes" column to record your thoughts.

Read and Reread   Quickly read the lyrics one time, marking unknown terms. Then reread more slowly and use the "Notes" column to record images and meanings that come to mind. Also write down any questions you have. Define unknown terms. Finally, listen to the song or read it aloud.

Tangled and Dark
Bonnie Raitt

Luck of the Draw

1   Gonna get into it
Where it's tangled and dark
Way on into it, Baby
Down where your fears are parked.
Gonna tell the truth about it
Honey that's the hardest part
When we get through it, Baby
You're gonna give up your heart

2   Gonna get into it, Baby
Gonna give them demons a call
Way on into it Baby
Gonna find out once and for all
Gonna get a little risky, Baby
Honey that's my favorite part
When we get through it, Baby
We're gonna give up our hearts.

3   Well, there's no turnin back,
No turnin back, this time
Well there's no turnin back,
No turnin back—

4   No use in runnin
It's always the same
You can count on the panic
It's the faces that change
We might have a chance
To get this love off the block

Notes

| So take a deep breath
Let's look under that rock.

Questions for Critical Thought

"Tangled and Dark"

1. What does the title of the song tell you? What images come to mind?

2. What is your general reaction to the lyrics? How do they make you feel? What details in the lyrics support your reactions?

3. Throughout the song Raitt refers to *it*. Circle all the *its* you can find. What do you think some of these *its* refer to?

4. In the last line Raitt says, "Let's look under that rock." What does she mean? Explain. (She's using figurative language here.)

5. What do you think is the general message in this song?

6. Do any of the lines or images in these lyrics remind you of yourself or your life? Explain.

Reading Assignment: *"Perfect"*

Preview   Read the title and the first two stanzas.

Anticipate   What do you think this song will be about? What kind of mood or message do you think it has? Respond in the "Notes" column.

Read and Reread   Quickly read the lyrics one time, marking unknown terms. Then reread more slowly and use the "Notes" column to record images and meaning that come to mind. Also write down any questions you have. Define unknown terms. Finally, listen to the song or read it aloud.

Perfect

Alanis Morissette

Jagged Little Pill

1   Sometimes is never quite enough
If you're flawless, then you'll win my love
Don't forget to win first place
Don't forget to keep that smile on your face

2   Be a good boy
    Try a little harder
    You've got to measure up
    And make me prouder

3   How long before you screw it up
    How many times do I have to tell you to hurry up
    With everything I do for you
    The least you can do is keep quiet

4   Be a good girl
    You've gotta try a little harder
    That simply wasn't good enough
    To make us proud

5   I'll live through you
    I'll make you what I never was
    If you're the best, then maybe so am I
    Compared to him compared to her
    I'm doing this for your own damn good
    You'll make up for what I blew
    What's the problem . . . why are you crying

6   Be a good boy
    Push a little farther now
    That wasn't fast enough
    To make us happy
    We'll love you just the way you are if you're perfect

Questions for Critical Thought

"Perfect"

1. What is your general reaction to the lyrics? How do they make you feel? (happy? sad? relaxed? energized? mad? or?) What lines in the lyrics can you point to that make you feel this way?

2. Think about the line in stanza 3, "How many times do I have to tell you to hurry up." Who might say words like these?

3. What do you think of these lines in stanza 5: "I'll live through you/I'll make you what I never was"? Who might say these words? How do you feel about these words?

4. Who do you think the speaker in the lyrics is? Is the speaker Morissette? Why, or why not?

5. What do you think of the last line in the song?

6. What do you think the general message is in this song?

7. Do any of the lines or images in this song remind you of yourself or your life? Explain.

Reading Assignment: *"Silent Legacy"*

Preview   Read the title and the first two stanzas.

Anticipate   What do you think this song will be about? What kind of mood or message do you think it might have? Respond in the "Notes" column.

Read and Reread   Quickly read the lyrics one time, marking unknown terms. Then reread more slowly and use the "Notes" column to record images and meanings that come to mind. Also write down any questions you have. Define unknown terms. Finally, listen to the song or read it aloud.

Silent Legacy
Melissa Etheridge

Yes I Am

1   Why did you steal the matches
From the one room motel
Once they gave you answers
Now they give you hell
They will never understand
They wonder where did they go wrong
How could you be so selfish
Why can't you get along

2   And as you pray in your darkness
For wings to set you free
You are bound to your silent legacy

3   You've seen it in the movies
And you've heard it on the street

Craving the affection
Your blood is full of heat
They don't listen to your reasons
As original as sin
Deny all that you feel
And they will bring you home again

Notes

4   And as you pray in your darkness
For wings to set you free
You are bound to your silent legacy

5   Your body is alive
But no one told you what you'd feel
The empty aching hours
Trying to conceal
The natural progression
Is the coming of your age
But they cover it with shame
And turn it into rage

6   And as you pray in your darkness
For wings to set you free
You are bound to your silent legacy
You are digging for the answers
Until your fingers bleed
To satisfy the hunger
To satiate the need
They feed you on the guilt
To keep you humble keep you low
Some man and myth they made up
A thousand years ago

7   And as you pray in your darkness
For wings to set you free
You are bound to your silent legacy

8   Mothers tell your children
Be quick you must be strong
Life is full of wonder
Love is never wrong
Remember how they taught you
How much of it was fear

Notes
> Refuse to hand it down
> The legacy stops here
>
> 9   Oh my child

Questions for Critical Thought

"Silent Legacy"

1. What does the title "Silent Legacy" suggest to you?

2. What is your general reaction to the music lyrics? How do they make you feel?

3. The following lines appear in stanza 1: "They wonder where did they go wrong / How could you be so selfish / Why can't you get along." Who might ask "Where did we go wrong?" or "How could you be so selfish?" or "Why can't you get along?" Look at the other times "they" is used. Who do you think "they" refers to in this song?

4. Read through the song and note where the words "sin," "shame," and "guilt" show up. What do you think the person in this song is struggling with?

5. The last stanza in this song is distinctly different in tone and message. Explain.

6. What do you think the "silent legacy" is?

7. Do any of the lines or images in these lyrics remind you of yourself or your life? Explain.

Journal Assignment

An Informal Response to the Songs

Write out your thoughts about two or three of the songs in this book. What do they mean? What clues do you have for the meaning? During class discussion, did any of your classmates point out things you hadn't seen in the songs? After reading someone else's journal, just say, "Thank You," when you return it.

Explore the Writing Assignment

Here, again, is your writing assignment. Review it carefully before continuing. Underline the important terms in the assignment.

Write an essay about one of the songs in this book or a song you have chosen and reviewed with your instructor. In your essay, summarize what you think the song is about. Then choose a couple of the most interesting parts to support your point and show that you have read the lyrics carefully and have good reasons for your interpretation.

Brainstorm   Review your work so far in this chapter. What song do you want to write an essay about? Write freely in response to the writing assignment and explore your reasons for choosing your selected song. What message(s), images, and emotions in this song interest you? What clues in the song support your interpretation of the song?

Activity

Analyzing a Song

A chart like the one that follows may be used to help you move from stanza to stanza in order to analyze the lines and better understand the song you've chosen to write about. "Silent Legacy" is used as an example here, but you can use a similar chart to analyze any song.

On a separate piece of paper, create a chart like the one below. Moving stanza by stanza or even line by line, list images or language that suggests the meaning of the song:

	Image/Language	Possible Meaning
Stanzas 1–2	"hell"	place of torment
	"bound to silent legacy"	tied to something passed down but unspoken
Stanzas 3–4		
Stanzas 5–7		
Stanzas 8–9		

In a sentence or two, sum up what these images suggest:

Who is the speaker addressing? What clues suggest this?

Who is the audience? What clues reveal the audience?

Consider Your Audience   You should not assume that your audience knows the song you'll be writing about. Write a brief summary of the song that lets your audience know what the song is basically about.

Notes

You may find that all or part of this summary fits into the introduction of your essay.

Create Your Thesis   Review your writing assignment, notes, brainstorm, and summary. Your thesis should tell the reader the general message of the song you've chosen. Experiment with several thesis statements until you find one that clearly states your conclusions about the song.

Outline   Consider now how you'll support your thesis statement. Remember that in an analytical essay, a writer must break the larger topic down into smaller pieces that can be studied. One approach to song lyrics is to study one stanza per paragraph. However, you may not want to cover all the stanzas. Perhaps you feel there are three or four key stanzas you want to focus on. Another approach might be to cover any or all of the following in separate paragraphs: mood, message, audience, speaker, or images.

Take time now to think critically about what your major supporting points will be, and write topic sentences that express these supporting points.

Next, think about the order of your main points. Experiment with your outline until you have found a method of organization that makes sense to you. Show your outline to a classmate, tutor, or your instructor, and see if that reader can see a focused, organized essay emerging.

Draft

Remember that you should direct your thoughts to a reader who is unfamiliar with the song you are writing about. In your introduction, you'll need to "introduce" the song and the songwriter and tell why you decided to write about this song. Then state what you intend to explain through analysis. In the body of your paper, you should go into more detail about a few parts of the song. Be sure to use vocabulary and figurative language as important parts of your explanation. As you write multiple drafts, your explanation will become clearer. In your conclusion, explain what you hope the reader learned from your essay.

Revise

Activity

Share Your Writing

Find a classmate to work with. Read each other's essay and apply the following questions to each essay.

- Have you explained the overall message of the song?

- Have you then offered smaller pieces of the song that you have studied in detail?

- Does each paragraph have a clear topic sentence?

- Are your paragraphs in a logical order? Have you used transitions where you need them?

- Have you offered the reader specific information from the song to support your major points?

- Have you explained that specific information fully? (What is obvious to you may not be obvious to the reader.)

- What areas of writing has your instructor suggested you work on?

After working with your classmate, make a list of improvements you want to make. Rank them from most important to least, and then tackle one task at a time.

Edit

Read your essay aloud and look for (and listen for) awkward spots and typographical errors.

Review your essay again slowly and consider the following:

- Look for errors you tend to repeat, focusing on one type of error at a time.

- Does your instructor have a certain area he or she wants you to focus on?

- Put song titles in quotation marks.

- When you quote lines from a song lyric, put a slash between lines. For example, if you quoted these lines from "Imagine," you

Notes

would use the slash like this: "Imagine there's no countries/It isn't hard to do."

After completing the work on pages 375–387, consider the following question:

- Have you combined sentences with coordinators and subordinators to better express your ideas?

Writing Assignment #2: *Analyzing Poetry*

In this assignment, you'll sharpen your analytical and inferential skills as you study poetry. This analysis requires you to study the details of the poems so that you can draw conclusions about what they mean.

Here, in brief, is the writing assignment you are preparing for.

Choose one of the poems in this book, or a poem you and your instructor have agreed upon, and write an essay in which you reveal the meaning of the poem to your reader. In your essay, you'll need to summarize the poem and then take the reader through the poem, stanza by stanza or line by line, in order to explain the poem's meaning.

Keep this assignment in mind as you proceed to analyze the poems presented in this chapter.

Discuss and Engage

Activity

Discuss Poetry

Discuss the term *poetry* with your classmates and develop a group definition of poetry. Think about what a poem should contain or do in order to be called a poem. Also talk about the kind(s) of poetry you enjoy reading or writing. Discuss any poems you remember having learned in the past.

Get Involved!

Go online to www.poems.com or www.emule.com/poetry and find two or three poems that would be interesting and challenging to analyze. Bring the poems to class and share them with your classmates.

Journal Assignment

Thinking About Poetry

Write out your own definition of a what a poem is. Be sure to include what you believe to be the essential elements of a good poem. Are there similarities between music lyrics and poems? (This is for your eyes only. Refer back to this journal when you are getting ready to write your essay on poetry.)

It may help you to know one of the official definitions of *poetry:*

> A term applied to the many forms in which human beings have given rhyth-mic expression to their most imaginative and intense perceptions [or views] of the world, themselves, and the relation of the two.
> —*C. Hugh Holman and William Harmon,*
> *A Handbook to Literature, 5th ed.*

As Holman and Harmon point out, poetry expresses humans' most creative views of themselves and the world.

Before moving on, check your definition with Holman and Harmon's. How does it compare? What are the differences? You may wish to revise your definition to include new information.

Read, Discuss, Think Critically

This section of the chapter contains five poems. The poems were all written by well-known poets and represent a variety of concerns that you'll explore as you discuss and analyze the poems in class.

Reading Assignment: *"Incident"*

Preview   Read the title and the first two stanzas.

Anticipate   What do you think this poem will be about? What kind of mood or message do you think it has? Respond in the "Notes" column.

Read and Reread   Quickly read the poem one time, marking un-known terms. Then reread more slowly and use the "Notes" col-umn to record images and meanings that come to mind. Also write down any questions you have. Define unknown terms. Finally, read the poem aloud.

Incident
Counteé Cullen (1903–1946)

A graduate of Harvard University, Cullen wrote poetry reflecting racist attitudes of the day.

(For Eric Walrond)

1   Once riding in old Baltimore,
        Heart-filled, head-filled with glee,

Notes

> I saw a Baltimorean
>   Keep looking straight at me.
>
> 2 Now I was eight and very small,
>   And he was no whit bigger,
> And so I smiled, but he poked out
>   His tongue, and called me, "Nigger."
>
> 3 I saw the whole of Baltimore
>   From May until December;
> Of all the things that happened there
>   That's all that I remember.

Questions for Critical Thought

"Incident"

1. What is your general reaction to the poem? How does it make you feel? What word(s) create this feeling?

2. Cullen uses the term "Nigger" in this poem. Explain the effect of the derogatory term on the speaker in the poem.

3. How does the tone of the poem shift following the use of this single term?

4. What do you think Cullen would like you to learn from the poem? What would he like you to think about?

5. Did the images or words make you think about an "incident" that's happened in your own life? If so, explain.

Reading Assignment: "Wild Nights"

> **Preview**   Read the title and the first two stanzas.
>
> **Anticipate**   What do you think this poem will be about? What kind of mood or message do you think it has? Respond in the "Notes" column.
>
> **Read and Reread**   Quickly read the poem one time, marking unknown terms. Then reread more slowly and use the "Notes" column to record images and meanings that come to mind. Also write down any questions you have. Define unknown terms. Finally, read the poem aloud.

Wild Nights

Emily Dickinson (1830–1886)

Considered one of America's greatest poets, Dickinson did not follow conventional poetic forms but constructed her own special form of verse. The dashes included are hers.

1 Wild Nights—Wild Nights
Were I with thee
Wild Nights should be
Our luxury!

2 Futile—the Winds—
To a Heart in port—
Done with the Compass—
Done with the Chart!

3 Rowing in Eden—
Ah, the Sea!
Might I but moor—Tonight—
In Thee!

Questions for Critical Thought

"Wild Nights"

1. What is your general reaction to the poem? How does it make you feel? What words create this feeling?

2. What is happening to the speaker in this poem? How do the words and sea imagery help to describe the speaker's feelings?

3. What are your favorite lines in this poem? Why?

4. Have the images or words made you think about your own life or experiences? If so, explain.

Reading Assignment: *"Refugee Ship"*

Preview   Read the title and the first two stanzas.

Anticipate   What do you think this poem will be about? What kind of mood or message do you think it has? Use the "Notes" column to record your thoughts.

Read and Reread   Quickly read the poem one time, marking unknown terms. Then reread more slowly and use the "Notes" column to record images and meanings that come to mind. Also write down any questions you have. Define unknown terms. Finally, read the poem aloud.

Refugee Ship
Lorna Dee Cervantes (b. 1954)

Of Native American and Mexican ancestry, Cervantes is a poet, editor, and teacher.

mi abuelita's is Spanish for "my grandmother's."

1 like wet cornstarch
   I slide past *mi abuelita's* eyes
   bible placed by her side
   she removes her glasses
   the pudding thickens

2 *mama* raised me with no language
   I am orphan to my Spanish name
   the words are foreign, stumbling on my tongue
   I stare at my reflection in the mirror
   brown skin, black hair

refugee ship is a boat carrying people who are fleeing to another country for safety.

3 I feel I am a captive
   aboard the refugee ship
   a ship that will never dock
   a ship that will never dock

Questions for Critical Thought
"Refugee Ship"

1. What is your general reaction to this poem? How does it make you feel? What words create this feeling?

2. Describe your image of the grandmother in this poem. What words make this image in your mind?

3. What do you think Cervantes means when she says, "I am orphan to my Spanish name/the words are foreign, stumbling on my tongue"?

4. What do you think the speaker is saying in the last stanza?

5. Do any of the lines, images, or messages in this poem connect to your life? Explain.

Reading Assignment: *"The Road Not Taken"*   Notes

Preview   Read the title and the first two stanzas.

Anticipate   What do you think this poem is about? What kind of mood or message do you think it has? Record your thoughts in the "Notes" column.

Read and Reread   Quickly read the poem one time, marking unknown terms. Then reread more slowly and use the "Notes" column to record images and meanings that come to mind. Also write down any questions you have. Define unknown terms. Finally, read the poem aloud.

The Road Not Taken
Robert Frost (1874–1963)

American poet

1   Two roads diverged in a yellow wood,
And sorry I could not travel both
And be one traveler, long I stood
And looked down one as far as I could
to where it bent in the undergrowth.

2   Then took the other, as just as fair,
And having perhaps the better claim,
Because it was grassy and wanted wear;
Though as for that the passing there
Had worn them really about the same,

3   And both that morning equally lay
In leaves no step had trodden black,
Oh, I kept the first for another day!
Yet knowing how way leads on to way,
I doubted if I should ever come back.

4   I shall be telling this with a sigh
Somewhere ages and ages hence:
Two roads diverged in a wood, and I—
I took the one less traveled by,
And that has made all the difference.

Questions for Critical Thought

"The Road Not Taken"

1. What is your general reaction to this poem? How does it make you feel? What words or images in the poem promote this feeling?

2. Describe the movements of this traveler (the speaker) in the poem. Describe what the speaker sees and then does in response.

3. It is possible that this "road" that the speaker did not take is an example of figurative language. Perhaps the speaker is not thinking of an actual road. What could he or she be speaking of? Do any other lines in the poem suggest that this interpretation might be right?

4. What is significant about the fact that he or she took the road "less traveled by"? If this is another example of figurative language, what does this road "less traveled by" represent?

5. Can you relate to what Frost is saying in his poem? Have you had a similar experience?

Reading Assignment: *"A Work of Artifice"*

Preview   Read the title and the first seven lines of the poem.

Anticipate   What do you think this poem will be about? What kind of mood or message do you think it has? Record your thoughts in the "Notes" column.

Read and Reread   Quickly read the poem one time, marking unknown terms. Then reread more slowly and use the "Notes" column to record images and meanings that come to mind. Also write down any questions you have. Define unknown terms. Finally, read the poem aloud.

A Work of Artifice
Marge Piercy (b. 1936)

American poet and novelist

1   The bonsai tree
    in the attractive pot
    could have grown eighty feet tall

on the side of a mountain
till split by lightning
6 But a gardener
carefully pruned it.
It is nine inches high.
Every day as he
whittles back the branches
11 the gardener croons,
It is your nature
to be small and cozy,
domestic and weak;
how lucky, little tree,
16 to have a pot to grow in.
With living creatures
one must begin very early
to dwarf their growth:
the bound feet,
21 the crippled brain,
the hair in curlers,
the hands you
love to touch.

Questions for Critical Thought

"A Work of Artifice"

1. Carefully consider the title. What does the word *artifice* mean?

2. Read the first five lines aloud. What picture do you see in your mind?

3. Read lines 6 through 8 aloud. What picture do you see now?

4. Read lines 9 through 16 aloud. What do you think of the gardener? Do you agree that the tree is lucky "to have a pot to grow in"? Explain.

5. Toward the end of the poem, the image changes, and we are no longer focusing on a tree. What do you see? What do you think Piercy is saying in this poem?

Journal Assignment

Thinking About the Poems

Write out your thoughts about two or three of the poems in this book. What does each poem reveal? What clues do you have to unlock the meaning in each poem? During class discussion, did any classmates reveal an unusual

Get Involved!

Two additional poems appear in Supplemental Readings. "Annabel Lee" by Edgar Allan Poe (pages 442–443) and "I Want to Write" by Margaret Walker (page 444) expand the themes presented in Chapter 8. After reading both poems, use your analytical skills to interpret them. Be ready to explain your interpretations to classmates.

interpretation of one of the poems? Which poem do you like the best? Why? After reading someone else's journal, just say, "Thank You," when you return it.

Explore the Writing Assignment

Here, again, is your writing assignment. Review it carefully before continuing. Underline the important terms in the assignment.

Choose one of the poems in this book, or a poem you and your instructor have agreed upon, and write an essay in which you reveal the meaning of the poem to your reader. In your essay, you'll need to summarize the poem and then take the reader through the poem, stanza by stanza or line by line, in order to explain the poem's meaning.

Brainstorm   Review your work so far for this assignment. What poem do you want to write an essay about? Write freely in response to the writing assignment and explore your reasons for choosing your selected poem. What message(s), images, or emotions in this poem interest you? What clues in the poem support your interpretation?

Activity

Analyzing a Poem

A chart like the one that follows may be used to help you move from stanza to stanza in order to analyze the lines and better understand the poem you've chosen to write about.

Create your own chart. Then moving stanza by stanza or even line by line, list images or language that suggests the meaning of the poem:

	Image/Language	Possible Meaning
Stanza 1		
Stanza 2		
Stanza 3		
Stanza 4		
Stanza 5		

In a sentence or two, sum up what these images suggest:

Who is the speaker addressing? What clues suggest this?

Who is the audience? What clues reveal the audience?

Consider Your Audience   You should not assume that your audience knows the poem you are writing about. Write a brief summary of the poem that lets your audience know what the poem is about. You may find that all or part of this summary fits into the introduction of your essay.

Create Your Thesis   Review your writing assignment, notes, brainstorm, and summary. Your thesis should tell the reader what the general message of the poem is. Experiment with several thesis statements until you find one that clearly states your analytical conclusions about the poem you have chosen.

Outline   Now think about how you'll support your thesis statement. Remember that in an analytical essay, a writer must break the larger topic down into smaller pieces that can be studied. One approach to poems is to study one stanza per paragraph. However, you may not want to cover all the stanzas. Perhaps you feel there are three or four key stanzas you want to focus on. (If you analyze "A Work of Artifice," which only has one stanza, you could select particular lines that work together to create an image or message and cover these groups of lines, each in a different paragraph.) Another approach might be to cover any or all of the following in separate paragraphs: mood, message, audience, speaker, or images.

Take time now to think critically about what your major supporting points will be and write topic sentences that express these supporting points.

Next, think about the order of your main points. Experiment with your outline until you have found a method of organization that makes sense to you. Show your outline to a classmate, tutor, or your instructor and see if that reader can see a focused, organized essay emerging.

Draft

Remember that you should direct your thoughts to a reader who is unfamiliar with the poem you are writing about. In your introduction, you'll need to "introduce" the poem and poet and tell why you decided to write about this poem. Also, mention what you intend to explain through analysis. In the body of your paper, you should go into more detail about a few parts of the poem. Be sure to use vocabulary and figurative language as important parts of your explanation. As you write multiple drafts, your explanation will become clearer. In your conclusion, explain what you hope the reader learned from your essay.

Activity

Study a Student Sample

Review the following introduction and conclusion from one student's essay. Mark what you like in each paragraph. Then respond to the questions and statements which follow.
(The title of the essay is "The Art of Deception.")

(Introduction)

My personal interpretation of the poem "A Work of Artifice" by Marge Piercy is that the poem is about stunting growth and the deceitfulness used to accomplish it. Basically, some people often stunt other people's growth for their own personal gains. The reason I chose this poem is because I can relate from my own personal experience. My ex-husband used the same type of deception toward me to fulfill his own idea of the person I should be. Just as the gardener stunts the growth of the bonsai tree, he determines the shape and size of the tree. The gardener even selects the tree's pot, all to his liking. I will explain as follows.

(Conclusion)

This poem in my opinion is clearly not about the tree's or creature's wants, desires, or capabilities. Therefore it is about what the gardener and the person who is crippling the brain want. These people are doing the deceiving and stunting of growth, creating their own expectations of their ideals. I feel this is an injustice that happens all too often in life, far too many times, all in the name of love. I can say I have been that bonsai/creature. I speak from my own horrible experience; I have been left scarred by the treachery and deceit of such an act of love. I fell prey to the crooning and whittling until it almost cost me my life. I believed and trusted this individual, that he had my best interest at heart, only to learn that it was purely a selfish motive that drove him. Yet with every branch they whittle and prune, they still croon.

—Ruth

1. The writing assignment asks that you summarize the poem and your reasons for writing in the introduction. Highlight Ruth's summary and reasons for writing.

2. A conclusion should connect back to the introduction without repeating the introduction. Underline the sentences in the conclusion that connect most closely to the introduction.

3. Note in Ruth's conclusion where she borrows words from the poem. Why is this effective?

Revise

Activity

Share Your Writing

Find a classmate to work with. Read each other's essays and consider the following questions in relation to each essay.

- Have you explained the overall message of the poem?

- Have you then offered smaller pieces of the poem that you have studied in detail?

- Does each paragraph have a clear topic sentence?

- Are your paragraphs in a logical order? Have you used transitions where you need them?

- Have you offered the reader specific information from the poem to support your major points?

- Have you explained that specific information fully? (What is obvious to you may not be obvious to the reader.)

- What areas of writing has your instructor suggested you work on?

After working with your classmate, make a list of improvements you want to make. Rank them from most important to least, and then tackle one task at a time.

Edit

Read your essay aloud and look for (and listen for) awkward spots and typographical errors.

Notes

Review your essay again, slowly, and consider the following:

- Look for errors you tend to repeat, focusing on one type of error at a time.
- Does your instructor have a certain area he or she wants you to focus on?
- Put poem titles in quotation marks.
- Put a slash between lines of the poem. (For example, if you were to quote these lines from "The Road Not Taken," you would use a slash like this: "Two roads diverged in a yellow wood,/And sorry I could not travel both/And be one traveler, long I stood.")

After completing the work on pages 375–387, consider the following questions:

- Have you used coordinators and subordinators to shape your sentences?

SUMMARY OF CHAPTER 8

In this chapter, you have

- strengthened your analysis and inference skills as you studied song lyrics and poetry;
- learned that analysis and inference require you to break larger subjects down into smaller pieces;
- learned that after careful study of the smaller pieces, you can infer information; and
- learned that when writing analytical essays, you must present your major point or conclusion, the pieces of proof that support the conclusion, and explanations of each piece of proof.

COMBINING SENTENCES WITH COORDINATORS AND SUBORDINATORS

Reviewing Coordinators
Sentence Combining
Reviewing Subordinators

In this chapter, you'll review some of what you learned in Chapter 4 about clauses, coordinators, and subordinators. Then you'll take that knowledge one step further by completing a number of sentence combining exercises. You'll find that soon you are using more coordinators and subordinators in your writing without even having to think about them.

Reviewing Coordinators

Coordinators, as you may remember, are special words that you can use to join independent sentences. These words help you show how the idea in one sentence relates to the idea in another sentence. So to use these words effectively, you must choose them carefully.

There are seven coordinators:

for	and	nor	but	or	yet	so
f	a	n	b	o	y	s

One way to remember these seven words is to remember the acronym *FANBOYS*.

Here are a few points to remember about coordinators.

- The *co* in *coordinators* is a prefix that tells us that they create *equal* relationships between the ideas that they join. Think about the equal relationships expressed by these words: *coworkers, coauthors, coexist.* All these words suggest equality. (Neither coworker is more important. Coauthors are equal partners, and to coexist is to live together without one dominating.) When you join sentences with coordinators, you will be showing how they relate to another, but you will *not* be emphasizing one idea over the other, nor will you be making either sentence a dependent clause.

- Each of the FANBOYS expresses a different relationship.

  for: expresses a relationship of *effect-cause.* The idea in the first sentence is the effect. The idea in the second sentence is the cause.

Notes

She chose this song, <u>for</u> it makes her feel happy.

and: expresses a relationship of *addition*. The idea in the first sentence is added to the idea in the second sentence.

She enjoys this song, <u>and</u> she wants others to enjoy it.

nor: expresses a relationship of *negative addition*. The idea in the first sentence is negative, and it is added to a negative idea in the second sentence.

I do not like her guitar playing, <u>nor</u> does he like her guitar playing. (*Note:* When you use *nor,* the subject and verb in the second sentence switch positions. Also, the *nor* in the second half expresses "not," so you don't need another "not.")

but: expresses a relationship of *opposition*. The idea in the first sentence is the opposite of the idea in the second sentence (or the first idea *contrasts* with the second idea).

I told her I didn't like her guitar playing, <u>but</u> she played anyway.

or: expresses a relationship of *alternatives*. The idea in the first sentence is one option. The idea in the second sentence is another option.

She should stop playing, <u>or</u> she should go where I can't hear her.

yet: expresses a relationship of *opposition*. The idea in the first sentence is the opposite of the idea in the second sentence (or the first idea *contrasts* with the second idea).

She heard my opinion, <u>yet</u> she didn't stop playing.

so: expresses a relationship of *cause-effect*. The idea in the first sentence causes the idea in the second sentence.

She said I hurt her feelings, <u>so</u> she stopped talking to me.

• You may use coordinators to begin sentences. Writers do this occasionally to add a little emphasis to the second sentence.

She should stop playing. <u>Or</u> she should go where I can't hear her.

• You must apply Punctuation Rule #2 when joining sentences with coordinators.

Punctuation Rule #2 (Review)

When you join two complete sentences with a coordinator (FANBOYS), you must put a comma after the first sentence.

- She said I hurt her feelings, so she stopped talking to me.

Sentence Combining

As you work through the sentence combining exercises in this chapter, keep the following points in mind.

- You'll benefit the most when doing these exercises if you write out your complete sentences. (Don't just draw arrows or insert words.) By practicing these sentence patterns and paying attention to the punctuation rules, these sophisticated patterns will eventually become second nature to you.

- Often the sentences in these exercises can be joined in more than one way. Follow the directions. (If the exercise asks you to use coordinators to join sentences, do that—even if you can think of other ways to join the ideas.)

- You and your classmates may sometimes disagree on precisely which joining word should be used. That's okay as long as you can each defend your choice.

Practice #1   Music Tastes

Using carefully selected coordinators, join the sentences that follow and express the relationships given to you. (Make sure that you combine two *complete* sentences.) Use each of the coordinators once.

Example:

(Express a relationship of addition.)
Music is a wonderful way for people to communicate their ideas.
They can express their feelings.

- Music is a wonderful way for people to communicate their ideas, and they can express their feelings.

1. (Express a relationship of alternatives.)
   Music can sound sad.
   It can sound happy.

2. (Express a relationship of opposition.)

My favorite music sounds energetic.

Occasionally I like to listen to mellow tunes.

3. (Express a relationship of effect-cause.)

My dad is dancing.

He hears his favorite country song.

4. (Express a relationship of cause-effect.)

My sister is blaring her rap music.

The dog hides under the rug.

5. (Express a relationship of negative addition.)

I don't like classical music.

I don't like big band music.

6. (Express a relationship of opposition.)

My mother loves rock and roll.

My father loves country and jazz.

Practice #2   Mozart

Using carefully chosen coordinating conjunctions (or coordinators), join the sentences that follow.

(Austrian composer Wolfgang Amadeus Mozart lived from 1756 to 1791.)

1. He was unusual.

He began to compose music at the age of 5.

2. He wrote music for the piano, violin, French horn, and string quartets.

He wrote wonderful symphonies, operas, serenades, sonatas, and religious music.

3. He was famous during his lifetime.

He was quite poor.

Practice #3   Louis Armstrong, a.k.a. Satchmo

Using carefully selected coordinators, join the sentences that follow. Sentences 1–11 will create three paragraphs. The italicized sentences add extra information. You do not have to change (or join) the italicized sentences in any way. When you write your completed paragraphs, include the italicized sentences.

1. Louis Armstrong was born in 1918.

   He lived in New Orleans, Louisiana.

   When he was 7 years old, his parents separated.

2. He and his mother needed money.

   He began singing.

3. He sang on the streets of New Orleans.

   He earned only pennies.

4. At age 13 he was arrested.

   He was sent to a home for street children.

   While living there, he learned to play the cornet (an instrument similar to the trumpet).

5. Two kind teachers helped him learn to play the cornet.

   They were not professional musicians.

   They accidentally taught him some bad habits.

   One of those habits was puffing up his cheeks when he played the cornet.

6. Later in life when he visited London as a well-known musician, the people called him Satchelmouth.

   He blew his cheeks as large as a "satchel" (a bag for carrying books or clothing).

   That name later turned into his nickname "Satchmo."

   [end of first paragraph]

   As one of the most famous jazz trumpet players, Armstrong was a true creative artist.

7. He was known for his ability to improvise on stage.

   He created "scat" singing where the human voice is used like an instrument.

8. Most singing relies on words.

   Instruments produce musical notes.

   Scat singing requires the singer to pronounce nonsense syllables.

   [end of second paragraph]

   Finally, some remember Armstrong as a pioneer in music.

Notes

9. He was part of the Creole Jazz Band.

    They were the first black jazz ensemble band to record an album.

10. Later, he had his own band.

    They performed as Louis Armstrong and His Hot Five.

    Even though he accomplished so much in his lifetime, one private dream was left unfulfilled.

11. He wanted to sing the national anthem at Shea Stadium where his favorite team, the New York Mets, played.

    He practiced all his life.

    He was never invited to sing.

    He died in 1971.

Practice #4   Selena

Using carefully selected coordinators, join the sentences that follow. Use a variety of coordinators. Sentences 1–5 will create one paragraph. The italicized sentences add extra information. You do not have to change (or join) the italicized sentences in any way. When you write your completed paragraph, include the italicized sentences.

1. Selena Quintanilla-Perez was born in 1971 in South Texas.

    She began performing professionally when she was only 10 years old.

2. She sang Tejano music.

    She was extremely popular in the Tejano culture of the South.

3. She sang in Spanish.

    She couldn't actually read Spanish.

    She grew up speaking English in a school system that discouraged speaking Spanish.

    When she began singing Tejano music, she had to learn the Spanish lyrics phonetically.

4. Her band, Los Dinos, was a family band.

    Her sister Suzette played the drums.

    Her brother A. B. played bass and wrote songs.

    Her father Abraham was the manager.

    Critics say she had a strong jubilant voice that was intoxicating in its joy and liveliness. Tragically, in 1994 she was shot and killed in a Corpus Christi motel by the president of her fan club.

5. She did not reach her goal of breaking into the "mainstream" music scene.

She did not see an album reach number one.

However, in July 1995 her posthumous album Dreaming of You *reached number one on* Billboard's *album chart. She is greatly missed by her family and fans.*

Practice #5 Create Sentences with Coordinators

Create three sentences that might show up in an essay about one of the lyrics or poems you analyzed. (You might use sentences you wrote in response to "Questions for Critical Thought.") These sentences must each have two independent clauses joined by a coordinator.

Reviewing Subordinators

You may remember that a *subordinator* is a word that can attach to an independent sentence and make that sentence a dependent clause. A dependent clause cannot stand on its own but can be joined to an independent clause, making a longer, more expressive sentence. Consider the prefix "sub." "Sub" means under or lower. Think of the words *submarine, subconscious, subfreezing, subhuman, submerge.* All these words suggest the idea of being under or lower: a *submarine* travels underwater. *Subfreezing* is below freezing. *Subhuman* means being beneath the human race in development, and to *submerge* means to place underwater. So, when you use a *subordinator,* you will be lowering one idea, making it dependent.

There are many subordinators, and you don't need to memorize them. As you work through the exercises in this section you'll learn the important points about how to use them to combine sentences and how to punctuate these new sentences correctly.

To review the subordinators that allow you to make concessions in your writing, see pages 277–281.

Here is a list of subordinators:

although	*since*
after	*though*
because	*unless*
even though	*when*
if	*while*

Notes

Like the coordinators you just studied, these subordinators help you express specific relationships between ideas. You must choose them carefully when joining sentences. Refer to the following explanations when completing the subordinator exercises.

- Subordinators expressing *opposition and concession:* although, though, even though, while
- Subordinators expressing *time* relationships: after, since, when, while
- Subordinators expressing *effect-cause* relationships: because, since
- Subordinators expressing *conditions:* if, unless

Punctuation Rule #5 (Review)

*When you **begin** a sentence with a subordinated clause, you must put a comma after the subordinated clause.*

- <u>Although the poem began with an interesting image,</u> the rest of the poem was really quite boring.

Punctuation Rule #6 (Review)

*If the subordinated clause comes **after** the independent clause, you do not need a comma.*

- The poem began with an interesting image <u>although the rest of the poem was quite boring.</u>

Practice #6   Edgar Allan Poe

- Join the sentences that follow using subordinators that express the relationship given to you.
- Use as many different subordinators as possible.
- In some instances, the subordinator will fit best at the beginning of the first sentence. In other instances, the subordinator will fit best at the beginning of the second sentence.
- Your final product will be one paragraph. (Include the italicized sentences when you write out your paragraph.)

Notes

Edgar Allan Poe was born in 1809.

1. (Express a relationship of time.)

   He was very young.

   He became an orphan.

2. (Express a relationship of effect-cause.)

   He had nowhere to go.

   His godfather took him in, and they lived in England from 1815 to 1820.

3. (Express a relationship of opposition.)

   He had the opportunity to attend a number of different schools during the years 1820–1831.

   He left these schools before completing his education.

4. (Express a relationship of opposition.)

   He also joined the army.

   He left that too.

5. (Express a relationship of opposition.)

   In 1836 he married his cousin.

   She was only 13 years old.

6. (Express a relationship of time.)

   His wife died at age 24.

   He wrote his famous poem "Annabel Lee."

   His other famous works include "The Raven," "The Tell-Tale Heart," and "Pit and the Pendulum." Poe had a drinking problem that seriously affected his health, and in 1849 he died at the age of 40.

Practice #7   Reading Poe's Poetry and Short Stories

- Join the sentences that follow using subordinators that express the relationship given to you.
- Use as many different subordinators as possible.
- In some instances, the subordinator will fit best at the beginning of the first sentence. In other instances, the subordinator will fit best at the beginning of the second sentence.
- Your final product will be one paragraph.

Notes

1. (Express a relationship of opposition.)

   I enjoy reading his poems and short stories.

   They scare me a little.

2. (Express a condition.)

   I won't read them.

   The lights are on.

3. (Express a condition.)

   My brother likes to read them.

   The electricity goes out.

4. (Express a relationship of effect-cause.)

   I think my brother enjoys this.

   He likes to scare me.

Practice #8   Emily Dickinson

- Join the sentences that follow using carefully chosen subordinators.
- Use as many different subordinators as possible.
- In some instances, the subordinator will fit best at the beginning of the first sentence. In other instances, the subordinator will fit best at the beginning of the second sentence.
- Your final product will be one paragraph. Include the italicized sentences when you write your paragraph.

   Emily Dickinson was born in 1830.

1. Growing up, she was exposed to a large, powerful social circle.

   She grew up in a politically active family concerned with civic issues.

   In fact, her family had a role in founding the Amherst Academy and the Amherst College.

2. She was ready for school.

   She attended Amherst Institute and Mount Holyoke Female Seminary.

3. She completed only one year at the seminary.

   She spent most of her time in her room in the family home.

4. She did not enjoy visiting in person.

She kept up a constant correspondence with a number of friends.

5. She wrote poems throughout her life.

No one realized how many until after her death.

Her sister found 1,147 poems in a dresser in Dickinson's room.

6. She wrote almost 2,000 poems as an adult.

Only two poems were published during her lifetime.

Practice #9   Reading Dickinson

- Join the sentences that follow using carefully chosen subordinators.

- Use as many different subordinators as possible.

- In some instances, the subordinator will fit best at the beginning of the first sentence. In other instances, the subordinator will fit best at the beginning of the second sentence.

- Your final product will be one paragraph.

1. I love reading Dickinson's short, intriguing poems.

They are very challenging.

2. I can't understand them.

I read them several times.

3. I read them aloud.

I get a clearer idea of what she is saying.

4. I'd like to take a class on Dickinson.

There's so much to learn about her and her poems.

Practice #10   Creating Sentences with Subordinated Clauses

Create three sentences that you might use in an essay about music or poetry. These sentences must each contain a subordinated clause and an independent clause.

Practice #11   Maya Angelou

This is a coordinator and subordinator review exercise.

- Carefully choose the best coordinators and subordinators and combine the sentences below.

- Use a variety of coordinators and subordinators and be sure to punctuate your sentences correctly.
- In some instances, the subordinator will fit best at the beginning of the first sentence. In other instances, the subordinator will fit best at the beginning of the second sentence.
- Your final product will be two paragraphs. Be sure to include the italicized sentences in your final paragraphs.

1. Maya Angelou was born in 1928.
   Her name was Marguerite Johnson.

2. She was very young.
   Her parents divorced.
   She moved to Arkansas with her brother Bailey.

3. She was 7 years old.
   She was sexually assaulted.

4. She told who assaulted her.
   He was killed.

5. She felt guilty for what she thought her words had done.
   She quit talking for 6 years.
   [end of first paragraph]
   When she was older, she lived with her mother in San Francisco.

6. Angelou ran away.
   She lived with other homeless children in a junkyard.
   Later she became the city's first black streetcar conductor.

7. She was 16.
   She had a son.
   However, a difficult childhood, trauma, and poverty haven't stopped her from enjoying life and trying new things.

8. She has worked as a Creole cook, singer, songwriter, dancer, and actress.
   She has been an educator, social activist, and writer.
   She read her poem "On the Pulse of the Morning" at President Clinton's inauguration.

Practice #12   Listening to Maya Angelou

This is a coordinator and subordinator review exercise.

- Carefully choose the best coordinators and subordinators, and combine the sentences below.

- Use a variety of coordinators and subordinators, and be sure to punctuate your sentences correctly.

- In some instances, the subordinator will fit best at the beginning of the first sentence. In other instances, the subordinator will fit best at the beginning of the second sentence.

1. I have read Angelou's *I Know Why the Caged Bird Sings.*

   I enjoyed it.

   I enjoy her poetry even more.

2. I could listen to her read aloud.

   That is the ultimate in enjoying her words.

   She has a stunning, deep, rich voice.

3. I heard her speak once.

   I was in college.

   I have never heard a voice that magical since.

4. I heard her in person.

   I bought some audio recordings of her telling stories about her life.

5. She will always be a person I admire greatly.

   She has strength, compassion, humor, a sense of joy, and a beautiful voice to tell us about life.

Your Own Writing: Using Coordinators and Subordinators

Study a piece of your writing (a journal or a paragraph from an essay). Underline any coordinators or subordinators that you find. Revise this piece of writing and clarify the relationships between ideas by joining independent clauses with coordinators or subordinators. Underline your revisions.

Combining Sentences with Coordinators and Subordinators

Notes

END-OF-TERM PROGRESS JOURNAL

Completing a college writing course is an admirable accomplishment. Take time in this final journal to reflect on your growth as a writer, reader, and critical thinker. (Draw comparisons between your skills and processes at the beginning of the term to your skills and processes now at the end of the term. Be specific.)

- How has your reading process changed? Explain.
- How has your writing process changed? Explain.
- How have your critical thinking skills improved? Explain.
- Have your attitudes toward reading, writing, and critical thinking changed? Explain.
- Which specific writing skills have improved the most? (Think about your ability to focus, organize, and develop ideas.)
- How have your sentence skills changed?
- What skills and processes do you still need to work on?
- What writing assignment from this term are you most proud of? Why?

We recommend that you share this journal with your classmates. We hope that your class has become a community of writers who are interested in each other's progress.

Good luck in your future writing, reading, and critical thinking endeavors!

This section of Connections *offers you a selection of supplemental readings that connect to the themes in this book. Your instructor might assign readings from this section, and/or you might choose to read these pieces to strengthen your reading and critical thinking skills and deepen your knowledge about a particular topic.*

THE VALUE OF LEARNING

Reading Assignment: *"The Most Precious Gift"*

Questions for Critical Thought follow this reading.

Preview   Read the first three paragraphs of this journalistic article.

Anticipate   What do you think this article will be about? Use the "Notes" column to record your thoughts.

Read and Reread   Read the entire article, marking unknown terms. Then reread more slowly and use the "Notes" column to write your responses to the reading. Mark important and interesting points and define unknown terms.

The Most Precious Gift
by Hank Whittemore

This article was published in *Parade Magazine*, December 22, 1991.

1   "Sometimes I do wonder where I came from," muses Robert Howard Allen of West Tennessee, who had never seen the inside of a classroom until, in 1981 at age thirty-two, he entered college. No, he was not a late-blooming genius; but last May, after just a decade of school, he graduated from Vanderbilt University in Nashville with a master's degree and a Ph.D. in English. A gentle, unworldly spirit who plays the banjo and loves to make puns, he adds with an enigmatic grin, "Maybe I just fell out of the sky."

2   When Allen first appeared on the campus of Bethel College, a small Presbyterian school in McKenzie, fifteen miles from his backwoods home, administrators were even more baffled. Here was a grown man who had never been to grammar school or high school, yet he had "blown the lid off" his college placement test. He stood six feet tall, with unkempt red hair, and his tattered sweater was held together by safety pins. There were holes in his shoes and his front teeth were gone. He had rarely set foot outside Carroll County, 120 miles west of Nashville, where he was born. He lived in a ramshackle farmhouse—one of three homes in the tiny hamlet of Rosser—without indoor plumbing. He had never ridden a bicycle or been inside a movie theater or out on a date.

3   With an aura of innocence, however, Allen's blue eyes sparkled from behind his steel-rimmed glasses as if he had a secret. And it turned out that he did—a secret that amounts to a triumph of faith.

Notes

4   From the age of seven, Robert Allen read books. Not just several books or even a few hundred, but thousands of every description—from Donald Duck comics to the Bible, from Homer to James Joyce—to the point where his head was filled with history and classical literature. The scope of his learning was far greater than that of any professor at Bethel, where he was invited to skip most of his freshman courses and enter as a sophomore. Yet, having spent his whole life in virtual isolation with elderly relatives, Allen himself had no idea how special he was.

5   He turned up at Bethel on a whim. "I'd started my own upholstery business in the back of the house," he recalls, "but when the 1980 recession came on, there was no more work. So I thought I'd give education a whirl. I didn't think I could succeed at it, though. I just assumed that people in college knew more than I did."

6   In three years, he graduated summa cum laude.

7   Without realizing it, Robert Allen had proved the power of reading to transform an individual life. In circumstances that otherwise would have been unbearable, he had read as an unconscious act of sheer survival. "Books were my great comfort," he says simply. "They were my pastime and my playmates." Reading whatever he could get his hands on, he traveled freely across time and space, meeting the world's greatest philosophers and poets down through the ages.

8   "He's at home in mythological Babylon and in eighth-century Judea," says Dr. William Ramsay, one of his Bethel advisers. "He became a citizen of the world without ever leaving Tennessee."

9   "Robert retains everything," says Prof. Vereen Bell, who teaches English at Vanderbilt, "so his head is just full of all this historical and mythological stuff that he has accumulated. In a sense, he missed the 20th century. He's in a kind of time warp, and I think he forever will be."

10   Allen's triumph had its seeds in suffering. His parents were divorced a few months before he was born. He yearned for his father but, to this day, has never seen him. His mother, Hazel, worked as a waitress and all but ignored him. "She was in the generation between the farmers and me," he says, "so I think she felt caught in that condition." When Robert was six, his mother abandoned him, running off with a traveling shoe salesman. She left him to be raised by elderly relatives—his grandfather and three great-aunts and a great-uncle—living in the same household.

11   Even today, Allen can express his youthful pain only through his poetry, as when he writes that the mother "had no love for her stray mistake of a child" and that his grandmother "died just one spring later, too soon to fill my childhood with any love." It was Uncle Eddie Jones, his guardian, who decreed that school was "a waste of time" and blocked authorities from enrolling him.

Notes

12   "I never entirely understood it," Allen says, adding that he was also told that his father might return "to kidnap me, even though there was no evidence that he even knew I existed." In any event, he adds, "They kept me home. I really was pretty much isolated."

13   The county sent teachers for the homebound twice weekly for a year, but from age seven the boy's formal education was over. In a house where at least one of his relatives was always sick or dying, growing up without friends, Allen listened to endless family stories; and Aunt Bevie Jones, Uncle Eddie's wife, began reading to him. "She had gone up to the eighth grade," he says, "but that was the only education in our family." Aunt Bevie taught him to read; his grandfather taught him to write; and the boy, in turn, read the King James Bible to his blind Aunt Ida, going through it twice from cover to cover.

14   Allen's male ancestors had been farmers, but since the 30s the men had become carpenters and house painters. The boy was destined to pick up these trades; but at age twelve, while he was helping care for sick relatives at home, he began reading an old set of Shakespeare's works. "I opened it up and just about read it through at a sitting," he says, and today he'll quote long passages from *King Lear* and *The Tempest*—to name just two of his favorites—at a moment's notice.

15   Hungry for more, he began picking up books at yard sales for pennies apiece—works of mythology, history, poetry and anything else he could find. By his early 20s, Robert had some 2000 volumes and a goal: "I followed a vague, overall plan, which I more or less fulfilled," he recalls, "to study literature in the context of history from the earliest times to the present."

16   When he saw the Carroll County Library in nearby Huntingdon, it was like discovering gold. "Sometimes his Grandfather Jim and Aunt Bevie came with him," recalls Claudine Halpers, the staffer who eventually encouraged him to try for college. "They showed up every week or two, regular as clockwork. They were poor but not ashamed. Robert was his own person—unassuming, but very bright with a keen sense of humor."

17   On the shelves, Allen found the complete set of Will and Ariel Durant's *The Story of Civilization* and spent the next two years wading through its ten massive volumes, simultaneously reading histories and classics for each period. Out of pure enjoyment, he worked his way through the entire library, also teaching himself to read Greek and French to better absorb original versions. The works of Milton, Burns, Keats, Whitman, Wordsworth and other poets continued to feed his insatiable appetite for knowledge and what he now calls "language used to its highest potential."

18   At age thirty, Robert Allen took a high school equivalency test and easily earned his diploma. Two years later, when Bethel College officials saw his placement scores, they eased his way with a work-study grant combining scholarship funds and a campus job.

19   By 1984, after three years as an amiable, older and unquestionably "different" figure on the Bethel campus, he topped his senior class with straight As in all but typing. He scored 3.92 out of a possible 4.0 grade-point-average. As graduation presents, the faculty bought him his first suit—which he accepted reluctantly, saying they should give it to "someone who really needs it"—and a set of new front teeth. Aunt Bevie, by now 77, attended ceremonies where he received his diploma. The newspaper ran a story about him.

20   The publicity, however, led to a crushing blow. One Sunday, while attending the local Baptist church, Allen recalls in a soft tone of wonderment, "The pastor got up and preached a sermon on 'the sinfulness of these arrogant people who get their picture in the paper,' obviously meaning me. It was a very unpleasant experience."

21   Accepting a fellowship from Vanderbilt, with an eye toward ultimately teaching, Robert Allen packed up his belongings that fall and moved with Aunt Bevie to Nashville. It was his first venture beyond the green hills of West Tennessee and his entrance into the modern world of a "big city," where he took his first elevator ride.

22   While coping with noise and traffic, along with adjusting to university life, Allen decided it was time to reconcile with his mother, who had remarried and settled in Missouri. For three years, he had phoned her on Mother's Day, although she always seemed annoyed and even hostile. He told his friends, "There's a new chance for us, because I can finally forgive. I just want to be a son to her." Near Christmas in 1984, he and Aunt Bevie drove to Missouri uninvited.

23   The incident is still hard for him to discuss. "We spent about an hour with her," he recalls, "and basically she was angry. She blamed everyone for not treating her well. I think she felt guilty. It was a tirade about how badly she had been raised." Allen left with Aunt Bevie while his mother was still shouting from the doorway. He cried all the way back to Tennessee.

24   The following summer, no longer able to take care of ailing Aunt Bevie, he was forced to put her into a nursing home in Huntingdon. He drove to visit her every other weekend until she died in 1988, leaving him to face the rest of his remarkable odyssey alone.

25   Aunt Bevie had lived long enough to see him earn his master's degree at Vanderbilt in 1986. Allen's thesis was a collection of his poetry, most of it autobiographical or based on the family tales he had heard as

Notes

Notes

a child. For his doctoral dissertation, he began studying an early poem by William Butler Yeats, "The Wanderings of Oisin."

26   In 1990, on the verge of earning his Ph.D., he drove alone to Missouri to see his mother and try once more. He called from a nearby pay phone to announce his arrival, only to be told that she had died ten days earlier. No one had notified him. He visited her grave, then drove back to Nashville.

27   During the first half of 1991, aside from attending graduation ceremonies at Vanderbilt, Robert Allen taught a semester of English at Bethel College. During the summer, he continued to live alone in McKenzie. There, he set aside a copy of *War and Peace* one afternoon to talk about the future. "I'd like to continue teaching and writing poetry," he told me. "In the past year I've been turning family history into a long series of poems, loosely linked together." What does the Ph.D. mean to him? "Well," he shrugged, "it means I can get a job." Any thoughts of eventually getting married? "No," he said with a smile—as if that were a possibility too far down the road to see.

28   "Robert is struggling with great courage to make himself more a part of the contemporary world," says Professor Bell, "so his story is going to go on and on."

29   At the doorway of his small, rented home, Robert Allen, age 42, stands with his Tolstoy edition in one hand, waving with the other. He smiles his enigmatic smile before turning and disappearing, at least for a while, into a distant time and place. Reading is what saved him; writing poetry about his family is both an exorcism of painful experiences and a bold journey of personal evolution. His secret seems to lie at some unfathomable depth, as if he were not only destined but determined, to finally solve the mystery for himself—to keep on falling out of the sky.

Questions for Critical Thought

"The Most Precious Gift"

1. Why did Robert Allen read so much as a child? What purpose did reading serve?

2. Why does Robert Allen write poetry now?

3. Have you ever used reading or writing in ways that are similar to how Allen used reading and writing? Explain.

4. What did you find most interesting about Allen's life?

ROLES AND RELATIONSHIPS

Reading Assignment:
"Sexual Revolution, Cohabitation, and the Rise of Singles"

This reading assignment is followed by activities to help you complete an academic summary.

Preview   Read Paragraphs 1–2 of this textbook excerpt.

Anticipate   What do you think this piece will be about? Record your thoughts in the "Notes" column.

Read and Reread   Read the entire excerpt, marking unknown terms. Then reread more slowly and use the "Notes" column to interact with the essay. Mark important and interesting points and look up unknown terms.

Sexual Revolution, Cohabitation, and the Rise of Singles
by William E. Thompson and Joseph V. Hickey

This excerpt is from the textbook, *Society in Focus: The Essentials.*

1   The twentieth century has witnessed several *revolutions* in sexual norms and behaviors that have brought dramatic changes to courtship, marriage, and family relationships. The first occurred in the Roaring Twenties, with greater sexual freedom and more diverse marriage and family forms. More dramatic changes occurred in the 1960s due to the widespread availability of birth control pills, the youth protest movement, the reemergence of *feminism* and a *proliferation* of mass media images and messages that proclaimed the "joy of sex" (Stengel, 1986; Masters et al., 1988).

2   These changes brought dramatic increases in the rate of premarital sexual intercourse, beginning at earlier ages for both boys and girls. In 1990, for example, by age 15, one-quarter of females and one-third of males had had sexual intercourse, and by age 19, the figure was over 80 percent for both sexes (Miller and Moore, 1990). Likewise, the double standard that once tolerated greater sexual freedom for men than women loosened considerably, and rates of pregnancy and out-of-wedlock childbearing among young women aged 15 to 19—especially white women—increased dramatically (Hofferth et al., 1987; Beeghley, 1994; Masters et al., 1994). For example, in 1990, "The percentage of children born to unmarried parents had risen to 28 percent" (Seltzer, 1994:235).

3   One impact of the sexual revolution has been a major increase in **cohabitation,** *two people living together as husband and wife without being legally married.* Since the 1960s, Americans have become more tolerant of alternative lifestyles; the fear of sexually transmitted diseases has also encouraged many people to opt for long-term relationships that include cohabitation. Likewise, greater employment and educational opportunities for young people, economic hardships, the decision of large numbers of women to delay marriage to pursue careers, and higher divorce rates also have contributed to an increase in the number of unmarried couples living together. . . .

4   Between 1970 and 1993, the number of unmarried couples who lived together quadrupled, and in 1993, approximately 3.5 million couples, or 6 percent of the population, lived in this type of relationship (Bumpass and Sweet, 1989; U.S. Bureau of the Census, 1993a). Research *dispels* several popular stereotypes about cohabitation and the people who practice it. For example, cohabitation is not confined to college campuses; it is in fact more common among working couples. Most cohabitants are young adults aged 35 or younger, but almost 7 percent are aged 65 and older. Moreover, although 53 percent have never married, 34 percent are divorced, and 40 percent of all cohabiting couples have one or more children present in the household (Spanier, 1983; Bumpass et al., 1989; Surra, 1990).

5   Likewise, the belief that living together as a form of "trial marriage" results in happier and more stable marriages is not supported. In fact, research shows slightly higher divorce rates for cohabitants who later marry as compared to other couples—perhaps not because of some flaw in cohabitation but because people who cohabit tend to have less conventional ideas and are less attached to traditional beliefs about marriage and the family, including the view that marriage is "for life" (Surra, 1990).

6   Researchers have also found cohabitation unions to be brief and unstable; most last a little more than a year. About one-third of all men and women in their thirties have lived with someone before marriage, a statistic that supports the view that cohabitation has become a new stage in the courtship process, one that for about half of all cohabitants is the final step before marriage (Gwartney-Gibbs, 1986). When cohabitant relationships dissolve, however, many men and women enter or reenter the singles populations.

7   Over the past few decades, the number of single adults, including the never married, the divorced, and the widowed, has increased dramatically. In the late 1980s, for example, there were over 22 million single-person households in the United States—almost a quarter

of all households. Some of the rise can be attributed to a growing tendency for young adults to postpone marriage. For example, in 1960, 28 percent of women and 53 percent of men aged 20 to 24 were unmarried; by 1990, more than 61 percent of women and 79 percent of men in that age group were still singles (U.S. Bureau of the Census, 1990b). . . .

8   Widowhood has contributed to the growth in the singles populations since the elderly have become better able to care for themselves and maintain independent households. Divorce, however, has been much more significant, with "6 million of the 26.8 million rise in the number of singles between 1960 and 1979 due to divorce" (Lamanna and Riedmann, 1988:149).

Activities

Distinguishing Between General and Specific Statements

1. Read "Sexual Revolution . . ." again, keeping the following questions in mind: What are the main (or general) statements? What are the specific statements that contain support for main ideas?

2. Working with a partner, decide which are the general statements and clearly mark each with a "G." Next, decide which are the specific statements and mark each with an "S." Are you and your partner in agreement?

3. Write down any words or phrases (such as "for example") that indicate that specific support follows.

Identifying Main Points in "Sexual Revolution . . ."

If someone asked what you had learned from "Sexual Revolution, Cohabitation, and the Rise of Singles," what would you say? You would certainly want to share the most important points of the piece. To help you determine what these points are, complete steps 1–3 below:

1. Look back at how you've marked general and specific statements in "Sexual Revolution, Cohabitation, and the Rise of Singles." Which statements appear to be the most important, or main, ideas? Highlight only these statements and review them carefully. Leave out details.

2. Now set the excerpt aside and from memory make a list of these main ideas. (You don't need to quote them exactly. In fact, you should put these main points in your own words.)

Notes

3. Go back to the excerpt and double-check to see that you've included all of the main points. Add necessary information to your list.

Drafting a Summary of "Sexual Revolution . . ."

Once you have listed the main points of the work, you are ready to begin writing your summary. Remember that a summary should

- open with a statement that introduces what is being summarized (including the author and title),

- provide an overview of the piece,

- include all of the main points (even those you may not agree with), and

- end with the author's conclusions on the subject.

Drawing from your list of main ideas, write a summary of "Sexual Revolution, Cohabitation, and the Rise of Singles."

Revising Your Summary of "Sexual Revolution . . ."

Once you have prepared a draft of your summary, it's a good idea to look at the article a final time to make sure you've accurately explained the main ideas as the author intended. If you discover that you haven't explained an idea correctly, then you need to *revise* (rewrite) parts of your summary to more accurately reflect the main ideas presented in the original. Return to "Sexual Revolution, Cohabitation, and the Rise of Singles." Compare the main ideas that you highlighted to those you have relayed in your summary. Have you explained the most important points accurately? If not, revise your summary to reflect the main ideas in the original.

Reading Assignment: "Sex Has Many Accents"

This reading assignment is followed by activities to help you complete an academic summary.

Preview   Read Paragraph 1 and the first sentence of each body paragraph.

Anticipate   What do you think this article will be about? Record your thoughts in the "Notes" column.

Read and Reread   Read the entire article, marking unknown terms. Then reread more slowly and use the "Notes" column to mark important and interesting points. Look up unknown terms.

Sex Has Many Accents

by Anastasia Toufexis

with reporting by Ulla Plon and Hiroko Tashiro

This article appeared as a 1994 *Time* magazine cover story.

1   Around the world, there are almost as many ways to teach sex as there are languages. At the two extremes are the conservative attitude in Japan and the bold approach in Scandinavian countries.

2   The Japanese seem embarrassed to discuss sex. Parents avoid the subject, though their offspring, like adolescents everywhere, are obsessed with it. "My parents aren't stiffs," allows Ayumi Suzuki, 17, from Togane, near Tokyo, "but it's just not something to talk about with them. I just talk about it with friends." Admits Yumiko Kaga, the mother of two adolescent daughters: "We never discuss sex at home. I feel we should, but . . . I do remember giving my children a book on where babies come from."

3   Schools are just as uncomfortable teaching about sex, though instruction is mandated beginning at age 10 or 11. But the curriculums resemble animal-reproduction lessons in biology class, with menstruation and ejaculation the primary topics. Teenagers say they learn about sex mostly from magazines and their peers.

4   Japanese teens are chaste compared with American youngsters. While a quarter of U.S. girls and a third of U.S. boys have had sex by age 15, in Japan it is just 4% for girls and 6% for boys.

5   "Why are Japanese children so good?" asks Hisayo Arai of the Japanese Association for Sex Education. "Partly because they're so busy with their college entrance examinations. Also, people are always keeping a watch on each other." While there are no religious taboos against premarital sex, Japanese culture has strongly urged youngsters, particularly girls, to wait until marriage. That tradition is slipping, however, because the average age for marriage among women has risen to 26, from 24 in 1970.

6   Whether adolescents become sexually active seems to depend to a large extent on peer pressure at a particular school. Some schools go so far as to ban dating, but at others "it's embarrassing if you haven't had sex, and you're under pressure to lose your virginity quickly," says Tsunetsugu Munakata, associate professor of health at Tsukuba University. "At one school I heard students would go to love hotels in their uniforms," declares Tetsuya Lizuka, 19, who lost his virginity four years ago, an experience "that made me the center of attention in high school."

Notes

7   In contrast to Japan's youngsters, Scandinavia's teens almost take sex for granted. "There is not much talk about sex between teenagers," notes Stefan Laack of the Swedish Association for Sex Information, "yet it is widely accepted that they sleep with their boyfriends or girlfriends in their homes."

8   Scandinavians believe that teens may be more receptive to sex education at school than at home. "When teenagers get in contact with their sexuality, they are about to break loose from their parents," says Laack. "This is only natural and shouldn't be disturbed."

9   Rather than confining instruction to special classes, schools integrate lessons throughout the curriculum. In Denmark sexual matters must be discussed whenever appropriate in any class. So too in Sweden, where sex education has been compulsory since 1956. Starting when the children are between ages 7 and 10, it is formally incorporated into different subjects. "In biology, for example, the physical side is discussed," explains Peter Karlberg of Sweden's Ministry of Education. Courses that cover geography, history or politics tackle ethics and gender roles. In Finnish schools, all 15-year-olds receive an introductory sexual package put together by the Population and Family Welfare Federation. Its contents: an information brochure, a condom and a cartoon love story.

10   The intense preparation has not pushed youngsters to having sex earlier. In Sweden youngsters typically lose their virginity at age 17, exactly the same age as 15 years ago.

Activities

Distinguishing Between General and Specific Statements in "Sex Has Many Accents"

1. Begin by labeling the basic parts—introduction, body, and conclusion.

2. As you read through the article again, mark any general statements with a "G." Then identify the statements that contain specific information and mark each with an "S."

3. Write down any clues that suggest that specific information follows.

Identifying Main Points in "Sex Has Many Accents"

After distinguishing between general and specific information in the article, you are now prepared to identify the most important points. As you complete steps 1–3 keep in mind that main ideas in magazine articles usually appear in general statements just as in academic writing.

1. Look back at how you've marked general and specific statements in "Sex Has Many Accents." Which statements appear to be the most important, or main, ideas? Highlight only these statements and review them carefully. Leave out the details.

2. Set the article aside, and from memory write a list of the main points. (Don't worry about getting them down exactly. These should be in your own words.)

3. Return to the article and check to see if you've included all of the main points on your list. Add any you left out.

Drafting a Summary of "Sex Has Many Accents"

As you know, the next step in writing a summary is to put the main points into paragraph form. Working from your list of main ideas, write your summary. First, introduce the author, title, and overall main idea. Follow with the most important points. End your summary with the author's conclusions on the subject.

Revising Your Summary of "Sex Has Many Accents"

Review "Sex Has Many Accents" again. Compare the main ideas you highlighted earlier to those that appear in your summary. Have you included the most important points? If not, revise your summary to agree with the original.

Reading Assignment:
"Feminism: The Struggle for Gender Equality"

Activities and a journal assignment designed to reinforce the reading process and vocabulary development accompany this reading.

Preview   This excerpt is from a sociology textbook, so you should expect it to follow basic essay form. Consider the title, authors, and introductory information. Next, read the introduction and topic sentences to get a sense of what this segment is about.

Anticipate   What do you anticipate this segment will be about? Use the "Notes" column to record your answer.

Read   Now read through the excerpt quickly, using your anticipation skills to guess what's coming next. Highlight unknown terms and write your own questions in the "Notes" column.

Feminism: The Struggle for Gender Equality
by William E. Thompson and Joseph V. Hickey

This textbook excerpt from *Society in Focus: The Essentials* comes from the chapter titled "Sex, Gender, and Age."

1   The struggle for women's rights has been a long and hard-fought battle in the United States. The first major wave of **feminism,** *an ideology aimed at eliminating patriarchy in support of equality between the sexes,* was linked to the pre–Civil War abolitionist movement. When it became clear that emancipation leaders were not seeking the same rights for women as for black men, however, Elizabeth Cady Stanton, Susan B. Anthony, and Lucretia Mott organized a convention on women's rights at Seneca Falls, New York, in 1848. The main thrust of the early feminist movement was women's suffrage (the right to vote) and with the passage of the Nineteenth Amendment in 1920, much of the movement's fervor dissipated.

2   The second wave of feminism arose in the 1960s, and again it was initially linked to the struggle for civil rights for blacks and other minorities. Social activism of the times provided the milieu for contemporary feminism, and Betty Friedan's book *The Feminine Mystique* (1963) ignited public consciousness. Friedan described the relative isolation, discontent, and alienation of American women trapped in the stereotypical roles of housewife and mother. Many American women identified with the plight Friedan described, and in 1966 the National Organization for Women (NOW) was formed. This organization and the women's movement attracted large numbers of women and men into their ranks.

3   Although the feminist agenda is diverse and feminists disagree about how best to accomplish its goals, there is consensus that laws, policies, regulations, and programs that discriminate against women should be abolished. A major goal of the contemporary feminist movement was the passage of the Equal Rights Amendment (ERA) to the U.S. Constitution. Initially proposed in 1923, the ERA simply states that equality under the law cannot be denied or abridged on the basis of sex. The amendment passed both houses of Congress in 1972, but despite widespread support from both men and women, it fell three states short of the 38 needed for ratification, with feminists' only consolation being that women are protected by the Fourteenth Amendment.

4   Within the feminist movement, a more radical faction emerged that not only endorsed all reforms proposed by more moderate elements but also sought revolutionary social change. The ideological basis for radical feminism was spawned by Kate Millett's book *Sexual Politics* (1970) and Germaine Greer's work *The Female Eunuch* (1972), which concluded that the goals of feminism could not be accomplished without abandoning the institution of the family.

5   The feminist movement, especially in its more radical forms, has met
with social resistance. In the early 1970s, Phyllis Schlafly became identified as the leader of the antifeminist movement, arguing that passage of
the Equal Rights Amendment and the rest of the feminist agenda would
destroy the American family. She and other antifeminists not only fear
change but also believe that feminist ideas are "unnatural" because they
violate traditional sex roles. In her book *Backlash,* Susan Faludi (1991:x)
asserted that virtually every positive stride women have made toward
achieving equality has met a social backlash from those who want to
maintain the status quo; folk wisdom has it that "women are unhappy
precisely *because* they are free." This, Faludi asserted, amounts to no less
than an "undeclared war against women."

6   Despite resistance, feminism persists, and feminist scholarship is making an important contribution to virtually all fields of study, especially sociology. Feminists argue that gender, like social class, is one of the most
important dimensions of social organization. Thus gender refers not only
to the ways that sex differences become socially significant but also to social relationships between men and women and the differential allocation
of social power based on sex. Simply put, from the feminist perspective,
power is a central aspect of gender relations; women have less access to
most types of power than men, and most stereotypical gender differences are a result of this imbalance of power (Laslett and Brenner, 1989;
Vance and Pollis, 1990; Lips, 1991, 1993; Andersen, 1993; Wood, 1994).

Notes

Activities

Reread

Complete a thorough second reading. Answer any questions you wrote in the
"Notes" column. Look up new words and write definitions in your notebook.

Consider adding the following words to your vocabulary notebook. Use
context clues to try to figure out what they mean. Then check their meanings by looking them up in the dictionary.

Par. 1: feminism; patriarchy; abolitionist; emancipation; women's suffrage; fervor; dissipated

Par. 2: milieu; discontent; alienation

Par. 3: consensus; abolished; abridged; ratification

Par. 4: faction; endorsed

Par. 5: antifeminist movement

Par. 6: differential

Think Critically

Enhance your reading process by answering the following questions:

1. What is feminism? What was the main focus of the early feminist movement in America?

2. What caused a "second wave of feminism" in the 1960s?

3. What does ERA stand for? Who was in favor of the ERA? Who was against it?

4. According to authors Thompson and Hickey, the antifeminist movement arose in opposition to the feminist movement. Who led the antifeminist movement? What were the basic beliefs of this group?

5. From the feminist perspective, who has the most power in our society, males or females? Do you believe that an "imbalance of power" exists in America today? Explain your position.

6. Who is the audience for this piece? What is the authors' purpose in presenting this reading to this particular audience?

Summarize

Now that you've read and discussed the excerpt, make a list of the main points. (Remember, in a summary your job is to include all the main points of the original and to leave out your opinion.) Then write a summary of the article. Identify author and title first as well as the overall main idea of the excerpt. Relay the main points from your list. Once you've written your summary, return to the original and check to see that you've included all the main points and have stated them correctly. Revise as necessary.

Journal Assignment

"Feminism: The Struggle for Gender Equality"

Now that you've gone through the stages of an effective reading process, take the time to respond to what you've read. Think about feminism and how it affects our lives. You might share a personal belief about feminism. You could share a personal insight or talk about your own experience. Write for ten to 15 minutes about what interests you most.

Reading Assignment:
"In India, Men Challenge a Matrilineal Society"

Activities and a journal assignment designed to reinforce the reading process and vocabulary development accompany this reading.

Preview   This article appeared in a magazine, so you should expect shorter paragraphs and fewer topic sentences. Review the title, author, and publication information. What do you know about this magazine? Who would most likely be the audience for this particular article? Read the first two paragraphs.

Anticipate   What do you think this magazine article will be about? Use the "Notes" column to record your answer.

Read   Now quickly read the article. Practice your anticipation skills as you read. Highlight unfamiliar terms and write questions in the "Notes" column.

In India, Men Challenge a Matrilineal Society
by Kavita Menon

Kavita Menon wrote this article for the September/October 1998 issue of *Ms.* magazine.

1   Meghalaya, a district tucked away in the remote northeastern corner of India, is home to the Khasi, one of the largest surviving matrilineal societies in the world. In this hill tribe of nearly 650,000, descent is traced through the mother's line and women have an honored place in the society. Here, baby girls are quite welcome, and, some argue, even more highly prized than boys. Since the woman's family holds the cards when arranging a marriage, the question of dowry—paying a man's family for accepting the "burden" of a wife—would never even arise. No social stigma is attached to women, whether they choose to divorce, remarry, or stay single.

2   Anthropologists say the Khasi matriliny developed as a practical measure: the men were often away fighting in wars, so it made sense for the women to hold all that was precious to a family. Money, land, and lineage were passed from youngest daughter to youngest daughter, since it was expected she would be the last to marry.

3   But a growing number of Khasi men are not interested in the logic of the old system. They say the matriliny has empowered women at the expense of men and the community as a whole. The epicenter of this dissent is a tiny office in a pleasant residential neighborhood in Shillong, Meghalaya's capital city. This is where the Syngkhong Rympei Thymmai (SRT)—which means "organization for the restructuring of Khasi society"—has its

Notes

headquarters. The SRT, which was formed eight years ago and has a membership of about 400, including a handful of women, aims to dismantle the matriliny. It wants property to be equally divided among all the children in a family, and children to carry their father's surname. . . .

4   Many SRT members, like Lyngdoh, believe it is both a biological and a divine imperative for a man to be the head of the family. They argue that it is the man who plants the seed that becomes the child and that for this reason almost all children resemble their fathers. For many, passing on their titles—or establishing ownership of their children and their wives—is even more important than the matter of inheritance.

5   SRT members believe the Khasi matriliny has favored the development of Khasi women to the detriment of the men. "Women have all the inheritance and therefore all the power," says SRT vice president Pilgrim Lakiang. "They are making more progress than the men and boys."

6   Women are indeed prominent in Khasi life. There are more Khasi women doctors than men, more Khasi women graduating from colleges, more Khasi women conducting business in the market places. Women are now even seen in the traditional governing bodies, or durbars, which were once off-limits to them.

7   In contrast, Khasi men are said to be drinking too much, and are increasingly worried about losing their jobs, their land, and their women to migrants from West Bengal and Bangladesh. "Well-to-do families give their daughters to nontribals instead of to Khasi boys, and property and other assets that belong to the Khasi society pass to them," bemoans the writer of an article in one SRT booklet. . . .

8   Donakor Shanpru is a single woman in her late forties whose family home is situated on the same block as the SRT headquarters. She lives in the home of her youngest aunt, who is also unmarried, with other members of the extended family including her father, a widower; a brother, who has left his wife and child; and two sisters (whose husbands have both left them, then tried to return, only to be turned away) and their children.

9   Shanpru, who teaches Khasi literature at one of Shillong's four women's colleges, has no patience with the SRT or its views. As far as she's concerned, it is a minority group expressing a minority position, and she's happy to let you know that its president has been kicked out of her house three times for "talking nonsense." For all the SRT's huffing and puffing, Shanpru says, Khasi men have been invested with important duties, as husbands, fathers, and maternal uncles in the clan. Maternal uncles in particular exercise a lot of clout—though the youngest daughter holds the purse strings and her opinions matter, it is typically the oldest maternal uncle who decides when and how to spend the clan's money.

10   But while the SRT positions are seen as extremist by some, they do fit into a larger debate within the society and attract some unexpected sympathizers. Patricia Mukhim, a journalist from Shillong, agrees to some extent with what the SRT is saying. She believes that giving boys an equal share of the family property will boost their self-esteem and encourage them to be more responsible, industrious husbands and citizens. Mukhim also blames the matriliny for making Khasi marriages "very brittle." Divorce has become too easy, she says, because husbands and wives can always return to their respective clans.

11   Where Mukhim disagrees with the SRT is in the speed of change. "We can't turn the system inside out so suddenly," she says. But change must come, she feels, since the problems that the men are facing affect everybody in the end.

12   A traditional society is being pressured to adjust to a modern world that is increasingly urban, and one in which families are smaller and more distant. Although the men's movement and the anxiety it expresses are city-based—men's roles are less of an issue in the villages where the traditional system still serves people's needs—the debate is widespread. . . .

13   Even though the matriliny has been the norm in Khasi society, that doesn't mean there are no gendered roles. In one traditional Khasi dance, for instance, the women are required to creep slowly forward by wriggling their toes like inchworms. They move in large groups, chins upturned and eyes downcast, looking very regal in their elaborate headdresses and long gowns. The role of the men is to "protect" the women—and they look like they're having great fun galloping, skipping, and spinning in circles around the women, while madly waving long, feathered whisks.

14   In the dance, the women are locked into the lines and circles assigned them, a reminder that in addition to being doctors and teachers and shopkeepers, they are still expected to be dutiful daughters, good mothers, and patient wives. And, for all the SRT members' talk of being downtrodden, men in a traditional Khasi home are still served the top of the rice bowl as a blessing on the family—and they very rarely cook or clean.

Activities

Reread

Read Menon's article a second time. Take your time as you read, stopping to look up definitions and to answer your questions.

Add the following new terms to the vocabulary section of your notebook. Use context clues and your dictionary to find word meanings.

Par 1: matrilineal; dowry; stigma

Notes

Notes

Par. 2: matriliny; lineage

Par. 3: epicenter; dissent; dismantle; surname

Par. 4: divine imperative

Par. 5: detriment

Par. 6: durbars

Par. 7: assets

Par. 9: clout

Par. 14: downtrodden

Think Critically

Enhance your reading process as you answer the following questions:

1. What is a matrilineal society? How has the Khasi clan developed into a matriliny, according to anthropologists?

2. Who is most concerned about the system being dominated by women? Why?

3. What have been some of the positive results of such a system? What have been the negative results? Does this system seem fair? Why, or why not?

4. What does SRT stand for? What does this group propose?

5. Writer Kavita Menon includes a variety of perspectives on whether or not the Khasi system is fair. List two of the people interviewed and explain their perspectives.

6. According to Menon, in what instances do women still take on traditional roles?

7. This article appeared in *Ms.,* a magazine that supports women's rights. Knowing this, who would most likely be the audience for this article? Do you think this audience would be sympathetic to the men of the Khasi clan? Why, or why not?

Summarize

Now that you've read the article at least twice, list the main ideas from the article and write a summary. Be sure to include the author, title, and publication. Begin with a general introductory statement and follow with the main points of the piece. Return to the article to make sure you've relayed the main ideas accurately. Make any necessary revisions.

> ### *Journal Assignment*
>
> #### *Respond to "In India, Men Challenge a Matrilineal Society"*
>
> Write a ten to 15 minute response to Menon's article. What do you think of the Khasi's matrilineal system? How does their system compare to our American system today? What do you think of the viewpoints expressed in the article? Write about what interests you most.

HEROES AND ROLE MODELS

Reading Assignment:
"How One Woman Became the Voice of Her People"

> *Questions for Critical Thought follow this reading.*
>
> Preview   This is a long essay. Begin previewing and reading when you have time to read the entire essay without being interrupted. Read the introductory information in italics, the title, and the first four paragraphs. Read and highlight topic sentences.
>
> Anticipate   What do you anticipate this essay will be about? Write your thoughts in the "Notes" column.
>
> Read and Reread   Read the essay quickly and mark unknown terms. Reread more slowly, using the "Notes" column and a highlighter to record and mark important ideas. Define unknown terms.

How One Woman Became the Voice of Her People
by David Wallechinsky

This article was first published in *Parade Magazine*, January 19, 1997.

Aung San Suu Kyi was forty-three and living outside her native Burma in England, as a housewife and mother of two. Then, almost overnight, she became the heart of her people's struggle for freedom and democracy.

1   In the exotic southeast Asian nation of Burma, a country of forty-six million people, a battle of wills of heroic proportions is taking place. On one side is a brutal military dictatorship known as SLORC (State Law and Order Restoration Council). On the other is a slim, fifty-one-year-old mother of two named Aung San Suu Kyi, who is leading her people in a nonviolent struggle for democracy.

2   For six years, from 1989 to 1995, Aung San Suu Kyi (pronounced Awng-Sahn-Soo-Chee) was kept in isolation under house arrest for

speaking out against the government, which has used torture and forced labor and which refuses to hand over power, even though it lost a national election. In 1991, still under house arrest, Aung San Suu Kyi was awarded the Nobel Peace Prize.

3   Following her release in 1995, she continued to challenge the junta, every weekend addressing the thousands of followers who congregated in front of the gate to her house and across the street. It had become the only forum for free speech in the country. But since September the government has cracked down on these gatherings. It has arrested more than 1000 people—usually in the middle of the night. And Aung San Suu Kyi is again restricted to her home.

4   Aung San Suu Kyi has been an inspiration, but the personal cost has been great: Since her struggle began, she has been allowed to see her husband and children only infrequently. While under house arrest, she did not see her children for two and one-half years.

5   Aung San Suu Kyi comes from a politically prominent Burmese family, but until the age of forty-three she had been leading a quiet life in England as a housewife and academic. How did she transform herself into the leading speaker for democracy and a symbol of freedom? And what gave this woman, by all accounts a devoted mother, the strength to sacrifice the satisfactions of marriage and motherhood, as well as the courage to risk her life again and again?

6   For the Burmese people, much of Aung San Suu Kyi's power comes from her being a living link to history. She is the daughter of Burma's greatest modern hero, Aung San, who founded the Burmese Army in 1941 and is considered the father of his nation. At the end of World War II, Aung San, like George Washington, made a successful transition from military leader to political leader. He negotiated with the British and arranged for national independence to be proclaimed by Jan. 4, 1948. But before that day arrived, Aung San was assassinated by political rivals. He was thirty-two. His daughter was barely two years old.

7   Besides his wife and daughter, Aung San left two sons: One died while still a child; the other is now an American citizen, an engineer living in San Diego. "Although I was too young to retain a direct memory of my father," Aung San Suu Kyi told me, "my mother taught me about his life and his principles, as did his old friends." (As an adult, she wrote a biography of Aung San.)

8   At fifteen, Aung San Suu Kyi moved to New Delhi when her mother, Khin Kyi, was appointed ambassador to India. Later, she studied at Oxford University in England. After graduating with a degree in philosophy, politics and economics, she worked for almost three years at the United Nations in New York City. It was a time of political and social tur-

Notes

moil in the U.S. "The young people were for love and not for war," she recalled. "There was a feeling of tremendous vigor. I had been moved by Martin Luther King's 'I Have a Dream' speech and how he tried to better the lot of the black people without fostering feelings of hate. It's hate that is the problem, not violence. Violence is simply the symptom of hate."

9   In 1972, Aung San Suu Kyi married Michael Aris, a British scholar specializing in Tibetan studies. He is now a don at Oxford. Prior to their marriage, she wrote these words to him: "I only ask one thing, that should my people need me, you would help me to do my duty by them."

10   In the meantime, she lived a reasonably normal life. She gave birth to two sons, Alexander in 1973 and Kim in 1977. For several years, she devoted herself to raising her family and continuing her studies. Then her life changed dramatically.

11   In April 1988, she received word from Burma that her mother was gravely ill. She returned to Rangoon to care for her. This visit coincided with unusual political activity in Burma. In March, riot police had shot to death 200 demonstrators, most of them students, who had protested government policies and repression. Despite the shootings, the demonstrations grew. Increasingly, protesters demanded free multiparty elections.

12   "Government leaders are amazing," Aung San Suu Kyi said. "So they are the last to know what the people want." Many demonstrations were staged in front of the U.S. embassy, because the U.S. was seen as a symbol of democracy. Between Aug. 8 and 13, 1988, the police killed nearly 3000 people.

13   Aung San Suu Kyi watched these developments with growing concern. Many of the pro-democracy demonstrators carried signs with pictures of her father. On Aug. 26, a general strike was called and several hundred thousand attended a rally in front of Rangoon's Shwedagon pagoda. Here, for the first time, Aung San Suu Kyi spoke to the crowd.

14   Recalling her father's assassination, she said, "People have been saying I know nothing of Burmese politics. The trouble is, I know too much." As the crowd warmed to her, she concluded, "I could not, as my father's daughter, remain indifferent to all that is going on. The national crisis could, in fact, be called the second struggle for independence."

15   Overnight, Aung San Suu Kyi became the leading representative of the movement for freedom and democracy. In September, the military seized control of the government, declared martial law and killed 1000 demonstrators. Aung San Suu Kyi joined with other anti-government leaders to form the National League for Democracy (NLD). She traveled the country, giving more than 1000 speeches.

16   During this period she was involved in a dramatic incident. On the evening of April 5, 1989, as they were returning home, she and a group of pro-democracy organizers were stopped and ordered off the road by government soldiers. Aung San Suu Kyi waved the others away and kept walking toward the soldiers. "It seemed so much simpler," she later explained, "to provide them with a single target." A captain ordered his troops to raise their rifles and shoot. She continued advancing. At the last second, a major ran forward and overruled the captain.

17   Three and a half months later, exasperated by her growing popularity, the Burmese dictators placed Aung San Suu Kyi under house arrest. She was not allowed to see her children for more than two and one-half years.

18   "I felt very guilty about not looking after them," she said. "The antidote to such feelings was knowing that others had it much worse. I knew that my children were safe with my husband in England, whereas a lot of my colleagues were in the terrible position of being in prison themselves and not knowing how safe their children were going to be."

19   She described seeing her younger son for the first time in almost three years: "I would not have recognized him if I had seen him on the street."

20   Later, in England, her husband told me that he supports his wife fully but could not talk on the record for fear that the Burmese government will accuse him of being a foreigner interfering in their affairs. I also met in London with Burmese women who had been arrested by SLORC and kept apart from their families. They confirmed what Aung San Suu Kyi had told me. One woman I met, who had been jailed for three years, gave birth in prison and immediately had the baby taken away from her.

21   In 1990, SLORC agreed to hold an election—an attempt to satisfy potential foreign investors. Only the military leaders were surprised by the results: Aung San Suu Kyi herself was not allowed to run for office, but her party, the NLD, won eighty percent of the vote and seats. The party of the military won only ten seats out of 485 contested.

22   SLORC announced that the election didn't count. Since then, it has followed "the Chinese model": liberalize the economy while keeping a tight lid on political dissent. Unfortunately, only a small percentage of the population has become richer, while most Burmese, suffering from spiraling inflation, actually have seen their lives become harder.

23   But even if the economy were to improve, Aung San Suu Kyi stressed that there is more to life than material success. "This is something you Americans would be in a better position to talk about," she told me, "because there is certainly material prosperity in the United States. And yet material prosperity has not insured happiness and harmony or even contentment. I do believe in the spiritual nature of human beings. To some it's a strange or outdated idea, but I do believe there is such a

thing as a human spirit. There is a spiritual dimension to man which should be nurtured."

24   Aung San Suu Kyi is adamant about sticking to her policy of nonviolence. "There are those," she explained, "who believe the only way we can remove the authoritarian regime and replace it with a democratic one is through violent means. But then, in the future, those who do not approve of a democratic government would be encouraged to try violent means of toppling it, because we would have set a precedent that you bring about political change through violence. I would like to set strongly the precedent that you bring about political change through political settlement and *not* through violence."

25   The government, meanwhile, is trying to persuade foreign investors to bring their business to Burma. They also have declared 1996–97 "Visit Myanmar[1] Year" for tourists. Aung San Suu Kyi's advice: "Tourists should wait until Burma is a freer and happier country." Foreign investors, she said, "will get better returns for their money if they invest in a country that is stable and which has a strong framework of just laws."

26   I asked what Americans can do. Although Aung San Suu Kyi stressed that it is up to the people of Burma to solve their own problems, it *is* possible for others to help. "Don't support businesses which are supporting injustice in Burma," she said. In the U.S., support for Aung San Suu Kyi has united liberals and conservatives. Groups promoting democracy in Burma have been formed on more than 100 American college campuses.

27   The day before I left Burma, I talked in Aung San Suu Kyi's garden with her cousin Aye Win, who served as her press secretary. (He has since been sentenced to twenty years in prison.) I was concerned that customs officials might confiscate my photos and tapes of Aung San Suu Kyi. "You have nothing to worry about," he reassured me, "because you have the power of the U.S. government behind you. It is we Burmese who have to worry." He nodded in the direction of Aung San Suu Kyi, who was walking toward us. "All we have," he added, "is Aung San's daughter."[2]

---

[1]Burma was renamed Union of Myanmar in 1989, but is still frequently referred to as Burma.

[2]Since the publication of this article, Aung San Suu Kyi has continued to live in Burma and fight for a democratic government. Her husband, Michael Aris, died in England in March of 1999. The Burmese government would not allow Aris to visit Kyi before his death. Kyi refused a visa to attend her husband's funeral in England because she feared the military government in Burma would not allow her to return. In May of 2002, Aung San Suu Kyi was released from house arrest and has been allowed to travel around her country. She is currently rebuilding her party, the NLD (National League for Democracy).

Questions for Critical Thought

"How One Woman . . ."

1. How did Aung San Suu Kyi become a hero to the people of Burma? List her specific actions and beliefs.

2. In what ways does she fit the profile of the traditional hero?

3. Does everyone in Burma think of her as a hero? If not, who doesn't and why?

4. Do you believe (as she does) that it's her duty to help her people?

5. The writer of this article, David Wallechinsky, composed some wonderful paragraphs that mirror the paragraph structure you've been studying. Select Paragraph 6, 17, 23, or 24; copy it in your notebook; and discuss Wallechinsky's use of topic sentence, detail, and wrap-up sentence. Describe how Wallechinsky stays focused on one idea in the paragraph you selected.

Reading Assignment: *"Who Is Great?"*

Questions for Critical Thought follow this reading.

Preview Read the first three paragraphs and then all the subheadings.

Anticipate What do you think this article will be about? Write your response in the "Notes" column.

Read and Reread Read the entire article, marking unknown terms. Then reread more slowly and use the "Notes" column to interact with the essay. Mark important and interesting points and define unknown terms.

Are the people we call "great" really different from you and me?
Here's what experts find when they ask . . .

Who Is Great?
by Michael Ryan

This article was published in *Parade* magazine, June 16, 1996.

1   As a young boy, Albert Einstein did so poorly in school that teachers thought he was slow. The young Napoleon Bonaparte was just one of the hundreds of artillery lieutenants in the French Army. And the teenage

George Washington, with little formal education, was being trained not as a soldier but as a land surveyor.

2   Despite their unspectacular beginnings, each would go on to carve a place for himself in history. What was it that enabled them to become great? Were they born with something special? Or did their greatness have more to do with timing, devotion and, perhaps, an uncompromising personality?

3   For decades, scientists have been asking such questions. And, in the past few years, they have found evidence to help explain why some people rise above, while others—similarly talented, perhaps—are left behind. Their findings could have implications for us all.

4   **Who is great?** Defining who is great depends on how one measures success. But there are some criteria. "Someone who has made a lasting contribution to human civilization is great," said Dean Keith Simonton, a professor of psychology at the University of California at Davis and author of the 1994 book *Greatness: Who Makes History and Why.* But he added a caveat: "Sometimes great people don't make it into the history books. A lot of women achieved great things or were influential but went unrecognized."

5   In writing his book, Simonton combined historical knowledge about great figures with recent findings in genetics, psychiatry and the social sciences. The great figures he focused on include men and women who have won Nobel Prizes, led great nations or won wars, composed symphonies that have endured for centuries, or revolutionized science, philosophy, politics or the arts. Though he doesn't have a formula to define how or why certain people rise above (too many factors are involved), he has come up with a few common characteristics.

6   **A "never surrender" attitude.** If great achievers share anything, said Simonton, it is an unrelenting drive to succeed. "There's a tendency to think that they are endowed with something super-normal," he explained. "But what comes out of the research is that there are great people who have no amazing intellectual processes. It's a difference in degree. Greatness is built upon tremendous amounts of study, practice and devotion."

7   He cited Winston Churchill, Britain's prime minister during World War II, as an example of a risk-taker who would never give up. Thrust into office when his country's morale was at its lowest, Churchill rose brilliantly to lead the British people. In a speech following the Allied evacuation at Dunkirk in 1940, he inspired the nation when he said, "We shall not flag or fail. We shall go on to the end. . . . We shall never surrender." After the war, Churchill was voted out of office but again demonstrated his fighting spirit when he delivered his famous "Iron Curtain" speech at Westminster College in Missouri in 1946. This time, at the dawn of the Cold

Notes

War, he exhorted the entire Western world to stand up to communism: "We hold the power to save the future," he said. "Our difficulties and dangers will not be removed by closing our eyes to them."

8   **Can you be born great?** In looking at Churchill's role in history—as well as the roles of other political and military leaders—Simonton discovered a striking pattern: "Firstborns and only children tend to make good leaders in time of crisis: They're used to taking charge. But middle-borns are better as peacetime leaders: They listen to different constituencies better and make the necessary compromises. Churchill, an only child, was typical. He was great in a crisis, but in peacetime he was not effective—not even popular."

9   Timing is another factor. "If you took George Washington and put him in the 20th century, he would go nowhere as a politician," Simonton declared. "He was not an effective public speaker, and he didn't like shaking hands with the public. On the other hand, I'm not sure Franklin Roosevelt would have done well in Washington's time. He wouldn't have had the radio to do his fireside chats."

10   **Can you be *too* smart?** One surprise among Simonton's findings is that many political and military leaders have been bright but not overly so. Beyond a certain point, he explained, other factors, like the ability to communicate effectively, become more important than innate intelligence as measured by an IQ test. The most intelligent U.S. Presidents, for example—Thomas Jefferson, Woodrow Wilson and John F. Kennedy—had a hard time getting elected, Simonton said, while others with IQs closer to average (such as Warren G. Harding) won by landslides. While political and economic factors also are involved, having a genius IQ is not necessary to be a great leader.

11   In the sciences, those with "genius level" IQs do have a better shot at achieving recognition, added Simonton. Yet evidence also indicates that overcoming traditional ways of thinking may be just as important.

12   He pointed to one recent study where college students were given a set of data and were asked to see if they could come up with a mathematical relation. Almost a third did. What they did not know was that they had just solved one of the most famous scientific equations in history: the Third Law of Planetary Motion, an equation that Johannes Kepler came up with in 1618.

13   Kepler's genius, Simonton said, was not so much in solving a mathematical challenge. It was in thinking about the numbers in a unique way—applying his mathematical knowledge to his observations of planetary motion. It was his boldness that set him apart.

14   **Love your work.** As a child, Einstein became fascinated with the way magnets draw iron filings. "He couldn't stop thinking about this stuff,"

Notes

Simonton pointed out. "He became obsessed with problems in physics by the time he was sixteen, and he never stopped working on them. It's not surprising that he made major contributions by the time he was twenty-six."

15   "For most of us, it's not that we don't have the ability," Simonton added, "it's that we don't devote the time. You have to put in the effort and put up with all the frustrations and obstacles."

16   Like other creative geniuses, Einstein was not motivated by a desire for fame, said Simonton. Instead, his obsession with his work was what set him apart. Where such drive comes from remains a mystery. But it is found in nearly all creative geniuses—whether or not their genius is acknowledged by contemporaries.

17   "Emily Dickinson was not recognized for her poetry until after her death," said Simonton. "But she was not writing for fame. The same can be said of James Joyce, who didn't spend a lot of time worrying about how many people would read *Finnegans Wake.* Beethoven once said, when confronting a musician struggling to play some of his new quartets, 'They are not for you, but for a later age.'"

18   Today, researchers have evidence that an intrinsic passion for one's work is a key to rising above. In a 1985 study at Brandeis University conducted by Teresa Amabile, now a professor of business administration at Harvard University, a group of professional writers—none famous—was asked to write a short poem. Each writer was then randomly placed in one of three groups: one group was asked to keep in mind the idea of writing for money; another was told to think about writing just for pleasure; and a third group was given no instruction at all.

19   The poems then were submitted anonymously to a panel of professional writers for evaluation. The poetry written by people who thought about writing for money ranked the lowest. Those who thought about writing just for pleasure did the best. "Motivation that comes from enjoying the work makes a significant difference," Amabile said.

20   **What price greatness?** Many great figures have had poor personal relationships, perhaps a result of their drive to excel, said Simonton. And great people, he added, often can be unbearable: "Beethoven, for instance, was tyrannical with servants and rude to his friends. His personal hygiene was not particularly great either. When working, he would go for days or weeks without bathing."

21   Yet one common belief about greatness—that it often is accompanied by mental imbalance—seems unfounded.

22   "Certain types of psychopathology are more common in some professions than in others," explained Dr. Arnold M. Ludwig, a psychiatrist at the University of Kentucky Medical Center and author of a new book, *The Price of Greatness.* "Poets, for example, have high rates of

Notes

depression. But architects as a group are very stable. Fiction writers and jazz musicians are more likely to abuse drugs and alcohol. But when you go outside the artistic fields, you find phenomenal creative achievements among scientists, social activists, and politicians. It is certainly possible for people to achieve great things without corresponding mental illness."

23   Dr. Ludwig did some personal research on the issue as well. "I have two children who are very creative and artistic," he said. "I decided to find out whether they would have to be crazy if they were to grow up to be geniuses. I was happy to find out that they would not."

Questions for Critical Thought

"Who Is Great?"

1. Referring back to the reading, list some of the "great" people mentioned. Who were they, and what did they do?

2. Now list some of the qualities of a "great" person.

3. If you are currently working in the *hero* chapter (Chapter 5), explain which qualities a "great" person and a hero have in common.

4. In Paragraph 2, the author, Michael Ryan, asks three questions. Why does he ask all of these questions? How do they help him communicate with us?

5. In Paragraph 4, Ryan tells us about Keith Simonton. Ryan tells us where Simonton works and the title of a book. Why did Ryan choose to include this information?

Reading Assignment:
"Civil Rights Movement Was the Sum of Many People"

Questions for Critical Thought follow this reading.

Preview   Read Paragraphs 1–3.

Anticipate   What do you think this article will be about? Write your response in the "Notes" column.

Read and Reread   Read the entire article, marking unknown terms. Then reread more slowly and use the "Notes" column to record your responses to the essay. Mark important and interesting points and define unknown terms.

Civil Rights Movement Was the Sum of Many People

by Paul Rogat Loeb

Notes

This article by Paul Rogat Loeb, who authored *Soul of a Citizen: Living with Conviction in a Cynical Time*, appeared in the *Sacramento Bee* on January 16, 2000.

1   Seattle—We learn much from how we present our heroes. A few years ago, on Martin Luther King Jr. Day, I was interviewed on CNN. So was Rosa Parks, by phone from Los Angeles.

2   "We're very honored to have her," said the host. "Rosa Parks was the woman who wouldn't go to the back of the bus. She wouldn't get up and give her seat in the white section to a white person. That set in motion the yearlong boycott of city buses in Montgomery. It earned Rosa Parks the title of 'mother of the civil rights movement.'"

3   I was excited to hear Parks' voice and to be part of the same show, but it occurred to me that the host's description—the story's familiar rendition—stripped the Montgomery boycott of its most important context.

4   Before the fateful December day in 1955 when Parks refused to obey a law designating segregated seating on buses, she had spent 12 years helping lead the local NAACP chapter, along with union activist E.D. Nixon, from the Brotherhood of Sleeping Car Porters; teachers from the local Negro college; and a variety of members of Montgomery's African American community. Parks allowed her arrest to be used to spark a boycott, which was led by King. That 382-day boycott ended on Dec. 20, 1956, when the U.S. Supreme Court declared segregated seating on city buses unconstitutional.

5   The summer of 1954, Parks had attended a 10-day training session at Tennessee's labor and civil rights organizing school, the Highlander Center, where she'd met an older generation of civil rights activists and discussed the Supreme Court's *Brown* decision banning "separate but equal" schools.

6   Parks didn't make a spur-of-the-moment decision that gave birth to the civil rights movement. She was part of an existing force for change when success was far from certain. Her tremendously consequential act might never have occurred without all the humble and frustrating work she and all the others had been doing. Her initial step of involvement 12 years before was just as courageous and critical as the moment she refused to move further back in the bus.

7   People such as Parks shape our models of social commitment. Yet the conventional retelling of her story creates a standard so impossible to meet, it may actually make it harder for us to get involved.

8   This portrayal suggests that social activists come out of nowhere to make sudden, dramatic stands. It implies that we make the greatest impact when we act alone, or at least alone initially; that anyone who takes

a committed public stand, or at least an effective one, has to be a larger-than-life figure—someone with more time, energy, courage, vision or knowledge than any normal person could ever possess. The beliefs pervade our society, in part because the media rarely represent historical change as the work of ordinary human beings.

9   Parks' real story conveys a far more empowering moral. In the 1940's, she goes to a meeting and then another. Hesitant at first, she gains confidence as she speaks out. She keeps on despite a profoundly uncertain context as she and others act as best they can to challenge deeply entrenched injustices with little certainty of results. Had she and others given up after her 10th or 11th year of commitment, we might never have heard of Montgomery.

10   Once we enshrine our heroes on pedestals, it's difficult for mere mortals to measure up. When individuals speak out, we're tempted to dismiss their motives, knowledge and tactics as insufficiently grand. We fault them for not being in command of every fact and figure. We fault ourselves as well for not knowing every detail, or for harboring uncertainties and doubts. We find it hard to imagine that flawed human beings might make a critical difference in worthy social causes.

11   Our culture's misreading of Parks' story hints at a collective amnesia in which we forget the examples that might most inspire our courage and conscience. Most of us know next to nothing of the old grass-roots movements in which ordinary men and women fought to preserve freedom, expand the sphere of democracy and create a more just society: the abolitionists, the populists, the women's suffrage campaigns, the union movements that ended 80-hour work weeks at near starvation wages. These movements could teach us how their participants successfully shifted public sentiment, challenged entrenched institutional power and found the strength to persevere. But their stories are buried.

12   In the prevailing myth, Parks decides to act on a whim, in isolation. She's a political innocent. The lesson seems to be that if any of us suddenly got the urge to do something equally heroic, that would be great. Of course most of us don't, so we wait our entire lives to find the ideal moment.

13   Parks' journey suggests that change is the product of deliberate, incremental action, whereby we join together to try to shape a better world. Sometimes our struggles will fail, as did many earlier efforts of Parks, her peers and her predecessors. Other times they may bear modest fruits. And at times they will trigger a miraculous outpouring of courage and heart—as happened with her arrest and everything that followed. Only when we act despite all our uncertainties and doubts do we have the chance to shape history.

Questions for Critical Thought

"Civil Rights Movement Was the Sum of Many People"

1. What is Loeb's reason for writing this essay? What do you believe he hopes to accomplish?

2. Loeb claims the CNN host had "stripped" the Montgomery boycott of its "most important context" in describing Parks as the woman who refused to "get up and give her seat in the white section to a white person." Explain what Loeb believes the interviewer should have said about Parks instead. Also explain why Loeb believes this.

3. According to Loeb, how might oversimplified portrayals of heroes discourage the average person from becoming a social activist?

4. What can we learn from knowing the history of Rosa Parks's activism? Why is this significant?

Reading Assignment: *"The Wrong Examples"*

Questions for Critical Thought follow this reading.

Preview   Read the introduction and the topic sentences.

Anticipate   What do you think this article will be about? Write your response in the "Notes" column.

Read and Reread   Read the entire article, marking unknown terms. Then reread more slowly and use the "Notes" column to interact with the essay. Mark important and interesting points and define unknown terms.

The Wrong Examples
by David L. Evans

An engineer and a native of Helena, Arkansas, Evans is a senior admissions officer at Harvard.

This article was published in *Newsweek*, March 1, 1993.

1   As a college admissions officer I am alarmed at the dearth of qualified black male candidates. Often in high schools that are ninety percent black, *all* the African-American students who come to my presentation are female! This gender disparity persists to college matriculation where the black male population almost never equals that of the female.

Notes

2   What is happening to these young men? Who or what is influencing them? I submit that the absence of male role models and slanted television images of black males have something to do with it.

3   More than half of black children live in homes headed by women, and almost all of the black teachers they encounter are also women. This means that most African-American male children do not often meet black male role models in their daily lives. They must look beyond their immediate surroundings for exemplary black men to emulate. Lacking in-the-flesh models, many look to TV for black heroes.

4   Unfortunately, TV images of black males are not particularly diverse. Their usual roles are to display physical prowess, sing, dance, play a musical instrument or make an audience laugh. These roles are enticing and generously rewarded. But the reality is that success comes to only a few extraordinarily gifted performers or athletes.

5   A foreigner watching American TV would probably conclude that most successful black males are either athletes or entertainers. That image represents both success and failure. Success, because the substantial presence of blacks in sports, music and sitcoms is a milestone in the struggle begun almost fifty years ago to penetrate the racial barriers of big-league athletics and television. It is a failure because the overwhelming success of a *few* highly visible athletes, musicians and comedians has type-cast black males. Millions see these televised roles as a definition of black men. Nowhere is this more misleading than in the inner city, where young males see it as "the way out."

6   Ask a random sample of Americans to identify Michael Jordan, Bo Jackson, Magic Johnson, Hammer, Prince, Eddie Murphy or Mike Tyson. Correct responses would probably exceed ninety percent. Then ask them to identify Colin Powell, August Wilson, Franklin Thomas, Mike Espy, Walter Massey, Earl Graves or the late Reginald Lewis and I doubt that ten percent would respond correctly. The second group contains the [former] chairman of the Joint Chiefs of Staff, a Pulitzer Prize–winning playwright, the president of the Ford Foundation, the secretary of agriculture, the director of the National Science Foundation, the publisher of Black Enterprise magazine and the former CEO of a multi-million-dollar business.

7   The Democratic National Convention that nominated Bill Clinton brought Ron Brown, Jesse Jackson, David Dinkins, Kurt Schmoke and Bernard Shaw into living rooms as impressive role models. Their relative numbers at the convention were in noticeable contrast to the black baseball players who made up nearly half of the All-Star teams on the Tuesday night of the convention.

8   This powerful medium has made the glamour of millionaire boxers, ballplayers, musicians and comedians appear so close, so tangible that,

to naive young boys, it seems only a dribble or dance step away. In the hot glare of such surrealism, schoolwork and prudent personal behavior can become irrelevant.

9   Impressionable young black males are not the only Americans getting this potent message. *All* TV viewers are subtly told that blacks are "natural" athletes, they are "funny" and all of them have "rhythm." Such a thoroughly reinforced message doesn't lie dormant. A teacher who thinks every little black boy is a potential Bo Jackson or Eddie Murphy is likely to give his football practice a higher priority than his homework or to excuse his disruptive humor.

10   **Neck jewelry:** Television's influence is so pronounced that one seldom meets a young black man who isn't wearing paraphernalia normally worn by athletes and entertainers. Young white men wear similar attire but not in the same proportion. Whites have many more televised role models from which to choose. There are very few whites in comparison to the number of blacks in the NBA. Black males are twelve and one-half percent of the American male population but constitute seventy-five percent of the NBA and are thereby six times overrepresented. That television presents poor role models for *all* kids doesn't wash.

11   These highly visible men's influence is so dominant that it has redefined the place of neck jewelry, sneakers and sports apparel in our society. The yearning to imitate the stars has sometimes had dire consequences. Young lives have been lost over sneakers, gold chains and jackets. I dare say that many black prison inmates are the *flotsam and jetsam*[1] from dreamboats that never made it to the NBA or MTV.

12   Producers of TV sports, popular music and sitcoms should acknowledge these "side effects" of the American Dream. More important are the superstars themselves. To a man, they are similar to lottery winners and their presence on TV is cruelly deceptive to their electronic protégés. Surely they can spend some of their time and resources to convince their young followers that even incredible talent doesn't assure fame or fortune. An athlete or performer must also be amazingly lucky in his quest for Mount Olympus.

13   A well-trained mind is a surer, although less glamorous, bet for success. Arthur Ashe spent his whole life teaching precisely this message. Bill Cosby and Jim Brown also come to mind as African-American superstars who use their substantial influence to redirect young black males. At this time, when black men are finally making some inroads into the upper echelons of American society, we need more than ever to encourage the young to look beyond the stereotypes of popular culture.

———————

[1]*Flotsam and jetsam:* Shipwrecked objects floating aimlessly.

Notes

Questions for Critical Thought

"The Wrong Examples"

1. What is Evans's reason for writing this essay? What do you believe he hopes to accomplish?

2. What kinds of media images is Evans concerned about, and why? Do his concerns seem legitimate to you? Why, or why not?

3. What kinds of heroes would he like to see young black males look up to? Explain why Evans believes such heroes would be effective role models for young black males.

4. Choose a well-developed paragraph from this essay and explain the kinds of evidence Evans uses to support his paragraph point.

TELEVISION AND THE MEDIA

Reading Assignment: "Guilt Free TV"

Questions for Critical Thought follow this reading.

Preview   This is a lengthy selection, so be sure to set aside plenty of time to complete a thorough reading process. Begin by reading the introduction and the topic sentences.

Anticipate   What do you think this article will be about? Write your response in the "Notes" column.

Read and Reread   Read the entire article, marking unknown terms. Then reread more slowly and use the "Notes" column to interact with the essay. Mark important and interesting points and define unknown terms.

Guilt Free TV

In the beginning, there was Big Bird. Now, thanks to intense competition from Disney and Nick, there are more quality shows for preschoolers than ever.

by Daniel McGinn

This article appeared in the November 11, 2002, edition of *Newsweek*.

1   When Alicia Large was growing up, her parents rarely let her watch television. Even the Muppets were off-limits, she says, because her parents disliked the sexual tension between Kermit and Miss Piggy. Now 31 and raising her own sons—ages 2 and 3—Large views TV more benevolently.

Her boys love *Dora the Explorer,* so when she takes them on errands, she draws a map—the bank, the grocery store—so they can track their progress as Dora does. Among Large's friends, kids' TV—what and how much are yours watching?—is a constant conversation. Yes, many parents still use TV as a babysitter. But increasingly, she says, parents are looking to TV to help them do a better job of raising kids. "Our generation is using it completely differently," she says.

2   Parents have felt conflicted about television since its earliest days. Even Philo T. Farnsworth, TV's inventor, fretted over letting his son watch cowboy shows, according to biographer Evan I. Schwartz. That anxiety continues. In a survey released last week by Public Agenda, 22 percent of parents said they'd "seriously considered getting rid of [their TV] altogether" because it airs too much sex and bad language. But at the same time, for parents of the youngest viewers—ages 2 to 5—there are new reasons for optimism. Now that PBS, which invented the good-for-kids genre, has new competition from Nickelodeon and Disney, there are more quality choices for preschoolers than ever.

3   Inside those networks, a growing number of Ph.D.s are injecting the latest in child-development theory into new programs. In Disney's *Stanley,* meet a freckle-faced kid who's fascinated with animals; in one episode, he and his pals explore the life and habitat of a platypus. Nickelodeon now airs 4.5 hours of quality preschool shows daily (in addition to learning-free fare like *SpongeBob* for older kids). Shows like *Dora* and *Blue's Clues* goad kids into interacting with the television set; studies show this improves problem-solving skills. Even the granddaddy of this genre, *Sesame Street,* has undergone a makeover to better serve today's precocious viewers. The newcomers provide stiff competition to Mister Rogers, whose show stopped production in 2000 (it still airs on PBS). But he welcomes his new TV neighbors. "I'm just glad that more producers—and purveyors of television have signed the pledge to protect childhood," says Fred Rogers, who now writes parenting books.

4   That's the good news. The bad news is that working these shows into kids' lives in a healthy way remains a challenge. Much of what kids watch remains banal or harmful. Many kids watch too much. There are also troubling socioeconomic factors at work. In lower-income homes, for instance, kids watch more and are more likely to have TV in their bedrooms, a practice pediatricians discourage. But even as some families choose to go TV-free, more parents are recognizing that television can be beneficial. In the Public Agenda survey, 93 percent of parents agree that "TV is fine for kids as long as he or she is watching the right shows and watching in moderation."

5   When it comes to the right shows, *Sesame Street* remains the gold standard. Last week, as the crew taped an episode for its 34th season, the set looked comfortably familiar: while Telly and Baby Bear worked

on a skit near Hooper's Store, Snuffleupagus hung from the rafters, sleeping under a sheet. The show's longevity is a testament to the research-driven process founder Joan Ganz Cooney invented in the late 1960s. Then, as now, each season begins with Ph.D.s working alongside writers to set goals and review scripts. Any time there's a question—will kids understand Slimey the Worm's mission to the moon?—they head to day-care centers to test the material.

6   When *Sesame* began reinventing kids' TV in the early '70s, Daniel Anderson was a newly minted professor of psychology at the University of Massachusetts, Amherst. Like most child-development pros at that time, he assumed TV was bad for kids. Then one day Anderson taught his class that young children have very short attention spans. One student challenged him: "So why do kids sit still for an hour to watch 'Sesame Street'?" "I genuinely didn't know the answer," Anderson recalls. So he went to a lab and placed kids in front of TVs to find it.

7   What he found surprised him. Like most researchers, he assumed that fast-moving images and sounds mesmerized young viewers. But videotapes of kids' viewing showed that their attention wandered most during transitions between segments and when dialogue or plotlines became too complex. He hypothesized that even young children watch TV for the same reason adults do: to enjoy good stories. To test that theory, he sliced up *Sesame Street* skits so the plot no longer made sense. Even 2-year-olds quickly realized the story was amiss and stopped watching. Some knocked on the TV screen. Others called out: "Mommy, can you fix this?" Over years of research, Anderson reached a startling conclusion: "Television viewing is a much more intellectual activity for kids than anybody had previously supposed."

8   This research might have stayed hidden in psych journals if it hadn't been for the work of two equally powerful forces: the U.S. Congress and a purple dinosaur named Barney. In 1990 Congress passed the Children's Television Act, increasing demand for quality kids' shows. Then *Barney & Friends* was launched as a PBS series in 1992. Kids went wild, and merchandise flew off shelves. Until then, Nickelodeon and Disney had been content to leave preschool shows to the do-gooders at PBS. Now they saw gold. "The success of *Barney* just changed everybody's feeling—it became 'OK, we should be able to do that, too,'" says Marjorie Kalins, a former *Sesame* executive.

9   It was a profitable move. By 2001 Nick and Disney's TV businesses had generated a combined $1.68 billion in revenue, according to Paul Kagan Associates. Everyone admits that licensing money influences programming decisions. (Ironically, merchandisers at Nickelodeon lobbied against *Dora* because they believed that another show would generate more sales.) Ads and toys can detract from many parents' enthusiasm

for the shows; no matter how much your kid may learn from *Sagwa* or *Rolie Polie Olie,* the characters are hard to love when you can't get through Wal-Mart without a giant case of "I-WANT-itis."

10   Until there's a way to make shows free, that overcommercialization will continue. But for parents, there's some comfort from knowing that more TV producers are applying the latest research to make their shows better. This happened partly because researchers of Anderson's generation helped grow a new crop of Ph.D.s, who began graduating into jobs at *Sesame* and Nickelodeon. And like seeds from a dandelion blown at by a child, folks who'd trained at *Sesame* began taking root inside other networks. Anne Sweeney, who'd studied at Harvard with *Sesame* co-founder Gerald Lesser, interned with television activist Peggy Charren and spent 12 years at Nickelodeon, took over the Disney Channel in 1996. She hired a team (led by ex-Nick programmer Rich Ross) to design preschool shows. By 1999 Disney had a full block of little-kid programming it branded Playhouse Disney. Today it uses a 28-page "Whole Child Curriculum" detailing what shows should teach.

11   To see how research can drive these new-generation shows, come along, neighbor, as we visit a day-care center on Manhattan's Upper West Side. Dr. Christine Ricci sits in a child-size chair, holding a script and tapping a red pen against her lip. Ricci, who holds a psychology Ph.D. from UMass, is research director for *Dora the Explorer,* which airs on Nick Jr., Nickelodeon's preschool block. In each episode Dora, an animated Latina girl, goes on a journey with a monkey named Boots. Using a map to guide them (which helps kids' spatial skills), they visit three locations ("Waterfall, mountain, forest!" kids yell) and solve problems. As in *Blue's Clues,* Nick Jr.'s groundbreaking hit in which a dog named Blue and the host Joe help kids solve puzzles, *Dora* encourages kids to yell back at the screen (often in Spanish) or do physical movements (like rowing a boat).

12   Today Ricci shows 4-year-olds a crudely animated *Dora* episode slated for next season. As they watch, Ricci's team charts, moment by moment, whether the kids are paying attention and interacting with the screen. At first the kids sit transfixed, but during a pivotal scene (in which Swiper the fox, Dora's nemesis, throws a boot down a hole) their attention wanders. One child picks up a Magic Marker, and suddenly every child is seeking out toys. All the while the researchers scribble furiously. When the episode ends, an adult asks the children questions: "What color button on the fix-it machine matched the tire?" Their recall is astonishing. *Sesame Street* has done this kind of testing off and on since the '70s. Ricci's team, however, is relentless, testing and revising every *Dora* episode repeatedly.

13   The following afternoon, Ricci, *Dora* creator Chris Gifford and their team study a bar graph showing how kids interacted with the episode minute by minute. To boost the numbers, sometimes they suggest better

Notes

animation. Sometimes they call for a better "money shot": a big close-up of Dora. Fixing one segment—"Only 15 out of 26 kids were still watching," Ricci informs them gravely—requires more drastic measures. Gifford stands up, motioning like a cheerleader, to suggest livelier movements to get kids moving along with Dora during a song. "So often when you work on a TV show for kids, you forget about your audience," Gifford says. "We've set up a system where we can't ignore them." Similar work goes on at *Blue's Clues.* Says Nick Jr. chief Brown Johnson: "It's science meets story."

14   For a parent, it's natural to get excited when kids shout back at the TV during *Dora* or dance to *The Wiggles,* a music-and-dance show that airs on Disney. That leads some parents to look at their TVs the way a previous generation looked to Dr. Spock. Colleen Breitbord of Framingham, Mass., sees these programs as so vital to the development of her children, 7 and 2, that she installed a TV in the kitchen so they can watch *Arthur* and *Clifford* while they eat. "They learn so much," Breitbord says. "I think children who don't have the opportunity to watch some of this excellent programming miss out." In Ansonia, Conn., Patti Sarandrea uses Playhouse Disney, Nick Jr. and PBS "to reinforce what I teach the kids: colors, shapes, counting." At 3 1/2, her daughter can count to 25. Thanks to *Dora,* her 18-month-old says "Hola."

15   As kids that young start tuning in, even *Sesame* is rethinking its approach. The show was originally designed for kids 3 to 5, but by the mid-1990s, many viewers were 2 or younger. The tykes seemed to tire of 60 minutes of fast-paced Muppet skits (the pacing was originally modeled after *Laugh-In* and TV commercials). So in 1999 *Sesame* introduced "Elmo's World," a 15-minute segment that ended every show. Even after that change, *Sesame* VP Lewis Bernstein noticed how today's little kids would sit still to watch 90-minute videotaped movies. So last February *Sesame* unveiled more longer segments. In "Journey to Ernie," Big Bird and Ernie play hide-and-seek against an animated background. Today ratings are up. The cast likes the new format, too. Before, stories were constantly cut short. "It was a little discombobulating," says Kevin Clash, the muscular, deep-voiced Muppet captain who brings Elmo to life. Now Elmo l-o-o-o-ves the longer stories.

16   So just how much good do these shows do? On a recent afternoon five undergrads sit around a table in the Yale University psychology department, playing a bizarre variation of bingo to try to find out. Together they watch three episodes of *Barney & Friends,* each filling in hash marks on six sheets of paper. After each screening, they tally how many "teaching elements" they've counted. "I've got 9 vocabulary, 6 numbers . . . 11 sharing," says one student. Afterward Yale researcher Dorothy Singer will crunch the data and compare them with past seasons'. Her work has shown that the higher

an episode's score, the more accurately children will be able to recount the plot and use the vocabulary words.

17   PBS does more of this postproduction "summative" research than other networks. Study after study shows *Sesame* viewers are better prepared for school. *Dragon Tales,* a *Sesame*-produced animated show, helps kids become more goal-oriented, and *Between the Lions,* a puppet show produced by Boston's WGBH, helps kids' reading. Nick research offers proof of the effectiveness of *Dora* and *Blue's Clues.* Disney doesn't do summative research; Disney execs say for now they'd rather devote resources to creating more shows for new viewers. Competitors suggest another reason: Disney's shows may not measure up. "It's scary to test," says *Sesame* research chief Rosemarie Truglio. "Maybe that's a piece of it—they're afraid."

18   Network-funded research won't change the minds of folks who say kids are better off with no television at all. That view gained strength in 1999, when the American Academy of Pediatrics began discouraging any television for kids under 2. But when you parse the pro- and anti-TV rhetoric, the two sides don't sound as far apart as you'd suspect. The pro-TV crowd, for instance, quickly concedes that violent TV is damaging to kids, and that too many kids watch too many lousy shows. The anti-TV crowd objects mostly to TV's widespread overuse. Like Häagen-Dazs, TV seems to defy attempts at moderation, they suggest, so it's safer to abstain entirely. They believe overviewing especially affects children because of what Marie Winn, author of *The Plug-In Drug,* calls the "displacement factor." That's when kids watch so much TV that they don't engage in enough brain-enhancing free play as toddlers or read enough during elementary school. Although pro-TV researchers say there are no data to support those fears, they agree it could be true. In fact, Anderson is currently conducting an experiment to measure whether having adult shows (like *Jeopardy!*) playing in the background interferes with children's play. Bad news, soap-opera fans: the early data suggest it might.

19   Even shows the academics applaud could be better. In his UMass office, Anderson pops in a videotape of *Dora.* It's one of the handful of shows that he advised during their conception. In this episode, Dora and Boots paddle a canoe down a river, around some rocks, toward a waterfall. Toward a waterfall? "If I'd read this script I'd have completely blocked this," he says, because it models unsafe behavior. Anderson has his arms crossed, his eyebrows scrunched; occasionally he talks to the screen, like an NFL fan disputing a bad call. "Oh, God, another dangerous thing," he says as Dora and Boots canoe under downed tree limbs. He still likes *Dora,* but not this episode. "The education is a little thinner than I would wish,

Notes

Notes

and it's a little dubious sending them on such a dumb journey." Then he watches *Bear* and *Blue's Clues,* still nitpicking but happier.

20   Even as the kids' TV environment improves, shortcomings remain. Only PBS airs educational shows for older elementary kids (examples: *Zoom* and *Cyberchase*). In focus groups, says Nickelodeon president Herb Scannell, older kids say they get enough learning in school; what commercial broadcaster is going to argue with the audience? Producers have other worries. Mitchell Kriegman, creator of *Bear in the Big Blue House,* says parents could grow too enamored of obviously educational, A-B-C/1-2-3–type shows. One of the most successful episodes of *Bear* involves potty training. "The [network's] reaction was 'Oh, my God, you can't say poop and pee on TV,'" Kriegman says. *Bear* did, and families loved it. Tighter curricula could dampen that creativity.

21   But those are worries for the future. For now, it's worth celebrating the improvements—however incremental—in shows for TV's youngest audience. Not everyone will want to raise a glass: like alcohol or guns, TV will be used sensibly in some homes and wreak havoc in others. Debating its net societal value will remain a never-ending pursuit. In the meantime parents live through these trade-offs daily. A recent issue of *Parenting* magazine offered the following question to help assess parenting skills: "I let my child watch TV only when . . . A) There's an educational show on public television, B) I have time to narrate the action for him . . . or C) I want to take a shower." The scoring code rates the answers: "A) Liar, B) Big fat liar, and C) You may not be perfect, but at least you're honest." As kids' TV raises the bar, parents who choose a different answer—D) All of the above—have a little less reason to feel guilty.

Questions for Critical Thought

"Guilt Free TV"

1. How has children's TV improved in recent years according to McGinn? Do you agree or disagree with his reasoning?

2. What are some of the negative effects mentioned in the article? Are there others not mentioned by McGinn? If so, explain.

3. What are the methods McGinn uses to prove to the reader that quality TV is being produced today?

4. What kinds of research is being done on children's TV? What do the sponsors of such research hope to find out? What are some of their goals in conducting research? Why might some avoid conducting research?

5. Besides the programming itself, what other problems might people have with children's TV? Why?

6. In Paragraph 18, McGinn mentions Marie Winn's concern about TV's "displacement factor." Explain what this means and whether or not you agree this is a problem.

7. McGinn suggests that recent improvements in children's TV are "worth celebrating." Do you agree? Why, or why not?

Reading Assignment: "Why We Tuned Out"

Questions for Critical Thought follow this reading.

Preview   Read the introduction and the topic sentences.

Anticipate   What do you think this article will be about? Write your response in the "Notes" column.

Read and Reread   Read the entire article, marking unknown terms. Then reread more slowly and use the "Notes" column to interact with the essay. Mark important and interesting points and define unknown terms.

Why We Tuned Out

"When Jazzy was 1 year old, her babysitter asked if TV was OK. We thought about it, and we said, 'No.'"

by Karen Springen

This article appeared in the November 11, 2002, edition of *Newsweek*.

1   "What's your favorite TV show?" our girls' beloved ballet instructor asked each pint-size dancer in her class. Our oldest daughter, Jazzy, didn't know how to answer. She shrugged. Her moment of awkwardness results from a decision my husband, Mark, and I made five years ago. We don't allow our kids to watch TV. Period. Not at home, not at friends' houses; and they don't watch videos or movies, either. We want our daughters, Jazzy, now nearly 6, and Gigi, 3, to be as active as possible, physically and mentally. So when a babysitter asked whether Jazzy, then 1 year old, could watch, we thought about it— and said no.

2   When we look at our inquisitive, energetic daughters, we have no regrets. And our reading of the research makes us feel even better. Nielsen Media Research reports that American children 2 through 11 watch

Notes

three hours and 16 minutes of television every day. Kids who watch more than 10 hours of TV each week are more likely to be overweight, aggressive and slow to learn in school, according to the American Medical Association. For these reasons, the American Academy of Pediatrics recommends no TV for children younger than 2 and a maximum of two hours a day of "screen time" (TV, computers or videogames) for older kids. We are convinced that without TV, our daughters spend more time than other kids doing cartwheels, listening to stories and asking such interesting questions as "How old is God?" and "What makes my rubber ducks float?" They also aren't haunted by TV images of September 11—because they never saw them.

3   Going without TV in America has its difficult moments. When I called my sister, Lucy, to make arrangements for Thanksgiving, she warned that her husband was planning to spend the day watching football. We're going anyway. We'll just steer the girls toward the playroom. And some well-meaning friends tell us our girls may be missing out on good educational programming. Maybe. But that's not what most kids are watching. Nielsen Media Research reports that among children 2 through 11, the top-five TV shows in the new fall season were *The Wonderful World of Disney, Survivor: Thailand, Yu-Gi-Oh!, Pokemon* and *Jackie Chan Adventures.*

4   Will our happy, busy girls suffer because they're not participating in such a big part of the popular culture? Will they feel left out in school when they don't know who won on *Survivor?* "Kids are going to make fun of them," warns my mother-in-law. And a favorite child psychiatrist, Elizabeth Berger, author of *Raising Children with Character,* cautions that maintaining a puritanical approach may make our kids into social outcasts. "Part of preparing your children for life is preparing them to be one of the girls," she says. "It's awful to be different from the other kids in fourth grade."

5   Our relatives all watch TV. So did we. I was born in 1961, the year Newton Minow, then the chairman of the U.S. Federal Communications Commission, called television a "vast wasteland." But I loved it. My sister, Katy, and I shared a first crush on the TV cartoon hero Speed Racer. Watching *Bewitched* and *The Brady Bunch* and, later, soap operas gave us an easy way to bond with our friends. Am I being selfish in not wanting the same for our children?

6   So far, our daughters don't seem to feel like misfits. We have no problem with the girls enjoying products based on TV characters. The girls wear Elmo pajamas and battle over who can sit on a big Clifford stuffed animal. From books, they also know about Big Bird, the Little Mermaid

and Aladdin. And they haven't mentioned missing out on *Yu-Gi-Oh!* cartoon duels. Dr. Miriam Baron, who chairs the American Academy of Pediatrics committee on public education, says I'm helping our kids be creative, independent learners and calls our decision "awesome." And Mayo Clinic pediatrician Daniel Broughton, another group member, says that "there's no valid reason" the girls need to view television.

7 As the girls grow older, we can't completely shield them from TV anyway. We'll probably watch Olympic rhythmic gymnastics; the girls love it. And if Jazzy's favorite baseball team, the Cubs, ever make the World Series, we'll tune in. Last Monday Jazzy's music teacher showed *The Magic School Bus: Inside the Haunted House.* Though *Magic School Bus* is a well-regarded Scholastic product, I still cringed, wondering why the kids weren't learning about vibrations and sounds by singing and banging on drums. But I kept silent; I'd never require my kids to abstain in school. Like Jean Lotus, the Oak Park, Ill., mom who founded the anti-TV group the White Dot and who also reluctantly allows her kids to view TV in school, I'm wary of being seen "as the crusading weirdo." But some public ridicule will be worth it if I help get even a few people to think twice before automatically turning on the tube. Now it's time for me to curl up with the girls and a well-worn copy of *Curious George.*

Questions for Critical Thought

"Why We Tuned Out"

1. According to Springen, why did she and her husband ban TV in their home? Do you believe they've made a positive decision for their family? Why, or why not?

2. What kinds of activities do the Springens want their daughters to engage in?

3. In your opinion, how might the Springen's daughters benefit from their parents' decision? Might they suffer from their parents' decision? Explain.

4. Why might the Springens allow their daughters to enjoy the products based on TV characters but not allow them to view these characters on TV? Does it seem contradictory for the Springens to allow their daughters to enjoy the products but not allow them to view characters on TV? Explain.

5. What advantages does Springen believe her children have that other children might not? Explain.

TECHNOLOGY

Reading Assignment: *"Reality Writes—Web Is but a Tool"*

Questions for Critical Thought follow this reading.

Preview   Read the first four paragraphs of the article and the topic sentences of all the other paragraphs.

Anticipate   What do you anticipate this article will be about? Record your thoughts in the "Notes" column.

Read and Reread   Quickly read the entire article, marking unknown terms. Then reread more slowly and use the "Notes" column to interact with the essay. Mark important points and define unknown terms.

Reality Writes—Web Is but a Tool
by Susan Swartz

Susan Swartz is a columnist for the *Press Democrat* in Santa Rosa, California.

This essay appeared in the *Sacramento Bee* newspaper, January 8, 1998.

1   The finest place to gather words is in the home of the story teller. In a room with pictures on the wall and food smells.

2   This is not to take away from the Internet, which provides virtual visits that can deliver everything from instant family news to RSVPs and keep the dialogue going with new and old correspondents.

3   And certainly when it comes to words, the computer is a wizard. When we are writing a story, we can dip into an encyclopedia and thesaurus and find the ultimate word without waiting, the ideal quote from famous people living or dead. The computer is full of appropriate, vibrant and lyrical choices, containing more words than what's in all our bookshelves put together.

4   But the words that tell a story must first come from the source and that requires being there. These words count most—the ones a person gives directly to a writer, sometimes whispered, sometimes shouted, words carefully sought through squeezed-shut eyes to define a life.

5   They may be as drab as a person's yellow wallpaper or as flip as the pink camellia bush scraping across their window. The writer, recording the words and the moment, makes sure they stay in context with the life.

6   The writer will be there to note that when the businessman talks about his father he rubs his knee hard. The oldest daughter of the flooded family twists her ring. The feminist leader wears fuchsia-colored lipstick.

7   The writer must be actually, not virtually, present in order to wrap smells and noises around the words so that, later, the reader will be able to imagine the subject in a kitchen that smells like sage and intuit something about a man who keeps pictures of his dead sister on the piano.

8   As reporters, we make our livings off other people's words. We start out with nothing to report and find someone to tell us something. We are constantly listening for words to tell a story, solve the crime, remember the victim, describe the rescue. We think if we look in a subject's eyes we'll know if they're telling the truth. They think if they look in our eyes they'll know if they can trust us.

9   Then we hope for a "bingo" quote that will end up in the first paragraph of the story or the clincher line in a column and even screamed in large type in a headline.

10   The computer, it is true, is a wonderful tool, but writers get our best stuff away from our desks. Once we get the information, the computer can make us sound better and smarter than we did before. It can analyze our data, find the numbers we need to prop up a story, search out expert commentary to lend strength to the story. With a few keystrokes it can change our words around and spell them right.

11   But we still need to go out and get the words, which to me is the most seductive and satisfying part about being a writer.

12   In search of someone's story, I have spent time in living rooms and kitchens that I would never have stumbled upon or been invited into without a notebook.

13   I have sat at the bed of a dying woman, perched on a pillow with a pagan priestess, discussed menopause with a prize-winning poet.

14   If you're going to write about people, you have to walk in, in the middle of their lives, sometimes before they have time to clean up the dishes or get the dog off the only good chair.

15   People give us entree to ask our questions and we get to stay for small talk. We scrape our feet on the mud mat outside and enter the farmhouse through the kitchen door and talk about lemonade. Or sometimes we sip tea from china cups and talk about men and roses.

16   Sometimes when I'm being the reporter I ask something unnecessary just to gain time to scribble down not their answer but the extra details—their hair color, the magazine on the coffee table, the political cartoon on the refrigerator.

17   The storyteller's words are unique to them and the moment. If they had a spokesman, most people's words might end up prettier or stronger, but they wouldn't be sincere or intimate.

18   As much as I now rely on the Internet to provide research and the word processor to groom my sentences, I will always prefer word gathering by foot and notebook.

Notes

Notes

19   The computer delivers the world, but it's not as real as what you find down a street you've never driven talking to people you've never met.

20   I get to say, "Can I ask you a few questions?" and sometimes they say "sure" and sometimes they say "why?" but seldom do they say "no."

21   And the story begins.

Questions for Critical Thought

"Reality Writes . . ."

1. What is Swartz's main point in this essay? Where does she express this idea most clearly?

2. What does Swartz use the Internet and the word processor for?

3. Swartz enjoys using detail to make her ideas come alive. An example of this is the sentence "The feminist leader wears fuchsia-colored lipstick" (Par. 6). What image comes to your mind when you read this sentence? Why does Swartz find this image interesting?

4. List some other examples of when Swartz uses detail to paint an image in our minds. (Consider doing this in your own essays.)

Reading Assignment: "The Great Unwatched"

Questions for Critical Thought follow this reading.

Preview   Read the introduction and the topic sentences.

Anticipate   What do you think this article will be about? Write your response in the "Notes" column.

Read and Reread   Read the entire article, marking unknown terms. Then reread more slowly and use the "Notes" column to interact with the essay. Mark important and interesting points and define unknown terms.

The Great Unwatched

Stipulated: The protection of our capital, its monuments and centers of authority, is a vital national interest.

by William Safire

This article, dated February 18, 2002, appeared on the *New York Times* website, www.nytimes.com.

1   Early in our history, when faced with a potential rebellion of unpaid officers, one of our leaders employed an uncharacteristic emotional trick—

Notes

pretending to be going blind—to appeal to the infuriated military men not to march on the capital. He soon had them in tears and in hand.

2   In another time, another leader risked all by turning the capital's defense over to the man most opposed to his political aims, gambling that he could later overcome the nation's gratitude to a man on horseback.

3   In our time, after the Pentagon was hit, the White House targeted and the Capitol anthraxed, D.C. again saw itself besieged. But now, in terror of an external threat, our leaders are protecting our capital at the cost of every American's personal freedom.

4   Surveillance is in the saddle. Responding to the latest Justice Department terror alert, Washington police opened the Joint Operation Command Center of the Synchronized Operations Command Complex (S.O.C.C.). In it, 50 officials monitor a wall of 40 video screens showing images of travelers, drivers, residents and pedestrians.

5   These used to be the Great Unwatched, free people conducting their private lives; now they are under close surveillance by hundreds of hidden cameras. A zoom lens enables the watchers to focus on the face of a tourist walking toward the Washington Monument or Lincoln Memorial.

6   The monitoring system is already linked to 200 cameras in public schools. The watchers plan to expand soon with an equal number in the subways and parks. A private firm profits by photographing cars running red lights; those images will also join the surveillance network.

7   Private cameras in banks and the lobbies and elevators of apartment buildings and hotels will join the system, and residents of nursing homes and hospitals can look forward to an electronic eye in every room. A commercial camera atop a department store in Georgetown catches the faces of shoppers entering malls, to be plugged into omnipresent S.O.C.C.

8   Digital images of the captured faces can be flashed around the world in an instant on the Internet. Married to face-recognition technology and tied in to public and private agencies around the world, an electronic library of hundreds of millions of faces will be created. Terrorists and criminals—as well as unhappy spouses, runaway teens, hermits and other law-abiding people who want to drop out of society for a while—will have no way to get a fresh start.

9   Is this the kind of world we want? The promise is greater safety; the tradeoff is government control of individual lives. Personal security may or may not be enhanced by this all-seeing eye and ear, but personal freedom will surely be sharply curtailed. To be watched at all times, especially when doing nothing seriously wrong, is to be afflicted with a creepy feeling. That is what is felt by a convict in an always-lighted cell. It is the pervasive, inescapable feeling of being unfree.

Notes

10   As the law now stands, there is no privacy in public places; that's why sports stadiums are called "Snooper Bowls." A whisper to your spouse on your front porch is the public's business, say the courts; and on that intrusive analogy, long-range microphones may soon be allowed to pick up voice vibrations on windowpanes.

11   When your government, employer, landlord, merchant, banker and local sports team gang up to picture, digitize and permanently record your every activity, you are placed under unprecedented control. This is not some alarmist Orwellian scenario; it is here, now, financed by $20 billion last year and $15 billion more this year of federal money appropriated out of sheer fear.

12   By creating the means to monitor 300 million visits to the U.S. yearly, this administration and a supine opposition are building a system capable of identifying, tracking and spying on 300 million Americans. So far, the reaction has been a most un-American docility.

13   It's Presidents' Day. To save the capital and thus the nation, the leader who manipulated his rebellious officers with an emotional pretense of incipient blindness was George Washington, and the one who risked creating a Caesar out of a necessary general was Abraham Lincoln. Neither would sacrifice our freedom to protect his monument.

Questions for Critical Thought

"The Great Unwatched"

1. What is surveillance? Why is Safire concerned about surveillance technology?

2. Look up the word "unwashed" in the dictionary to see what it means when used as an adjective. Safire is playing with words when he uses "unwatched" in the title and in Paragraph 5 because he knows many readers will think of the word "unwashed." He is drawing a connection between the "unwatched" and the "unwashed." What is the connection? Explain why Safire chose the word "unwatched."

3. What are some of the surveillance systems available currently?

4. What are some of the advantages and disadvantages of surveillance technology?

5. What new technology is on the horizon?

6. Why is "being recorded" comparable to "being controlled" according to Safire? Do you agree or disagree? Why?

7. Examine the structure of the article (particularly the introduction and conclusion). Explain how such a structure helps Safire reinforce his main idea.

Reading Assignment: *Excerpt from* 1984

Questions for Critical Thought follow this reading.

Preview   Read the introductory sentences and paragraphs 1–2.

Anticipate   What do you think this excerpt will be about? Write your response in the "Notes" column.

Read and Reread   Read the entire excerpt, marking unknown terms. Then reread more slowly and use the "Notes" column to respond to what you read. Mark important and interesting points and define unknown terms.

Excerpt from *1984*
by George Orwell

In his futuristic novel, *1984* (which he wrote in 1949), Orwell envisions a world in which the individual's right to privacy has been stripped away. In this excerpt from Chapter 1, Orwell invites us to observe his main character's life.

1   It was a bright cold day in April, and the clocks were striking thirteen. Winston Smith, his chin nuzzled into his breast in an effort to escape the vile wind, slipped quickly through the glass doors of Victory Mansions, though not quickly enough to prevent a swirl of gritty dust from entering along with him.

2   The hallway smelt of boiled cabbage and old rag mats. At one end of it a coloured poster, too large for indoor display, had been tacked to the wall. It depicted simply an enormous face, more than a metre wide: the face of a man of about forty-five, with a heavy black moustache and ruggedly handsome features. Winston made for the stairs. It was no use trying the lift. Even at the best of times it was seldom working, and at present the electric current was cut off during daylight hours. It was part of the economy drive in preparation for Hate Week. The flat was seven flights up, and Winston, who was thirty-nine and had a varicose ulcer above his right ankle, went slowly, resting several times on the way. On each landing, opposite the lift-shaft, the poster with the enormous face gazed from the wall. It was one of those pictures which are so contrived that the eyes follow you about when you move. BIG BROTHER IS WATCHING YOU, the caption beneath it ran.

Notes

3   Inside the flat a fruity voice was reading out a list of figures which had something to do with the production of pig-iron. The voice came from an oblong metal plaque like a dulled mirror which formed part of the surface of the right-hand wall. Winston turned a switch and the voice sank somewhat, though the words were still distinguishable. The instrument (the telescreen, it was called) could be dimmed, but there was no way of shutting it off completely. He moved over to the window: a small-ish, frail figure, the meagreness of his body merely emphasized by the blue overalls which were the uniform of the party. His hair was very fair, his face naturally sanguine, his skin roughened by coarse soap and blunt razor blades and the cold of the winter that had just ended.

4   Outside, even through the shut window-pane, the world looked cold. Down in the street little eddies of wind were whirling dust and torn paper into spirals, and though the sun was shining and the sky a harsh blue, there seemed to be no colour in anything, except the posters that were plastered everywhere. The blackmoustachio'd face gazed down from every commanding corner. There was one on the house-front immediately opposite. BIG BROTHER IS WATCHING YOU, the caption said, while the dark eyes looked deep into Winston's own. Down at streetlevel another poster, torn at one corner, flapped fitfully in the wind, alternately covering and uncovering the single word INGSOC. In the far distance a helicopter skimmed down between the roofs, hovered for an instant like a bluebottle, and darted away again with a curving flight. It was the police patrol, snooping into people's windows. The patrols did not matter, however. Only the Thought Police mattered.

5   Behind Winston's back the voice from the telescreen was still babbling away about pig-iron and the overfulfilment of the Ninth Three-Year Plan. The telescreen received and transmitted simultaneously. Any sound that Winston made, above the level of a very low whisper, would be picked up by it, moreover, so long as he remained within the field of vision which the metal plaque commanded, he could be seen as well as heard. There was of course no way of knowing whether you were being watched at any given moment. How often, or on what system, the Thought Police plugged in on any individual wire was guesswork. It was even conceivable that they watched everybody all the time. But at any rate they could plug in your wire whenever they wanted to. You had to live—did live, from habit that became instinct—in the assumption that every sound you made was overheard, and, except in darkness, every movement scrutinized.

6   Winston kept his back turned to the telescreen. It was safer, though, as he well knew, even a back can be revealing. A kilometre away the Ministry of Truth, his place of work, towered vast and white above the grimy landscape. This, he thought with a sort of vague distaste—this was London, chief city of Airstrip One, itself the third most populous of

the provinces of Oceania. He tried to squeeze out some childhood memory that should tell him whether London had always been quite like this. Were there always these vistas of rotting nineteenth-century houses, their sides shored up with baulks of timber, their windows patched with cardboard and their roofs with corrugated iron, their crazy garden walls sagging in all directions? And the bombed sites where the plaster dust swirled in the air and the willow-herb straggled over the heaps of rubble; and the places where the bombs had cleared a larger patch and there had sprung up sordid colonies of wooden dwellings like chicken-houses? But it was no use, he could not remember: nothing remained of his childhood except a series of bright-lit tableaux occurring against no background and mostly unintelligible.

Questions for Critical Thought

Excerpt from 1984

1. George Orwell, a British writer, uses a few terms in ways that may be new to you. For example, in Paragraph 2, Orwell uses "lift" and "flat" as nouns. Look these words up in the dictionary and look for the noun definitions that come after the italicized words "chiefly Brit." ("Chiefly Brit" means that the meaning listed is most often used by people in Britain.) What does Orwell mean when he uses the words "lift" and "flat"? (*Note:* Some smaller dictionaries won't give the "chiefly Brit" definition. You may have to go to a larger dictionary.)

2. Review the reading and underline all the descriptive words and phrases that help paint a picture of the setting. Then write a paragraph describing the world in which Winston, the main character, lives. In a second paragraph, describe your reaction to his surroundings.

3. How is the word *party* being used in Paragraph 3? What does this usage suggest to you about the society in which Winston lives?

4. What surveillance device is used to watch people like Winston? What is the device capable of seeing, hearing, or recording?

5. How would you feel about living under constant surveillance? How might such living conditions change your life and your view of society?

6. What are some of the advantages and disadvantages of surveillance technology according to Orwell? Explain.

7. How accurate do you think Orwell was in imagining what the year 1984 would be like? How close is he to accurately describing the current year?

THE POWER OF POETRY

Reading Assignment: *"Annabel Lee"*

Questions for Critical Thought follow this reading.

Preview   Skim the poem once. Notice that the lines are numbered (every fith line) and an extra space appears between stanzas.

Anticipate   What does it appear to be about? Write your response in the "Notes" column.

Read and Reread   Read the poem again, marking unknown terms. Then reread more slowly and use the "Notes" column to write down your impressions. Define unknown terms.

Annabel Lee
by Edgar Allan Poe

This poem, dating from 1849–1850, is believed to focus on the past practice of arranged marriage and the treatment of disobedient daughters.

It was many and many a year ago,
    In a kingdom by the sea,
That a maiden there lived whom you may know
    By the name of ANNABEL LEE;
5 And this maiden she lived with no other thought
    Than to love and be loved by me.

I was a child and *she* was a child,
    In this kingdom by the sea,
But we loved with a love that was more than love—
10   I and my ANNABEL LEE—
With a love that the winged seraphs of heaven
    Coveted her and me.

And this was the reason that, long ago,
    In this kingdom by the sea,
15 A wind blew out of a cloud, chilling
    My beautiful ANNABEL LEE;
So that her highborn kinsman came
    And bore her away from me,

To shut her up in a sepulchre
20   In this kingdom by the sea.

The angels, not half so happy in heaven,
        Went envying her and me;
Yes! that was the reason (as all men know,
        In this kingdom by the sea)
25 That the wind came out of the cloud by night,
        Chilling and killing my ANNABEL LEE.

But our love it was stronger by far than the love
        Of those who were older than we—
        Of many far wiser than we—
30 And neither the angels in heaven above,
        Nor the demons down under the sea,
Can ever dissever my soul from the soul
        Of the beautiful ANNABEL LEE:

For the moon never beams without bringing me dreams
35   Of the beautiful Annabel Lee;
And the stars never rise, but I feel the bright eyes
        Of the beautiful ANNABEL LEE;
And so, all the night-tide, I lie down by the side
Of my darling—my darling—my life and my bride,
40   In the sepulchre there by the sea—
        In her tomb by the sounding sea.

Questions for Critical Thought

"Annabel Lee"

1. If you were going to argue that this poem is about the old practice of arranged marriage and the punishment of disobedient daughters, what evidence from the poem would you use to support this position? What images contribute to this idea?

2. Do you see any other possible meanings? If so, what evidence from the poem would you use to support this meaning? What images, words, or themes contribute to this idea?

3. Explore the images of life and death in the poem. Which images suggest life or living to the fullest? Which suggest death or the end of life as once known?

4. What do you believe the poem says about love? Using evidence from the poem, explain.

Reading Assignment: *"I Want to Write"*

Questions for Critical Thought follow this reading.

Preview   Skim the poem. Notice that this is a single-stanza poem.

Anticipate   What do you think this poem is about? Write your response in the "Notes" column.

Read and Reread   Read the poem, marking unknown terms. Then reread more slowly and use the "Notes" column to record your impressions. Define unknown terms.

I Want to Write

by Margaret Walker

Walker, a widely published poet, is a professor of English and director of the Institute for the Study of History, Life, and Culture of Black People at Jackson State College in Mississippi.

I want to write
I want to write the songs of my people.
I want to hear them singing melodies in the dark.
I want to catch the last floating strains from their sob-torn throats.
I want to frame their dreams into words; their souls into notes.
I want to catch their sunshine laughter in a bowl;
fling dark hands to a darker sky
and fill them full of stars
then crush and mix such lights till they become
a mirrored pool of brilliance in the dawn.

Questions for Critical Thought

"I Want to Write"

1. What does the speaker want to write? Why does the speaker want to write? How do you know?

2. Which images reinforce the speaker's desire? Describe how these images work in the poem.

3. What is the purpose of writing down people's experiences?

4. If you were asked to write about your own family or people, what would you write? What stories would you tell? Why?

This section of Connections *offers you information and exercises to help you sharpen some important skills.*

- Discovering your learning style

- Using the dictionary

- Building your vocabulary

- Spelling matters

- Reading aloud: a trick of the trade

- Using outside sources

- Writing in class/Writing the argument

DISCOVERING YOUR LEARNING STYLE

Each person has his or her own **learning style**—a method that makes learning easier. Researchers have found that there are basically four styles: **visual, auditory, tactile,** or **kinesthetic.**

- **Visual learners** learn best when they see the material.
- **Auditory learners** learn best when they hear the material.
- **Tactile learners** learn best when they can write down the material.
- **Kinesthetic learners** learn best when they can involve their bodies in the learning process.

If you know what your learning style is, you will have an advantage in college because then you can study in the way that is best for you. For example, if you are a visual learner, you will want to use charts and to review cards and pictures when you are studying. However, if you know that you are an auditory learner, you know that lecture classes will be easier for you, and you might even tape record information to play back to yourself. If you are a tactile learner, you will want to find ways to learn information that involves taking notes or tracing letters. And if you're a kinesthetic learner, you will want to learn through physical movement: building models, organizing ideas by organizing note cards, and so on. (You'll notice in this textbook that we offer activities and approaches that work for all kinds of learners: charts to express and organize ideas, reading aloud to help you edit your essays, note cards to organize your thoughts in an essay, and many more.)

No one learns *only* one way. You may learn best with visual materials, second best with auditory materials, third best with tactile materials, and so on. The key is knowing how you learn best, making the most of that method, and strengthening your other styles as you go along.

Discovering Your Learning Style

Take the test that follows and find out what your strongest learning style is. Then carefully review the study tips for each learning style.

Barsch Learning Style Inventory
by Jeffrey Barsch, Ed.D.

To gain a better understanding of yourself as a learner you need to evaluate the way you prefer to learn. We all should develop a style which will enhance our learning potential. The following evaluation is a short, quick way of assessing your learning style.

This is not a timed test. Try to do as much as you can by yourself. You surely may, however, ask for assistance when and where you feel you need it. Answer each question as honestly as you can. There are thirty-two questions.

When you are finished, transfer each number to its proper place on page 450. Then, total each of the four columns on that page. You will then see, very quickly, what your best method of learning is, i.e., whether you are a **visual, auditory, tactile** or **kinesthetic** learner. By this we mean, whether you as an individual learn best through seeing things, hearing them, through the sense of touch, or through actually performing the task.

For example:
- If you are a visual learner, that is, you have a high visual score, then by all means be sure you see all study materials. Use charts, maps, filmstrips, notes, and flashcards. Practice visualizing or picturing spelling words, for example, in your head. Use brightly colored markers to highlight your reading assignments. Write out everything for frequent and quick visual review.
- If you are an auditory learner, that is, have a high auditory score, then be sure to use tapes. Sit in the lecture hall or classroom where you can hear lectures clearly. Tape your class or lecture notes so that you can review them frequently. After you have read something, summarize it on tape. Verbally review spelling words and lectures with a friend.
- If you are a tactile learner, that is, if you have a high tactile score, you might trace words, for example, as you are saying them. Facts that must be learned should be written several times. Keep a supply of scratch paper just for this purpose. Taking and keeping lecture notes will be very important.
- If you are a kinesthetic learner, that is, if you have a high kinesthetic score, it means you need to involve your body in the process of learning. Take a walk and study your notes on flashcards at the same time. It is easier for you to memorize school work if you involve some movement in your memory task.

If several of your scores are within 4 or 5 points of each other, it means that you can use any of those senses for learning tasks. *When you are in a hurry, use your best learning styles. When you have extra time, improve your weak sensory areas.* Discuss the results of this test with your teacher or counselor. You will develop through conversation other helpful ways to study more efficiently. Good luck in your efforts to identify and use a more effective study pattern.

Place a check on the appropriate line after each statement.

Notes

Notes		**Often**	**Sometimes**	**Seldom**
	1. I can remember more about a subject through listening than reading.	___	___	___
	2. I follow written directions better than oral directions.	___	___	___
	3. Once shown a new physical movement, I perform it quickly with few errors.	___	___	___
	4. I bear down extremely hard with pen or pencil when writing.	___	___	___
	5. I require explanations of diagrams, graphs, or visual directions.	___	___	___
	6. I enjoy working with tools.	___	___	___
	7. I am skillful with and enjoy developing and making graphs and charts.	___	___	___
	8. I can tell if sounds match when presented with pairs of sounds.	___	___	___
	9. I can watch someone do a dance step and easily copy it myself.	___	___	___
	10. I can understand and follow directions on maps.	___	___	___
	11. I do better at academic subjects by listening to lectures or tapes.	___	___	___
	12. I frequently play with coins or keys in my pockets.	___	___	___
	13. I enjoy perfecting a movement in sports or dancing.	___	___	___
	14. I can better understand a news article by reading about it in the paper than by listening to the radio.	___	___	___
	15. I can chew gum, smoke, or snack during studies.	___	___	___
	16. I feel the best way to remember is to picture it in my head.	___	___	___
	17. I enjoy activities that make me aware of my body's movement.	___	___	___
	18. I would rather listen to a good lecture or speech than read about the same material in a textbook.	___	___	___

	Often	Sometimes	Seldom	Notes
19. I consider myself an athletic person.	____	____	____	
20. I grip objects in hands during learning period.	____	____	____	
21. I would prefer listening to the news on the radio rather than reading it in a newspaper.	____	____	____	
22. I like to obtain information on an interesting subject by reading relevant materials.	____	____	____	
23. I am highly aware of sensations and feelings in my hips and shoulders after learning a new movement or exercise.	____	____	____	
24. I follow oral directions better than written ones.	____	____	____	
25. It would be easy for me to memorize something if I could just use body movements at the same time.	____	____	____	
26. I like to write things down or take notes for visual review.	____	____	____	
27. I remember best when writing things down several times.	____	____	____	
28. I learn to spell better by repeating the letters out loud than by writing the word on paper.	____	____	____	
29. I frequently have the ability to visualize body movements to perform a task, e.g., correction of a golf swing, batting stance, dance position, etc.	____	____	____	
30. I can learn spelling well by tracing over the letters.	____	____	____	
31. I feel comfortable touching, hugging, shaking hands, etc.	____	____	____	
32. I am good at working and solving jigsaw puzzles and mazes.	____	____	____	

Scoring Procedures:

OFTEN = 5 points
SOMETIMES = 3 points
SELDOM = 1 point

On page 450 place the point value on the line next to its corresponding item number. Next, add the points to obtain the preference scores under each heading.

	Visual		Auditory		Tactile		Kinesthetic	
	No.	Pts.	No.	Pts.	No.	Pts.	No.	Pts.
	2 ___		1 ___		4 ___		3 ___	
	7 ___		5 ___		6 ___		9 ___	
	10 ___		8 ___		12 ___		13 ___	
	14 ___		11 ___		15 ___		17 ___	
	16 ___		18 ___		20 ___		19 ___	
	22 ___		21 ___		27 ___		23 ___	
	26 ___		24 ___		30 ___		25 ___	
	32 ___		28 ___		31 ___		29 ___	

VPS = _____   APS = _____   TPS = _____   KPS = _____

VPS = Visual Preference Score
APS = Auditory Preference Score
TPS = Tactile Preference Score
KPS = Kinesthetic Preference Score

Notes

Scoring Tips: Try moving down one column at a time. Begin with the VISUAL column where the #2 is listed. Look back at your answer for #2 of the survey. If you answered OFTEN, you would put 5 points next to #2 in the Pts. column. If you answered SOMETIMES, you would put 3 points next to #2. And if you answered SELDOM for #2, you would list 1 point in the Pts. column. Work your way down the VISUAL column until you've recorded your scores for numbers 7, 10, 14, 16, 22, 26, and 32 of the survey. After recording the scores in this column, add up the points in the VISUAL column and record the total at the bottom next to VPS=. Move next to the AUDITORY column and insert the appropriate number of points for each survey statement. Total the points at the bottom next to APS=. Then complete the TACTILE column and finally the KINESTHETIC column. Your highest score will tell you what your preferred learning style is.

Study Tips for Different Learning Styles

Directions: Use the study tips outline for your first learning preference and then reinforce what you are learning with tips from your second preference. When you have extra time, work on strengthening your weaker sensory areas. Remember that if several of your scores are within 4 or 5 points of each other, then you can use any of those senses for learning.

I. Tips for Visual Learners (those who learn by seeing/visualizing)

1. Write down anything you want to remember, such as a list of things to do, facts to learn for a test, etc.

2. Try to write down information in your own words. If you don't have to think about the material and restate it in your own words, you won't really learn it.

3. Underline or highlight important words you need to learn as you read.

4. When learning a new vocabulary word, visualize the word.

5. When you have a list of things to remember, keep the list in a place where you will be sure to see it several times a day. Suggestions: bulletin board by your desk at home, in your notebook, on the mirror in the bathroom, etc.

6. Try drawing a picture of any information you want to learn. Try making a diagram, a chart, or actually drawing people, things, etc.

7. Always read any material in the textbook before going to class so you have a chance to visually connect with the information before hearing it.

II. Tips for Auditory Learners (those who learn through hearing/listening)

1. Use a tape recorder to record notes when reading instead of writing facts down. Play it back while you are riding in the car, doing dishes, washing the car, jogging, etc.

2. Subvocalize—that is, talk to yourself about any information you want to remember. Try to recite it without looking at your notes or the book.

3. Discuss with others from your class and then quiz each other on the material. Really listen to yourself as you talk.

4. When learning a new vocabulary word, say it out loud. Then spell it out loud several times. See if it rhymes with a word you know. You could even try singing the word in a song.

5. To learn facts, say them out loud, put the facts to music or read them into a tape recorder. Then listen often to what you have recorded.

6. When writing, talk to yourself. First, tell yourself what you will write, say it out loud as you write it, and then read aloud what you have written or tape record it.

7. Always read material in your textbook to be learned after hearing the information first in the class lecture (unless the instructor assigns the reading first before class so you can participate in class discussions).

III. Tips for Tactile Learners (those who learn through touch/tracing)

1. Try to study through practical experiences, such as making models or doing lab work.

2. Trace words and letters to learn spelling and to remember facts.

3. Use the computer to reinforce learning through the sense of touch.

4. Recopy your notes as you study for an exam.

5. Write facts to be learned on 3″ x 5″ cards, with a question on one side and the answer on the other.

6. When working with a study group, think of T.V. quiz games (*Jeopardy,* etc.) as ways to review information.

IV. Tips for Kinesthetic Learners (those who learn through physical activity)

1. Take frequent, short breaks (5–10 minutes) in study periods.

2. Memorize or drill while walking, jogging, or exercising.

Notes

3. Try expressing your abilities through dance, drama, or sports.

4. Try standing up when you are reading or writing.

5. Write facts to be learned on 3" x 5" cards, with a question on one side and the answer on the other. Lay out the cards, quiz yourself, shuffle them, lay them out again, and quiz yourself again.

6. When working with a study group, think of T.V. quiz games (*Jeopardy,* etc.) as ways to review information.

7. Study through role playing.

IV. Tips for Multisensory Learners (Any Combination of the Above Styles)

Use any combination of the above study tips. It may take some experimentation before you find the best techniques for you.

Activity

Making the Most of Your Learning Style

Find other classmates who share your learning style. (If you don't get the chance to do this with classmates, work individually or with a tutor.) Review the study tips for your learning style and try to rewrite each tip so that it applies specifically to the work you do in this class. Then choose another class you are taking and rewrite the tips so that they specifically work for that class. You may also want to do this for your second learning style.

USING THE DICTIONARY

The following section on using the dictionary will help you see what an important tool the dictionary is to the writer, the student, and the person in the work world.

Every college student should own (and carry, if possible) a good dictionary, because the dictionary can help you

- spell,
- define words,
- find the right verb forms, and
- find other forms of a word.

The next four subsections will help you understand how the dictionary works and how you can use the dictionary for the purposes listed above.

Using the Dictionary to Spell

Imagine that you are working on an essay about Anne Frank's diary. You have typed the following quote into your essay and returned Frank's diary to the library. You're editing your essay, and you want to make sure you've spelled *recapture* correctly.

> I can shake off everything if I write; my sorrows disappear, my courage is re-born. But, and that is the great question, will I ever be able to write anything great, will I ever become a journalist or a writer? I hope so, oh, I hope so very much, for I can recapture everything when I write, my thoughts, my ideals, and my fantasies.
>
> —*Anne Frank (1929–1945)*
> *diary entry 4/4/44,* Diary of a Young Girl

A word like *recapture* is fairly easy to look up in a dictionary. By sounding out the word, you know to begin by looking up words beginning with *re*. Then you can narrow your search to words beginning with *reca* or *reka,* and by scanning the entries on the page, you will find *recapture.*

Other words might be more difficult to find when you are unsure of the spelling. Do your best to sound them out and then scan the dictionary pages. Other options include asking a tutor, instructor, or friend to help you get started. You can also try using an electronic dictionary or a computer dictionary. The advantages to these two kinds of dictionaries is that you can type in a word by the way it sounds to you, and often, but not always, the electronic or computer dictionary can figure out what you are looking for.

Be aware, too, that sometimes you may look up a word in the dictionary and not find it because it is in a form that is not listed. For example, if you looked up *recapturing,* you would not find it listed in bold print in its own entry in the dictionary. With *recapturing,* you would simply look for a form of the word that is listed in bold print, then check that entry to see if the form you want is listed. In other words, you'd look up *recapture* and find *-turing* toward the front of the entry. This tells you the word is spelled *recap + turing.* In other situations, you may find the form you want listed at the end of an entry.

Finally, if you are using a computer to complete your essays, you can use spell check. This is a program that will check your writing for you. But be careful of relying on it too much. A spell-check program cannot catch wrong word errors. (For example, if you typed in *recapturing* instead of *recaptures,* spell check would see nothing wrong with your work. A more

Notes   common problem is when a writer mixes up words like *their/there* or *to/too* or *its/it's*. Spell check does not help in these situations, either.)

Activity

Using the Dictionary to Correct Misspellings

Look up the following misspelled words in a dictionary to find the correct spellings. If you can, use an electronic or computer dictionary for three of them. Write down the correct spelling next to each word and where you found it (book, computer, or electronic dictionary).

assend (to climb upwards)

bankrupped (having no money)

filanthropist (someone who gives to charities)

rationnaly (reasonably)

gord (like a squash or pumpkin)

cresent (shape of a partial moon)

seperate (to keep apart)

perpatrator (someone who commits a crime)

Using the Dictionary to Find Word Meanings

Imagine that you're unsure just what *recapture* means in the Frank quote. You want to find the meaning in the dictionary.

> I can shake off everything if I write; my sorrows disappear, my courage is re-born. But, and that is the great question, will I ever be able to write anything great, will I ever become a journalist or a writer? I hope so, oh, I hope so very much, for I can recapture everything when I write, my thoughts, my ideals, and my fantasies.
>
> —Anne Frank (1929–1945)
> diary entry 4/4/44, Diary of a Young Girl

The dictionary says,

transitive verb

re•cap•ture (rē-kap′chər) *tr.v.* -tured, -turing, -tures. **1.** To capture again; retake or recover. **2.** To recall: *an attempt to recapture the past.* **3.** To ac-quire by the government procedure of recapture.

noun

—n. **1.a.** The act of recapturing. **b.** The condition of being recaptured. **2.** In-

ternational Law. The retaking of booty or goods. **3.** Anything recaptured. **4.** The lawful taking by a government of a fixed amount of the profits of a public-service corporation in excess of a stipulated rate of return.

When you look at a dictionary entry, you can't just pick any part of the entry and apply that information to the word and sentence you are interested in. *Recapture*, for example, can be a transitive verb or a noun. The *tr.v.* and the *–n.* tell us that. You have to figure out how the word you want to define is being used. In the quote above, *recapture* is being used as a verb, so you should pay attention to the first three definitions. The first definition seems to suggest that someone is actually taking some object back. That doesn't really fit what Frank is saying. The second definition, however, seems perfect because Frank is discussing *thoughts, ideals, and fantasies.* According to this definition, writing helps her recall, remember, and recapture things from the past.

So, remember that when you are looking up a word for meaning, look carefully at the other words in the sentence and surrounding sentences. These other words are the context that you must study so that you can choose the right definition in the dictionary.

Activity

Finding Meanings in the Dictionary

Find definitions for the eight words in italics in the following reading. This is part of the introductory section to Marie Winn's essay "The Trouble with Television." Make sure that the definitions you write down fit how the words are used in this *context.*

1 Of all the wonders of modern technology that have *transformed* family life during the last century, television stands alone as a universal source of parental *anxiety.* Few parents worry about how the electric light or the automobile or the telephone might *alter* their children's development. But most parents do worry about TV.

2   Parents worry most of all about the programs their children watch. If only these weren't so violent, so sexually *explicit,* so *cynical,* so unsuitable, if only they were more innocent, more educational, more worthwhile.

3   Imagine what would happen if suddenly, by some miracle, the only programs available on all channels at all hours of day and night were delightful, worthwhile shows that children love and parents

wholeheartedly approve. Would this eliminate the nagging anxiety about television that troubles so many parents today?

4   For most families, the answer is no. After all, if programs were the only problem, there would be an obvious solution: turn the set off. The fact that parents leave the sets on even when they are *distressed* about programs reveals that television serves a number of purposes that have nothing to do with the programs on the screen.

5   Great numbers of parents today see television as a way to make child-drearing less *burdensome*. In the absence of Mother's Helper (a widely used nineteenth-century patent medicine that contained a hefty dose of the *narcotic* laudanum), there is nothing that keeps children out of trouble as reliably as "plugging them in."

Using the Dictionary to Find Verb Forms

I can shake off everything if I write; my sorrows disappear, my courage is reborn. But, and that is the great question, will I ever be able to write anything great, will I ever become a journalist or a writer? I hope so, oh, I hope so very much, for I can recapture everything when I write, my thoughts, my ideals, and my fantasies.

—Anne Frank (1929–1945)
diary entry 4/4/44, Diary of a Young Girl

Assume that you are writing an essay, and you want to relate your own experiences to what Anne Frank says in her diary entry. You like the way she says, "I can shake off everything if I write." You want to say, "I too have shaked (?) off troubles when I write." The problem is that you're not sure if *shaked* is the right form of the verb. Dictionary entries list verb forms so that you can easily find information like this.

The dictionary says,

shake (shāk) *v.* **shook** (sho͝ok), **shak•en** (shākən), **shak•ing, shakes.** –*tr.* **1.** To cause to move. . .

Dictionaries generally follow the same format. With an irregular verb like *shake*, a dictionary will first give its *base form* (**shake**), then its *past tense form* (**shook**), then its *have form* or *past participle form* (**shaken**), then (sometimes) its *present participle form* (**shaking**), and (sometimes) its *-s form* (**shakes**).

You can now see that the sentence is incorrect: "I too have shaked(?) off troubles when I write." The dictionary says that after the helping verb *have* you should use *shaken*. The correct sentence would read: "I too have shaken off troubles when I write."

Activity

Verb Forms in the Dictionary

Look up the following irregular verbs in the dictionary and make a chart that shows their base form, past tense form, and have form. (*Note:* With some irregular verbs, the past tense and the have form are the same. For example, *lose*—base form, *lost*—past tense form, and *lost*—have form.)

1.	arise	6.	hold
2.	bid	7.	keep
3.	burst	8.	leave
4.	forget	9.	prove
5.	hide	10.	slide

For a discussion of irregular verbs and a list of the most common irregular verbs, see pages 496–504.

Using the Dictionary to Find Other Forms of a Word

> I can shake off everything if I write; my sorrows disappear, my courage is re-born. But, and that is the great question, will I ever be able to write anything great, will I ever become a journalist or a writer? I hope so, oh, I hope so very much, for I can recapture everything when I write, my thoughts, my ideals, and my fantasies.
>
> —*Anne Frank (1929–1945)*
> *diary entry 4/4/44*, Diary of a Young Girl

One effective way to improve your vocabulary is to pay attention to the different forms a word can take. If, for example, you added the word *ideal* (from the Frank quote) to your vocabulary notebook, you might notice in the dictionary all the words listed before and after *ideal*: *idea, idealism, idealist, idealistic, ideality,* and *ideally.* Being aware of and studying word forms is key to communicating clearly, and your dictionary can help you.

Consider the following sentences where writers have used the wrong form of a word:

1. He is headed down a *destructional* way.

2. People are judged by what they *product* on the job.

3. He works without *supervise.*

(*from* Errors and Expectations, *Mina Shaughnessey*)

In sentence 1, the writer needs an adjective to describe *way.* In sentence 2, the writer needs a verb for the subject *they.* In sentence 3 the writer needs a noun to follow *without.*

These writers may have sensed that they weren't using the correct form of the word they wanted. When a writer knows or thinks that she has used the wrong form of a word, the dictionary is a perfect resource.

Activities

Correcting Word Forms

In the dictionary, look up the misused words in 1–3 on the previous page and list the different forms you find. Choose the correct forms for sentences 1–3 and rewrite the sentences.

Studying Word Forms

Write down the definitions of words 1–5 that follow and the different forms you find in the dictionary. Write down what part of speech each form represents: *n.* (noun), *v.* (verb), *adj.* (adjective), or *adv.* (adverb). Make sure that the new words you write down connect at least loosely in meaning to the word you look up.

> *Example:*
> a. organize:

- *organize (verb) to put together in an orderly fashion*

- *organizer (noun)* [found at the end of the entry defining *organize*]

- *organization (noun)*

(But don't include *organist.* It looks similar, but doesn't connect in meaning.)

1. illusive:

2. glorify:

3. simplify:

4. violent:

5. empathy:

BUILDING YOUR VOCABULARY

Writing, reading, and critical thinking grow more interesting, more complex, and more rewarding as your vocabulary grows. With a larger vocabulary, you'll do all of the following:

- Understand your readings more easily and more completely.

- Express your own thoughts more clearly and accurately.

- Think through complex concepts defined with difficult vocabulary more easily.

In this subsection, you'll study the steps to building a better vocabulary.

Read and Recognize Vocabulary Choices

The first step in working on your vocabulary is to read as much as you can. This is the most natural (and painless) way to improve your vocabulary. If you don't currently read much, begin by reading materials that seem easy and interesting to you. Make reading a regular part of your day. Periodically, push yourself to read something different or something that seems more difficult. This way you'll be exposed to a larger variety of words.

Enjoying what you read is key to improving your vocabulary because if you don't relax and enjoy, you probably won't read much. You should also get into the habit of recognizing the choices writers make when selecting their words. Writers want their writing to be clear and compelling, and, fortunately, the English language offers many word choices.

Consider what it would be like if we only had "good" and "bad" as our adjectives. ("Dinner was good. The band was bad. The dancing was bad. The dessert was good.") Not only would our language be repetitive, but we also would be incredibly limited in the feelings and information that we could communicate to others.

John Krakauer, author of *Into Thin Air*, demonstrates in the following paragraph the powerful results of making good vocabulary choices. He is describing how exhausted he was when he reached the top of Mount Everest and, consequently, how he couldn't quite appreciate the moment.

> Straddling the top of the world, one foot in China and the other in Nepal, I cleared the ice from my oxygen mask, hunched a shoulder against the wind, and stared absently down at the vastness of Tibet. I understood on some dim, detached level that the sweep of the earth beneath my feet was a spectacular sight. I'd been fantasizing about this moment, and the release of emotion that would accompany it, for many months. But now that I was finally here, actually standing on the summit of Mount Everest, I just couldn't summon the energy to care.

Instead of saying "standing at the summit," he says, "Straddling the top of the world, one foot in China and the other in Nepal." The image he paints with these words is clearer and more interesting. Instead of saying he "looked down into Tibet," he says he "stared absently down at the vastness of Tibet." With these words, we get a better sense of the incredible sight in front of him and, importantly, his inability at that time to really appreciate the view.

By noticing other writers' choices, you will deepen your understanding of how certain words are used, and you will become more aware of the choices you make in your own writing. You will begin to see opportunities to clarify your thoughts through your choice of vocabulary words.

Defining Words Through Context Clues

Of course, recognizing and admiring the choices other writers make is just the first step in building your vocabulary. The next step is for you to learn new words as you read, and contrary to what you might think, going to the dictionary is not the first step to understanding unfamiliar words.

It is important to be able to figure out the meanings of unfamiliar words by considering the *context* in which they appear. This means that you should consider the entire sentence and nearby sentences when trying to figure out the meaning of a word. Other words and other sentences will often give you clues as to what the unfamiliar word means. Doing this well will save you time—since you won't have to reach for the dictionary so often—and you are more likely to develop a deeper understanding of the word in question by studying how it is used.

For example, the word *banal* in the following paragraph might be unfamiliar to you. Read the entire paragraph, highlight the word *banal*, and study the rest of the paragraph for clues to the meaning of *banal*.

> [Krakauer has just reached the summit of Everest and has realized he is out of bottled oxygen; he is worried about how he will make it down the mountain with no extra oxygen.] I removed my now useless [oxygen] mask, planted my ice ax into the mountain's frozen hide, and hunkered on the ridge. As I exchanged banal congratulations with the climbers filing past, inwardly I was frantic: "Hurry it up, hurry it up!" I silently pleaded. "While you guys are [goofing around] here, I'm losing brain cells by the millions!"

Krakauer tells us clearly that he is frightened about what will happen to him. He is "frantic," "pleading," yelling at people in his mind. What kind of congratulations would he offer other people when he is feeling this way? Well, he wouldn't be offering sincere, joyful congratulations. He would probably be saying what was expected without really feeling the happy emotions. *Banal* is an adjective you can use to describe something unoriginal, worn-out, and flat.

Activity

Context Clues in Textbooks

Find a reading in this textbook that you have not read yet that has at least three words you are unfamiliar with. Read the entire selection. Write down the words that are unfamiliar to you, the context clues you find for each word, and the meanings you figure out on your own. (Also, write down the name of the reading, page numbers, and paragraph numbers.) Then compare your definitions to the dictionary definitions.

Keeping a Vocabulary Notebook

Whether you are confident that you have figured out what a word means through context clues or whether you have used a dictionary, the next step is to record the new word and information about the new word. Simply writing down information helps you remember it. Then referring back to and studying what you have written brings you even closer to the point at which these new words will become a part of your everyday vocabulary. (Be sure to enter in your notebook all unfamiliar words you come across in *all* of your classes—not just your English class.)

An entry in your vocabulary notebook should look like this:

demure (from *Into Thin Air*) ———————————————— vocabulary word

"Demure and reserved, the forty-seven-year-old Namba was forty minutes away from becoming the oldest woman to climb ——— sentence it showed up in Everest. . . "

I think it means quiet. ———————————————— meaning in context

It is an adjective.
Pronunciation: di•myoor′
Other forms of the word: demurely (adverb), ——— information from dictionary
demureness (noun)
Definition: Sedate in manner or behavior; reserved, shy

Notes   **Activity**

> **Vocabulary Notebook**
>
> Go back to the activity on page 461 where you selected words out of a reading in this textbook. Put those words into your vocabulary notebook. Be prepared to share your work with your instructor and classmates.

Writing out all this information will help you learn new words, but don't stop there. You must actually *use your notebook*. Study the words you enter in your notebook. Study words while brushing your teeth, riding the bus, ironing clothes, and so on. Quiz classmates.

Also, take a chance now and then and *use your new words* when you speak and write. The words might feel a little awkward at first, but you must use them to make them a permanent part of your vocabulary.

Special ESL Vocabulary Concerns

If English is not your first language, then you may have special vocabulary concerns. Consider the following suggestions:

A. Read and write in English as often as possible. Of course, you'll have required work in college, but you should also read for pleasure in English. Find a magazine or novel that interests you and read. Begin keeping a journal in English. You can write about what happens during your days; you could focus on your school experiences; you could write about what you're reading for pleasure. A journal simply gives you another opportunity to use your English.

B. Speak English as often as possible. Join study groups at your college. Work with an English-speaking tutor.

C. Listen to English. Television is helpful for this, but an even better choice is to listen to books on tape. You can rent these from libraries and video stores or purchase them at bookstores. Sometimes you can find unabridged novels on tape, and you can then read while also listening to the tape.

Here are some suggestions for audio books:

- *Into Thin Air: A Personal Account of the Mount Everest Disaster* by Jon Krakauer
- *To Kill a Mockingbird* by Harper Lee (story about race relations in the South, a young girl growing up, and the trial of a black man)

- *A Night to Remember* by Walter Lord (sinking of the *Titanic*)
- *Wouldn't Take Nothing for My Journey Now* by Maya Angelou (Angelou reflects on some of the lessons she has learned in her life.)

Note: Most contemporary best-sellers are on audiotape. (See books by Stephen King, John Grisham, and so on.)

D. Keep an idiom notebook. There are many English idioms, and the only way to learn them is by memorization since rules don't apply.

An **idiom** is an expression that may not make sense if you translate it directly word by word. Here are some sample idiom notebook entries.

kicked the bucket: died

got up on the wrong side of the bed: woke up in a bad mood

caught a movie: watched a movie

caught a bus or *took a bus:* rode a bus

dumped that class or *dumped that girl (or boy):* stopped attending that class or stopped dating that girl (or boy)

tie the knot: marry

SPELLING MATTERS

Developing spelling skills is an important part of your progress as a student, writer, and employee because often your writing meets people before you do.

- You may send a resumé or letter of inquiry about a job.
- You may fill out an application for college admission.
- You may communicate through letters or e-mail.

First impressions are important. Whether you think it's fair or not, you may be judged in the business world and in college by the number of spelling errors appearing in your writing because many see the ability to spell as an indication of intelligence and literacy.

In the age of computers and spell check, employers and professors consider spelling errors avoidable and unacceptable. In the business world, misspellings detract from the overall quality of an employee's work and could cost the company a client or business opportunity. In college, misspellings could result in a student receiving a lower score on an essay or project.

The fact is that many people struggle with spelling and dread the thought of memorizing endless lists of spelling words in order to improve. However, there are some strategies that you can learn and practice to improve your skills and reduce the number of spelling errors.

This section offers a combination of explanation and action strategies to help you strengthen your spelling skills:

- You'll discover why spelling errors occur.
- You'll learn some practical strategies for overcoming individual spelling issues.
- You'll review the spelling of plurals, verbs, and homophones.
- You'll learn when to use the apostrophe.

As you begin this section, it's important to recognize that spelling difficulties are unique to the individual. There is no one-size-fits-all solution, but there are some basic things that you can do to help yourself become a more accurate speller.

Understanding Spelling

English is a language that has been evolving over centuries. As written English developed, people were fairly relaxed when it came to spelling and simply spelled words according to sound. However, spelling according to pronunciation posed a communication problem, since the pronunciation of words varied from region to region. As the language evolved, some people began to fear that words would lose their connection to sounds.

By the late eighteenth century, Benjamin Franklin and others had begun to lobby for a standardized and more simplified system of spelling. Today, many still believe that spelling should be simplified. But for now, here are some basic facts that help explain why spelling can be difficult:

- In English, a single sound may be spelled in several different ways. For example, examine the different spellings of the sound *sh* in *shell, sugar, ration, anxious, occasion, pressure,* and *champagne.*
- Some letters in English are silent in certain situations. Think about the silent *k* in *k*nife as opposed to the spoken *k* in *k*ite, or the *p* in *p*neumonia as opposed to *p*arty.
- Spelling in English is less consistent than in some other languages, such as Spanish, in which letters and sounds are often matched.

- English contains many words that sound alike but have different spellings and meanings. Consider the difference in meaning between *here* and *hear*, or *to*, *too*, and *two*.
- English is a blend of many languages, which helps explain why our spelling system is inexact.

Even though English contains some irregular spellings, you should also know that most English spellings follow basic, rational patterns or "rules." Only a few vary completely from the patterns and must therefore be memorized.

Why Spelling Errors Occur

As you've seen, there are some reasons why spelling can be difficult in general. However, there are also reasons why spelling may be difficult for the individual.

- Those with less reading experience may have trouble recognizing misspellings in their own writing.
- Those with less writing experience may sometimes scramble letters within a word.
- Those with less experience speaking English or those who do not fully pronounce words may find it difficult to spell by sound.
- Those who don't know how to break words into syllables or form word variations (such as plurals or verb tenses) may make spelling errors that otherwise could be avoided.

Overcoming Spelling Problems

Although it may seem too easy to suggest that by writing, reading, and speaking more, your spelling will improve, the fact is that it will. Just as reading skills improve as you read more and writing skills improve as you write more, your spelling will improve as you read and write. But there are many other things you can also do to develop your spelling skills.

The Spelling Log   Perhaps one of the easiest ways to help yourself become a better speller is to carry a small 3" x 5" spiral notebook with you. In it, you would keep a list of problem words—words that cause *you* trouble—spelled correctly. When faced with a situation in

Notes

which you must write, you would have your personal spelling list with you. Of course, you would add to this list as you begin to be more aware of your spelling and the kinds of spelling errors you're making consistently.

- While editing essays in a workshop, a classmate finds a misspelling (not a typo) in your essay. You would add it to your list.

- When you receive your essay back from your instructor, you would check for any misspellings your instructor found and then add them to your list.

- As you're reading, you notice a word that you realize you've been misspelling. You would add it to your list.

Keeping a personal spelling list means that you're taking responsibility for your spelling and becoming more aware of your own repeated spelling errors.

Spell Check   Most computer writing programs today come with spell check, a program that identifies possible misspellings in papers and documents. Basically, spell check works by searching the computer's dictionary and highlighting any words that don't appear in the dictionary. In most cases, when spell check highlights a word, it will offer a list of suggested spellings. It's likely that the correctly spelled word is in that list. If so, you only need to select the correct spelling, and the program will replace the incorrect spelling in the paper. Spell check also identifies possible capitalization errors and repeated words errors. You should use spell check whenever you write on a computer, especially during the editing stage of the writing process. If your spelling skills are particularly weak, you should type out all of your homework on a computer (in addition to your essays) and then use spell check before turning it in. (There are many variations of spell check. If you're working in a computer lab, ask the computer technician to show you how to use it the first time.)

Spell check does have a few drawbacks, however. When a misspelling is highlighted, and you've been given a list of suggested spellings, don't assume the correct spelling for the word will always be on the list. It may not be. If it isn't, you'll need to go to the dictionary to find that word. Also, spell check will not catch words that sound alike but have different meanings (such as *to, too,* and *two*). If

Notes

you're trying to decide between using *hear* or *here,* for instance, go to the dictionary or to "Using the Right Word" in Section VI of this text and look up the meanings of the words. Finally, spell check won't identify errors in proper names and places, so when editing your paper, be sure to check these spellings yourself.

The Dictionary   The dictionary is an invaluable spelling tool. Not only does the dictionary give you the spelling of a word, but it also offers the plural of nouns, and, for verbs, the basic tenses. When in doubt about how to spell a word, you can always look it up in the dictionary.

But how do you look up a word if you don't know how to spell it? Usually you do so through trial and error, looking up the word by pronunciation and then trying slightly different variations of spelling until you find the word. If you find looking up words in the dictionary nearly impossible, however, you might benefit from a misspeller's dictionary.

The Misspeller's Dictionary   A misspeller's dictionary contains two columns of words: one column lists words as they are typically misspelled and a corresponding column lists the same words spelled correctly. For instance, in such a dictionary, you might see the following entries:

Incorrect	Correct
eco	echo
eightteen	eighteen

Often this type of dictionary also contains a section on **homophones** (words that sound alike but have different meanings) and their meanings, such as *find* (locate) and *fined* (given a penalty).

The Spelling List   Another speller's tool is a pocket-size spelling list. In it, words have been broken into syllables so that they're easier to look up according to pronunciation:

bi•og•ra•phy   re•cant   ty•po

Such spelling lists include the correct spellings for the most commonly misspelled words.

Both the misspeller's dictionary and the spelling list are light and small enough to carry with you everywhere.

A Review

The spelling log, spell check, dictionary, and misspeller's dictionary will certainly help you cut down on the number of spelling errors in your writing. But there are a few areas of spelling that students find particularly troublesome. In this subsection, we'll review the spellings of plurals, the past-tense form and have form of verbs, homophones, contractions, and possessives.

Plurals   Change a noun from singular to plural according to the following rules:

- To form the plural of most nouns, add *s* to the word: tree to trees, action to action*s*.

- To form the plural for nouns ending in *s, ss, sh, ch, x,* and *z* (a hissing sound called a **sibilant** sound), add *es* to the word: church to church*es*, hush to hush*es*, box to box*es*, kiss to kiss*es*.

- To form the plural for nouns ending in *o*, add *s* or *es* to the word, depending on the word: hero to hero*es*, stereo to stereo*s*. (*Note:* Since some of the words ending in *o* are followed by *s* and some are followed by *es*, you should look them up in the dictionary when you're uncertain.)

- To form the plural of a noun that ends in *y* when preceded by a vowel, add *s*: toy to toy*s*, monkey to monkey*s*.

- To form the plural of a noun that ends in *y* when preceded by a consonant, change the *y* to *i* and add *es*: party to part*ies*, rally to rall*ies*.

Not all plurals are formed by adding *s* or *es*. Some words are adopted from other languages and keep their original plural spellings. Others are simply irregular plurals, exceptions to the rules mentioned above. Here are a few examples:

Singular	Plural
analysis	analyses
child	children
criterion	criteria
datum	data
foot	feet
goose	geese

Singular	Plural
man	men
medium	media
moose	moose
mouse	mice
tooth	teeth
woman	women

When in doubt about forming a plural, look up the singular form of the word in the dictionary. You'll find the plural form of the word listed after the singular form.

Verb Tense   The past-tense form and the have form of verbs pose spelling problems for students only when these forms are irregular. In most cases, the past-tense form and have form are easy to spell. Simply add *ed* to the end of the base form or add just *d* if the base form ends in *e*.

Examples of regular verbs:

Base	Past	Have
generate	generated	generated
talk	talked	talked

Examples of irregular verbs:

Base	Past	Have
drive	drove	driven
sing	sang	sung

When you have questions about verb forms, you can look up the base form in the dictionary. After the base form, you'll find the past-tense form, the have form, and finally the *-ing* form. (If the past-tense form and have form are the same, the dictionary will list that form once.) Or you can check the "Irregular Verb Form Chart" on pages 499–500 of the text for spellings of the most common irregular verbs.

Homophones   **Homophones** are words that sound alike but are spelled differently and have different meanings. Homophones cause problems for students who may believe they're spelling words correctly when, in fact, they're spelling the *wrong* words correctly. This is another instance in which your dictionary is an invaluable tool. When in doubt about which spelling to use, look it up. Another resource in this text is "The Right Word" on page 534, which contains a listing of words that are often confused such as *to, too,* and *two. (To* means toward a

Notes

particular direction: *I traveled to Paris to see the Mona Lisa. Too* means also: *My husband went, too. Two* is the number: *We discovered two can travel for the price of one.)*

Apostrophe   The **apostrophe** is used in two very different ways in English. It's used to form possessives—my *daughter's* new car—and contractions—she *can't* drive yet. Because the apostrophe is used in such different ways, students are often confused by when and how to use the apostrophe. We'll examine both uses.

Contractions   A **contraction** is a word with an apostrophe in it. The apostrophe indicates where letters have been left out.

*   it + is = it's
*   had + not = hadn't
*   she + would = she'd

Notice that *it's* is a contraction of the words *it* and *is*. Also note that the apostrophe shows where a letter has been left out. In the second example, *hadn't* is a contraction of the words *had* and *not*. In this case, too, the apostrophe shows where a letter is missing. And the apostrophe in *she'd* is a contraction of *she* and *would*. The apostrophe shows where several letters have been left out. *In a contraction, the apostrophe indicates where a letter or letters have been left out.*

Activity

Practice in Forming and Using Contractions

Change the following word combinations into contractions. Look up any you're unsure of in your dictionary.

1. he + would =_____

2. what + is =_____

3. can + not =_____

4. will + not =_____

5. should + have =_____

6. I + have =_____

7. you + are =_____

8. do + not =_____

9. it + will =_____

10. we + are =_____

Now write four or five sentences that use all of the contractions you've just formed. (You can use more than one contraction in each sentence.)

Possessives A **possessive** is a word that shows ownership. In this sub-section, you'll learn to form the possessives of nouns and pronouns. In addition, you'll learn the special rules that apply when forming the possessive of proper nouns.

Forming the Possessive of Nouns
To form the possessive of a singular noun, use an apostrophe + *s.*

- The student's goal is to become a doctor.
- My puppy's tail wags whenever I pet her.

To form the possessive of a plural noun, just add an apostrophe.

- The students' desks are arranged in a circle.
- The ladies' lunches were delivered late.

Note: Irregular plurals (those not ending in s) require an apostrophe + *s.*

- The children's toys were scattered across the day care floor.
- The men's volleyball team challenged the women's volleyball team to a game.

Forming the Possessive of Proper Nouns
To form the possessive of a **proper noun** (a specific name or title), use an apostrophe + *s.*

- Eminem's new hit reached the top of the charts.
- Presidents Bush's State of the Union Address was telecast on all major networks.
- Jennifer Lopez's new film will be out next week.
- Ed Harris's Oscar nomination brought him lots of attention.

Notes

Activity

Practice Forming Possessives

Change the following nouns into possessives:

1. lady to_____

2. ladies to_____

3. man to_____

4. men to_____

5. child to_____

6. children to_____

7. actress to_____

8. actor to_____

9. twins to_____

10. instructors to_____

Change the following proper nouns into possessives:

11. Joie to _____

12. Hopkins to _____

13. Miles to _____

14. Inez to _____

15. Cruiz to _____

16. Lewis to _____

17. Olts to _____

18. Jones to _____

19. Thomas to _____

Once you've formed the possessive of each noun, use five of the newly formed possessives in two or three sentences.

Forming Possessive Pronouns

There are two basic types of pronouns: personal and indefinite. **Personal pronouns** (which refer to specific persons, places, or things) *do not need* apostrophes to show ownership, but **indefinite pronouns** (which refer to nonspecific persons or things) *do need* apostrophes to indicate ownership.

- Personal pronouns *do not need* apostrophes to show possession. They include *hers, his, its, mine, ours, theirs,* and *yours.* Consider this sentence: Samantha earned *her* degree. Because *her* is a personal pronoun, no apostrophe is necessary.

- Indefinite pronouns *do need* apostrophes to show possession. Add *'s* to indefinite pronouns when showing possession: *anybody's, anyone's, each's, everybody's, nobody's,* and *somebody's.* Study this sentence: *It was anybody's game.* Because *anybody* is an indefinite pronoun, an *'s* must be added to show possession.

Activity

Practice Using Personal and Indefinite Pronouns

Write five sentences that include personal pronouns (no apostrophes) and five that include indefinite pronouns (with apostrophes) that show possession.

READING ALOUD: A TRICK OF THE TRADE

Most professional writers routinely read their own writing aloud. They know that reading aloud will help them identify weaknesses in their writing.

Here is a writing scenario that might be familiar to you:

A student works hard on her essay. She follows all the process steps. The student is proud of the final version of her essay: it is interesting, thoughtful, carefully created. The student takes the time to proofread and is sure that the essay is nearly perfect.

The instructor reads the essay and appreciates the thoughtful meaning in the essay. The instructor responds to the ideas and offers suggestions about how to keep improving writing skills. The instructor sees places where the student needs more information and needs to delete or move information. The instructor also notes <u>many</u> spelling, grammatical, and typographical errors.

The student appreciates the instructor's writing suggestions, and wonders why she didn't see those spots that clearly need some improvement. And the student is shocked at the number of minor errors in what she thought was a perfect paper. How did the student miss all those spelling, grammar, and typing errors?! The student feels discouraged.

Notes

This scenario is fairly common. Sometimes writers are surprised that they didn't see the weak spots in their papers. Mostly, this is a normal part of acquiring good writing skills, but it can also be a sign that the writer hasn't been able to see her paper objectively.

Now, the mechanical errors (spelling, typing, and grammar errors) may seem minor, but they can confuse the reader, and they certainly ruin a professional image.

Being a good reviser and proofreader takes time and practice. The more you read and write, the better you will get, provided you don't rely on a tutor or friend to do your revising or proofreading work for you. However, there are a few ways to acquire good revising and proofreading skills *more quickly*. One method is to *read aloud*.

Reading Aloud Helps When You Revise

Students at California State University, Sacramento, were required one semester to read all of their essays aloud into tape recorders. Students were amazed at all the problems and errors they found in their essays. On the tapes they would say things like, "American students don't study enough. That's why they score lower than students in other countries. Hmm . . . I bet I need some proof here." Or, "The woman murdered her husband. She is against capital punishment. Oh, that sounds funny. That doesn't flow." Reading aloud helped these students see their writing more clearly, more objectively.

There are, in fact, many benefits to reading aloud. If you read your essays aloud frequently, you will find places

- to add information,
- to delete unnecessary information, and
- where transitions must be added or information moved.

And reading aloud while writing your essay will help you get going again if you lose focus or run out of things to say. Reading aloud is a tool professional writers rely upon:

> We spoke before we wrote, historically and individually. Writing is not quite speech written down but it is speech transformed so that it may be heard. The voice lies silent within the page, ready to be turned on by a reader.
>
> We know our language best by hearing it and speaking it. Writing is an oral/aural act and we do well to edit out loud, hearing the text as we revise and polish it. Should we add this, slow that down, speed it up here, take time to define this term, use this word, this construction? What is traditional and

expected by the reader? What best supports and communicates the meaning of the draft? These questions can often be answered by reading the line out loud, taking something out and reading it out loud, putting something in and reading it out loud. Hand, eye, and ear, a constant interplay.

—Donald Murray, American novelist, poet,
Pulitzer Prize–winning journalist, and writing instructor

Reading Aloud Helps When You Edit

Finally, when you are proofreading (editing) your essay, read aloud frequently. Don't leave this to the last minute because you may find areas where you left out a whole sentence, or you may find minor errors that you want to fix on the computer or typewriter before handing in your work. Look for these kinds of errors:

- Misspelled words
- Missing words/sentences
- Wrong words
- Words repeated or used too often
- Punctuation errors
- Subject-verb agreement errors
- Verb tense errors
- Run-ons, comma splices, and fragments

Activity

Reading Your Own Writing Aloud

Read aloud a piece of your writing that has not yet been seen by anyone else. (Ideally, you should read a draft of an essay, but a journal or even answers to reading questions will do.) Read your writing several times. Mark any errors or problems that you see now that you hadn't seen before.

Reading Aloud Helps You Develop a Writer's "Ear"

Experienced writers, like Donald Murray, who was quoted earlier in this section, have what we call an "ear" for language. They know what *sounds* good. By reading material aloud, they can easily hear punctuation errors, awkward sentences, and weak spots in focus, development, or organization. You can improve your "ear" for language by reading good pieces of writing aloud. Here are some recommendations:

- Choose an essay out of this textbook each week and read it aloud at home.
- Participate in class when your instructor wants to read an essay aloud.
- Choose something you really like to read (a newspaper, magazine, novel, or poem) and read aloud to your spouse, significant other, or children.
- Listen to books on tape (available at video stores and libraries).

If you do some or all of these activities, you will improve your

- vocabulary,
- sense of how sentences should flow, and
- sense of how writers can focus, develop, and organize writing.

Some Final Notes About Reading Aloud

- When a piece of reading is very difficult to understand, try reading it aloud. (Students find it especially helpful to read aloud such things as famous speeches, poetry, and works by Shakespeare because these were meant to be heard.)
- Read to your children. Your "ear" for language will improve and, besides, study after study shows that reading aloud to children helps children build their vocabularies, their "ear" for language, their problem-solving skills, and so on.
- When you read aloud in private, you will be preparing yourself for those situations at school and work when you must present oral reports.
- When you read aloud, note words that you are unsure about pronouncing. Look in a dictionary and study the pronunciation information. Ask a tutor or instructor how to pronounce these words. They are bound to show up again (perhaps when you need to make an oral report).

Activity

Reading Angelou Aloud

The following reading is a chapter from Maya Angelou's *Wouldn't Take Nothing for My Journey Now.* Angelou, a poet and writer, is well-known for the "voice" in her writing. Her vocabulary and sentence structure make her meaning nearly sing off the page. Read this aloud and enjoy the power of Angelou's voice. (Her book is available on audiocassette.)

Complaining

When my grandmother was raising me in Stamps, Arkansas, she had a particular routine when people who were known to be whiners entered her store. Whenever she saw a known complainer coming, she would call me from whatever I was doing and say conspiratorially, "Sister, come inside. Come." Of course I would obey.

My grandmother would ask the customer, "How are you doing today, Brother Thomas?" And the person would reply, "Not so good." There would be a distinct whine in the voice. "Not so good today, Sister Henderson. You see, it's this summer. It's this summer heat. I just hate it. Oh, I hate it so much. It just frazzles me up and frazzles me down. I just hate the heat. It's almost killing me." Then my grandmother would stand stoically, her arms folded, and mumble, "Uh-huh, uh-huh." And she would cut her eyes at me to make certain that I had heard the lamentation.

At another time a whiner would mewl, "I hate plowing. That packed-down dirt ain't got no reasoning, and mules ain't got good sense. . . . Sure ain't. It's killing me. I can't ever seem to get done. My feet and my hands stay sore, and I get dirt in my eyes and up my nose. I just can't stand it." And my grandmother, again stoically with her arms folded, would say, "Uh-huh, uh-huh," and then look at me and nod.

As soon as the complainer was out of the store, my grandmother would call me to stand in front of her. And then she would say the same thing she had said at least a thousand times, it seemed to me. "Sister, did you hear what Brother So-and-So or Sister Much-to-Do complained about? You heard that?" And I would nod. Mamma would continue, "Sister, there are people who went to sleep all over the world last night, poor and rich and white and black, but they will never wake again. Sister, those who expected to rise did not, their beds became their cooling boards and their blankets became their winding sheets. And those dead folks would give anything, anything at all for just five minutes of this weather or ten minutes of that plowing that person was grumbling about. So you

Notes

watch yourself about complaining, Sister. What you're supposed to do when you don't like a thing is change it. If you can't change it, change the way you think about it. Don't complain."

It is said that persons have few teachable moments in their lives. Mamma seemed to have caught me at each one I had between the ages of three and thirteen. Whining is not only graceless, but can be dangerous. It can alert a brute that a victim is in the neighborhood.

USING OUTSIDE SOURCES

Introduction to Outside Sources
Using Outside Information

Citing sources can get very complicated and must be done with precision. The guidelines here will help you use outside information for the assignments in this book. Other classes may require you to learn more about citing sources, so be sure to ask your instructor about the appropriate handbook for you to use in other classes.

Introduction to Outside Sources

An **outside source** is a person or publication that supplies you with information.

Outside information is any fact or idea that someone other than you came up with.

A writer often uses information from other sources when writing her own essay, book, or article. Sometimes a writer will use something she heard on television or in a speech. Sometimes a writer will use something she read in an encyclopedia, a newspaper, a textbook, or a magazine. There are many places to get useful information.

Guidelines A–E will help you get started on using outside sources.

A. Why Writers Use Outside Sources

- A writer may hear or read something interesting and want to discuss it in more detail.
- A writer may come across an idea she disagrees with and want to argue against it.
- A writer may find information that supports something she already wants to discuss.

B. Source of the Source

Of course, a writer can't use information from just anywhere. The source of the information must be one that readers will respect. For example, a writer should use information from a reputable publication or a recognized expert. Readers might not believe information that comes from a gossip magazine, and they might not be too interested in what your neighbor down the street once dreamt about aliens from outer space. Choose your sources carefully. When doing research, keep careful notes on where you get your information from. Write down the following source information whenever possible:

Notes

> author
>
> title (of book, or title of essay or article with the title of the magazine or newspaper it appeared in)
>
> date
>
> page number
>
> volume number (when the source is a journal or encyclopedia)

C. *Quantity of Outside Sources*

You can use a little outside information or a lot of outside information, depending on what you are writing. In a cover letter for your resumé, you probably wouldn't use many (if any) outside sources. In a scientific report, you'd probably use many outside sources. Most of the college essays you write will call for *some* outside information. Here's a good general rule: outside information should play a supporting role to what you have to say. That is, your ideas should come first and take center stage. If you are ever worried about having too many pieces of outside information in your writing, highlight all information that you borrowed from an outside source. If you highlight more than a third of your essay, you probably have too much outside information and too few of your own original ideas.

D. *Where to Use Your Outside Sources*

Generally, you want to use the quotes and borrowed information in the body of a paragraph. Sometimes you can start a paragraph with a quote, but usually you need your own topic sentence. Rarely, you can put outside information at the end of a paragraph. Usually, you, as the writer, must interpret outside information. You must explain it and analyze it for the reader. Otherwise, your reader might interpret the information in ways you don't expect.

E. *The Most Important Thing to Remember About Outside Sources*

Interpret, explain, and analyze your outside information. Readers don't want a bunch of quotes. They want your well-supported ideas.

Read the following paragraph.

> I think it is important to introduce my son to real-life heroes. My son cannot learn all he needs to from the Power Rangers. Dennis Denenberg, a professor of education at Millersville University of Pennsylvania, explained this very well: "Like junk food, popular fantasy and cartoon characters are sweet, enticing to the eye—and empty of real value. Like junk food, they displace what is more important." I think it is more important for my son to learn about the courage of Har-

riet Tubman, the dedication of Albert Einstein, and the spirit of Mother Teresa. My   *Notes*
son needs to feast on the nutrients that these real-life heroes can offer.

—Talia Fields

Activity

Following the Guidelines for Citing Sources

Review guidelines A–E. Explain whether or not Fields follows each of these guidelines. Discuss each guideline and how it is or is not followed.

Using Outside Information

When you use ideas and information that belong to someone else, you must give that person credit. If you do not do this, you'll be guilty of **plagiarism.** In some cultures, it is common practice to copy the words of an expert without mentioning the expert. Such a practice stems from the idea that copying these words is the writer's way of saying, "These are better words and ideas than I could ever come up with." However, in American colleges and businesses, writers are expected to give credit to the person who first came up with the idea or information. Plagiarism can be grounds for being dismissed from a college or job, so it is important that you know how to use outside information and give credit to the person who first stated the information. Giving credit to the original sources is called **citing your sources.** (The information that follows focuses mainly on how to use quotations. However, even if you put someone else's ideas into your own words and you don't use quotation marks, you must still say where you got these ideas from.)

First, you should know that information that is considered "general knowledge" doesn't have to be cited. For example, if you are writing an essay about George Washington, and you find his birthdate in an encyclopedia, you do not have to cite this encyclopedia. Washington's birthdate can be found in many different sources: it is considered general knowledge.

However, if you want to use a piece of information that cannot be found in many different places, you must say where you got the information from.

There are many ways of incorporating a quotation into your essay. Here are five of the most common patterns. The sample quotation comes from the essay "Move Over, Barney" by Dennis Denenberg, which appears on pages 195–200. (When you introduce a quotation, put a

Notes

Remember from your prepositional phrase work that nothing in a prepositional phrase can be the subject of a sentence. So, if you begin a sentence with "in" as shown in Pattern #2, you must supply a subject after that introductory prepositional phrase. In Pattern #2, the subject is *Dennis Denenberg*.

comma after the introductory phrase and capitalize the first word in the quotation. Pattern #5 is different because of the word *that*.)

Pattern #1 (from the earlier paragraph): *Dennis Denenberg, a professor of education at Millersville University of Pennsylvania, explained this very well: "Like junk food, popular. . . . "*
[Author's name], [author information], explained:

Pattern #2: *In "Move Over, Barney" Dennis Denenberg, a professor of education, explained this very well: "Like junk food, popular . . . . "*
In [name of the article] [author's name], [author's info.], explained:

Pattern #3: *According to Dennis Denenberg, a professor at Millersville University of Pennsylvania, "Like junk food, popular . . . . "*
According to [author's name], [author's info.],
or
According to [name of article],

If the writer had already introduced Dennis Denenberg and explained his status as an expert, the writer could have just said the following:

Pattern #4: *Denenberg noted, "Like junk food, popular . . . . "*
[Author's last name] noted,

Pattern #5: *Denenberg said that "like junk food, popular . . . . "*
[Author's name] said that [no capital letters at the beginning of the quote]

Note: The first time you use a source, it is a good idea to explain who or what your source is. If your source is a person and the person is an expert, what is this person's job title? Where does he or she work? If the source is a journalist, for what magazine or newspaper does the journalist write? If you are using statistics, from what government agency or private company did you get the statistics? Your reader is more likely to trust your information with these kinds of details.

Activity

Practice in Citing Sources

1. Choose some interesting quotes from "Move Over, Barney," pages 195–200. Write five sentences showing that you can use each of the

five different quoting patterns. Be very careful that you punctuate
correctly and use capital letters when necessary.

2. Review other readings and find some other patterns for using quotes.
   (Look in the newspaper, textbooks, magazines, and so on.) Write
   down three quotes you find that have slightly different patterns than
   the five mentioned here.

WRITING IN CLASS/WRITING THE ARGUMENT

So far in this text, you have been using the writing process to develop
your writing skills in out-of-class writing assignments. But there may be
times when you will be required to write essays in class within a specified
period of time such as an hour or two. Keep in mind that timed essays
are a key component of many college courses and may be used

- to determine entrance into a particular field of study,
- to determine entrance into or exit from a writing class,
- to determine basic writing proficiency for graduation, and
- to gauge students' development as writers at various points of
  the term.

The Writing Process in Timed Situations

Although the thought of writing an entire essay in an hour or two
may make you feel uneasy, you should know that the very same
strategies you have learned and practiced this semester in your out-
of-class writing assignments will serve you in your in-class writings
as well. This subsection will teach you how to use the same process
you have practiced in your out-of-class essays in timed-writing situations in class.

Preparing to Write

In order to write well in timed situations, you must be mentally and
physically prepared for the task. You must be as well rested and relaxed as possible. It's a good idea to arrive early to class on these days.
Then you'll have a few minutes to get out paper and pen, think about
the task, and envision yourself writing. It may help to do a quick five-
minute freewrite. Any topic will do. You could freewrite on how you're
feeling about writing in class. Or if you have an idea about what the
topic might be about, you could get the juices flowing by listing ideas
or by writing on the topic in general.

Notes

Utilizing the Writing Process in In-Class Writings

When writing an out-of-class essay, writers have ample opportunity to rethink ideas, revise, and make their essays better. However, with an in-class essay, writers are required to complete their essays in a set amount of time. Because of this time limit, writers sometimes panic and make one of the worst mistakes they could make—they just start writing. Writing without a plan is like traveling in unknown territory without a map.

In order to write a successful in-class essay, a writer must read and understand the prompt, brainstorm ideas, decide what main idea to present, and list supporting points—all before writing the essay. Experienced writers have learned to set aside a portion of class for these activities. (Be careful, however, not to spend so much time on these activities that there's no time left for writing. Students should spend no more than 20–25 percent of the time on these planning activities.)

The bulk of writing time, which is anywhere from 60 to 75 percent, should be devoted to proving the main idea set up in the first few minutes of class. At this time, the writer jots down the introduction and thesis, and then begins addressing the supporting points one by one. (When a reading has been assigned, the writer should bring it to class with important points and interesting quotations highlighted for easy reference.)

The final portion of class should be devoted to revision and then to editing. Although writers don't necessarily need to rewrite their entire essays (though some students do), they should go back and revise words, phrases, and sentences. If they've written on every other line, they can easily revise by drawing a line through a sentence that doesn't work and rewriting that sentence in the blank line above. For those on computers, the revision process is much easier. They need only go back to certain spots to insert new text and delete what doesn't work.

Editing is the very last stage of the process. Writers must be sure to leave the final few minutes of time to read for errors in spelling, capitalization, sentence boundaries, and verb tense. Writers should also look carefully for their own common grammar errors. If using a computer, they should use spell check before printing their essays.

Tips for Writing the In-Class Essay

- Ask your instructor for a sample of a previous essay exam to study and practice.
- Try to anticipate the kinds of questions that might be asked.
- If you know the topic beforehand, discuss it with classmates or friends.

- Arrive early so you can mentally prepare.
- Think positive thoughts—envision yourself writing a strong essay.
- Outline, list, or freewrite on potential topics.
- Neatness counts, but don't worry too much about penmanship.
- Write on every other line to allow for changes and revision.
- If writing on computer, use spell check (if permitted) before printing your essay.

Notes

Anticipating the Writing Prompt

Even if you have no idea what the writing prompt will be, you can still prepare to write. If you are taking a content course like sociology, for instance, you could review sections of your textbook and any lecture notes you had taken. Then you would be in a better position to *anticipate* the kind of essay question your instructor might assign. If your instructor had been lecturing on dating and how technology has entered into courtship, and if she had recently assigned the class an article to read entitled, "Love Online," you might anticipate that your instructor would be assigning an essay on contemporary dating trends.

You might even complete a cluster to see what area of the topic you would be most interested in writing on.

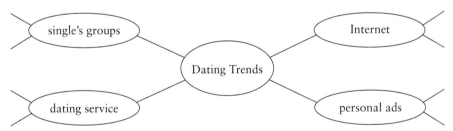

If you're in a class in which controversial issues are being discussed, you could complete a pro/con list on a topic from class:

Should High Schools Provide Students with Condoms?

Pro (For)	Con (Against)
—Yes, this would help ensure that teenagers would practice safe sex.	—No, this is the equivalent of giving teenagers permission to have sex.

It's important to do as much preparatory work as possible before an in-class essay. If you have read and done some brainstorming ahead of time, you'll feel much more confident about the in-class writing experience.

Notes   And even if you haven't been given a reading and don't have an idea of what the writing topic will be, remember that you can still "warm up" by brainstorming, summarizing chapters, studying your notes, and anticipating essay questions.

Activity

Warm-Up Topics

If you have no idea what the writing prompt will be, you can still practice your brainstorming and writing skills before the day of the in-class writing. Here are a few topics to practice on:

- Your favorite or most interesting class
- Your hero
- The best or worst job you ever had
- Your view on gun control
- Your first love
- Your view on living together before marriage
- Your favorite hobby
- Your view on censoring music lyrics
- The best or worst lesson you learned
- Your view on children's TV
- Your view on whether or not the United States should reinstate the draft
- Your view on whether or not grade school children should have Internet access at home (or at school)
- Your view on metal detectors in grade schools
- Your view on a current controversial issue

Understanding the Writing Prompt

Once you're in class and the writing prompt has been handed out, your most important task begins. In the first few minutes of class, you must read and break down the prompt to make sure that you understand it so that you can address its parts.

This first prompt has not been connected to an outside reading, so students would receive this topic "cold" on the day they write.

Write about what you see as one of the most serious problems in your city or state today. First, explain the problem. Then, discuss what you think can and should be done to try to solve it.

Breaking it down:

- Note the opening general statement. Students are being asked to write about "one of the most serious problems in your city or state today." (Notice *one*, not two or three; *today*, not yesterday; and *your city or state*, not the entire country.)

- That general statement is followed by two steps. The first asks students to *explain* or define one of the most serious problems.

- Students are then asked to *discuss* what they think *can* and *should* be done to solve the problem. In other words, they are being asked for a solution to the problem.

In the next prompt, students have been given a cartoon to consider and then analyze in an essay.

Prompt: Write an essay in response to the comic strip, "Why Johnny Can't Read."

For this prompt, students haven't been given much in the way of direction. What they have been told is to "write an essay in *response* to the comic strip," which means that students are expected to offer their opinions (agreeing or disagreeing with the comic strip's message).

- Before beginning to write, students should carefully consider the title of the piece, the picture, and the artist's message.

Notes
- They should also brainstorm (listing ideas or writing down their reactions to the cartoon), focus on the most important issue or idea they see, and then develop a thesis *before* writing.

- In developing the body of the essay, students should draw support from their own observations or experiences with television. Students should also refer to any articles about television they might have read.

Utilizing the Reading Process in In-Class Writings

Sometimes your instructor will give out a reading ahead of time and will expect you to come to the next class prepared to write about an issue raised in the reading. If this is the case, then you would read the piece as soon as possible so that you would have time to reread, think, and talk about the reading. You would be wise to practice your reading process and summary skills in preparation for writing.

Let's say that your instructor announces that you'll be writing an in-class essay during your next class period. She then assigns "The Most Precious Gift" by Hank Whittemore, which appears on pages 390–394, and she tells you to be prepared to write about the ideas expressed in the article. How would you prepare for such a writing task?

Well, first, you would follow the PARTS of the reading process (pages 80–81) to make sure that you understand the article. You would preview the article first, looking at the title, publication information, and main ideas. Next you would read quickly, anticipating what should come next, highlighting key terms and ideas, but not looking up any words yet. Then you would reread the article more slowly, looking up unfamiliar terms and making notes in the "Notes" column so that you would remember the main ideas. You would respond to the reading questions, too, which would give you a bit of practice writing about various aspects of the article. You would think about and discuss the reading and the ideas in the reading with classmates, friends, or family members. And, finally, you would write a summary of the piece, restating the most important points in your own words. By this point, you would know the article very well, so well in fact that you would probably have some strong opinions to express on the topic.

Activity

Preparing to Write

1. You're preparing to write an essay in your next class on a topic taken from "The Most Precious Gift," by Hank Whittemore, pages 390–394. Follow the reading process as you read the article.
2. Summarize the article.
3. Finally, take time to anticipate what the essay prompt might be about. Brainstorm ideas for possible prompts.

When reading a prompt, look for *key words* that indicate a certain kind of approach:

- If you see *take a position, take a stand,* or *argue for or against,* then you can be sure you're supposed to be persuading an audience to believe as you do about an issue.

- If you see *examine the sides* or *discuss,* you're being asked to provide a more balanced view of both sides of the issue.

- If you see *explain, describe,* or *define,* you're being asked to help your reader see and understand through your explanation.

Activities

Analyzing the Prompt

An in-class writing prompt for "The Most Precious Gift" follows. Your job is to analyze and then paraphrase the prompt.

> In the article "The Most Precious Gift," Hank Whittemore describes the incredible journey that comprises Robert Allen's life. Whittemore also focuses on reading as a life-sustaining source for Allen.
>
> *Write an essay in which you discuss the importance of reading in Robert Allen's life. Then examine the degree to which you believe reading has had the same transforming power in your own life. (It might help to imagine what your own life would be like if you were unable to read. How would being illiterate affect your ability to get a decent job, attend school, or achieve your life goals?) Support your discussion with evidence from the reading and from your own experiences and personal observations.*

Writing the In-Class Essay

Set aside a two-hour period to write an essay on the prompt for "The Most Precious Gift." Be sure to divide your time wisely so that you have time for prewriting, writing, revising, and editing.

Writing the Argumentative Essay in Class

Argument is an important part of many of the discussions you'll engage in as college students. When you argue, you try to persuade an audience to believe as you do about a cause, an issue, or an idea. Handling an argument in an essay can be tricky. On the one hand, you need to get across your point of view. On the other hand, you need to represent the opposition fairly without canceling out your own arguments. So how do you accomplish such a feat in a timed writing situation? In this section, you'll learn the strategies for writing an effective argument in class. But first you'll examine the essential elements of an argument.

In the Argumentative Essay

- The writer establishes a clear position on the issue.
- The writer presents the opposing view fairly. The writer doesn't ignore the opposing view but presents it, then tries to refute it (argue against it). (The writer who doesn't mention the opposing view has written a one-sided argument.)
- The writer supports his or her own position with evidence in the form of facts, examples, or experience.

The Writer Takes a Stand   When you've been given a writing prompt that asks you to argue an issue, you've been given a very specific task—take a position and prove your point. Consider the following writing prompts:

- Argue for or against testing college athletes for drug use.
- Argue for or against raising the national smoking age to 21.
- Argue for or against condoms being distributed to students at local middle schools and high schools.
- Argue for or against stricter handgun regulations.
- Argue for or against mothers nursing their babies in public.
- Argue for or against spanking as an effective method of discipline for children.
- Argue for or against children being required to wear uniforms at school.
- Argue for or against censorship of pornography on the Internet.
- Argue for or against mandatory military service for both males and females.

- Argue for or against continuing the NASA space program.
- Argue for or against legalization of marijuana for medical use.
- Argue for or against [add your own issue].

Before you could take a position on any of these topics, you would need to spend some time brainstorming. The pro/con list is an excellent tool for brainstorming argumentative topics.

Should College Athletes Be Drug Tested?	
Pro (For) —Yes, college athletes should be tested because they represent the school.	*Con (Against)* –No, it's a violation of privacy.

Once you've listed as many pros and cons as you can think of, you should be in a better position to decide where you stand on the issue. Have you come up with more pros than cons? Are some arguments more important than others? (Draw a line through less important ones.) At this point, ask yourself which side you agree with most. This will be the side to take in your argument.

The Writer Organizes the Arguments   Once you've established your position, you should identify and highlight the top two or three arguments on each side of the issue. These are the arguments you'll address as you write your essay.

Consider organizing your arguments in one of the following ways:

- Least important ideas first, most important ideas last
- Alternating pro/con arguments: pro argument, con argument, pro argument, con argument, and so on

Notes

- Pro arguments (divided into different paragraphs) and then con arguments (divided into different paragraphs)

To avoid a one-sided argument and to show your audience that you are fair and well educated, you should present your opponents' view as well as your own. You may even admit that your opponents have some legitimate points. However, you will want to point out that your points are more important, more persuasive, and probably more in number. How do you address the opposition without weakening your own argument?

Here are a few methods:

- Mention fewer of your opponents' ideas compared to the number of your ideas.
- Mention your opponents' ideas early and then focus the rest of your essay on your ideas.
- Mention your opponents' ideas and then explain why these ideas are not as strong as yours or why your ideas are better.

Strategies for Writing the Argument in Class

As discussed earlier in this chapter, sometimes students will be given a writing prompt at the start of class and will be expected to write an essay on the topic from their general knowledge. Such is the case with the argument prompt that follows.

> *Some people believe that spanking is an effective method of disciplining children. Others feels that spanking is cruel and only teaches children to be violent. In your opinion, is spanking a good way to punish children? Argue your point of view and support your reasons with facts and examples.*

Action Strategies

- Read and analyze the prompt.
- Develop a pro/con list on the topic.
- Establish your position.
- Highlight the most important points on both sides of the issue.
- Decide on an organizational pattern to follow.
- Draft the essay, presenting pros and cons, but make sure your position is clear and well supported.
- Revise your essay.
- Edit your essay.

Activity

Writing the In-Class Argument

Using the action strategies mentioned, respond to the argument prompt on spanking. Set a time limit of two hours to complete the essay.

At other times, students will be given an essay to read, think about, and discuss as preparation for writing an argument in class.

Activity

Writing the In-Class Essay

Arguing "No TV"

1. In preparation for writing an in-class essay, read "Why We Tuned Out," by Karen Springen, pages 431–433. Be sure to follow the prereading instructions and answer the questions at the end of the piece.

2. Consider other—perhaps less drastic—bans on television that parents might impose such as limiting the amount of time children spend watching television, not allowing children to watch television until homework is done, and banning television after family hour.

3. Using the action strategies for writing in-class arguments, *write an essay in which you argue for or against children being allowed to have their own televisions in their bedrooms.* Be sure to support your position with evidence, example, or observation. Set a time limit of two hours to complete the essay.

Arguing the Value of Children's TV

1. In preparation for writing an in-class essay, read "Guilt Free," by Daniel McGinn, pages 424–430. Be sure to follow the prereading instructions and answer the questions at the end of the piece.

2. Using the action strategies for writing in-class arguments, *write an essay in which you argue for or against the value of children's television.* Be sure to support your position with evidence, example, or observation. Set a time limit of two hours to complete the essay.

Notes

A Final Note

Not all of your in-class writing will be done in writing classes. Many instructors across the disciplines use the in-class essay to test students' knowledge of the course material as well as students' writing ability. The things you've learned in this chapter should help you with in-class writing in all of your courses.

Understanding, Correcting, and Avoiding Sentence Errors

This section of Connections *reviews six different kinds of sentence errors that can do the most damage to clear communication. The information and exercises in this section will help you understand why writers sometimes make these errors, how to correct each kind of error, and how to avoid making these errors in the future.*

- Understanding, correcting, and avoiding verb form errors

- Understanding, correcting, and avoiding verb tense errors

- Understanding, correcting, and avoiding subject-verb agreement errors

- Understanding, correcting, and avoiding fragments

- Understanding, correcting, and avoiding run-ons

- Understanding, correcting, and avoiding comma splices

UNDERSTANDING, CORRECTING, AND AVOIDING VERB FORM ERRORS

In this section, you'll study verb form errors. In particular, you'll work on

- understanding verb form errors,
- correcting verb form errors, and
- avoiding verb form errors.

Understanding Verb Form Errors

A verb form error occurs when a writer uses the wrong form of a verb. Here are examples of verb form errors:

Yesterday, I <u>beginned</u> my assignment.

The cook <u>freezed</u> the leftover meat.

Simone <u>choosed</u> the most challenging task.

Here are those same sentences using correct verb forms:

Yesterday, I <u>began</u> my assignment.

The cook <u>froze</u> the leftover meat.

Simone <u>chose</u> the most challenging task.

This subsection reviews verb tenses and then focuses on two verb forms that can be a little tricky for writers.

As you may remember, verbs can come in a number of different forms depending on what tense they are in. In Chapter 2, you reviewed the simple tenses: the present, past, and future. Here are sentences using those tenses and a few other tenses you may not have studied yet (although you already use them when you speak and write).

Today, I <u>walk</u> to the river. (present tense)

Yesterday, I <u>walked</u> to the river. (past tense)

Tomorrow, I <u>will walk</u> to the river. (future tense)

I <u>have walked</u> to the river every day since I was 15. (present perfect tense)

(The *present perfect tense* helps you show that an action took place in the past and continues to take place.)

After I <u>had walked</u> to the river, I decided to call the game warden. (past perfect tense)

(The *past perfect tense* shows that an action took place at a non-specific time in the past or that the action took place before another time or action.)

I <u>am walking</u> to the river. (present progressive tense)

(The *present progressive tense* shows that an action is continuing.)

I <u>was walking</u> to the river. (past progressive tense)

(The *past progressive tense* shows that an action started and continued in the past.)

There are even a few more tense variations not listed here!

Don't worry; you don't need to memorize all of these different tenses! To avoid the most common verb form errors, you really only need to study and be aware of three verb forms: the *base form*, the *past tense form*, and the *have form* (also called the *past participle form*) which is used with the perfect tenses.

The base form of a verb is the form you would look up in the dictionary. It is in the present tense and has no special endings.

work

I <u>work</u> for the school district.

print

I <u>print</u> my name neatly.

save

The firefighters <u>save</u> the child.

The **past tense form** is the form you use when writing in the past tense. Verbs in the past tense usually end in *-ed*.

worked

Last year, I <u>worked</u> for the school district.

printed

Yesterday, I <u>printed</u> my name neatly.

saved

Yesterday, the firefighters <u>saved</u> the child.

The have form (or the **past participle form**) is the form you would use when writing in one of the perfect tenses mentioned earlier. The **present perfect tense** is formed by using *has* or *have* plus the verb in the have form. This tense will tell the reader one of two things: the action took place in the past and continues to take place in the present, or the action took place at a nonspecific time in the past.

Notes

worked

He <u>has worked</u> for the school district for the last four years. (The action in this sentence took place in the past and continues to take place in the present so the <u>present</u> perfect tense fits.)

printed

I <u>have printed</u> my name neatly. (The action in this sentence occured at a nonspecific time in the past so the present perfect tense fits.)

The **past perfect tense** is formed by using *had* plus the verb in the have form. This tense tells the reader that the action took place before another time or action in the past. Most often, you will use this tense with words like *before* and *after.* Don't use the past perfect form unless you are comparing two past times. (It is a common mistake for students to use *had* unnecessarily.)

saved

After the firefighters <u>had saved</u> the child, the parents were arrested for child neglect. (The "saving" takes place in the past before the arresting.)

For a review of past participles (have form verbs) working as adjectives, see pages 330–331.

The have form of a verb can also be transformed into an adjective to describe nouns. When acting as an adjective, the have form will not have *has, have,* or *had* in front of it. In the next two examples, the verb is underlined twice. In the second sentence, you'll see a highlighted have form verb that has been transformed into an adjective.

I <u>have printed</u> three copies of the letter.

The printed word <u>is</u> not always true. (*Printed* is now an adjective describing *word.*)

The next two sentences also have have form verbs that have been transformed into adjectives. The verbs are underlined twice. The have form verbs that are working as adjectives are highlighted.

The watched pot never <u>boils.</u>

The disciplined student <u>studied</u> for hours.

So far we have focused on regular verbs. **Regular verbs** are verbs that change tense in a predictable way: add *-ed* to create the past tense or the have form (past participle form). The tricky part—which sometimes leads to a verb form error—comes when irregular verbs are used. **Irregular verbs** change form in unpredictable ways when they change tenses. The sentences at the beginning of this chapter all had irregular verbs: begin, freeze, and choose. You can look up these words in the chart that follows. (The chart does not name *all* irregular verbs, but it does name quite a few.) Notice how the past tense is not created by simply adding *-ed,* and notice that the have form is often different from the past tense (unlike with regular verbs.)

Common Irregular Verbs

Base	Past	Have Form
awake	awoke, awaked	awakened, awaked
be	was	been
become	became	become
begin	began	begun
bite	bit	bitten, bit
blow	blew	blown
break	broke	broken
bring	brought	brought
build	built	built
buy	bought	bought
catch	caught	caught
choose	chose	chosen
come	came	come
cost	cost	cost
cut	cut	cut
dive	dived, dove	dived, dove
do	did	done
draw	drew	drawn
dream	dreamed, dreamt	dreamed, dreamt
drink	drank	drunk
drive	drove	driven
eat	ate	eaten
fall	fell	fallen
feel	felt	felt
find	found	found
fit	fit, fitted	fit, fitted
fly	flew	flown
freeze	froze	frozen
get	got	got, gotten
give	gave	given
go	went	gone
grow	grew	grown
hear	heard	heard
hit	hit	hit
know	knew	known

Notes

The first column shows the base form, which is the form you'd look up in the dictionary. The second column shows the past tense of the verb. The third column shows the have form (also called the past participle form). You can use this chart as a reference tool. You can also find the correct form of any irregular verb by looking in the dictionary. The dictionary lists irregular verbs in this same order—base form, past form, and have form. See "Using the Dictionary" on pages 452–458 for more information.

Notes

lay [to put or place]	laid	laid
lead	led	led
let	let	let
lie [to recline]	lay	lain
pay	paid	paid
put	put	put
ride	rode	ridden
ring	rang	rung
rise	rose	risen
run	ran	run
say	said	said
see	saw	seen
set [to place]	set	set
shake	shook	shaken
shine	shone, shined	shone, shined
shrink	shrank	shrunk
sing	sang	sung
sit [to be seated]	sat	sat
speak	spoke	spoken
spring	sprang	sprung
steal	stole	stolen
swim	swam	swum
take	took	taken
teach	taught	taught
tear	tore	torn
throw	threw	thrown
wake	woke, waked	waked, woken
wear	wore	worn
win	won	won
write	wrote	written

There are no rules to explain irregular verbs. You have to memorize them or look them up in a dictionary. (Or you can refer to the chart provided here.)

Practice #1   Using the Correct Verb Form
In the following exercises, fill in the blanks with the correct verb forms.

• Read your answers aloud when you are done. (Reading these sentences aloud will help you check your work and will help you develop an "ear" for correct verb forms.)

Examples: Today I go to the farmer's market and buy all the vegetables for the week.

Using past tense verbs: Yesterday, I _____ to the farmer's market and _____ all the vegetables for the week.

• Yesterday, I _went_ to the farmer's market and _bought_ all the vegetables for the week.

Sharon catches a beautiful trout.

Using the have form to create the present perfect tense: Sharon _____ a beautiful trout.

• Sharon _has caught_ a beautiful trout.

Felix dives into the water.

Using the have form to create the past perfect tense: Before Felix _____ into the water, I sensed that this was not going to turn out well.

• Before Felix _had dived_ into the water, I sensed that this was not going to turn out well.

1. My neighbor's dog bites the mailman. Using a past tense verb: My neighbor's dog _____ the mailman.

2. The judge speaks to the media. Using a past tense verb: The judge _____ to the media.

3. The sun rises and wakes the campers. Using past tense verbs: The sun _____ and _____ the campers.

4. I feel that we need to rethink donating money to that cause. Using the have form to create the present perfect tense: For some time now, I _____ that we need to rethink donating money to that cause.

5. Kenny's act draws a huge crowd. Using the have form to create the past perfect tense: Before his trouble with the law, Kenny's act _____ a huge crowd.

6. My kids grow into responsible adults. Using the have form to create the present perfect tense: My kids _____ into responsible adults.

Notes

7. I am happy to volunteer on Saturday. Using a past tense verb: I _____ happy to volunteer on Saturday. (*Hint: Am* is a form of *be*.)

8. The father becomes worried about the kids. Using a past tense verb: (write the whole sentence)

_____

_____

9. He steals the last cookie from the plate. Using the have form to create the present perfect tense: (write the whole sentence)

_____

_____

10. Martin Luther King Jr. speaks his mind. Using a past tense verb: (write the whole sentence)

_____

_____

Practice #2   Creating Sentences with Have Form Verbs as Adjectives

Part One

Write the have form of each irregular verb in the blank.

break   _____

• break   *broken*

  1. freeze   _____
  2. choose   _____
  3. drive   _____
  4. steal   _____
  5. write   _____

Part Two

Referring to the list of have form verbs in Part One, use one have form verb as an adjective modifying the subject in each sentence.

Example: The bicycle was worthless.

• The *broken* bicycle was worthless.

For more practice on using past participles as adjectives, see pages 330–331. For a review of how participial phrases can be transformed into adjective phrases in sentences, see pages 328–330.

1. Her confession was a surprise to everyone.
2. The scientist dedicated his life to finding a cure.
3. The smile on her face didn't seem genuine.
4. The jewelry would be hard to sell.
5. Only a few would be allowed to visit the laboratory.

Practice #3   Creating Sentences Using Irregular Verbs
Create the sentences described in the following exercises.

1. Create a sentence that is in the past tense. Use an irregular verb.
2. Create a sentence that is in the present perfect tense. Use an irregular verb.
3. Create a sentence that is in the past perfect tense. Use an irregular verb.

Correcting Verb Form Errors

Practice #4   Correcting Verb Form Errors
In the following exercises, find the verb form errors and rewrite the sentences on another piece of paper, correcting the errors. Read the correct sentence aloud to check your work and further develop your "ear" for correct verb forms.

1. Last year, I builded an outdoor fireplace in my backyard.
2. Before I had drawed the final plans, my brother gave me some suggestions for making the fireplace more energy efficient.
3. After much consideration, I choosed the gray bricks.
4. The gray bricks costed a bit more than the standard red bricks.
5. After I had layed the last brick, I decided we should have a party to celebrate.
6. My project payed off nicely.
7. When we refinanced, the appraiser sayed that the fireplace added $15,000 to the price of our home.

Avoiding Verb Form Errors

If you tend to make verb form errors, you should check all of your verbs at the editing stage of your writing process. Keep a list of irregular verbs

Notes

that you have misused before, perhaps with your spelling words, so that you can easily check your work.

UNDERSTANDING, CORRECTING, AND AVOIDING VERB TENSE ERRORS

In this section, you'll study verb tense errors. In particular, you'll work on

- understanding and correcting verb tense errors and
- avoiding verb tense errors.

Understanding and Correcting Verb Tense Errors

For a further review of verb tense, go to Chapter 2, pages 72–74.

As you may remember from Chapter 2, verbs can change tense. In fact, they are the only types of words that can change tense. There are quite a few different tenses in English. Review the different verb tenses in the following sentences:

Present tense: I talk with my friends.

Past tense: Yesterday, I talked with my friends.

Future tense: Tomorrow, I will talk with my friends.

Present progressive tense: I am talking with my friends.

Past progressive tense: I was talking with my friends.

Future progressive tense: I will be talking with my friends.

See pages 496–498 to review the perfect tenses.

There are also the perfect tenses and the future progressive tenses, but for the purposes of this section, we will focus on just the simple tenses to help you understand, correct, and avoid unnecessary verb tense shifts.

Shifting between verb tenses unnecessarily can ruin clear communication. Your readers expect you to be consistent with your verb tenses. Shifting between verb tenses is like jumping around in time. Readers find this confusing. These sentences, for example, are confusing because they use different tenses:

Years ago, young women rarely <u>went</u> to college. They <u>expect</u> to be housewives.

The first verb, *went,* is in the past tense, which seems appropriate since the writer is looking back in history. The second verb, *expect,* is in the present tense. This is confusing. Is the writer now talking about modern society? Here are the sentences with consistent verb tenses:

Years ago, young women rarely <u>went</u> to college. They <u>expected</u> to be housewives.

Now both verbs are in the past tense, and the idea in the sentence is clearer.

These two sentences suffer from unnecessary shifts in verb tense:

I <u>volunteer</u> at the local soup kitchen. (present tense)

I <u>met</u> interesting people. (past tense)

The sentences are clearer when they are both written in the same tense:

I <u>volunteer</u> at the local soup kitchen. (present tense)

I <u>meet</u> interesting people. (present tense)

Occasionally, you may need to shift tenses within a paragraph or even a single sentence:

If I <u>am</u> late today, I <u>will lose</u> my job.

In this case, the first verb is in the present tense, and the second verb is in the future tense. However, this shift makes sense because the writer is thinking about being late now and what will happen in the future. The general rule, however, is to consistently use the same tense throughout a piece of writing.

Practice #1:   Correcting Shifts in Verb Tense

- Underline the verbs twice.
- Find the verb tense errors.
- On a separate piece of paper, correct the sentences so that the verbs in each pair of sentences are in the same tense.
- Underline the verbs twice.

For a review of verbs, see pages 28–37 and pages 72–78 in Chapters 1 and 2.

Example: The woman updates her resume. She sent it with a cover letter to two prospective employers.

- The woman <u>updates</u> her resume. She <u>sent</u> it with a cover letter to two prospective employers.
- The woman <u>updates</u> her resume. She <u>sends</u> it with a cover letter to two prospective employers.

1. Kevin cuts the article out of the newspaper. He wanted to show it to his roommate, Hal.

2. The article compares the salaries of college graduates to non-college graduates. Kevin wanted to encourage Hal to keep trying.

3. Recently, Hal failed a class. The bad grade surprises Hal.

4. He thought that he was doing okay in the class. However, he rushes through his final assignment.

5. Now, Hal wonders if he belongs in college. He thought about taking some time off.

6. Once, I thought about dropping out. My dad says okay—on one condition.

7. He said that I needed to have a good alternative plan. I do not have a better plan than finishing school.

8. I stayed in school, and I earn my degree.

9. Now, I am relieved to have my degree because the job I had required a degree.

10. Besides helping me to get a good job, earning my degree turned out to be a great experience. Last week, I apply to the graduate program at the university in town.

Practice #2:   Reviewing Verb Tense
Read the following paragraph and decide what tense it should be in.

- Then rewrite the paragraph on a separate piece of paper.
- Underline the verbs.
- Change the tense of any verbs that are not in the correct tense.

My last essay was about technology and required some research. I enjoy doing the research. In fact, I learn a lot about hidden surveillance cameras in stores and even schools. One store I visited had cameras hidden in plants. I share my findings with my classmates. One of my classmates interviews the security officer at an insurance firm. She learns about their fingerprint scanner and their voice recognition system. Another student described the high-tech security tools that she saw at the airport. Yesterday, the instructor handed back the essays. She said they were very interesting because we spend so much time researching and discussing the reading in the book.

Practice #3   Manipulating Verb Tense

Write a paragraph on any topic of your choice. Use the present tense. Then rewrite the paragraph using the past tense. Underline all verbs in both paragraphs.

Practice #4   Applying Your Verb Tense Knowledge

Select a piece of your writing—a journal or essay—that has verb tense errors in it. Rewrite the piece, correcting all verb tense errors.

Avoiding Verb Tense Errors

If you frequently make verb tense errors, you should check all your verbs at the editing stage of your writing process. You may want to place a piece of paper over your essay and reveal one sentence at a time. Find the verb in each sentence and see if it is in the right tense. With time and practice, you will find that you make fewer verb tense errors.

UNDERSTANDING, CORRECTING, AND AVOIDING SUBJECT-VERB AGREEMENT ERRORS

In this section, you'll learn about subject-verb agreement errors. In particular, you'll work on

- understanding and correcting subject-verb agreement errors and
- avoiding subject-verb agreement errors.

Understanding and Correcting Subject-Verb Agreement Errors

Subject-verb agreement errors can be very distracting to your reader. A **subject-verb agreement error** means you have used a plural subject with a singular verb or that you have used a singular subject with a plural verb. Both of these sentences have subject-verb agreement errors.

She ask a question. (singular subject with a plural verb)

They votes for the new program. (plural subject with a singular verb)

Notes

To insure clear communication, subjects and verbs must agree in number. If you have a singular subject, you must have a singular verb. If you have a plural subject, you must have a plural verb. **Plural** means more than one. For example, *they* and *we* are both plural.

This sentence has a singular subject and a singular verb:

<u>She</u> <u>asks</u> a question.

Now this sentence has a plural subject and a plural verb:

<u>They</u> <u>ask</u> a question.

Notice how the subject and verb change when you move from the singular to the plural:

<u>She</u> <u>votes</u> for the new program. (singular subject and verb)

<u>We</u> <u>vote</u> for the new program. (plural subject and verb)

Writers make subject-verb agreement errors for a couple of different reasons:

- When we speak, we may not hear how some verbs end in -*s* and some don't. Therefore, when we write, we might forget to pay attention to how verbs should end.

- If you speak in a dialect that has different rules for verb endings, you might not use the verb endings that standard American English requires. In academic writing, subjects and verbs must agree in number.

Third Person Singular, Present Tense

The most common time for people to make a subject-verb agreement error is when they are using third person singular, present tense. For example, these sentences have subject-verb agreement errors:

<u>Instructor Smith</u> <u>work</u> with students after class.

<u>She</u> <u>enjoy</u> getting to know her students.

Here are the sentences with no subject-verb agreement errors:

<u>Instructor Smith</u> <u>works</u> with students after class.

<u>She</u> <u>enjoys</u> getting to know her students.

The following chart demonstrates the rule to remember: When you use *he*, *she*, or *it* (or another third person singular word) in the present tense, put an -*s* or -*es* on the verb.

	Singular	Plural

First Person (the person speaking)	I
	    work
	    kiss
	    write
		we
		    work
		    kiss
		    write

Second Person (the person or people being spoken to)	you
	    work
	    kiss
	    write
		you
		    work
		    kiss
		    write

Third Person (the person or people being spoken about)	he, she, it
	
	Or any word that can be used instead of *he, she, or it* (examples: Mr. Smith, the police officer, the child)
	    works
	    kisses
	    writes
		they
		    work
		    kiss
		    write

The following chart shows some irregular verbs. (There are present tense *and* past tense verbs listed here.)

	Singular	Plural

First Person (the person speaking)	I
	    do
	    am
	    was
		we
		    do
		    are
		    were

Second Person (the person or people being spoken to)	you
	    do
	    are
	    were
		you
		    do
		    are
		    were

Third Person (the person or people being spoken about)	he, she, it
	
	Or any word that can be used instead of *he, she, or it* (examples: Mr. Smith, the police officer, the child)
	    does
	    is
	    was
		they
		    do
		    are
		    were

Notes

Practice #1   Practicing Subject-Verb Agreement

- On a separate piece of paper, rewrite these sentences in the third person singular. (Your subject in each new sentence will be *he, she, it,* or another word that can be used instead of *he, she,* or *it.*)

- Use the present tense.

- Underline the verbs twice.

Example: I write an essay about television.

- He <u>writes</u> an essay about television. (It would be acceptable to use a name like *Steven* or a phrase like *my classmate* instead of *he.*)

1. Analyzing the song, I decide to listen to it a couple more times.
2. I ask the tutor to respond to my analysis. (*Hint:* Remember to change *my* when you revise the sentence.)
3. We listen to George's explanation.
4. They are anxious to hear our response.
5. I enjoy analyzing songs and poems.
6. I am now interested in taking a film analysis class.
7. I begin my essay with a comparison of two different songs.
8. They recite the poem.
9. I go to the poetry reading.
10. I do an excellent job.

Practice #2   Creating Sentences with Subjects and Verbs That Agree

Create the sentences described below. Use the present tense only.

1. Create a sentence that uses *I* as the subject. Then write the sentence again and change the subject to *he.* Make sure your subjects and verbs agree in number.
2. Create a sentence that uses *we* as the subject. Then write the sentence again and change the subject to a proper name (like *Frank* or *Mrs. Carlisle*). Make sure your subjects and verbs agree in number.

Indefinite Pronouns

Writers often make mistakes with subject-verb agreement when using indefinite pronouns as subjects. For example, this sentence has a subject-verb agreement error:

Everyone <u>decide</u> to go to the theater.

Here is the same sentence written correctly:

Everyone <u>decides</u> to go to the theater.

This is the rule to remember: Generally, indefinite pronouns are considered singular and require singular verbs.

The following chart gives examples of indefinite pronouns.

any	everybody	no one
anybody	everyone	someone
anyone	nobody	something
anything	nothing	somebody

These sentences are written correctly:

Everybody <u>agrees</u> to turn off the television for a week.

Somebody <u>takes</u> notes.

Practice #3   Subject-Verb Agreement at the Movies

In the following sentences, the subjects are indefinite pronouns, and they do not agree in number with the verbs.

- Underline the subjects once.
- Underline the verbs twice.
- On another sheet of paper, rewrite these sentences, correcting the subject-verb agreement errors. Use *only* the present tense. Underline the verb twice.

Example: No one want to ask the first question.

- <u>No one</u> <u>want</u> to ask the first question.
- No one <u>wants</u> to ask the first question.

1. Nobody want to miss the movie.
2. Nothing scare him like a movie about spiders.
3. Everybody agree to meet after the movie.

Notes

4. No one like the movie.

5. Somebody suggest a comedy for the next film.

6. Something in this film remind me of an old Hitchcock film.

7. Someone in our group send a reminder to each of us.

8. Everyone gather for the next movie.

Practice #4   Using Indefinite Pronouns and Maintaining Subject-Verb Agreement

Create the sentences described below. Use the present tense.

1. Create a sentence that uses *everyone* as the subject.

2. Create a sentence that uses *no one* as the subject.

3. Create a sentence that uses *nothing* as the subject.

Phrases That Confuse Things

If a subject and verb are separated by a long phrase, it can be easy to make a subject-verb agreement error. For example, this sentence has a subject-verb agreement error:

A tutor from one of the learning centers <u>help</u> dedicated students.

Here is the sentence correctly written (with a singular subject and verb):

A <u>tutor</u> from one of the learning centers <u>helps</u> dedicated students.

Remember that you won't find your subject or verb in a prepositional phrase, so you can cross out the prepositional phrases and see your subject more clearly. You can then make sure that the subject and verb agree. (See pages 76–78 for a review of prepositional phrases.)

A <u>tutor</u> ~~from one of the learning centers~~ <u>helps</u> dedicated students.

This sentence has a subject-verb agreement error:

Computers in the classroom is an asset to writing students.

Crossing out the prepositional phrase makes it easier to see and correct the error. Here is the sentence correctly written.

<u>Computers</u> ~~in the classroom~~ <u>are</u> an asset ~~to writing students~~.

Also, remember that *-ing* words are not verbs unless they have a helper in front of them. Sometimes descriptive *-ing* phrases can cause confusion with subject-verb agreement. You may want to cross out descriptive *-ing* phrases to help you see the subject and verb more clearly. This sentence, for example, has a subject-verb agreement error:

> The students listening to music in the pub is taking a break from studying.

Here is the sentence again. The descriptive *-ing* phrase and the prepositional phrase have been crossed out and the subject-verb agreement error corrected:

> The <u>students</u> ~~listening to music in the pub~~ <u>are taking</u> a break ~~from studying~~.

Practice #5   Watching Out for Phrases

There are subject-verb agreement errors in these sentences.

- Cross out the prepositional and descriptive *–ing* phrases.
- Underline the verbs twice and the subjects once.
- On a separate piece of paper, rewrite these sentences (including the prepositional and *-ing* phrases) so that there are no subject-verb agreement errors.
- Underline the verbs twice.
- Use the present tense.

Example: The advertisement, representing the downtown stores, are printed in black and white.

- The <u>advertisement,</u> ~~representing the downtown stores~~, <u>are</u> printed ~~in black and white~~.
- The <u>advertisement,</u> representing the downtown stores, <u>is</u> printed in black and white.

1. The words at the top of the ad encourages people to come shopping for a special gift for Valentine's Day.

2. The pictures of chocolates and lingerie is at the top of the ad.

3. The words, describing a decline in romantic feelings over many years of marriage, brings your eye down to the last image—a vacuum.

4. The final sentences of the advertisement encourages people of all ages to come to the mall.

5. My mom, having been married for 35 years, think the ad is offensive.

6. My dad, laughing at the not-so-hidden messages, decide to go to the mall for a vacuum.

7. One of my classmates in my psychology class bring me two advertisements.

8. The ad advertising milk and its high content of calcium show a little girl standing next to an enormous dinosaur skeleton.

9. The colors and facial expressions in the ad about Cartier diamonds makes me think of romance.

10. The women in the commercial wearing the jewelry looks very happy.

Practice #6   Create Sentences with Phrases

Create the sentences described in the following exercises. Use only the present tense. Make sure your subjects and verbs agree.

1. Create a sentence that begins with these words: *The man explaining the rules to the children and their parents*

2. Create a sentence that begins with these words: *The children next to the fountain by the trees*

3. Create a sentence that has a descriptive -*ing* phrase (participial phrase) in the middle of the sentence.

4. Create a sentence that has two prepositional phrases that come right after the subject and before the verb.

There *and* Here *Sentences*

Sentences that begin with *there* or *here* don't have clear subjects; neither *there* nor *here* will be the subject, so subject-verb agreement errors are easy to make. This sentence, for example, has a subject-verb agreement error:

There <u>is</u> two people in the advertisement.

Here is the sentence correctly written:

There <u>are</u> two people in the advertisement.

With *there* and *here* sentences, the subject will come after the verb in the sentence. Find the subject and make sure that your subject and verb agree in number. For example, this sentence has a subject-verb agreement error:

> Here is the marketing information and the product description.

With the verb and subject identified, the error is clear:

> Here <u>is</u> the <u>marketing information</u> and the <u>product description.</u>

Here is the sentence correctly written:

> Here <u>are</u> the <u>marketing information</u> and the <u>product description.</u>

You may also want to revise the sentence and get rid of the *there* or *here* since *there* and *here* sentences aren't always effective. This sentence, for example, can be revised and made stronger:

> There <u>are</u> four people employed in this office.

The sentence can be revised and given a stronger, clearer verb and subject.

> <u>We</u> <u>employ</u> four people in this office.

> Four <u>people</u> <u>work</u> in this office.

Practice #7   Correcting Subject-Verb Agreement Errors in *There* and *Here* Sentences

These sentences have subject-verb agreement errors.

- Underline the verbs twice.
- Underline the subjects once.
- Then, on a separate piece of paper, rewrite the sentences so that they do not begin with *there* or *here* <u>and</u> so that they have no subject-verb agreement errors. You may add information to the sentences as you revise.
- Use the present tense.

Example: According to my analysis, there is two evil people in this story.

- According to my analysis, there <u>is</u> two evil <u>people</u> in this story.
- According to my analysis, two people in this story are evil.

1. There is different ways of looking at this story.
2. There is two ways for him to respond.
3. Here is the opinions of my classmates.
4. There are one very good reason for choosing this character as the most evil.
5. Here is two of my classmates' essays to read.

Notes

6. There are an Internet website offering essays for sale.

7. There is three ways of organizing these arguments.

8. Here is the draft and the revision.

9. There is a sample introduction and conclusion on page 32.

10. Here is the instructor's comments and my tutor's suggestions.

Practice #8   Creating and Revising *There* and *Here* Sentences

Create the sentences described in the following exercises. Use the present tense. Make sure your subjects and verbs agree.

1. Create a sentence that begins with *here*.

2. Revise the sentence you created in #1 so that it does not begin with *here*.

3. Create a sentence that begins with *there*.

4. Revise the sentence you created in #3 so that it does not begin with *there*.

Avoiding Subject-Verb Agreement Errors

If you frequently make subject-verb agreement errors, you should check all your verbs at the editing stage of your writing process. You may find it easier to see specific sentence errors if you place a piece of paper over your essay and reveal one sentence at a time. Find the verb in each sentence and see if it agrees in number with the subject. After you have checked your own work, you might want to ask a tutor to check your essay and then tell you how many (if any) subject-verb agreement errors he or she sees. Then see if you can find them and fix them on your own. With time and practice, you will find that you make fewer subject-verb agreement errors.

UNDERSTANDING, CORRECTING, AND AVOIDING FRAGMENTS

This section focuses on sentence fragments. You'll work on

- understanding fragments,
- correcting fragments, and
- avoiding fragments.

Understanding Fragments

A fragment is an incomplete sentence. It may be a phrase (a group of words missing a subject, a verb, or both). Or it may be a dependent clause (a group of words with a subject and verb that cannot stand on its own).

The following examples show fragments that are phrases. Following each fragment is a complete sentence. (The verbs are underlined twice and the subjects are underlined once in the complete sentences.)

After her divorce. (This fragment is a prepositional phrase.)

After her divorce, <u>she</u> <u>was</u> unsure about marrying again. (The prepositional phrase now introduces a complete sentence.)

The young, single man hoping to meet someone special. (This fragment is a noun phrase with an adjective phrase attached.)

The young, single <u>man</u> <u>was hoping</u> to meet someone special. (In this revision, the verb is now complete; *was hoping* is the verb. The fragment is now a complete sentence.)

Planning a singles dance party. (This fragment is a participial phrase.)

<u>Planning</u> a singles dance party <u>is</u> a lot of work. (*Planning* is now working as the subject in the complete sentence.)

These fragments are dependent clauses:

When I asked my grandparents about their courtship.
Since he plans on marrying later in life.
Although I hadn't yet met his family.

A dependent clause, as you may remember, has a subject and verb, but it cannot stand by itself because of the subordinator attached to it. Here is a list of subordinators that can create dependent clauses:

For a review of dependent and independent clauses, see pages 155–171 in Chapter 4 and pages 274–288 in Chapter 6.

if	though
since	although
while	even though
because	when

The dependent clauses listed above can be joined to independent clauses to create complete sentences, or the subordinators can be removed to change the dependent clauses into independent clauses.

Notes

When I asked my grandparents about their courtship, they were happy to share their memories. (The dependent clause has been joined to an independent clause.)

I asked my grandparents about their courtship. (The subordinator has been removed to create an independent clause.)

Since he plans on marrying later in life, he wants to buy his house in a family-oriented neighborhood. (The dependent clause has been joined to an independent clause.)

He plans on marrying later in life. (The subordinator has been removed to create an independent clause.)

Although I hadn't yet met his family, I was sure I would enjoy spending Christmas at his family's home. (The dependent clause has been joined to an independent clause.)

I hadn't yet met his family. (The subordinator has been removed to create an independent clause.)

Practice #1   Identifying Fragments

Place an "F" next to each sentence that is actually a fragment. Put a "C" next to complete sentences.

Example: If I want to research different marriage ceremonies.

• If I want to research different marriage ceremonies. F

1. When I think about the high divorce rate in this country.
2. Because her parents divorced when she was young.
3. Interviewing four recently married couples.
4. Jason will explain the history behind wedding rings.
5. By beginning the essay with historical information.
6. If I were writing that advice column.
7. She wonders about our society's insistence on monogamy.
8. Even though I thought he had a valid point.
9. Since my reading audience may not agree with me.
10. Discussing my essay with my tutor.

Correcting Fragments

There are a number of ways to correct fragments.

A. If you have a fragment that is missing a subject, a verb, or both, you can add the missing element. This fragment has no subject or verb:

> Speaking to the senior class.

Here the fragment has been revised by adding a verb and allowing the initial fragment to work as the subject.

> Speaking to the senior class was frightening.

In this revision, a subject and verb have been added and the initial fragment becomes the completing idea.

> I enjoyed speaking to the senior class.

B. If you have a fragment that is really a dependent (or subordinated) clause, you can get rid of the subordinator. This fragment is really a dependent clause because of the *when*.

> When the students asked questions.

To correct this fragment, remove the subordinator.

> The students asked questions.

C. Or if you have a fragment that is really a dependent (or subordinated) clause, you can finish the sentence by adding an independent clause. Here is the fragment again.

> When the students asked questions.

The fragment becomes a sentence when an independent clause is added.

> When the students asked questions, I realized that they had been listening closely to my speech.

Practice #2   Correcting Fragments

Correct each fragment below using one of these three different methods.

- Add the missing element(s).

- Get rid of the subordinator.

- Keep the subordinator and complete the idea. (You can add information before or after the subordinated clause.)

Write your new sentences on a separate piece of paper and *use each method at least once.*

Notes

Example: If you are concerned that your ideas don't flow.

• If you are concerned that your ideas don't flow, you should think about using transition words or phrases.

1. When we discussed good dating practices.
2. Because our modern lifestyle has changed.
3. Although my mom and dad were both pretty modern in their views.
4. Reviewing the next reading on advertisements.
5. Since I am not a good artist.
6. One of my friends who draws really well.
7. After three hours of scouring magazines.
8. If you want to work together on the advertisement.
9. Carefully choosing the words.
10. When my classmates reviewed my work.
11. Because I was nervous.
12. Professor Minturn from the history department.

Practice #3   Correcting Fragments in Your Own Writing
Select one of your paragraphs or essays that has fragments. Rewrite the paragraph or essay, correcting your fragments.

Avoiding Fragments

If you are writing fragments in your essays, see if there is a pattern.

• Do you create a fragment when you begin a sentence with an *-ing* word?
• Do you end up with a fragment when you use *because* or other subordinators?
• Don't stop using *-ing* words or subordinators. Just begin watching out for them and making sure that you complete your sentences.

When you reach the editing stage of your writing process, review your essay sentence by sentence, keeping an eye out for *-ing* words or subordinators that might create fragments. It is important for you to be able to find and fix your own fragments, but if you need help at first, ask a tutor to check for fragments. Find out how many you have—but not where they are—then find them and fix them on your own. Check your work with your tutor.

UNDERSTANDING, CORRECTING, AND AVOIDING RUN-ONS

This subsection focuses on run-on sentences. You'll work on

- understanding run-ons,
- correcting run-ons, and
- avoiding run-ons.

Understanding Run-Ons

A **run-on sentence** is really two sentences that run together with no punctuation between them. A run-on sentence is sometimes called a **fused sentence.** A writer may accidentally create a run-on when ideas in two sentences are closely related. In this situation, the writer may make the mistake of presenting two sentences as one. The following sentences are actually run-ons:

> I enjoyed Bobryk's essay he included interesting detail and humor. (The first sentence ends after the word *essay.*)
>
> Wong explains how she felt as a child then she expresses her feelings as an adult. (The first sentence ends after the word *child.* Remember that *then* cannot join sentences. It's a transition.)
>
> I was surprised to read that women still earn less than men I thought that wasn't true anymore. (The first sentence ends after the word *men.*)

Practice #1   Identifying Run-Ons

Identify which of the following sentences are actually run-ons. When you find a run-on, put an "R" next to the sentences, and use a slash to mark where one sentence ends and the other begins. Mark correct sentences with a "C."

Example: I need to develop a better writing process then my final essays might be stronger.

Notes

- I need to develop a better writing process / then my final essays might be stronger. R

1. I should take the first few steps of the writing process slower I misunderstood the last essay assignment.

2. During the Superbowl, they show the funniest advertisements.

3. I hate watching network television there are too many commercial interruptions.

4. My classmates and I got together to study the advertisements.

5. I'm going to take my outline to my tutor my last essay had some organizational problems because I didn't do an outline.

6. He did some great analysis he explained how a modern ad had hidden racist messages.

7. Until our class discussion, I hadn't realized how pervasive cheating is in college.

8. My classmate told everyone to watch a PBS special that is on tonight.

9. The program will show that many college students cheat regularly they say that cheating is the only way they can get into good graduate school programs.

10. If that television program is accurate, Jack isn't the only cheater out there.

Correcting Run-Ons

Consider this run-on:

The man was considered a hero he had stood up to the office bully.

There are four ways to correct run-on sentences.

A. Put a period after the first sentence and capitalize the first letter of the second sentence.

The man was considered a hero. He had stood up to the office bully.

B. Separate the two sentences with a semicolon. (A semicolon is just as strong as a period.)

The man was considered a hero; he had stood up to the office bully.

C. Join the two sentences with a comma and a coordinating conjunction, or coordinator. (The seven coordinating conjunctions are *for, and, nor, but, or, yet,* and *so.*)

> The man was considered a hero, for he had stood up to the office bully.

D. Add a subordinator and change one of the complete sentences to a subordinated clause. (Some subordinators are *if, when, because, although,* and *since.* If the new subordinated clause comes first, put a comma after it.)

> The man was considered a hero since he had stood up to the office bully.

Notes

See pages 156–158 and 375–381 for more information on using coordinators.

See pages 160–164, 274–279, and 381–387 for more information on using subordinators.

Practice #2   Correcting Run-Ons

Correct each run-on two different ways. Write your new sentences on a separate piece of paper.

Example: I haven't yet picked a hero to write about I'm really interested in three different people.

  a. Correct this run-on using method B.

  b. Correct this run-on using method D.

- a. I haven't yet picked a hero to write about; I'm really interested in three different people.

- b. I haven't yet picked a hero to write about since I'm really interested in three different people.

1. Perhaps I should check the resources at the library there might be more information available on one of my prospective heroes than on the others.

  a. Correct this run-on using method A.

  b. Correct this run-on using method C.

2. The personal hero assignment was cool I learned a lot about my dad.

  a. Correct this run-on using method B.

  b. Correct this run-on using method D.

3. Analyzing films can be tough I think I did a good job.

Notes

a. Correct this run-on using method A.

b. Correct this run-on using method C.

4. Bernie LaPlante is not your typical hero he doesn't look, talk, or even act like you expect.

a. Correct this run-on using method A.

b. Correct this run-on using method C.

5. I'm going to interview my uncle for my essay he's a fire investigator.

a. Correct this run-on using method B.

b. Correct this run-on using method D.

6. I saw another movie that deals with heroism I found some more information for my essay.

a. Correct this run-on using method B.

b. Correct this run-on using method D.

See pages 280–282 for more information on using transitions.

Using Transitions to Correct Run-Ons

A *transition* is a word or phrase that creates a meaningful bridge between ideas and sentences. Transitions can be very useful when correcting run-ons. Here are some common transitions:

however
consequently
therefore
then

This sentence is actually a run-on:

Winn's article made me see how television can be harmful to children I plan on making some new restrictions at our house.

The run-on can be corrected using a semicolon and a transition:

Winn's article made me see how television can be harmful to children; therefore, I plan on making some new restrictions at our house.

When using transitions, keep in mind that they are different from coordinating conjunctions or subordinators, which can join sentences with commas. Transitions do not join sentences. You must keep the two sentences separate by using a period or a semicolon.

These sentences show how to use transitions correctly. Notice that each transition is followed by a comma.

I don't have any day care on Mondays. Consequently, I have to let the television baby-sit the kids so I can get my homework done.

I don't have any day care on Mondays; consequently, I have to let the television baby-sit the kids so I can get my homework done.

I realize that television can be an unhealthy influence. However, I don't think that I need to throw the television set away.

I realize that television can be an unhealthy influence; however, I don't think that I need to throw the television set away.

Practice #3   Correcting Run-Ons with Transitions

Correct the following run-ons by using transitions and appropriate punctuation.

- Use each of the following transitions at least once.
  however
  consequently
  therefore
  then
- Use semicolons in some sentences.
- Use periods to separate other sentences.

Example: Obesity runs in my family I'm careful about making sure that my kids get exercise every day.

- Obesity runs in my family; therefore, I'm careful about making sure that my kids get exercise every day.

1. We wanted more time to read, do homework, talk, and play games we stopped watching television during the week.

2. I was impressed by all the research *Sesame Street* does I don't feel so bad about letting my kids watch it.

3. The kids have to do their chores and their homework first they can watch television or play on the computer.

4. I don't like my kids to watch anything other than G-rated movies they really like action movies that have the PG- or PG-13 ratings.

5. Stacey has fond memories of watching sitcoms in the evenings with her parents she doesn't want to eliminate television from her children's lives.

6. Each of my kids made a list of their favorite programs we made a schedule so that each child gets to watch two programs a week.

Notes

7. Most of the videos on MTV are too sexy I don't let the kids watch them.
8. My neighbors don't own a television their kids come to our house every afternoon to watch cartoons.
9. I know reality shows are the latest thing I just can't stand them.
10. My kids have to earn B averages at school I'll let them play video games.

Practice #4   Correcting Run-Ons in Your Own Writing
Select one of your paragraphs or essays that has run-ons. Rewrite the paragraph or essay, correcting your run-ons.

Avoiding Run-Ons

If run-ons are showing up regularly in your essays, look to see if there is a pattern.

• Do you create a run-on when you use transitions?
• Do you create a run-on when ideas seem closely related?

When you reach the editing stage of your writing process, review your essay sentence by sentence, keeping an eye out for transition words and closely related sentences that might be written as run-ons. It is important for you to be able to find and fix your own run-ons, but if you need help at first, ask a tutor to check for run-ons. Find out how many you have—but not where they are. Then find them and fix them on your own. Check your work with your tutor.

UNDERSTANDING, CORRECTING, AND AVOIDING COMMA SPLICES

This section focuses on comma splice errors. You'll work on

• understanding comma splices,
• correcting comma splices, and
• avoiding sentence comma splices.

Understanding Comma Splices

A **comma splice** is two sentences incorrectly joined with a comma. A writer may create a comma splice because the ideas in two sentences are closely related and the writer feels the need to pause. The writer might then insert a comma between the two sentences. However, a comma cannot do the job of a period, and the result is a comma splice error.

These sentences have comma splice errors. The comma in each example is separating complete sentences.

I am grateful for technology, I don't know what I'd do without my computer and cell phone.

My dad is really uncomfortable with high-tech stuff, he hasn't learned how to send or receive e-mail.

You may have heard that every time you "hear" a pause in your writing you should use a comma. This is *not* a good rule to follow. Where you "hear" a pause and where your reader "hears" a pause may be quite different, and scattering commas on your paper will cause confusion. There are specific reasons for using commas, and you shouldn't use a comma unless you can name a specific comma rule. Here is a brief list of comma rules.

Punctuation Rule #1 (see pages 112 and 326)
Put commas between items in a series.
- I rely on my cell phone, pager, and e-mail.

Punctuation Rule #2 (see pages 157 and 377)
When you join two complete sentences with a coordinator (FANBOYS), you must put a comma after the first sentence.
- I turned off my pager, for I didn't want to be interrupted.

Punctuation Rule #4 (see pages 159, 168, and 282)
When you begin a sentence with a subordinated or dependent clause, you must put a comma after the subordinated clause.
- When she got her cell phone bill, she nearly fainted.

Punctuation Rule #6 (see pages 162, 276, and 382)
When you introduce a sentence with a phrase, put a comma after the phrase.
- Wanting to save time, Felicia grabbed fast food on the way home.

Punctuation Rule #7 (see page 284)
Put commas around interruptive words and phrases in a sentence.
- Her brother, however, was not surprised.

Practice #1   Identifying Comma Splices

Identify which of the following sentences have comma splice errors.

- When you find a comma splice, put "CS" next to the sentence, put a period where the comma is, and begin the second sentence with a capital letter.

Notes

- If the sentence is correct, put a "C" next to the sentence.

Note: A few of the following sentences use commas correctly. Refer to the comma rules listed earlier to check how the commas are used.

Example: I was surprised by the Macionis article, I hadn't thought about the negative sides to modernization.

- I was surprised by the Macionis article. I hadn't thought about the negative sides to modernization. CS

1. The technology inventory assignment was interesting, we came up with a long list of high-tech gadgets.
2. Sharon hadn't ever been on the Internet, so she asked the librarian for help.
3. My roommate lives on frozen dinners, she doesn't ever eat fresh food.
4. Frozen dinners are convenient, but they cost a lot more than fresh ingredients.
5. Worried that the babysitter might be mistreating their child, the parents installed a hidden camera.
6. The company told its employees that they were being watched, the state law required the company to do so.
7. The character in the movie burned his own fingers on purpose, he wanted to eliminate his fingerprints.
8. Because his DNA revealed certain physical defects, the character in the book assumed another person's identity.
9. I don't like having surveillance cameras on our streets, I feel my privacy has been invaded.
10. Security is a priority at all airports, the government is trying to prevent terrorist attacks.

Correcting Comma Splices

There are four ways to correct comma splice errors. (Notice that these are the same methods you can use to correct run-ons.) Study this comma splice and methods A–D for correcting the comma splice:

George Orwell's book *1984* was interesting to read, many of the surveillance tools Orwell mentions are now being used.

A. Put a period after the first sentence and capitalize the first letter of the second sentence.

Notes

> George Orwell's book *1984* was interesting to read. Many of the surveillance tools Orwell mentions are now being used.

B. Separate the two sentences with a semicolon. (A semicolon is just as strong as a period.)

> George Orwell's book *1984* was interesting to read; many of the surveillance tools Orwell mentions are now being used.

C. Join the two sentences with a comma and a coordinating conjunction, or coordinator. (The seven coordinating conjunctions are *for, and, nor, but, or, yet,* and *so.*)

See pages 156–158 and 375–381 for more information on using coordinators.

> George Orwell's book *1984* was interesting to read, for many of the surveillance tools Orwell mentions are now being used.

D. Add a subordinator and change one of the complete sentences to a subordinated clause. (Some subordinators are *if, when, because, although,* and *since.* If the new subordinated clause comes first, put a comma after it.)

See pages 160–164, 274–279, and 381–387 for more information on using subordinators.

> George Orwell's book *1984* was interesting to read because many of the surveillance tools Orwell mentions are now being used.

Practice #2   Correcting Comma Splices

Correct each comma splice two different ways. Write your new sentences on a separate piece of paper.

Example: I enjoy writing songs, I express my feelings and comment on current political issues.

  a. Correct this comma splice using method B.
  b. Correct this comma splice using method D.

• a. I enjoy writing songs; I express my feelings and comment on current political issues.
• b. I enjoy writing songs because I express my feelings and comment on current political issues.

  1. I was surprised that her lyrics were so complex, I still didn't like the CD.

a. Correct this comma splice using method A.
b. Correct this comma splice using method C.

2. The lyrics were perfect for this assignment, their complexity would make the analysis interesting.
   a. Correct this comma splice using method B.
   b. Correct this comma splice using method D.

3. Steven's introduction wasn't clear, he didn't have enough detail.
   a. Correct this comma splice using method A.
   b. Correct this comma splice using method C.

4. I wanted to hear the song before writing my draft, I thought listening to it might help me understand it better.
   a. Correct this comma splice using method B.
   b. Correct this comma splice using method D.

5. I had always thought that I hated poetry, I found Frost's poem interesting.
   a. Correct this comma splice using method A.
   b. Correct this comma splice using method C.

6. I was surprised, my classmates thought I did a great job summarizing the lyrics.
   a. Correct this comma splice using method B.
   b. Correct this comma splice using method D.

Using Transitions to Correct Comma Splices

If you use method A or B to correct a comma splice, you must use a period or a semicolon to separate complete sentences. Occasionally, you may want to use a transition with these methods. (You cannot use these transitions with just a comma to join complete sentences.)

Here are some common transitions:

however

consequently

therefore

then

The first sentence in this group has a comma splice error. The second and third sentences show how a transition can be used to correct the comma splice error.

I needed evidence to back up my point, I carefully chose some quotes from the song lyric.

I needed evidence to back up my point; consequently, I carefully chose some quotes from the song lyric.

I needed evidence to back up my point. Consequently, I carefully chose some quotes from the song lyric.

As with the previous group of sentences, the first one here has a comma splice error. The second and third sentences show how a transition can be used to correct the comma splice error.

I don't think I'll ever be a professional writer, I feel confident that I can write better reports at work now.

I don't think I'll ever be a professional writer; however, I feel confident that I can write better reports at work now.

I don't think I'll ever be a professional writer. However, I feel confident that I can write better reports at work now.

Practice #3   Correcting Comma Splices with Transitions

The following sentences have comma splice errors. On a separate piece of paper, correct them using transitions.

- Choose transitions from this list:
  however
  consequently
  therefore
  then

- Use semicolons in some sentences.
- Use periods to separate other sentences.

Example: Ms. Stanley was pleased with Michael's improved writing skills, she offered him the promotion.

- Ms. Stanley was pleased with Michael's improved writing skills; therefore, she offered him the promotion.

1. I feel more confident about my speaking skills, I'm still not crazy about public speaking.

2. Jordan worked in the manufacturing department, he moved over to marketing.

Notes

3. Jenny knew that she could get her essays done faster if she had a computer, she used her Christmas bonus to buy one.

4. The new software is complicated, I need to take a training class.

5. I need to finish this book about Jesse Ventura, I want to start this novel called *Winter Prey.*

6. My classmate said the essay "The Most Precious Gift" was good, I decided to read it.

7. I knew she had a wonderful personal library, I asked if I could borrow a couple of books.

8. My grandmother and I had a great time discussing her heroic uncle, we've decided to write some more stories about family members.

9. Caleb didn't have much faith in himself, he bought an essay on the Internet.

10. The editor at the school paper offered me a job, I already have two jobs!

Practice #4   Correcting Comma Splices in Your Own Writing

Select one of your paragraphs or essays that has comma splices. Rewrite the paragraph or essay, correcting your comma splices.

Avoiding Comma Splices

If comma splices are showing up regularly in your essays, look to see if there is a pattern.

- Do you create a comma splice when you use transitions?
- Do you create a comma splice when ideas seem closely related?

When you reach the editing stage of your writing process, review your essay sentence by sentence, keeping an eye out for transition words and closely related sentences that might lead you to create comma splices. Remember that there are specific rules for using commas. See page 527 and pages 538–539 for a review of those rules.

It is important for you to be able to find and fix your own comma splices, but if you need help at first, ask a tutor to check for comma splices. Find out how many you have—but not where they are. Then find them and fix them on your own. Check your work with your tutor.

This section of Connections *offers rules that you can easily and quickly refer to when necessary.*

- The right word

- Capitalization

- Punctuation rules

Notes

THE RIGHT WORD

Sometimes words that are close in sound or meaning can be confusing. Yet using the right word in an essay or report can mean the difference between being understood or misunderstood. This section includes a list of commonly confused words (like *to, too,* and *two*) and their basic meanings. For additional information on these words, consult your dictionary.

a, an   Use **a** before words beginning with any consonant sound even if the word actually starts with a vowel: *a horse, a unicorn, a Cadillac.* Use **an** before words beginning with any vowel sound even if the word actually starts with a consonant: *an honor, an act, an evergreen tree.*

accept, except   **Accept** is a verb meaning to receive. *Hal accepted the invitation.* **Except** means but. *Everyone ate ice cream except Cheshire.*

advice, advise   **Advice,** a noun, is an opinion about a problem or issue. *His advice helped me make a decision about which car to buy.* **Advise** is a verb meaning to suggest. *He advised me to wait until interest rates are lower.*

advise, advice   See **advice, advise.**

affect, effect   **Affect,** a verb, means to have an influence on. *Studies suggest that TV violence affects behavior.* **Effect,** as a noun, means a result. *The negative effects of cigarette smoking have been documented.*

are, hour, our   **Are,** a verb, is the plural form of *to be. We are a team.* **Hour** refers to time. *The clock struck on the hour.* **Our** is the possessive form of *we. Our team won the tournament.*

effect, affect   See **affect, effect.**

hear, here   **Hear** means to be able to listen. *I hear knocking at the door.* **Here** means present at this time. *I arrived here this morning.*

here, hear   See **hear, here.**

hour, our, are   See **are, hour, our.**

its, it's   Its is the possessive form of *it. The canary chirped its song.* It's is a contraction meaning it is. *It's time to go.*

know, no   Know, a verb, means to understand. *I know how to study well.* No means not so. *No, I'm not eating now.*

no, know   See know, no.

one, own, won   One means a single thing. Own, a verb, means to possess. *Chandra owned one cat.* Won is the past tense of the verb *win. We won the tennis tournament.*

our, are, hour   See are, hour, our.

own, won, one   See one, own, won.

peace, piece   Peace, a noun, means the absence of disagreement. *In times of peace, the people live in harmony.* Piece refers to a portion of something. *I'll order a piece of pie.*

piece, peace   See peace, piece.

than, then   Than is used to indicate an unequal comparison between two things. *The A's maintained a better record than the Giants.* Then refers to a time in the past. *Back then, most people grew their own vegetables.* Then also means the next thing. *First is the polo competition; then, the gymnasts will perform.*

their, there, they're   Their is the possessive form of *they. Their faces turned in unison.* There refers to location. *The lid is there on the counter.* They're is a contraction for *they are. They're our favorite guests.*

then, than   See than, then.

there, they're, their   See their, there, they're.

they're, their, there   See their, there, they're.

Notes

threw, through   **Threw** is the past tense form of the verb *throw. He threw the baseball.* **Through** refers to something passing from one side to the other. *The baseball crashed through the window.*

through, threw   See **threw, through.**

to, too, two   **To** means toward. *I traveled to Paris to see the Mona Lisa.* It is also part of an infinitive. *They want to eat, then to sleep.* **Too** means also. *My husband went, too.* **Too** also means excessive. *There was too much noise for me to hear well.* **Two** is the number. *We discovered that travel for two is cheaper than travel for one.*

too, two, to   See **to, too, two.**

two, to, too   See **to, too, two.**

your, you're   **Your** is the possessive form of *you. Your heroism is inspiring.* **You're** is a contraction of *you are. You're going to receive a promotion.*

you're, your   See **your, you're.**

wear, where   **Wear** is a verb meaning to put on something. *Sandra wears her baseball cap.* **Where** means at or in what place. *Where is the morning newspaper?*

weather, whether   **Weather,** a noun, refers to atmospheric conditions. *The weather changed from rain to snow.* **Whether** suggests that a decision will be made between two alternatives. *Soleil had to decide whether or not to attend the conference.*

whether, weather   See **weather, whether.**

which, witch   **Which** refers to choice. *Which of these would you prefer?* A **witch** is a female sorcerer. *The witch cast a spell.*

when, win   **When** refers to time. *When will we take our vacation?* **Win,** as a verb, means to achieve victory. *We win every year.* As a noun, **win** is the victory. *Andre enjoyed a spectacular win.*

win, when   See **when, win.**

where, wear   See **wear, where.**

witch, which   See **which, witch.**

won, one   See **one, own, won.**

CAPITALIZATION

Capitalize proper nouns (naming *specific* people, places, or things).

San Francisco	Texas
Whitney Houston	*New York Times*

(But not **common nouns,** naming nonspecific people, places, things, or ideas: songwriter, newspaper, book, state, class.)

Capitalize the days of the week, months, and holidays.

Monday   November   Thanksgiving

Capitalize the first word in a sentence.

She traveled to Philadelphia by train.

Capitalize the first word of a quoted sentence.

The instructor said, "Essays are due Thursday."

Capitalize *specific* courses

Art 101   Biology 1A

(But not subject areas: history, geography.)

Capitalize *I* when used as a personal pronoun.

My writing improved as I learned to revise.

Capitalize language, nationality, and ethnicity.

Native American	Asian American	Swiss
French	Hispanic	African American

Capitalize the names of celestial bodies.

Mars   Milky Way

Capitalize the first and last words and other significant words in titles of books, films, movies, television series, compact discs, magazines, and journals.

The Color Purple	*South Park*	*A Short History of the World*
GQ	*Vogue*	*The Bridges of Madison County*

(Don't capitalize *a, an, the,* or prepositions unless they are the first or last word in a title.)

Notes

Capitalize names of wars and historical events.
the Vietnam War   the American Revolution

Capitalize names of government agencies, corporations, and institutions.

Bank of America   Microsoft

Department of Defense   Stanford University

Do not capitalize the seasons: summer, fall, winter, spring.

Do not capitalize centuries: the twenty-first century.

PUNCTUATION RULES

Punctuation Rule #1 (See pages 111, 326, and 527.)

Put commas between items in a series.

Example:
The exhausted, confused, and frustrated writer leaned back in his chair.
(The comma before the *and* is optional with a list like this.)

Punctuation Rule #2 (See pages 157, 377, and 527.)

When you join two complete sentences with a coordinator (FAN-BOYS), you must put a comma after the first sentence.

Example:
*At midnight he finally remembered his thrilling opening line, **and** he began to type.*

Punctuation Rule #3 (See pages 159, 282, and 527.)

You may use a semicolon to separate two complete sentences.

Example:
He needed to find the words now; his editor was waiting for his work.

Punctuation Rule #4 (See pages 159, 168, 282, and 527.)

Follow an introductory word or phrase with a comma.

Example:
Sitting at his computer, he brainstormed ideas.

Note: Punctuation Rules 3 and 4 are both applied when you join two complete sentences with a semicolon and transition.
He came up with three promosing topics; **then,** *he focused on a single idea.*

Punctuation Rule #5 (See pages 162, 276, 382, and 527.)

When you begin *a sentence with a subordinated or dependent clause, you must put a comma after the subordinated clause.*

Example:
If he could just remember that great opening line, *the rest would flow.*

Punctuation Rule #6 (See pages 284 and 527.)

If the subordinated clause comes after *the independent clause, you do not need a comma.*

Example:
The rest would flow **if he could just remember that great opening line.**

Punctuation Rule #7 (See page 284.)

Put commas around interruptive words or phrases in a sentence.

Example:
For two long hours, **however,** *no words came to his mind.*

Glossary

action verb: a word that expresses activity or movement (32).

activities: work that puts into practice new writing concepts or ideas (24).

adjectives: words that describe nouns (325).

adverbs: words that describe verbs, adjectives, other adverbs, and whole groups of words (332).

analyze: to break down a complex concept into smaller, less complex pieces and then study the pieces (339).

and: one of the seven coordinators. It expresses a relationship of addition (156).

antecedent: the noun that a pronoun refers to (218).

anticipate: a step in the reading process when the reader guesses what the reading will be about based on his or her preview of the reading material. Readers also anticipate (or guess what will come next) while reading the entire piece for the first time (80).

apostrophe: a punctuation mark used to show possession. An apostrophe can also be used in a contraction (two words joined as one) (470).

audience: any person or persons you are communicating to (9).

auditory learner: a person who learns best when listening to the material (446).

base form: the most basic form of the verb. It is in the present tense and has no special endings. It is the form you would look up in the dictionary (330).

body: the middle section of an essay or paragraph that supports the claim established in the introduction or topic sentence (39).

body paragraphs: paragraphs that appear after the introduction of an essay and before the conclusion. They contain information that helps support the claim established in the introduction (43).

brainstorming: writing freely on a topic without concern for grammatical correctness or form. The purpose of brainstorming is to let the writer explore ideas (133).

but: one of the seven coordinators. It expresses a relationship of opposition (156).

citing your sources: giving credit to the original source of information (481).

clause: a group of words with a subject and verb (155).

coherence: in a coherent essay, all the ideas fit together and support the thesis (143).

cohesion: in a cohesive essay, ideas are unified (260).

column: a piece of writing in which a columnist (the writer) expresses his or her own views (63).

columnist: a writer of a column (63).

columns: long vertical rows of newsprint in a newspaper (56).

comma splice: an error that is created when two complete sentences are joined as one with only a comma to separate them (526).

command sentences: sentences that give someone work to do. This type of sentence has the implied subject *you* (113).

common noun: a nonspecific person, place, thing, or idea (537).

complete sentence: a group of words containing a subject and verb and expressing a complete idea. A complete sentence is also known as an independent clause (28).

con argument: an argument against something (258).

concession: an instance in which the writer acknowledges the opponent's position (277).

conclusion: the final paragraph in a piece of writing. It sums up the most important points, restates

541

the writer's claim, and draws the piece to an end (40).

context: the surrounding words, sentences, and ideas in which another word/idea appears (88).

contraction: a word with an apostrophe in it that indicates where letters have been left out (470).

coordinating conjunction: a word that can be used to join independent sentences: *for, and, nor, but, or, yet, so* (156).

dependent clause: a group of words with a subject and verb that cannot stand alone. Also known as a subordinated clause (160).

detail: specific information that helps you understand ideas and helps paint a picture in your head (188).

development: the process of moving from a basic idea to a fully expressive, well-supported main idea that communicates to a specific audience for a specific purpose (234).

discuss and engage: the beginning stage of the writing process in which the writer talks about the general topic with others and becomes involved in the topic (120).

draft: the stage of the writing process in which the writer produces a rough, but complete, version of an essay (120).

edit: the stage of the writing process in which the writer works on improving sentence structure, usage, punctuation, and spelling. Editing usually occurs toward the end of the writing process and is also known as the "polishing" stage (121).

embed: to insert phrases into sentences to add more meaning (325).

essay: an organized, multiparagraph piece of writing in which the writer focuses on and develops a particular issue or theme for a specific audience for a specific purpose (26).

essay assignment: the writing assignment instructions. Also known as the essay or writing prompt (133).

essay prompt: the essay assignment instructions (133).

excerpt: a selected piece of a longer reading (45).

explore the writing assignment: the stage of the writing process in which the writer reviews the actual writing assignment and explores what kind of information should go into the essay. This stage may also include planning and/or outlining the essay (120).

FANBOYS: an acronym for the seven coordinating conjunctions (156).

feature story: a newspaper article that presents and discusses a timely issue (56).

figurative language: language that compares two things, helping to paint an image in the reader's mind (343).

focused: sticks to one point (175).

focused essay: an essay with a clear thesis and body paragraphs that directly support the thesis (177).

focused paragraph: a paragraph with a clear topic sentence and information that connects directly to the topic sentence (176).

for: one of the seven coordinators. It expresses a relationship of effect-cause (156).

fragment: an incomplete sentence (161).

freewriting: a form of brainstorming in which writers allow their thoughts about the writing assignment or topic to flow freely onto the page (133).

fused sentence: two sentences incorrectly joined as one with no punctuation separating them. Also known as a run-on sentence (521).

gerund: a name for an *–ing* word that is working as a noun (109).

have form: a verb form that often ends in *–ed*, but not always. This verb form is also called the past participle form (330).

helping verbs: verbs that work with other words to create complete verbs (35).

homophones: words which sound alike but have different spellings and meanings (469).

idiom: an expression that may not make sense if it is read literally or translated word for word (463).

implied subject: a subject that is not stated. Command sentences have the implied subject *you* (113).

imposters: words that look like verbs but really aren't (74).

indefinite pronouns: pronouns which refer to nonspecific people, places, or things (473).

independent clause: a group of words that can stand alone as a sentence (155).

infer: to draw a conclusion based on evidence (339).

infinitive: *to* + verb combination (76).

introduction: the opening paragraph or two of a piece of writing. It explains what the piece will be about and may suggest the order and direction of the body paragraphs that follow (39).

irregular verbs: verbs that change form in unpredictable ways (498).

journalism: news writing and reporting (56).

journals: "freewriting zones." They are an opportunity to explore ideas on paper without fear of judgment (23).

kernel sentence: the basic subject and predicate of a simple sentence (324).

kinesthetic learner: a person who learns best when involving the body in the learning process (446).

lead: the opening statement of a journalistic piece of writing designed to "hook" the reader (60).

learning style: a method by which the individual learns best (446).

linking verb: a verb that connects or links the subject to information in the sentence (32).

making a concession: acknowledging the opponent's position (277).

meter: a specific, formal rhythmic pattern used in poetry (342).

nor: one of the seven coordinators. It expresses a relationship of negative addition (156).

noun: a word that names a person, place, thing, or idea (108).

or: one of the seven coordinators. It expresses a relationship of alternatives (156).

outline: a formal and thorough list of all major points and supporting points in an essay, or a quick list of just the major points (134).

outside information: any fact or idea that someone else came up with (479).

outside source: a person or publication that supplies you with information (479).

parallel structure: having two or more items in a sentence arranged in a similar grammatical form (225).

participial phrase: a group of words consisting of a present or past participle and the words attached to that participle. A participial phrase can include prepositional phrases (166).

PARTS: the five stages of the reading process—preview, anticipate, read and reread, think critically, summarize (80).

past participle form: a verb form that often ends in *–ed*, but not always. This verb form is also called the have form (497).

past perfect tense: a verb tense formed by using *had* plus the verb in the have form. This tense tells the reader that the action took place before another time or action in the past (498).

past tense form: the form of the verb used when writing in the past tense. Verbs in the past tense usually end in *–ed* (497).

patterns of organization: methods for arranging ideas in a paragraph or essay (291).

personal narrative: a piece of writing in which an individual recounts an event or series of events from his or her life usually to make a point or to help the reader better understand an issue (91).

personal pronouns: pronouns which refer to specific people, places, things, or ideas (472).

phrase: a group of words that is missing a subject or verb or both (164).

plagiarism: using information that belongs to someone else without giving that other person credit (481).

plot line: a concise summary that retells the major events or actions in a story or a film (212).

plural: more than one (508).

possessive: a word that shows ownership (471).

predicate: in a sentence, the verb and all the words that come after the verb (28).

prepositional phrase: a group of words consisting of a preposition and its object (76).

present participles: words ending in –*ing* (74).

present perfect tense: a verb tense formed by using *has* or *have* plus the verb in the have form. This tense will tell the reader one of two things: the action took place in the past and continues to take place in the present, or the action took place at a nonspecific time in the past (497).

preview: the first step in the reading process in which the reader looks at the author, title, length, topic sentences, headings, subheadings, charts, pictures or diagrams in order to get a sense of what the reading will be about (80).

pro argument: an argument in favor of something (258).

process package: a collection of work—including class notes, all brainstorming, an outline, a draft, and more (122).

pronoun: a word that can be used instead of a noun in a sentence (217).

proper noun: a specific name, title, or organization (471).

purpose: the author's reason for writing (9).

questions for critical thought: questions that follow the readings in this book. These questions are designed to help you understand and analyze your readings and to help you consider the writer's message and strategies (25).

questions for development: a set of questions used by writers and journalists to "flesh out" ideas (237).

read and reread: the act of reading through a selection quickly (only marking unknown terms and interesting points) and then rereading a second time more carefully (responding to the text and looking up unknown terms) (80).

read, discuss, think critically: the stage of the writing process in which the writer reads about the assigned topic, discusses the readings and topic with classmates, and carefully considers how the ideas expressed relate to the writing assignment (120).

reading: an essay, article, or book excerpt presented to give you information on a theme and to help you strengthen your reading, writing, and critical thinking skills (25).

reading assignments: assignments that help you engage in the steps of the reading process (25).

reading process: a series of stages readers go through to help them comprehend (understand) and retain (remember) what they have read. There are five stages in this process: preview, anticipate, read and reread, think critically about, summarize (80).

regular verbs: verbs that change tense in predictable ways (498).

response: a written, thoughtful reaction to what you have read. It is a commentary on the most important or intriguing ideas presented in a piece (86).

revise/revising: the part of the writing process in which the writer evaluates his or her essay and then rewrites portions to strengthen focus, organization, or development (120).

run-on sentence: two sentences incorrectly joined as one with no punctuation separating them. Also known as a fused sentence (521).

sentence work: practice in developing and refining sentences (26).

sibilant sound: a hissing sound (468).

so: one of the seven coordinators. It expresses a relationship of cause-effect (157).

stanzas: paragraphs in music lyrics and poems (342).

subject: the person, place, thing, or idea that is performing the action expressed by the verb or that is being described by the verb (28).

subject-verb agreement error: a sentence error that occurs when the subject and verb in a sentence do not "agree" in number (507).

subordinated clause: a group of words with a subject and verb that cannot stand alone. Also known as a dependent clause (160).

subordinators: words that can attach to independent clauses and make them dependent (or subordinated) clauses (161).

summarize: restate the main ideas of a piece of writing in your own words; also the last stage of the reading process (81).

summary: a concise retelling of the main points of a longer piece of writing (51).

synonyms: words that have similar meanings (217).

tactile learner: a person who learns best when taking notes (446).

technology: a broad term encompassing anything that science has created, usually relating to industry and commercial items (299).

tenses: tell when the action (or linking) takes place (72).

test of time: the act of placing *yesterday, today,* or *tomorrow* at the beginning of a sentence to see which word (or words) must change tense. The word that changes is the verb (73).

thesis statement: the overall main idea of an essay, chapter, or article (42).

think critically: to look beyond the surface of an issue or action and examine the purpose or motivation behind it; also, the fourth stage of the reading process in which readers discuss important points with classmates or answer questions as they "make sense" out of their reading (8).

topic sentence: general statement that introduces the main idea of a paragraph (43).

transitions: words or phrases that help show relationships between ideas and add coherence to paragraphs or essays (143).

verb: the word that expresses the action in the sentence or links the subject to descriptive information. It tells when the action (or connecting) is taking place (28).

verb tense: tells the reader when the action (or linking) takes place (72).

visual learner: a person who learns best by seeing the material (446).

writing assignment: academic essay assignment (26).

writing process: the steps a writer takes when completing a writing assignment. There are six stages: discuss and engage; read, discuss, think critically; explore the writing assignment; draft; revise; edit (120).

writing-reading-critical thinking connection: the act of using your writing, reading, and critical thinking skills to understand an issue and communicate your ideas about the issue (3).

yet: one of the seven coordinators. It expresses a relationship of opposition (157).

Bibliography

SECTION I

Chapter 1:

Blum, Deborah. 1995. "Monogamy: Till-Death-Do-Us-Part is Rare for Mammals; What About Us?" *The Sacramento Bee,* 16 October, A16.

Chapter 2:

[Sources in Alex Thio's "Preparing for Marriage" from *Sociology: A Brief Introduction,* 3/e. 1997.] Kephart, William M., and Davor Jedlicka. 1988. *The Family, Society, and the Individual,* 6/e New York: Harper & Row. Simpson, Jeffrey A., Bruce Campbell, and Ellen Berscheid. 1986. "The association between romantic love and marriage: Kephart (1967) twice revisited." *Personality and Social Psychology Bulletin,* 12, pp. 363–372. Strong, Bryan, and Christine De-Vault. 1992. *The Marriage and Family Experience,* 5/e St. Paul, Minn. Whyte, Martin King. 1992. "Choosing mates—The American Way." *Society,* March/April, pp. 71–77. [Sources in William E. Thompson and Joseph V. Hickey's "Sexual Revolution, Cohabitation, and the Rise of Singles" from *Society in Focus: The Essentials.* 1996.] Beeghley, Leonard. *The Structure of Social Stratification in the United States.* Boston: Allyn and Bacon, 1989. Bumpass, Larry L., and James A. Sweet. "National Estimates of Cohabitation." *Demography* 26, 1989:615–625. Bumpass, Larry L., James A. Sweet, and Andrew Cherlin. *The Role of Cohabitation in Declining Rates of Marriage.* NSFH Working Paper No. 5. Madison: University of Wisconsin, 1989. Gwartney-Gibbs, Patricia A. "The Institutionalization of Premarital Cohabitation: Estimates from Marriage License Applications, 1970 and 1980." *Journal of Marriage and the Family* 48 (May), 1986:423–434. Hofferth, Sandra L., Joan R. Kahn, and Wendy Baldwin. "Premarital Sexual Activity Among U.S. Teenage Women over the Past Three Decades." *Family Planning Perspectives* 19, 1987:46–53. Lamanna, Mary A., and Agnes Riedmann. *Marriage and Families: Making Choices and Facing Changes,* 3/e Belmont, CA: Wadsworth, 1988. Masters, William H., Virginia E. Johnson, and Robert C. Kolodny. *Human Sexuality,* 3/e Glenview, IL: HarperCollins, 1988. Masters, William H., Virginia E. Johnson, and Robert C. Kolodny. *Heterosexuality.* New York: HarperCollins, 1994. Miller, Brent C., and Kristin A. Moore. "Adolescent Sexual Behavior, Pregnancy, and Parenting: Research Through the 1980s." *Journal of Marriage and the Family* 52 (November), 1990:1025–1044. Seltzer, Judith A. "Consequences of Marriage Dissolution on Children." *Annual Review of Sociology* 20, 1994:235–266. Spanier, Graham B. "Married and Unmarried Cohabitation in the United States, 1980." *Journal of Marriage and the Family* 45 (May), 1983:277–288. Stengel, Richard. "Resentment Tinged with Envy." *Time,* July 8, 1985:56. Surra, Catherine A. "Research and Theory on Mate Selection and Premarital Relationships in the 1980s." *Journal of Marriage and the Family* 52 (November), 1990:844–865. U.S. Bureau of the Census. *Population Studies.* Washington, DC: Government Printing Office, 1990b. U.S. Bureau of the Census. "Marital Status and Living Arrangements." *Current Population Reports.* Series, P-20, No. 478. Washington, DC: Government Printing Office, 1993a.

Chapter 3:

The American Heritage Dictionary. 2nd College Ed. 1991. Boston: Houghton Mifflin Co.

Chapter 4:

Elbow, Peter. 1995. *Peter Elbow on Writing,* Media Education Foundation. "The Most Evil Character," author unknown. Every attempt has been made to identify an author or original source. If the author/source can be identified, please contact the publisher listed on the title page of this text. [Sources in John Macionis's "When Advertising Offends" from *Sociology*, 5/e, 1995.] Simpson, Janice C. "Buying Black." *Time*. Vol. 140, No. 9 (August 31, 1992):52–53. Westerman, Marty. "Death of the Frito Bandito." *American Demographics*. Vol. 11, No. 3 (March 1989):28–32.

SECTION II

Chapter 5:
Frears, Steven. 1992. *Hero*. Motion Picture.

Chapter 7:
[Sources from John Macionis's "Modernization and Women: A Report from Rural Bangladesh" from *Sociology* 5/e, 1995.] Alam, Sultana. "Women and Poverty in Bangladesh." *Women's Studies International Forum*. Vol. 8 No. 4 (1985):361–371. Mink, Barbara. "How Modernization Affects Women." *Cornell Alumni News*. Vol. III, No. 3 (April 1989):10–11. Mumford, Lewis. *Camp's Unfamiliar Quotations from 2000 B.C. to the present*, Wesley D. Camp (New Jersey: Prentice Hall, 1990) 385.

Chapter 8:
Holman, C. Hugh, and William Harmon. 1986. *A Handbook to Literature*, 5/e New York: MacMillan. Bergreen, Laurence. 1997. *Louis Armstrong: An Extravagant Life*. New York: Bantam Books. *The New Encyclopedia Britannica*. Vol. 1. 1997. Louis Armstrong. Chicago: Encyclopedia Britannica, Inc. *The World Book Encyclopedia*. 1999. Louis Armstrong. Chicago: World Book Inc. *Knowledge Adventure Encyclopedia*. 1998. Louis Armstrong. http://www.letsfindout.com/subjects/art/louis-armstrong.html

SECTION III:
SUPPLEMENTAL READINGS

[Sources in William E. Thompson and Joseph V. Hickey's "Feminism: The Struggle for Gender Equality" from *Society in Focus: The Essentials*. 1996.] Andersen, Margaret L. *Thinking About Women: Sociological Perspectives on Sex and Gender*, 3/e New York: Macmillan, 1993. Faludi, Susan. *Backlash: The Undeclared War Against American Women*. New York: Crown, 1991. Laslett, Barbara, and Johanna Brenner. "Gender and Social Reproduction: Historical Perspectives." *Annual Review of Sociology* 15, 1989:381–404. Lips, Hilary M. *Women, Men, and Power*. Mountain View, CA: Mayfield, 1991. Lips, Hilary M. *Sex and Gender: An Introduction*, 2/e Mountain View, CA: Mayfield, 1993. Vance, Carole S., and Carol A. Pollis. "Introduction: A Special Issue on Feminist Perspectives on Sexuality." *Journal of Sex Research* 27 (February), 1990:1–5. Wood, Julia T. *Gendered Lives: Communication, Gender, and Culture*. Belmont, CA: Wadsworth, 1994.

SECTION IV
SKILL BUILDERS

Using the Dictionary:
Merriam-Webster's Collegiate Dictionary. 10th ed. 1993. Springfield: Merriam-Webster, Inc.

Building Your Vocabulary:
Frank, Anne. 1967. *The Diary of a Young Girl*. Translated from the Dutch by B.M. Mooyaart-Doubleday. New York: Doubleday & Company, 218. Shaughnessy, Mina P. 1977. *Errors & Expectations: A Guide for the Teacher of Basic Writing*. New York: Oxford University Press, 190. Krakauer, John. 1997. *Into Thin Air: A Personal Account of the Mount Everest Disaster*. New York: Anchor Books, 3 and 7.

Spelling Matters:
Shaughnessy, Mina P. 1977. *Errors & Expectations: A Guide for the Teacher of Basic Writing*. New York: Oxford University Press, 164–175. Bryson, Bill. 1990. *The Mother Tongue: English & How It Got That Way*. New York: Avon Books, 120, 129.

Reading Aloud:
Murray, Donald M. 1991. *The Craft of Revision*. Chicago: Holt, Rinehart, and Winston, Inc. 143.

Credits

TEXT CREDITS

CHAPTER 1

pp. 7–8: As seen in *Dear Abby* by Abigail Van Buren a.k.a. Jeanne Phillips and founded by her mother Pauline Phillips. Copyright © Universal Press Syndicate. Reprinted with permission. All rights reserved; **pp. 12–13, 15:** Mortimer J. Adler, from essay, "How to Mark a Book," 1940; **pp. 13–14:** James Kirby Martin, Randy Roberts, Steven Mintz, Linda O. McMurry, and James H. Jones, from *America and its People*, 2/e. Copyright © 1993 by HarperCollins College Publishers. Reprinted by permission of Addison-Wesley Educational Publishers, Inc; **p. 14:** Joshua Meyrowitz, from "Television: The Shared Arena," *The World & I*, July 1990, pp. 465–481. Copyright © 1990 by Joshua Meyrowitz. Reprinted with permission of the author; **pp. 15–17:** William H. Armstrong, from *Study is Hard Work*. Reprinted by permission of David R. Godine, Publisher, Inc. Copyright © 1995 by William H. Armstong.

CHAPTER 2

pp. 40–42: Frank D. Cox, from *Human Intimacy: Marriage, the Family, and its Meaning*. St. Paul, MN: West Publishing Company, 1979; **pp. 46–47:** Alex Thio, from *Sociology: A Brief Introduction*, 3/e. Copyright © 1997 by Longman Publishers. Reprinted by permission of Addison-Wesley Educational Publishers, Inc.; **p. 54:** James Kirby Martin, Randy Roberts, Steven Mintz, Linda O. McMurry, and James H. Jones, from *America and its People*, 2/e. Copyright © 1993 by HarperCollins College Publishers. Reprinted by permission of Addison-Wesley Educational

Publishers, Inc.; **pp. 57–60:** William R. Macklin, "Modern Marriage" as appeared in *The Sacramento Bee*, 1/30/99. Copyright © 1999 Knight Ridder/Tribune Media Services. Reprinted by permission. **pp. 64–65:** Maggie Bandur, "Women Play the Roles Men Want to See," *The Daily Northwestern*, 1/23/96. By permission of The Daily Northwestern at Northwestern University, Evanston, IL.

CHAPTER 3

pp. 82–84: Elizabeth Wong, "The Struggle to Be an All-American Girl" originally appeared in *The Los Angeles Times*, September 7, 1980. Reprinted by permission of the author; **p. 88:** William E. Thompson and Joseph V. Hickey, from *Society in Focus: The Essentials*. Copyright © 1996 by William E. Thompson and Joseph V. Hickey. Reprinted by permission of Addison-Wesley Educational Publishers; **p. 89:** James Kirby Martin, Randy Roberts, Steven Mintz, Linda O. McMurry, and James H. Jones, from *America and its People*, 2/e. Copyright © 1993 by HarperCollins College Publishers. Reprinted by permission of Addison-Wesley Educational Publishers, Inc.; **p. 90:** Kavita Menon, from "In India, Men Challenge a Matrilineal Society," *Ms.* Magazine, September/October 1998. Reprinted by permission of *Ms.* Magazine. Copyright © 1998; **pp. 88, 92–94:** Jim Bobryk, "Navigating My Eerie Landscape Alone." From *Newsweek*, March 8, 1999. All rights reserved. Reprinted by permission; **pp. 100–103:** Dave Murphy, "Not a Two-Bit Problem," *San Francisco Examiner*, 4/11/99. Copyright © 1999 San Francisco Examiner. Reprinted with permission.

CHAPTER 4

p. 142: John Macionis "When Advertising Offends" from *Sociology, 5/e,* p. 140. Copyright © 1995 by Prentice-Hall, Inc. Reprinted by permission of Pearson Education, Inc., Upper Saddle River, NJ; **pp. 147–148:** "The Most Evil Character," author unknown. Every attempt has been made to identify an author or original source. If the author/source can be identified, please contact the publisher listed on the title page of this text.

CHAPTER 5

pp. 185–187: Megan Burroughs, "A Hero in My Family." 1999 (with permission from Elaine Roberts and Geoffrey Burroughs.) By permission; **pp. 195–200:** Dennis Denenberg, "Move Over, Barney," *American Educator,* Fall, 1997. By permission of Dennis Denenberg; **pp. 201–203:** Sandy Banks, "It's Good to Know Real Heroes Are Still Revered," *Los Angeles Times,* April 20, 1998. Copyright © 1998, *Los Angeles Times.* Reprinted by permission.

CHAPTER 6

p. 235: Joshua Meyrowitz, from "Television: The Shared Arena," *The World & I,* July 1990, pp. 465–481. Copyright © 1990 by Joshua Meyrowitz. Reprinted with permission of the author; **p. 236:** Douglas Gomery, from "As the Dial Turns," *The Wilson Quarterly,* Autumn, 1993, pp. 41–46. Copyright © 1993 by Douglas Gomery. Reprinted by permission of the author; **pp. 401–403:** Neil Hickey, from "How Much Violence," *TV Guide,* August 22, 1992. Reprinted with permission from TV Guide Magazine Group, Inc. Copyright © 1992 TV Guide Magazine Group, Inc. *TV Guide* is a registered trademark of TV Guide Magazine Group, Inc.; **pp. 240–241:** Nancy Signorielli, from "Television, the Portrayal of Women, and Children's Attitudes" in G. Berry and J. Asamen (Eds.) *Children and Television: Images in a Changing Sociocultural World,* pp. 229–242. Copyright ©

1993 by Sage Publications, Inc. Reprinted by permission of Sage Publications, Inc.; **pp. 245–253:** Marie Winn, "The Trouble With Television" from *Unplugging the Plug-In Drug.* Copyright © 1987 by Marie Winn. Used by permission of Viking Penguin, a division of Penguin Putnam Inc.; **pp. 264–266:** Daniel R. Anderson, "How TV Influences Your Kids," *TV Guide,* March 3, 1990. Reprinted by permission of the author.

CHAPTER 7

pp. 295–296: John J. Macionis "Modernization and Women: A Report from Rural Bangladesh" from *Sociology 5/e,* p. 311. Copyright © 1995 by Prentice-Hall, Inc. Reprinted by permission of Prentice-Hall, Inc., Upper Saddle River, NJ; **pp. 301–303:** Amy Wu, "Stop the Clock" from *Newsweek,* 1/22/96. All rights reserved. Reprinted by permission of Newsweek; **pp. 308–316:** Ivan Amato "Big Brother Logs On" from *Technology Review,* September, 2001. Copyright 2001 by MIT Technology Review. Reproduced with permission of MIT Technology Review in the format textbook via Copyright Clearance Center.

CHAPTER 8

pp. 340–341: From *The World Almanac and Book of Facts 1998,* reprinted with permission. Copyright © 1997 PRIMEDIA Reference Inc. All rights reserved; **pp. 344–345:** Langston Hughes, "Evenin' Air Blues" from *Collected Poems* by Langston Hughes. Copyright © 1994 by the Estate of Langston Hughes. Reprinted by permission of Alfred A. Knopf, Inc; **pp. 349–350:** John Lennon, "Imagine." Words and music by John Lennon. © 1971 (Renewed 1999) LENONO MUSIC. All rights controlled and administreed by EMI BLACKWOOD MUSIC INC. All rights reserved. International copyright secured. Used by permission; **pp. 351–352:** Joe Chambers and Larry Jenkins, "Old 8 x 10." Words and music by Joe Chambers and Larry Jenkins. Copyright

© 1988 Universal-MCA Music Publishing, Inc., a division of Universal Studios, Inc. (ASCAP) International copyright secured. All rights reserved. By permission of Universal Music Publishing Group; **pp. 352–354:** Bonnie Raitt, "Tangled and Dark." Copyright © 1991 by Kokomo Music (ASCAP). All rights reserved. Used by permission of Bonnie Raitt, administered by Gold Mountain Management; **pp. 354–355:** Alanis Morissette and Glen Ballard, "Perfect." Words and music by Alanis Morissette and Glen Ballard. Copyright © 1994 Universal - MCA Music Publishing, Inc., a division of Universal Studios, Inc. (ASCAP) International copyright secured. All rights reserved. By permission of Universal Music Publishing Group; **pp. 356–358:** Melissa Etheridge, "Silent Legacy." Words and Music by Melissa Etheridge. Copyright © 1993 MLE Music (ASCAP). All rights reserved. Used by permission; **pp. 363–364:** Counteé Cullen, "Incident." Reprinted by permission of GRM Associates, Inc., Agents for the Estate of Ida M. Cullen. From the book *Color* by Counteé Cullen. Copyright © 1925 by Harper & Brothers; copyright renewed 1953 by Ida M. Cullen; **pp. 364–365:** Emily Dickinson, "Wild Nights," c. 1861; **pp. 365–366:** Lorna Dee Cervantes, "Refugee Ship". Reprinted with permission from the publisher of *A Decade of Hispanic Literature: An Anniversary Anthology.* (Houston: Arte Publico Press-University of Houston, 1982); **pp. 367–368:** Robert Frost, "The Road Not Taken," 1915; **pp. 368–369:** Marge Piercy, "A Work of Artifice" from *Circles on the Water* by Marge Piercy. Copyright © 1982 by Marge Piercy. Reprinted by permission of Alfred A. Knopf, Inc.

SUPPLEMENTAL READINGS

pp. 390–394: Hank Whittemore, "The Most Precious Gift." First published in *Parade,* 12/22/91. Copyright © 1991 by Hank Whittemore. Reprinted by permission of *Parade* and Scovil Chichak Galen Literary Agency on behalf of the author; **pp. 398–400:** Anastasia Toufexis, "Sex Has Many Accents," *Time,* May 24, 1993. Copyright © 1993 by Time, Inc. Reprinted by permission; **pp. 401–403:** William E. Thompson and Joseph V. Hickey, from *Society in Focus: The Essentials.* Copyright © 1996 by William E. Thompson and Joseph V. Hickey. Reprinted by permission of Addison-Wesley Educational Publishers, Inc.; **pp. 405–407:** Kavita Menon, from "In India, Men Challenge a Matrilineal Society," *Ms. Magazine,* September/ October 1998. Reprinted by permission of *Ms.* Magazine, Copyright © 1998; **pp. 409–413:** David Wallechinsky, "How One Woman Became the Voice of Her People," *Parade,* 1/19/97. Reprinted with permission from *Parade* and David Wallechinsky. Copyright © 1997; **pp. 414–418:** Michael Ryan, "Who Is Great?" First published in *Parade,* 6/16/96. Copyright © 1996 by Michael Ryan. Reprinted by permission of *Parade* and Scovil Chichak Galen Literary Agency on behalf of the author; **pp. 418–420:** Paul Rogat Loeb, "Civil Rights Movement Was the Sum of Many People," *The Sacramento Bee,* January 16, 2000. Reprinted by permission of the author; **pp. 421–423:** David L. Evans, "The Wrong Examples" from *Newsweek,* 3/1/93. All rights reserved. Reprinted by permission of *Newsweek;* **pp. 424–430:** Daniel McGinn, "Guilt Free TV." From *Newsweek,* November 11, 2002. All rights reserved. Reprinted by permission; **pp. 431–433:** Karen Springen, "Why We Tuned Out." From *Newsweek,* November 11, 2002. All rights reserved. Reprinted by permission.; **pp. 434–436:** Susan Swartz, "Reality Writes— Web is But a Tool," originally published as "Words Up Close and Non-Virtual," *The Press Democrat,* January 2, 1998. By permission of *The Press Democrat;* **pp. 436–438:** William Safire, "The Great Unwatched," *The New York Times,* February 18, 2002, Op-ed. Copyright © 2002 by The New York Times. Reprinted with permission; **pp. 439–441:** Orwell, George. Excerpt from *Nineteen Eighty-Four* by George Orwell. Copyright 1949 by Harcourt, Inc. and

PHOTO CREDITS

Subject Index

553

Index of Authors and Titles